Lafayette

LAFAYETTE

PRISONER OF STATE

Paul S. Spalding

The University of South Carolina Press

© 2010 University of South Carolina

Published by the University of South Carolina Press
Columbia, South Carolina 29208

www.sc.edu/uscpress

Manufactured in the United States of America

19 18 17 16 15 14 13 12 11 10   10 9 8 7 6 5 4 3 2 1

LIBRARY OF CONGRESS CATALOGING-IN-PUBLICATION DATA

Spalding, Paul.
  Lafayette : prisoner of state / Paul S. Spalding.
     p. cm.
  Includes bibliographical references and index.
  ISBN 978-1-57003-911-9 (cloth : alk. paper)
  1. Lafayette, Marie Joseph Paul Yves Roch Gilbert Du Motier,
marquis de, 1757–1834—Imprisonment. 2. France—History—
Revolution, 1789–1799. 3. Generals—France—Biography.
4. Political prisoners—Austria. I. Title.
DC146.L2S64 2010
940.2'77—DC22   2010002601

This book was printed on Glatfelter Natures, a recycled paper
with 30 percent postconsumer waste content.

To Almut

CONTENTS

ILLUSTRATIONS

PREFACE

The story of Lafayette's captivity is a key chapter in the life of a leading actor in the democratic struggles of the time. The prison years, 1792–97, form a sharp break between his activities on the public stage, where he played prominent political and military roles on both sides of the Atlantic, and his life as an exile and gentleman-farmer who continued to exercise influence mostly behind the scenes.

Lafayette's political captivity is extensively documented. Indeed, because of the victim's fame and the duration of his incarceration, the primary sources are the most extensive documentation of any captivity in early modern times.[1] The case inspired a wealth of correspondence, military and civil records, memoirs of participants, articles, and pamphlets.

The story illustrates how private individuals and unofficial groups can frustrate powerful systems and move governments to act. The printing revolution and religious reformations and wars had long shaken orthodoxies backed by political power. Lafayette's incarceration and eventual release offer a detailed case study of how state mechanisms tried to suppress dissent and shape public discourse in early modern Europe, only to inspire ever more creative counterstrategies by their opponents. Pressure from the French government and its military brought about Lafayette's release, but credit must also be given to the private individuals and groups who lobbied the powerful and shaped public opinion. They gained and persisted in keeping the attention of French authorities who could take the final steps, including the Directory, Foreign Minister Charles de Talleyrand, and Generals Napoléon Bonaparte and Henri Clarke.

Despite its significance, much about Lafayette's captivity has remained poorly understood, particularly his supporters' international cooperation to attain his release. Typically biographers have covered the story briefly, vaguely, and inaccurately. There are several reasons for their confusion and neglect. The original source materials were widely dispersed because of international interest in Lafayette among his contemporaries. The materials became even more scattered as a result of political changes in Europe[2] and collectors' acquisition of manuscripts. Participants or eyewitnesses published brief accounts in relatively ephemeral forms such as journal articles, anonymous pamphlets, or third-rate poems.[3] Lafayette worked on memoirs covering his prison years, including original correspondence, but did not publish them in his lifetime. When they appeared, they included only a portion of available correspondence, and then in expurgated form.[4] Voluminous archives from Lafayette's family homes—Chavaniac near Le Puy-en-Velay (Haute-Loire) and La Grange near Rozay-en-Brie (Seine-et-Marne)—did not become available to scholars until the twentieth century.[5] Other key manuscript collections, particularly the relevant Habsburg Austrian military archives in Vienna and civil archives in Brno, Czech Republic, are written in idiosyncratic Gothic German script illegible to the vast majority of current German speakers.[6] Until recently political barriers made access to some documents and inspection of key prison sites difficult or impossible.

This book seeks to reconstruct the progress, circumstances, and end of Lafayette's captivity with greater precision and accuracy than previous authors have attempted. It draws on firsthand accounts, many never published, as well as ground surveys and secondary literature of the time's larger struggles. It describes how Lafayette became a prisoner, how he and his supporters maintained communication, and how they sought and eventually achieved his release. It reveals how an elaborate modern system of ideological control operated to suppress its opponents and how in the end Lafayette and his partisans on both sides of the Atlantic were able to defeat it.

Lafayette's status remained ambiguous for a time after his arrest, changing definitively to that of "prisoner of state" only when he refused to cooperate with his captors. An extraordinary Coalition tribunal sentenced him and three fellow officers to an imprisonment of open duration in the Prussian Rhineland. This sentence was based not only on alleged political crimes he had committed in the past but also on alleged political dangers he could present in the future. Two subsequent developments sent the prisoners much further east and back into Austrian hands: French military successes and Prussian preoccupation with seizing a major portion of Poland. Despite the harsh conditions that Lafayette's party endured, their captors showed leniency that tended to grow over time. Sympathetic officials on both sides of the Atlantic, acting primarily in their governments' interests, avoided formal approaches to Lafayette's captors, though made some noteworthy efforts on the prisoner's behalf behind the scenes. Private individuals and unofficial circles formed overt and secret conduits of money, communications, and projects to free him. Finally, while the French Republic and Napoléon Bonaparte eventually forced Lafayette's release, they did so in response to a public opinion shaped and articulated by the dramatic deeds and impassioned words of persons typically without political office, Fayettists female and male, European and American.

A dilemma in telling this story concerns the names of places in central Europe. In Lafayette's time, most of Silesia and some of Bohemia and Moravia were predominately German speaking. The Prussian and Austrian regimes used German names, often even for places where Polish or Czech was the most widely spoken language. At the end of World War II, the Polish and Czechoslovakian republics expelled most Germans and made Polish and Czech place designations the standard. The following account follows manuscript sources in using the German names but provides Polish and/or Czech equivalents in parentheses.

Many people made this book possible. My home institution, Illinois College, provided generous support. College grants enabled not only extensive archival research but also visits to Lafayette's former prison sites. Former dean Dr. Frederik Ohles and present dean Dr. Elizabeth Tobin gave much encouragement, information, and advice. Illinois College students gave critical aid: Eckhart Spalding in scanning pictures and creating maps and Karun Gyawali in final preparation of visuals. Librarian Laura Sweatman was tireless in her pursuit of interlibrary loan requests over many years.

The staffs of many archives were also generous with their time and expertise. Among those whom I wish especially to thank are Diane Shaw, special collections librarian and college archivist at Lafayette College Library; Laurent Ferri, curator of the French Collections at Cornell University Library; PhDr. Bohdan Kaňák, director of the District State Archive of Olomouc; Colonel Mojmír Sklenovský, director of the Czech Army Administrative Archive in Olomouc; Yasmine Houssenbay of the Josée and René de Chambrun Foundation in Paris; and Marion Sommer of the Manuscript Collection, State and University Library Carl von Ossietzky, Hamburg. Ernst-Peter Wieckenberg of Munich shared private papers.

Other colleagues contributed advice and help. Dr. Robert Crout of Charleston College, chair of the Lafayette Papers Project and president of the American Friends of Lafayette, was prominent among them. The American Friends of Lafayette, from many walks of life, encouraged this project with their shared passion for the man, his age, and the values that he represented. At the University of South Carolina Press, Alexander Moore cleared the project for review, and Linda Fogle and Karen Rood shepherded it to completion with great expertise.

Most of all, family members have given emotional and practical support every step of the way. Among them are my three sons: Peter, a skillful writer, who evaluated a late draft and made countless detailed, specific, astute suggestions; Eckhart, who applied his considerable technical and historical skills to the visuals; and Alex, whose honesty and good humor always kept the project in context. My parents-in-law, Prof. Dr. Peter and Frau Helga Grützner of Darmstadt, Germany, mediated transatlantic payments, reconnoitered Olomouc, and helped with photographs. My mother, Virginia Spalding, reminded me not to assume that readers had previous knowledge about the man who is the object of this book: excellent advice indeed.

Above all I owe all good results of the project to the expert aid, passionate interest, and limitless inspiration of my wife and colleague, Dr. Almut Spalding of the Department of Modern Languages at Illinois College. I dedicate this book to her, with feelings akin to those Lafayette expressed about his own wife, a woman who reminds me so much of Almut: "Her tenderness, her goodness, the elevation, delicacy, generosity of her spirit have charmed, embellished, honored my life."

INTRODUCTION

Fleeing into Captivity

A cold drizzle fell through the evening in Belgian Rochefort on 19 August 1792. Outside the town's northwest gate, fifteen auxiliary Flemish troops under Austrian command stood guard, warming themselves over campfires.

The appearance of military routine on a peaceful evening was deceptive. For months the monarchs of Austria and Prussia had been assembling vast forces in the southern Netherlands and western Rhineland to invade France and end its Revolution. In the last hours, at no great distance from Rochefort, the Coalition's main army had begun crossing the French frontier.[1]

Sometime after 9:00 P.M., a mounted stranger in French uniform hailed the Rochefort sentries. He introduced himself as Jean de Bureaux-Pusy, recently captain of engineers in France's Northern Army. Pusy was seeking safe passage to Holland as a noncombatant refugee. A corporal led him to the guards' commander, Captain Count Philippe d'Harnoncourt. Pusy explained that the recent radical Jacobin coup in Paris had forced him to leave his homeland. He requested rights of transit, which other people had received in similar circumstances. Harnoncourt assured him that would be no problem. Pusy then revealed that he was not alone, that several other former officers were waiting some distance behind him. Harnoncourt extended his offer of safe passage to the entire group. Pusy returned to his companions, and around 10:00 P.M. their contingent of more than forty men rode into town.[2] They found armed soldiers lining both sides of the town's single street, as it ascended steeply under a massive castle.[3] Harnoncourt lodged the visitors in the Pelican Inn (Auberge du Pélican) near the southeast gate.[4]

The group's leader was the recent commander of the Northern Army, General Lafayette. His appearance was so widely known that someone recognized him

Lafayette as commander. Engraving based on an October 1790 pastel portrait by Jean Baptist Weyler. Marquis de Lafayette Prints Collection, Special Collections and College Archives, Skillman Library, Lafayette College

shortly after he passed through the city gate. Warned of this fact and knowing that he could only gain by candor, Lafayette ordered Pusy to inform Harnoncourt of his presence.[5]

Harnoncourt reconsidered. His superiors might deem Lafayette's custody strategically necessary. He posted guards, had the Frenchmen searched, and collected arms and names. The men could not proceed, he said, without a passport from the regional commandant, Major General Johann von Moitelle, in nearby Namur.[6] The travelers protested that Harnoncourt had violated his word of honor. Lafayette's aide and friend, the volatile César de Latour-Maubourg, shouted that the Austrian captain was a scoundrel deserving a sound caning, which Maubourg would have been glad to administer.[7] The men vainly composed and signed a declaration that, having renounced military status, they were no longer combatants and that they sought transit to a country at peace with their own, which they considered to be a universal human right.[8]

News of Lafayette's capture spread quickly among Coalition forces. That same evening Harnoncourt sent reports to Moitelle as well as to the cogovernor and commander of defense forces in the Austrian Netherlands (Belgium and Luxembourg), Field Marshal Duke Albert of Saxe-Teschen, in Mons. Early the following day, Harnoncourt sent Pusy with the courier to Moitelle, allegedly for the passport. On reading Harnoncourt's words and before Pusy could explain his errand, Moitelle began shouting in glee, "Lafayette! Lafayette!" Amid further invocations of the famous name, Moitelle ordered the news sent to Teschen, the French émigré princes, and all the Austrian generals he could think of. Meanwhile Harnoncourt was writing to the commander of Austrian invasion forces, General Count Carl von Clerfayt, who was linking up with Prussian forces at Longwy in the southeast, and General Prince Louis de Bourbon, commander of French émigré troops at Brussels. From Brussels, Count Franz von Metternich, chief minister of the Austrian Netherlands, notified Vienna and asked for instructions. King Frederick William II of Prussia received word in the field at Longwy. The French king's brothers, Counts Louis de Provence and Charles d'Artois, learned of the arrest at their headquarters in Stadtbredimus, near Luxembourg. Teschen issued a war bulletin on 22 August, and a French royalist published a Brussels pamphlet to celebrate the capture.[9]

In Paris the Jacobins heard what they wanted to hear, interpreting the news to mean that Lafayette had abandoned France to join enemy forces. In the National Assembly, a deputy proclaimed: "Lafayette has just escaped the law, but he cannot escape the hatred of the nation and the horror of posterity." Another proposed razing Lafayette's house and erecting a pillar on the spot to commemorate his crime. The Paris newspaper *Moniteur* quoted an officer in the Northern Army as saying, "Finally Lafayette has unmasked himself; the traitor has abandoned us after having taken along with him all this mess of aides-de-camp, adjutants, gathered from the streets of Paris. His last maneuver is the height of villainy." Minister of Justice Georges Jacques Danton denounced Lafayette before the Jacobin Club as "this vile eunuch of the Revolution."[10] Mobs destroyed the bust of Lafayette in the Paris town hall; the hangman broke the die of a Lafayette medallion; and authorities seized his property.[11]

News of Lafayette's flight and arrest reached neutral Europe and America as quickly as horses and ships allowed. From The Hague, British envoy William Eden, Lord Auckland, notified Foreign Minister Lord William Grenville in London. William Short and Gouverneur Morris, U.S. envoys in The Hague and Paris, sent reports to Secretary of State Thomas Jefferson in Philadelphia. Others informed the German imperial diet in Regensburg (Ratisbonne) and the courts at Madrid and Warsaw.[12]

Few of Lafayette's contemporaries had such fame. Still known often as the Marquis de La Fayette, he had adopted a simpler, humbler surname, "Lafayette," when the French National Assembly had abolished the aristocracy two years before. The only title he used thereafter was one he had earned through his own efforts: "general."[13] Some enemies saw him as a chief rebel, if not the chief of all rebels, against divinely ordained authority. Others saw him as a conspiratorial monarchist. To admirers he was an apostle of liberty, the "Hero of Two Worlds."

Lafayette had helped to lead America's struggle for independence from Great Britain. As a nineteen-year-old captain and one of the richest men in France, he bought his own ship to cross the Atlantic and join American forces in 1777. Desperate for foreign aid, the Continental Congress appointed him a major general. He spent a sizeable portion of his fortune to equip troops and subsidize the American cause in its darkest hour. He was wounded at Brandywine in September 1777, endured the cold winter at Valley Forge, and fought alongside George Washington at Monmouth in June 1778. He successfully lobbied the French court for funds, arms, and troops. He helped trap British forces under General Charles Earl Cornwallis in Virginia, which brought about their decisive surrender at Yorktown in 1781 and ended the American Revolution. After this time Lafayette "could call every important American figure a friend."[14]

Europe provided a new stage for Lafayette. He inspired and encouraged the Dutch patriots who opposed an autocratic prince of Orange in 1783–87. He assisted the Belgian Brabant Revolution of 1789–90, which arose when the Austrian emperor abrogated a charter of rights. Lafayette helped to lead the early phases of the French Revolution. He proposed a national assembly, helped to draft the Declaration of the Rights of Man, and devised the red-white-blue cockade. As commander of the French National Guard, he provided security during demolition of the notorious Bastille,[15] and sent Washington a key to the main prison door. In 1791 he campaigned in the so-called Constituent Assembly to write a French constitution.

But in Europe, Lafayette did not have the same good fortune that he had enjoyed in America. The Prussian army suppressed the Dutch patriot movement, and Austrian troops put down the Brabant Revolution. In France, Lafayette's role as a unifying figure dissolved in 1791–92. Conservative Royalists saw him as appeasing those who would destroy political legitimacy and shred the social fabric. Radical Jacobins despised him for supporting a constitutional monarchy and cultivating a base of personal power; they attacked him with ever greater vituperation than did the Royalists.

The French constitutional order collapsed in summer 1792. The Austrian emperor and the Prussian king planned to invade, allegedly to rescue the royal family but with confidential plans to acquire territory. Lafayette rushed to prepare his troops along France's northeast frontier.[16] Jacobins took advantage of the hysteria aroused by the prospect of invasion to attack the constitution and its supporters, bringing Lafayette to believe that they were conspiring with the foreign enemy. Lafayette returned briefly to the capital to denounce the Jacobins before the National Assembly. When they tried to indict Lafayette for dereliction of duty, two thirds of the Assembly voted to vindicate him. But only two days later, on 10 August, the Jacobins organized a successful coup. A mob stormed the royal palace of the Tuileries and slaughtered its defenders. The new regime arrested Louis XVI and stripped him of his functions, ended the constitution, and continued massacring suspected opponents.

An officer who had escaped the Tuileries rushed the news to Sedan. On 12 August, Lafayette wrote Minister of War Charles d'Abancourt for details, but the insurgents had already deposed Abancourt and soon murdered him.

Lafayette did not intend to obey the usurpers holding Assembly and king hostage, "armed brigands" at whose hands he could expect only death. He issued a bulletin calling on all to rally around the constitution; if necessary, to die defending it. He wrote Sedan's council to warn of commissioners approaching from a National Assembly composed of insurgents and to call for "all measures that can support resistance to oppression, the prime duty of all free souls." On the afternoon of 14 August, the commissioners appeared at Sedan, equipped with power to dismiss and replace Lafayette and his fellow officers. But with Lafayette's support, the city council arrested the emissaries on grounds that they lacked constitutional authority. Lafayette tried to organize resistance among other regional authorities. He wrote officials of the Department of the Ardennes that in face of "the recent events that have soiled the capital," he held fast to his constitutional duties. He summoned troops to join Sedan officials in affirming loyalty to the constitution and resisting the usurpers. He packed a cart and covered wagon at his headquarters villa and prepared to march.[17]

As news of Lafayette's defiance reached the Assembly, Jacobin deputies derided him as "an enemy of the people," "a rebel," "a traitor to the country," and "the most infamous of conspirators." They called for his head to avenge patriots who fell in taking the Tuileries palace. On 17 August 1792 the new Provisional Executive Council relieved Lafayette of command and summoned him to explain his conduct. A mob pillaged his townhouse.[18]

That Lafayette was in mortal danger later became even clearer. Less than two years after his flight, on the Parisian Place de la Révolution, authorities executed twenty-seven members of the Sedan council and twelve administrators of the Ardennes Department for alleged complicity in Lafayette's treason.[19]

In the week after 10 August 1792, Lafayette realized that rebels had undermined his authority, that opposition was hopeless, and that he was facing certain arrest and execution by the new regime. On 18 August he invited some aides, particularly those in mortal danger, to escape with him to the Dutch Republic. "Come with me tomorrow, my dear Pusy, in the whirligig I have to ride," he wrote one of them. "Leave Sedan for Bouillon, where you'll have to be before noon. Have a good horse."[20] He hoped to claim diplomatic protection from U.S. envoy Short at The Hague and to find refuge in Rotterdam with his close friend Pieter Paulus, minister of the Dutch province of Maas (Meuse). Ultimately Lafayette hoped to retire to England, gather his family, and possibly sail to America.[21]

Lafayette rode out of Sedan early the next morning with aides, servants, and a hussar escort. Among the company was Lafayette's companion and childhood friend, Brigadier General César de Latour-Maubourg. Lafayette pretended that they were going to inspect the front beyond Bouillon, capital of a small, sovereign border duchy under French military protection. He abandoned most possessions, including new military equipment and much of his salary, to give the appearance that his departure was routine and temporary. Still he carried along a handsome sum of some twenty thousand francs.[22]

That day, the National Assembly ordered Lafayette's arrest and prohibited the army from recognizing his authority.[23] Coalition forces also began to invade France, the largest thrust coming from Luxembourg.[24]

Lafayette's party rode into Bouillon toward noon. Four other officers met them at an inn, including Captain Jean de Bureaux-Pusy and Brigadier General Alexandre de Lameth. Lameth had outridden two pursuers armed with an arrest order. Lafayette sent back his escort with orders for final troop dispositions and with a note to Sedan's mayor and council, announcing his departure, absolving them of responsibility, and declaring his refusal ever to "bow under any despotism."[25]

Around 3:00 P.M. the Frenchmen left Bouillon, crossed its bridge over the Semois, turned north, and ascended into heavily forested hills. They entered the neutral prince-bishopric of Liège, pursuing a route to Maastricht, the southernmost town of the Dutch Republic.[26] Other officers tried to join Lafayette. When former French Assembly deputy Colonel Jean d'Averhoult could not escape his pursuers, he shot and killed himself.[27] Brigadier General Nicolas Duroure and five

Lafayette and staff officers of the Northern Army fleeing their camp at Sedan on 19 August 1792. Marquis de Lafayette Prints Collection, Special Collections and College Archives, Skillman Library, Lafayette College

aides were more fortunate. They learned of Lafayette's route and tracked him down, which increased the group to twenty-one officers, twenty-three servants, and fifty-nine horses.[28]

Lafayette's officers had a diverse history. Three, like him, had served in the American War of Independence: Brigadier Generals Lameth and Jean de Laumoy, and Captain Louis de La Colombe.[29] Three—Maubourg, Pusy, and Lameth—had served in the Constituent Assembly during the early phases of the French Revolution. Maubourg and Pusy were Lafayette's close political allies, and coming events only deepened their friendship. Lameth, on the other hand, had opposed Lafayette from the left in the Constituent Assembly. Though Lameth eventually broke with the Jacobins, Lafayette mistrusted him and never forgave his earlier opposition.[30]

The company rode in rain and cold through thick, hilly woods broken occasionally by fields. They spotted riders whom they took to be French émigrés hostile to the Revolution and did not hail them. Though their map was the best available, their bearings became uncertain. Lafayette ordered his men to stop threatening a peasant who refused to serve as their guide.[31]

As darkness fell and the horses showed signs of exhaustion, the company caught sight of the campfires outside Rochefort, still on the allegedly neutral territory of Liège. Lafayette sent Pusy, a German speaker, to reconnoiter and negotiate their safe passage. What awaited them was what Lafayette later called "the imperial & royal fangs."[32]

Thus Lafayette fled the Revolution for his life, only to fall captive to the Revolution's enemies. For the next five years, these enemies led him across western and central Europe from Rochefort to Namur, Nivelles, and Arlon in present-day Belgium; Luxembourg in the present-day Duchy of Luxembourg; Trier, Koblenz, Wesel, and Magdeburg in Germany; Neisse (Nysa) in present-day Poland; and Olmütz (Olomouc) in today's Czech Republic.[33]

Lafayette's supporters never forgot him or allowed him to be forgotten. They formed networks of assistance stretching from Philadelphia to Hamburg, London to Vienna, Paris to Milan, and Basel to Dresden. They maintained communication with him, sent him money, petitioned political authorities, plotted breakouts, and aroused public opinion. In the course of these five years, Lafayette became the world's most famous political prisoner.[34] Partisans eventually managed to move a more moderate French Republic to make his release a condition of European peace.

1

PRISON ROAD INTO PRUSSIA

Critical events continued to sweep over France and Europe during the year and a half following Lafayette's arrest. For this reason, after the initial condemnations of Lafayette's alleged treason, his fate made little impact on French politics for many months to come.

During this time France had to reorganize its government and, in the face of invasion, fight for her life. In late September 1792, the National Convention became the new French government. Charged with writing a new constitution, the Convention declared France to be a republic. Happily for this new republic, the invaders, Austria and Prussia, had "entered upon the war with insufficient agreements, insufficient conceptions of the magnitude of the task, insufficient forces, and . . . insufficient confidence in one another."[1] On 20 September French forces repelled the Coalition invasion at Valmy, south of Sedan, and carried the fighting into the enemy's own territories. The counterattack lost steam soon after mid-March 1793, when Charles Dumouriez, Lafayette's successor as commander of the Northern Army, lost the Battle of Neerwinden in the Austrian Netherlands. Britain, the Dutch Republic, and Spain entered the war against France. In the meantime the French Convention had laid a foundation for military victory by ordering a mass military draft. That summer the battles of Tourcoing and Fleurus turned the tide again in France's favor, forcing British and Austrian forces to abandon the Netherlands and retreat east of the Rhine. Much farther east, Prussia became absorbed in cooperating with Russia to partition and devour huge swaths of Polish territory. King Frederick William II of Prussia considered this Polish war more important than fighting France. He made clandestine overtures of peace to France and ended Prussia's effective participation in the western war long before concluding an official peace in early spring 1795. Poland's destruction brought France's salvation.

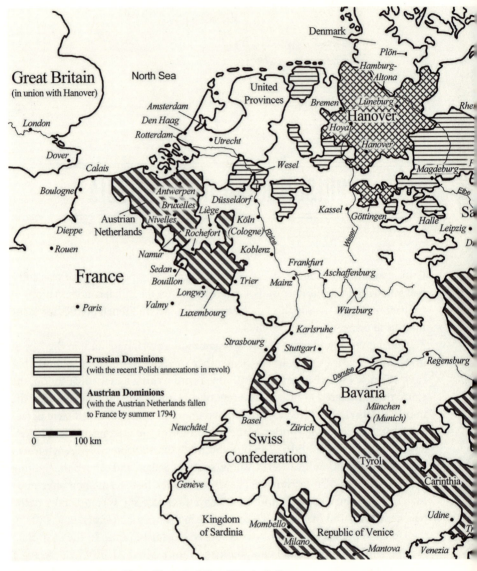

Europe in 1794. Prepared by Eckhart Spalding, Illinois College

For some time after Lafayette and his men rode into arrest at Rochefort, the Austrian-Prussian Coalition treated them as prisoners of war. After Lafayette refused to cooperate, however, the Coalition declared that he and three companions, all once politically prominent in the Revolution, were "prisoners of state" for uncertain duration.

Captain Harnoncourt, the officer who arrested Lafayette and his men at Rochefort, had reason to label them prisoners of war. Except for the servants in the

Baltic Sea

Gdańsk (Danzig, annexed 1793)

(annexed from Poland 1772)

(annexed from Poland 1793)

Warszawa

Vistula

Oder

Görlitz

Breslau

Silesia

Poland

Zittau

Brieg

Hirschberg

Neisse *Tarnowitz*

Waldenburg

Glatz

Ratibor

Kraków

Galicia

Schweidnitz

Troppau

nia

Olmütz

(annexed from Poland 1772)

Brünn Moravia

Znaim

Austria

Hungary

Wien (Vienna)

Pressburg

Eger

Klagenfurt

Ofen (Buda)

Croatia - Slavonia

Map by Eckhart A. Spalding

group, they had all been enemy officers just hours before and had arrived at Rochefort armed and in uniform. Harnoncourt could have taken them at their word and allowed them to proceed, but instead he had judged that his superiors would want to decide the Frenchmen's fate.

On 22 August one hundred imperial Hungarian hussars arrived from Brussels with orders to transfer the captives deeper into the Belgian provinces. Lafayette alerted his wife by letter, expressing confidence in his rectitude and affection as

Francis II, Emperor of the Holy Roman Empire of the German Nation. Engraving, 1792. Bildarchiv Preussischer Kulturbesitz / Art Resource, New York

well as hope for early release: "I am making no apology at all, either to my children or to you, for having ruined my family. Not a single one of you would have wanted to benefit from my having acted against my conscience. Come join me in England; let us establish ourselves in America; we will find there the liberty that no longer exists in France, and my love will try to compensate you for all the joys you have lost."[2]

Lafayette was sure he would find a sympathetic hearing for his argument that he and his men were refugees and that the prince-bishop's territory where they had been traveling was neutral. He hoped to clear up the misunderstanding quickly and convince authorities to allow his party to proceed on its way.

The cavalry escort moved the Frenchmen to the small fortress town of Namur at the confluence of the Meuse and Sambre. Their overnight domicile was the Hôtel d'Hariscamp, a former Franciscan monastery attached to Notre Dame church.[3] Lafayette became aware of hostile French monarchists in the area, "émigrés with the white cockade." He expressed relief that his guards kept them at a distance.[4]

Meanwhile, sixty kilometers to the northeast, authorities in Brussels were conferring. Although Teschen hoped to consult Lafayette about French conditions, his chief minister, Metternich, advised against it. Metternich maintained that Lafayette was a dangerous man who had declared insurrection to be "the holiest of duties" and that any information he gave would be untrustworthy. Metternich provided a letter from the resident Prussian minister, which suggested that Lafayette's ideas threatened all Europe. Metternich also wrote the Austrian chancellor, Count Wenzel von Kaunitz, that Lafayette's challenges to authority, in word and deed, "demand that he be treated as a prisoner of state by all the governments into whose power he fell."[5] In other words some officials wanted to convert Lafayette's status to that of political prisoner because of his past activities and future threat as a revolutionary ideologue.

The Vienna court could make a foreigner a "prisoner of state" if it deemed him ideologically dangerous or guilty of political crimes. Though the former emperor Leopold II had abolished this legal category, his successor, Francis II, revived it on coming to the throne early in 1792. Within a year it had been applied to twenty-four people held in various Bohemian and Moravian fortresses.[6]

General Moitelle having left Namur for the front, his replacement as commandant was Lieutenant Colonel Marquis Gabriel de Chasteler. Chasteler received the French captives with exquisite courtesy, praising Lafayette as a noble defender of liberty and declaring himself flattered to do homage to Washington's friend.[7] When Chasteler tried to address Lafayette as "marquis," Lafayette corrected him. Having voted with the majority in the National Assembly to abolish all aristocratic titles for French citizens in 1790, he wanted to emphasize his consistency.[8] Lafayette also told Chasteler that he preferred to be the victim of "arbitrary governments" rather than of "the people," the violent mobs he had escaped. Though forced to flee his own country, he still proudly saw himself as an enemy of the Coalition.[9]

Chasteler alerted Lafayette that General Prince Charles de Lorraine, formerly Lambesc, had come from Brussels for a talk. When the prince entered the room, there was a momentary silence, which ended as Lafayette expressed astonishment at the prince's visit, given their political differences. The prince tried to assure him that their views were not so far apart as to prevent an agreement and that all Europe supported the Constitutionalist cause that Lafayette had advocated in France. Furthermore, the prince asserted, the Austrian crown was not necessarily hostile to Lafayette, would follow international law in dealing with him, and would surely come through with passports to a neutral country. But when Lorraine asked about France's military arrangements with an implicit offer of quid pro quo, Lafayette erupted in anger at the implication that he would turn against his principles and homeland.[10]

Chasteler tried to mediate. He visited the captive shortly after Lorraine's visit, bringing a letter he claimed to have written for Duke Teschen and his cogoverning wife, Archduchess Marie Christine. The letter described Lafayette's "most reasonable principles," but Lafayette argued that he was much more democratic than the note indicated. Chasteler tried to persuade him to support the note in order to gain release, but Lafayette refused.[11]

Teschen may well have directed Chasteler to flatter Lafayette into compliance. It is clear that he initially rejected Metternich's advice and sought to engage Lafayette's help. When two appeals for Lafayette's collaboration failed, however, Teschen had the captives moved northwest. Though the ultimate destination seemed uncertain, Lorraine opined it to be the citadel at Antwerp (Antwerpen/Anvers). Late the morning of 23 August, the hussars escorted the Frenchmen out of their domicile at Namur, through a gawking crowd that filled its courtyard. From there they made their way to the town of Nivelles.[12]

Teschen may have tried to soften Lafayette's intransigence even here, this time through the escort commander, Major von Paulus. Paulus withdrew guards from the captives' quarters and declared the men free to walk the streets as long as they gave their word of honor not to flee. Though Lafayette expressed appreciation, he refused to acknowledge imperial officers' authority to coerce him and his men and stated that his companions could act as they wished. The other Frenchmen followed their commander's example and accepted house arrest.[13] "We are guarded to the point that I have a sentry at my door and cannot go walking in a small garden at the end of my stairway. We go walking only in the courtyard," Lafayette wrote, neglecting to note that this was his choice.[14]

Aides of Teschen arrived to examine and seize the captives' possessions. They were disappointed not to find a rich army chest. "How can I help laughing?" Lafayette said when one commissioner admonished him to take the search more seriously. "For all that I can understand of your demand is that had your Prince been in my place he would have run away with the military chest." The aides made a list of cash, papers, and other belongings, and had them confiscated to join the weapons seized earlier. Even a toothpick was taken from Alexandre de Lameth with the explanation, "You could make a quill of it." Lafayette claimed that the inspectors found on him "only a watch out of order and a very simple wallet," but the wallet was quite full. Other impounded items were evidence of Lafayette's prosperous and prestigious past: a gold repeater watch, two gold military medals, a gold neck buckle, and gold spurs. Still, the captives' total belongings did not amount to anywhere near the rumored "8 million in cash and effects." After seizing what they could find, the commissioners formally declared the men prisoners of war destined for Antwerp.[15]

Lafayette never again saw some personal equipment with ideological significance. An Austrian officer or officers soon bartered it away to Prussian counterparts

Frederick William II,
King of Prussia. Painting
by Anton Graff, ca. 1795.
Bildarchiv Preussischer
Kulturbesitz / Art
Resource, New York

at Verdun. Cabinet minister Lieutenant General Count Friedrich von der Schulenburg carried away "a set of colours, & a sword which belonged to M. de la Fayette
made of the bars of the Bastille, & ornaments with various emblematic figures, &
suitable mottos." The haul went on display in Berlin, initially at the queen's palace,
Monbijou, for the king's birthday in late September, then at the arsenal on Unter
den Linden avenue. Yet the bulk of Lafayette's effects remained under lock and
key, destined to follow him through his captivity.[16]

King Frederick William II had special plans for Lafayette. As crown prince he
had received Lafayette in Prussia in 1785, but Lafayette's subsequent role in the
French Revolution had convinced the king that the Frenchman was a threat to
regimes throughout Europe, including Prussia. The king agreed on this point with
his minister resident in Brussels and with Teschen's chief minister. From royal field
headquarters at Witry, behind invading forces, the king had notified Teschen that
Lafayette was not a military but a political prisoner; that the Austrian monarch,
Emperor Francis II, would surely see Lafayette as "one of the guiltiest" revolutionaries, "disposed to do harm where he could"; and that holding him would prevent
him from being able "to foment insurrection everywhere he believes it his duty
to preach." Lafayette deserved incarceration not only for his role in ending the Old
Regime in France, but because his message and activities threatened regimes elsewhere. The king asked for Lafayette to be transferred to Luxembourg or Koblenz

until Louis XVI could be restored to the French throne to decide the captive's fate.[17]

Teschen's aides had arrived at Nivelles with orders that reflected a consensus at the top. The Austrians would release twelve of the Frenchmen who had been mere National Guards and order them immediately to leave the Austrian Netherlands. Most of the other officers were to be interned in Antwerp's citadel as war prisoners. Yet another destination awaited Lafayette and three others who had served as deputies in the French Constituent Assembly, Alexandre de Lameth, César de Latour-Maubourg, and Jean de Bureaux-Pusy: the fortress city of Luxembourg, where a special tribunal would consider their political crimes.[18]

At the last moment, Lafayette, convinced that execution awaited him, was able to embrace and say goodbye to only one of his friends, Louis Romeuf. In tears Romeuf received Lafayette's declaration that death at the hands of tyrants was better than at the hands of fellow citizens. Moreover, Lafayette said, "The truths that I have spoken and the efforts that I have made in the two worlds are not lost. Aristocracy and despotism are mortally wounded, and my blood, crying vengeance, will bring liberty new defenders." He requested that Romeuf publish a memorial testifying to Lafayette's "steadfast political religion."[19]

Lafayette had long considered the possibility that he might one day face execution, and he continued to do so. Seven years before his arrest, during a visit to Potsdam, Lafayette had heard a warning about the lethal implications of his political views from Frederick II, the Prussian hero-king known to English speakers as Frederick the Great. When Frederick claimed that a monarchy and aristocracy would one day re-establish themselves in America, Lafayette took exception. Both institutions seemed to him superfluous. After a pause Frederick continued: "'I once knew a young man who came back from his travels with ideas of liberty and equality, and wanted to introduce his principles into his homeland. Do you know what happened to him?' 'No, Sire.' 'He was hanged.'" In captivity Lafayette often thought of this threat.[20] On the first anniversary of the American Declaration of Independence following his arrest, he wrote that his "fructifying blood on a scaffold" would promote the downfall of European tyranny.[21] Until his release he had to consider facing "an exemplary death."[22]

At the beginning of September, a major, three infantry officers, and an attachment of hussars took Lafayette, the three other former Assembly deputies, and their servants to the southeastern corner of the Austrian Netherlands. Noting that security had tightened since their arrest, Lafayette concluded that they were already being treated as state prisoners rather than prisoners of war. At every overnight stop, the escort posted two guards outside his door and two at the bottom of the stairs.[23]

The day after a stay in Arlon, the men arrived in Luxembourg, chief operational headquarters for the invasion. Austrian authorities placed the captives in separate quarters. Lafayette was housed over the shop of a family named Lontz. The morning after his arrival, several émigrés tried to force their way past guards, cursed Lafayette, and chanted threats under his windows. On the ground floor, Madame Lontz effectively wielded a broomstick and cried out for help. Lafayette saw the incursion as an assassination attempt. Major Count Rochefort d'Ailly, the garrison's executive officer and an old acquaintance of Lafayette's, strengthened security. He banned Frenchmen from the street and ordered guards to warn off anyone trying to insult the captive or stop under his windows. To avoid exposing Lafayette at a public inn, he arranged for him to eat with the Lontz family.[24]

At Nivelles, Lafayette had demanded his release in letters to Frederick William and Teschen. The king never replied, but the duke sent a response to Luxembourg. "It is with regret that I am determined not to grant you the liberty you have demanded. We certainly did not arrest you, Monsieur, as a prisoner [of war], nor as a Constitutional, nor as an émigré; but because it is you who were the instigator of the Revolution that overturned France; because it is you who put fetters on your King, after having stripped him of all his legitimate rights and powers, and held him captive; because it is you who were the principal instrument of all the disgraces that are overwhelming this unhappy monarch. It is only too just that those who are working to reestablish his dignity detain you until the moment when your master, having recovered his liberty and his sovereignty, will be able to render judgment on your fate, according to his justice and clemency."[25] It was an indictment for the highest political crimes, one that exaggerated Lafayette's responsibility for the Revolution and disregarded his persistent defense of the royal family's lives, the king's constitutional role, and the rule of law.[26]

Even at Luxembourg, Austrian authorities seemed to hope for Lafayette's cooperation. When Lafayette requested an audience with Archduchess Marie Christine, Prince Heinrich XV zu Reuss (an aide to Teschen) and Prince Paul von Eszterházy (the commander of troops in Austria's Rhineland province of Breisgau) came to interview him. The men were surprised to discover that Lafayette hoped for Louis XVI's salvation, either through Coalition victories or by a Frenchman who could defend the king effectively.[27] Still no deal emerged.

The tribunal, which included Prussian minister Schulenburg and an alleged representative of the imprisoned Louis XVI, Baron Louis de Breteuil, did not consider the possibility that Lafayette might be innocent. The hearing was not a trial, but a legal facade for decisions reached previously by the Coalition partners. Lafayette seems never to have been called to defend himself before it. Breteuil called for holding Lafayette until Louis XVI could regain power and prosecute him for crimes against the throne. Schulenburg told the captive that the commission considered him culpable for both his political ideas and his actions. Lafayette was "not only the man of the French Revolution, but of universal liberty," and had proved "his projects and his values" in America and Europe alike. While Prussia had

César de Latour-Maubourg.
Bibliothèque nationale de
France (46.B.2455)

crushed the Dutch patriots, his "mere presence" would "electrify all of Holland."[28]
The Vienna court fully agreed that Lafayette had "made himself answerable to all
Sovereigns by solemnly preaching the holiness of insurrection against them all, in
the broadest sense" and had applied his ideas in concrete actions. These actions
included supporting the Brabant revolt in the Austrian Netherlands and treating
Marie Antoinette, not only queen of France but also an Austrian archduchess,
"with the most outrageous insolence."[29] The tribunal agreed that his ideas were
dangerous. Lafayette recalled that "after each member had sung my praises in the
name of his government, it was decided *that the existence of M. de Lafayette . . . was
incompatible with the security of the governments of Europe.*"[30]

　　For his royal captors, Lafayette embodied the Revolution they were fighting.
His arrest seemed to be a first, prestigious victory in a campaign that had little to
show for itself as yet on the battlefield. They believed his captivity would help contain the spread of Revolutionary ideas beyond France, ideas that menaced traditional monarchy and aristocracy.

　　Lafayette had indeed been prominent among Frenchmen articulating what a
later observer called "the global and universal value of the American experience."
He directly threatened European monarchs claiming absolute powers from God,
as classically expressed in Lafayette's 1789 draft for a French declaration of human

rights. Among the "inalienable rights" Lafayette listed in this document was "resistance to oppression." He insisted on freedom of religion, thought, writing, and the press. He claimed that "all sovereignty resided in the nation," rather than in a monarch or noble class. "No group and no individual can have any authority except that which emanates expressly from the nation," he declared, adding that "a person can be subject only to laws that either he or his representatives have first promulgated and legally applied" and that application of these laws must be "clear, precise, and uniform for the citizens." People made government for the "sole purpose" of "the common good." The government's powers—"legislative, executive, and judicial"—were "distinct and defined," with a king limited to the executive power. Though Lafayette still maintained in his 1789 draft that "the person" of the French king was "sacred," this did not apply to his agents, who received their authority from the nation and were responsible to the nation. Finally Lafayette recognized the right and, at times, the need of people to change their government entirely. Thus "there should be explicit constitutional means that provide in certain cases for an extraordinary convocation of representatives, whose sole object is to examine and modify, if necessary, the form of government."[31]

The Austrian emperor and Prussian king did not have any motive to use Lafayette as a hostage or pawn. The new French Republic did not want him, except to execute him, and its attention was on fighting for its life. The weak, distant American republic and its wishes were insignificant in the strategic plans of central European powers. In Britain the administration of Prime Minister William Pitt the Younger shrugged off Lafayette's fate. There was never any evidence that the Austrians and Prussians thought they could pressure the Poles or anyone else by bargaining over Lafayette.

Other motives for holding Lafayette are possible. Despite Lafayette's initial refusals to share information of military importance, at least the Prussian king later tried again to persuade him by offering the prospect of improvements in his incarceration if not release. There might have been some initial consideration to breaking Lafayette's will in order to destroy his reputation and hurt the attraction of his ideas. Lafayette did not prove amenable; yet his incarceration continued.

One is left with the explicit explanation that his captors gave for their central motives: Lafayette's ideas and those of his comrades were toxic. They had already led to rebellions in the Austrian Netherlands and Dutch Republic and to overthrowing the rightful sovereign of France. They threatened to have a similar effect wherever they were free to spread their gospel.

The sentence of the Luxembourg tribunal came down precisely as Frederick William and Breteuil had demanded: to hold Lafayette, Maubourg, Lameth, and Pusy as prisoners of state until such time as a restored French king could render final judgment. At least some of Lafayette's enemies expected that the eventual royal judgment would bring execution. Marie Christine maliciously sent Lafayette

Jean de Bureaux-Pusy.
Bibliothèque nationale
de France (69.B.49225)

Alexandre de Lameth.
Bibliothèque nationale
de France (66.B.41184)

word that authorities "were keeping him for the scaffold."[32] Some of her fury was at his earlier support of republicans in the Netherlands. Some derived from anxiety over her sister, the imprisoned Marie Antoinette.[33]

That his enemies did not execute him immediately may have betrayed confidence that the war would soon be over and the French throne restored. Such confidence was groundless. Even if indeterminate incarceration was not the worst outcome for Lafayette, it was, as he put it, a most "gloomy fate."[34] The captivity could last the rest of Lafayette's life.

Tribunal members did not decide the prison site. Frederick William did that with the concurrence of his Austrian counterpart, Emperor Francis. It would not be Luxembourg, but Wesel in the Prussian king's Rhineland duchy of Cleves, near the Dutch border. It was still close enough to France to enable a prompt return to Paris once the Revolution was crushed and the king restored. Frederick William later claimed that he had the men taken to Wesel to protect them from attack by royalist French émigrés. The kernel of truth in this assertion was that such people had tried to attack Lafayette in Luxembourg, and they could conceivably try again. Elsewhere the king alleged that authorities of the Austrian Netherlands had asked him to take the captives because Luxembourg was vulnerable to the French. This was a more convincing motive: to move the prisoners away from the war front and prevent their release by enemy forces. Ironically those forces would have taken Lafayette's party to the guillotine, a fact Frederick William also later cited in self-justification. The tribunal ordered the Frenchmen transferred to Prussian custody, the hand-over occurring on 12 September.[35]

The captives' servants continued to follow them and were accepted as appropriate for prisoners of high rank. The attendants could relieve Prussian soldiers from caregiving. Maubourg had brought along a twenty-year-old valet, Jules Grugeon, and Lafayette had three servants. Two were also valets: Jean Pierre Compte and another identified as Demanges. Compte was a barely literate twenty-five-year-old tailor's son nicknamed "Chavaniac" after his hometown of Chavaniac near Lafayette's family château in the Auvergne. The third was Félix Pontonnier, Lafayette's sixteen-year-old secretary and son of his coachman.[36] Though Pusy had originally lacked a valet and had never requested one, authorities assigned him one at departure from Luxembourg: an old illiterate servant named Nicolas Jandel.[37] Jailors came to call these men "prisoners of state" along with their masters.[38]

Prussian troops drove the four chief prisoners down the Moselle River valley, under vineyards famous since Roman times, to the Rhine. The captives encountered crowds of the curious, well-wishers, and antagonists. They also had foretastes of rigors to come. A firm, polite escort commander sat beside Lafayette, while other officers accompanied his companions in each of three other coaches. Sixteen noncommissioned cavalry officers preceded and followed. Only during brief stopovers were the Frenchmen able to talk to each other. At the first overnight stay, in a Trier seminary, each prisoner was lodged in a separate room furnished only with table and pallet and guarded by a soldier, "pistol in hand," who had his eyes on him at all times. Other soldiers stood watch in the corridor and outside, under captives' windows.[39] When they arrived at Koblenz on the Rhine, Lafayette recorded that the escort had "double sentries set at our doors and around the house." He ended the note with a cry from the heart, underlined and in English: "I can't get out."[40]

After a few nights' rest, the captives and their escort embarked on the final leg of the journey, down the Rhine. Following a layover in Cologne (Köln),[41] they reached Wesel late in the afternoon of 19 September. They docked in a small bay and entered a star-shaped brick citadel adjacent to the fortress town, the largest stronghold in Prussia's western provinces. The citadel alone had five bastions surrounding an inner courtyard 175 meters across. Many barracks served as a military hospital. Space that could have accommodated five hundred soldiers had been set aside and furnished at considerable cost for secure custody of the four arrivals, resulting in crowded conditions for the garrison.[42]

The servants left Luxembourg a day after their employers, meeting them at Koblenz and accompanying them to Wesel "despite the dismal prophecies that people made to them along the way."[43] Given such predictions, their persistence showed a striking devotion. At Wesel they stayed under guard in local inns.[44]

Conditions were miserable in the citadel of Wesel, "a disgusting place" for Lafayette. The Prussians held the four chief prisoners in isolation to keep them from communicating with each other or the outside world. Every day at opening parade and review, the officer on guard repeated aloud an oath to refuse the captives' questions. A noncommissioned officer's constant gaze, relieved every two hours day and night, was "an inexpressible torture" for Lafayette. A corrugated iron stove always illuminated his small cell. Vermin tormented him as he lay on his pallet. These conditions aggravated Lafayette's chest and sinus congestion, night sweating, and fevers that had plagued him for years. He found it hard to sleep, and the prison physician feared for his life. Lafayette's fellow prisoners suffered similarly. Lameth nearly died, but Maubourg was told that not even at a deathbed could the captives see each other. Physicians appealed to the king, but he refused to let the Frenchmen walk outside. The fortress commandant, Colonel Friedrich von Tschirschky, embezzled funds at Lafayette's disposal. The colonel never allowed Lafayette to send or receive mail but still charged him for "postage."[45]

Based on reports "from more than one source and through absolutely impartial persons," Count Christoph von Keller, special Prussian envoy at The Hague, protested to cabinet minister Schulenburg in Berlin about the prison conditions. Keller noted that Tschirschky "has the general reputation of being quite brutal" and that the poor treatment may have lost Berlin potential allies among high-ranking French officers alienated from the Jacobin regime. Schulenburg responded

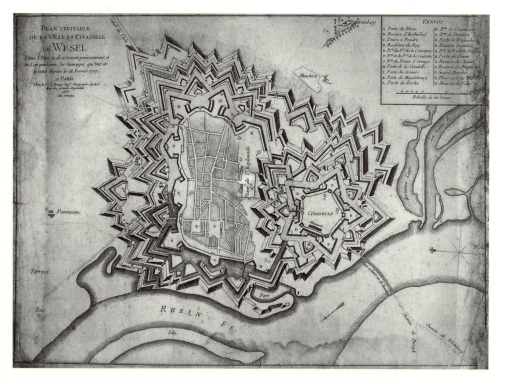

Wesel fortress-city in 1757. Preussen-Museum Nordrhein-Westphalen, Wesel

that he was not in a position to help as the king had issued personal confidential orders about the captives and commanded the Cabinet Ministry and Supreme War Council not to interfere. Schulenburg could only refer the envoy to chief minister Marchese Girolamo di Lucchesini, who was at the king's field headquarters in Frankfurt.[46] Little came of the protest.

The king may well have intended to make life miserable for Lafayette in order to force his cooperation. Tschirschky and a legal officer brought a letter from the king offering to improve conditions if Lafayette were to partner with the Coalition against France. These men had no better luck than had Teschen. "The king is quite impertinent to associate my name with such an idea," said Lafayette. When authorities allowed the prisoners to write the king's general adjutant of infantry and childhood friend, Major Hermann von Manstein, Lafayette tried in his letter to restrain his pride and request release in a reasonable, moderate tone. Still he did not wish to give enemies the sense that he considered their crimes against him justified, that he would ever renounce his involvement in the American and French revolutions, or that their opposition to liberty would prove productive.[47]

The Coalition had assumed that Wesel would be the Frenchmen's prison throughout the war, but they spent only three months there.[48] Lafayette and company had barely arrived in Wesel when, on 20 September, the new French Republic halted the invading Coalition forces at Valmy and forced a retreat. Republican forces advanced rapidly into and across the Austrian Netherlands, entered Westphalia, and threatened the Prussian Rhineland. On 10 October, Frederick William ordered Wesel's commandant to set palisades before the town.[49]

The king knew of Wesel's vulnerability and badly needed space for more soldiers. He ordered the captives moved east to his fortress city of Magdeburg. It was the country's mightiest bastion, a place that Lafayette had visited years before as guest of the Prussian crown.[50] Early on 22 December, Lafayette and company embarked under escort of an officer and some eight soldiers. They rode in two rented wagons supplied with chains and handcuffs in case of trouble. The captives were glad to see each other and breathe fresh air.[51]

The route crossed a series of Prussian territories. From the duchy of Cleves, it crossed the county of Mark to enter Hamm, where Frederick William had provided shelter to the recently deposed French king's brothers, Counts Provence (soon dubbed Louis XVIII) and Artois (later Charles X). The captives' party stopped at a Hamm inn just as the two French princes arrived from Düsseldorf. Both sides seemed to have felt a mixture of emotions rather than pure hostility. Lafayette and Artois had been adolescent friends at the Academy of Versailles and emerged on opposite political sides only during mutual service in the Assembly of Notables in 1787. Provence allowed his aide Count Charles de Damas, brother of Lafayette's close friend Countess Diane de Simiane, to talk to the captives. Damas shared news and thanked Lafayette for his help during the count's arrest the previous year.[52] Lafayette's party then continued to Soest and Lippstadt. Lafayette's servant Demanges escaped at Lippstadt, apparently aided by two sympathetic Germans. He carried a message asking Lafayette's friends to attempt a rescue.[53] Other signs of support appeared along the way. "Our passage through Germany, whatever may have been the original intention," Lafayette wrote, "was most highly honorable to the martyrs of a glorious cause."[54] Shortly after Christmas, a new escort from Magdeburg met the captives at Minden and transferred them to rented wagons of its own.[55]

Journey's end was the Citadel in Magdeburg. The Citadel dominated a small island in the Elbe River, within the city's wider fortifications. Like the Wesel fort, this one took the form of a star, with a bastion at each of five points and casemates along the perimeter. Because of its island location, the Citadel was less regular in shape than the one at Wesel. Its earthen walls, faced in red brick and topped by a sandstone cornice, rose eight meters high and ran more than two hundred meters between bastions. Inside was a courtyard with auxiliary buildings and two main gates. The custodians lodged Lafayette and Maubourg next to one another, apparently on the southern corridor.[56] Secret orders affirming Lafayette's status as "state prisoner" went to the city commandant, Major General Otto von Hüllesen, and the

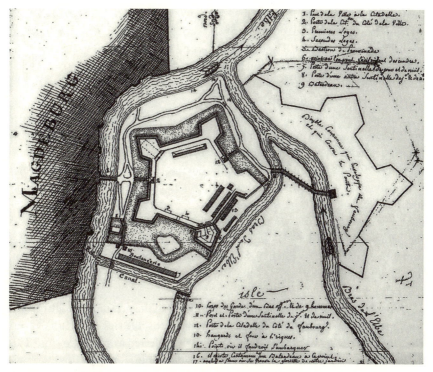

Magdeburg Citadel as sketched by Maubourg in preparation for an escape attempt. In reality the Citadel was much less symmetrical because it had to fit the narrow contours of the island it occupied in the Elbe River. Collection of the Josée and René de Chambrun Foundation

vice commandant, Major Senfft von Pilsach, also superintendent of the Citadel. The prisoners spent a full year here, 4 January 1793–4 January 1794.[57]

Lafayette's early descriptions of the Citadel indicate that the king's instructions, eventually "enough to fill two volumes,"[58] were to continue close and wretched confinement. To enter Lafayette's small casemate cell of six by four paces, a person had to pass four chained, locked, and barred gates, to which a fifth was later added. A rhyming French verse on one wall announced how the captive's destiny was "to suffer and die" (*souffrir et mourir*), a cruel jest on an early Revolutionary slogan, "to live free or die" (*vivre libre ou mourir*). Since the Citadel stood on the river, Lafayette's room was dank and dark. It reminded him of the hold of a prison ship he had visited in New York Harbor during the American war. Only indirect light came from "a small but closely grated window," through which he once saw an executed soldier's head displayed. In addition to the regular guard detail, two sentinels stood outside on platforms beyond a high palisade. The men watched the cell windows to prevent communication among the captives. By royal command the Citadel commandant also watched Lafayette while he ate, kept the room keys on his person, and slept in rooms nearby. At each guard change, an officer reported all that Lafayette had said. The captive expressed satisfaction that at least the generals in Berlin knew what he thought, observed that "these gentlemen here must think they are holding the Devil in prison," and cursed the place as "this latrine of despotism, servitude, ignorance, and espionage."[59]

The captives' health had recovered to a degree during the transfer to Magdeburg. However, it deteriorated again in the first weeks, when weather was coldest. Lafayette's asthma and fevers returned and increased despite his determination to survive.[60] His companions fared similarly. "I doubt if Lameth will long hold out; he was dying at Wesel, and is but little better here," Lafayette noted. "M. de Pusy suffers much, although he is less ill. The same may be said of Maubourg." Lafayette shared a corridor with Maubourg. In the afternoon, staff opened gates for airing while the Citadel commandant looked on. During that time Lafayette sometimes managed to catch sight of his friend, observing "with much pain, that his appearance is greatly changed." Incarceration seemed a "slow death" for them all.[61]

Lafayette felt that the king might be trying to kill the prisoners unobtrusively: "the unwholesomeness of our subterranean dungeons, the lack of air and of exercise, and every form of mental agony have been preferred as a slow poison." This suspicion grew with time and "the very confidential opinion of an honest physician" that slow murder could be at work. Lafayette stated that if he were to die by poison, then it could only have been at the king's behest.[62]

Indeed Lafayette came to experience incarceration itself as a form of death. It felt as if he had been "buried" and was "dead to the world," as if the subterranean cells were "tombs."[63] It did not help him to hear rumors of his own death. A Prussian officer told Lafayette how French prisoners of war claimed that their leaders had assured them of Lafayette's demise, and stories of his death appeared in journals of London and Philadelphia.[64]

Eventually Frederick William made plans to transfer the prisoners again. Their custody was one more cost in a war whose pursuit, as his ministers constantly reminded him, surpassed Prussia's resources. He needed more space to accommodate prisoners of war. Behind these irritations were two developments affecting his chief political concern: to seize territory. One development was deepening military plight in the west as France scored victory after victory, making territorial gains in that direction most unlikely. The other development, by far more important, was Frederick William's efforts in concert with Russia to seize Polish territory in the east. He decided to withdraw entirely from hostilities against France, thus freeing up resources for his eastern projects. Even the alleged motive for holding the four state prisoners, to prevent the spread of their ideas and to keep them for a restored French king to judge, had disappeared in the victories of the French republican armies. The prisoners' ideas had spread everywhere, it seemed, and the prospect of a royal restoration in France had receded completely out of sight.

Frederick William could return the four state captives to France or Austria, or he could release them. He chose to return them to Austria. On 25 November 1793, he directed his Foreign Affairs Department to write to Lucchesini, his envoy to Vienna, that he "may petition the Vienna court to take back the said prisoners, since they actually belong to it." He soon repeated this redefinition of status in a note to Lucchesini, stating that these were Austrian rather than Prussian prisoners. Less openly he began to blame the emperor for Lafayette's imprisonment.[65]

Francis II agreed to the transfer. For him too the chief purpose of holding these captives had ended. Lafayette and his companions had no negotiable value because Paris had never shown interest in their release or transfer to French custody. America's interest still counted for little with Francis. Still he did not suggest freeing the prisoners. In his view the French Revolution had done and was still doing great damage. It had attacked Francis's own family by murdering his aunt, Marie Antoinette. It had assaulted the Austrian Empire and was seeking its destruction. To Francis's way of thinking, Lafayette held responsibility for that Revolution, even embodied it, and he deserved indeterminate incarceration. Continuing to hold him behind bars was just one more battle Francis was fighting against the revolutionary hordes.

Initially Frederick William was willing to share custody with Francis by extraditing just two captives. On 18 December 1793, as some one thousand prisoners of war were to arrive in Magdeburg, Frederick William ordered Lafayette sent to Neisse (Nysa) and Lameth to Glatz (Kłodzko). Both places were in Prussian Silesia, near Austrian Bohemia and Moravia. Frederick William hoped that this placement would be only temporary, before extradition to an Austrian fortress city, perhaps Prague or Brünn (Brno). He told Vienna that he wanted "to be entirely discharged from guarding these two prisoners" and dubbed them again "not Prussian but Austrian prisoners." Lafayette heard of plans almost two weeks before the transfer but dismissed them as unfounded rumor.[66]

In the first days of 1794, Lafayette learned that what he had taken as hearsay was true. The extradition was to include all four prisoners, but since Lameth was too ill to travel, only three would be making the trip for the time being. Two days after the government transferred Lafayette to Neisse, Maubourg went to Glatz. Pusy soon followed Maubourg, occupying a separate cell.[67]

Beginning on 4 January, Lafayette's trip to Neisse took a week and a half for a journey of 450 kilometers. It offered him much needed exercise and fresh air. As he entered Silesia, he beheld mountains he had seen under quite different circumstances on his August 1785 trip as an honored guest of Frederick II. On arriving at Neisse, the strongest fortress in the province, the escort installed Lafayette in casemates of a star-shaped, brick-surfaced northern outwork known as Fort Prussia, across the Neisse River from town.[68]

Many conditions at Neisse resembled those of Wesel and Magdeburg. Lafayette had an elongated, subterranean cell with "a very low ceiling and barred ventilation shafts extending through eight-foot walls." It looked out upon a narrow courtyard through openings in two iron grilles. Lafayette alluded to "bad" air although he added, perhaps to help his letter pass censorship, that other captives had it worse. He noted that there were three guards posted before his cell by day and five at night, representing a "small" guard in addition to the "large" guard of the fort as a whole. Sentries shouted to relay information and orders, making the place not only unsightly and restrictive, but noisy.[69]

Added to physical discomfort was the mental anguish that Lafayette suffered for family and friends during this time of the Terror in France, when the Jacobin regime was incarcerating and executing adversaries by the thousands. On 17 September 1793, the new Law of Suspects empowered committees to draw up lists of persons to arrest without further judicial process, prime targets being former nobles. "This frightful news brought back my insomnia and has caused me more pain than all the efforts of my persecutors could approach," Lafayette confessed. "I have much more energy to resist any personal situation and to defy the vengeance directed at me, but I simply do not have the energy to sustain the dangers threatening those I love." He agonized over the fate of his wife, children, and aunt in the Auvergne. He wanted Countess Simiane and Princess Anne de Poix, his wife's cousin by marriage, to leave Paris at once. He wondered about the mother and wife of a murdered friend, Duke Louis de La Rochefoucauld, and about his wife's brother-in-law, Marquis Alexandre de Grammont. News of the arrests of colleagues and friends arrived: former Paris mayor Jean Bailly, former minister Chrétien de Malesherbes, and Princess Poix. Then news of executions arrived: Bailly (12 November 1793), Duke Louis d'Haraucourt du Châtelet (13 December 1793) and his wife, Diane (22 April 1794), and Malesherbes (22 April 1794). Lafayette found the horror wrenching.[70]

Meanwhile Frederick William had solicited Emperor Francis's assent to accept the prisoners back into Austrian custody. On 6 February 1794, Prussian ambassador Lucchesini reported to the Austrian director general of foreign affairs, Baron Francis von Thugut, about "the Expense and Inconvenience that attended the detaining of M. de la Fayette and his Companions" and "His Prussian Majesty's wish that the Emperor would allow them to be transported to one of the Prisons in His Dominions." Prussian ministers brought up the matter with the Austrian ambassador in Berlin, Count Ludwig von und zu Lehrbach. Francis II consented to negotiations. On 6 March, Vienna's cabinet agreed to accept all of Lafayette's party. The following week Frederick William declared that he "has now agreed with the

Vienna court that, in the future, it alone has to take over the detention and support of the 4 French state prisoners Lafayette, Lameth, Latour-Maubourg, and Pusy." The king ordered his foreign and war departments to work out arrangements. Berlin asked Vienna where to deliver the men. The Austrian War Council deemed accommodations insufficient in its Bohemian strongholds, so it decided to send the prisoners to a place in Moravia.[71] The Austrians misled their Prussian counterparts by claiming the final choice to be the Spielberg fortress in Brünn when it was actually Olmütz.[72]

Prisoners of state had resided at Olmütz since August 1793.[73] They included former French war minister Pierre de Beurnonville, his servant Marchand, and French National Convention deputy Henri Bancal. In April of that year, Beurnonville and four Convention deputies had come to Belgium as an official delegation to arrest Lafayette's successor as commander of the French Northern Army, Charles Dumouriez, on suspicion of plotting a coup. Instead Dumouriez arrested the delegation, fled to the enemy on 5 April, and turned them over to an Austrian commander. While Vienna interned three of the men at Brünn's Spielberg citadel and four at Königgrätz, it brought Beurnonville and his valet, Marchand, as well as Bancal to Olmütz, where Beurnonville and Marchand shared quarters at a former Jesuit college, so that Marchand could aid his ill employer at all times. Bancal occupied a room in a former Clarissan convent nearby.[74]

Including servants, Lafayette and company added seven more state prisoners to the three already at Olmütz. In preparation for their arrival the night of 18–19 May 1794, the interim fortress commandant, Lieutenant General Baron Gabriel von Splényi, issued orders that he was soon repeating daily to administrative officer Lieutenant Caspar Jacob and the provost or prison bailiff, Sergeant Johann Platzer: to take more precautions in dealing with ten prisoners than they had with only three. Jacob and Platzer repeated the orders daily to the guards and guard commander, stressing that if a mishap occurred, they could expect life imprisonment or even execution.[75] In exchange the guards received double pay for the onerous responsibility.[76]

Complications arose with Lameth, whose poor health forced Berlin to delay extradition. The government was sensitive to foreign protests of the captivity and was concerned that Lameth's death en route would cause "a new embarrassment." On 20 March, Prussia's Supreme War Council finally ordered Pusy to leave for Glatz without Lameth. The locks rattled at 5:00 A.M. a week later, followed by the sounds of Pusy packing, alerting Lameth to his companion's departure. Meanwhile Frederick William ordered an updated report on Lameth's health, hoping that he had recovered enough to be extradited. He had not. Although Lameth could walk and ride, the report claimed that his emaciation would demand extraordinary attention from the escort officer and a surgeon or caregiver, and it might lead to his death on the road. The king ordered that Lameth remain in Magdeburg while the others departed. Both the king and the Austrians still expected Lameth to follow.[77]

It was not to be. When Prussia formally withdrew from war with France on 5 April 1795, ministers who found the king's leniency ill-advised still considered handing Lameth over to Austria. They pointed out that Austrian custody would expose him to less danger than a transfer to French hands and that, as a state prisoner, he was not subject to the article in the Peace of Basel governing exchange of war prisoners. On the other hand, if Vienna refused to accept Lameth at this late date, Foreign Affairs declared, "In our humble opinion there would perhaps remain no other choice for us to avoid inconvenience than to connive in his escape." The king decided not to indulge in this subterfuge. On 17 May he ordered Lameth released on the emperor's agreement. Negotiations with Vienna on the point delayed release until 15 November, when Lameth set off for Hamburg and England. Lameth's fellow captives heard that he had written a political memorandum for Berlin, became convinced that he had offered valuable intelligence and advice about French affairs, and broke off further relations with him.[78]

Had they been able to read the memorandum, their suspicions would have dissipated immediately. Far from divulging military secrets, Lameth encouraged Frederick William to recognize Austria and Russia rather than France as Prussia's natural enemies. He advised the king to break his alliance with Austria, withdraw from war with France, and begin building a Baltic coalition against Russia. Indeed, he concluded, "the natural, essential, permanent interest of the Prussian monarchy is its alliance with France."[79]

In early April 1794, when it had become clear that Lameth could not join the other captives, extradition of them started up again. Berlin transferred Pusy, Maubourg, and their servants from Glatz to Neisse by midmonth, into separate cells near Lafayette's. Maisonneuve followed. An Austrian, a Prussian, and each man's aide met at Neisse to arrange the handover. Field Marshal Marchese Giacomo Botta d'Adorno of Austrian Moravia solicited from the Prussian, Major Karl von Hanff, commandant at Neisse, a report on the captives' identities and Prussian standards of treatment. The two sides urged one another to act quickly.[80]

The extradition order went into effect on 12 May, as the king left Berlin to take over command of troops fighting Polish insurrection. At 4:30 P.M. that day, Field Marshal Botta in Brünn, Austrian Moravia, alerted Major Hanff in Neisse, Prussian Silesia, that the prison rooms were ready in Olmütz. Despite the king's command that the captives not be informed, Lafayette learned that he was going to a Moravian fortress.[81] He had now been a prisoner of state in Prussian custody for more than a year and a half. He was about to face a much longer period of time in Austrian hands.

2

LAFAYETTE'S ATLANTIC BASE

The war that enveloped much of continental Europe during the months of Lafayette's Prussian incarceration also drew in, to differing degrees, Britain and the United States. Though Britain tried initially to maintain armed neutrality, French violation of treaties governing Dutch defenses in November 1792 provoked the British to make swift preparations for war. Charles James Fox, leader of the Whig opposition in Parliament, continued to maintain public sympathy for the French Revolution, only to see his political support erode with every new report of Jacobin aggression. France and Britain exchanged formal declarations of war in February 1793. Concluding alliances with Prussia, Austria, Russia, and smaller European powers, Britain sent troops to the Netherlands. The British also issued rules by which they would board neutral ships trading with France and seize what they deemed to be war contraband. France sought to hold the United States to the Alliance of 1778, hoping to draw the Americans into the war on the French side. President George Washington insisted on a policy of neutrality for the United States, but Britain's seizures of American ships and French attempts to sponsor attacks on Britain from U.S. harbors and territory made the policy difficult to maintain.

Within this world of war, Lafayette's incarceration awakened supporters on both sides of the Channel and the Atlantic. American officials, French Constitutionals, British Whigs, and German democrats began to cooperate to ease his predicament.

U.S. diplomats were among the first to respond and had to do so on their own initiative. The president, his cabinet, and Congress could react only belatedly, as the young republic's capital, Philadelphia, was six week's sailing away from Europe.

After rebuffing Coalition approaches, Lafayette concluded at Nivelles that his incarceration would last longer. As he considered sources of help, he decided that his military service in America and honorary awards of U.S. civil status sanctioned his assuming an American identity "exclusively"[1] and requesting diplomatic protection. As the Austrians allowed him to write and receive correspondence, he was able to turn to an envoy who was geographically and personally an obvious choice: William Short, the American minister resident in the Dutch Republic. Short had served as private secretary to Thomas Jefferson when he was the American ambassador in Paris and then as first American chargé d'affaires to France. He had visited Lafayette frequently. Lafayette had three requests of Short: to publish the protest that the captives signed the night of their arrest; to demand that the Austrian viceregal government in Brussels allow him a personal interview with Lafayette as "an American citizen, an American officer, no more in the French service"; and to work with other U.S. diplomats to bring about Lafayette's release. *"No time is to be lost,"* Lafayette stressed.[2]

Short responded with sympathy and goodwill, describing himself as "mortified" by news of the arrest. He had the Rochefort declaration published in Europe's leading political news journal, the Dutch *Gazette de Leyde,* and promised that he would try to visit. However, he doubted the prospects for overt diplomatic initiatives. He had no influence with the Austrian government; indeed it would never allow his visit. Nevertheless, while he asked Secretary of State Jefferson to send instructions, he also asked colleagues Thomas Pinckney, ambassador to Great Britain, and Gouverneur Morris, ambassador to France, to consider an immediate, joint approach to Austria. He was appalled that a man devoted so long to America might not receive its help on the first occasion he asked for it.[3]

Short and his colleagues knew that Lafayette's request for diplomatic action confronted two harsh realities. While the three envoys accepted him as "our fellow Citizen,"[4] his recent service as a French military officer took legal precedence, preventing formal diplomatic protection and giving the United States no grounds to demand his release. The United States was still a young, weak republic, little respected and often despised by the European powers. In the midst of war between the Coalition and France, President Washington insisted that America pursue strict neutrality. Even before Lafayette's capture, the president had instructed U.S. diplomats to avoid any action that might involve the country in European disputes.[5]

Pinckney was quite willing to apply his considerable cultural, legal, and political experience on Lafayette's behalf and to do so in cooperation with Short and Morris. Still he could not imagine any effective strategy. The situation gave him the most "painful Sensations." A South Carolinian educated in Britain and France, Pinckney had been captured and paroled by the British during the American war, spending more than a year in exile from his native state. He had become friends

Thomas Pinckney, U.S. ambassador to Great Britain. Library of Congress

with Lafayette in the Virginia war theater, and after the war he had worked as a lawyer and served as a state legislator and governor of South Carolina. He then took over the London embassy, the preeminent U.S. diplomatic post. Pinckney sympathized deeply with Lafayette but doubted that a joint appeal could persuade Vienna. The appeal "can at best serve as a testimonial of national gratitude, and may be a consolatory tribute to the feelings of a man of whose services and zeal for our country there is I believe but one sentiment in America." Pinckney did conclude that at least a gesture was in order, so he drew up the draft of a diplomatic note affirming Lafayette's American credentials and requesting his release.[6]

Morris's objections doomed the draft. He voiced the same concerns that Pinckney had expressed: even if Lafayette were technically a U.S. citizen, his French army service at time of arrest had priority; Austria's rejection of the request, Morris argued, would dishonor the United States, offend its government, and hurt Lafayette more than help; furthermore, he asserted, to "meddle in the great Quarrel which agitates Europe" was against America's vital interests. Morris concluded that the note's harm would outweigh its benefits and that "although the private feelings of friendship or Humanity might properly sway us as private Men we have in our public Character higher Duties to fulfil than those which may be dictated by Sentiments of Affection towards an individual."[7] Short and Pinckney reluctantly agreed.[8]

A fourth U.S. envoy, who neither participated in his colleagues' correspondence nor agreed with their consensus, took a desperate step on his own after Lafayette was transferred into Prussian hands. In mid-October 1792, William Carmichael, an old Lafayette comrade and current chargé d'affaires in Spain, sent Lafayette an open letter via Prussian minister Schulenburg, with a cover letter explaining that he also intended it for Schulenburg's eyes. He declared to Lafayette that "I will sacrifice my life & the little fortune which I still possess to aid & assist you to the utmost of my power" and assured him that the four million other Americans felt similarly. Carmichael then alluded to threats against Frederick William. Carmichael claimed to have stopped "a project of assenation [assassination]" against the king, but said he was willing to use violence himself if "the necessity is *extreme*." Indeed, he confided allegedly to Lafayette, "for you my dear friend I will go to greater lengths than for any person under heaven & I have a few *chosen* friends that are determined—let princes think." Carmichael claimed to have made plans for allies to risk their lives to avenge any hurt or wrong done to Lafayette. "I have said enough, you will understand me," he concluded. He also used the threatening tone in the cover letter to Schulenburg: "I would if possible prevent the terrible consequences. I have all in my power." The language was extreme for a diplomat. Schulenburg gave the king the original letters with translations but stated that "they appear to me only to merit contempt."[9] The court took the incident as a fluke and did not respond further.

Carmichael's act was the odd exception to the rule of overall harmony between the president's policy and his envoys' actions. Short, Pinckney, and Morris knew that any steps they took would have to be sensitive to Lafayette's ambiguous legal status and to remain within the strictures of formal neutrality. Still they indulged in "hope that a Moment will soon offer in which Something may be done for [Lafayette's] relief."[10] They found the moment by engaging eventually in collaboration with the president, cabinet, and legislators in Philadelphia, in low-profile, allegedly informal activity.

One project was arranging monetary support. In November 1792 Morris advanced Lafayette ten thousand Dutch guilders (then equivalent to four thousand dollars) from U.S. accounts at Amsterdam. After Lafayette's transfer to Magdeburg, Short placed the money in a Magdeburg bank for the captive's use. The prison commandant could withdraw funds with Lafayette's permission, but money left over on the captive's departure would revert to U.S. control. Morris assured Madame Lafayette and her family "that the United States would take care of them" and loaned her one hundred thousand livres from his own pocket. Washington gave her two hundred guineas from his personal funds, deposited at Amsterdam, explaining, "This sum is, I am certain, the least I am indebted for services rendered me by Mr. de la Fayette, of which I have never yet received the account." He seemed quite willing to send more.[11]

It proved unnecessary. American officials found a way to send much more substantial amounts while removing any grounds for Coalition protest; they gave Lafayette back pay for his service as an American major general in 1777–83.

Jefferson noted that, although Lafayette had relinquished in writing any "particular allowance or pension" at the beginning of his American service, the wording of his declaration did not exclude regular pay. Also Congress had never officially accepted Lafayette's offer. Jefferson consulted the war department on the amount of unpaid salary, apart from accrued interest, and the administration made a formal proposal to Congress. Washington signed the act into law shortly before the Prussians extradited Lafayette to Austrian Moravia. Secretary of State Edmund Randolph placed the money in Pinckney's hands to disburse on Lafayette's behalf.[12]

U.S. envoys also conducted informal talks with Austrian and Prussian representatives. Short asked the emperor's minister in Holland about his sovereign's intentions.[13] After Austria handed Lafayette over to Prussia, Pinckney approached the Prussia minister in London, Baron Constanz von Jacobi, "unofficially and expressly in my private capacity," to ask for information and awaken interest in more humane treatment and release. Jacobi promised to request news of Lafayette. He also promised to ask that the captive be allowed to correspond with family members by "open" letters, messages that the authorities would read and approve for delivery. At least the Lafayettes would know each other to still be alive.[14]

President Washington explicitly authorized this sort of low-key diplomatic action, to which he alluded in reply to Adrienne Lafayette's plea for a special envoy: "The measures you were pleased to intimate . . . are perhaps not exactly those which I could pursue, perhaps indeed not the most likely, under actual circumstances, to obtain our object. But be assured that I am not inattentive to his condition, nor contenting myself with inactive wishes for his liberation."[15] Washington bade Jefferson to instruct U.S. envoys "to neglect no favorable opportunity of expressing, *informally,* the sentiments and wishes of this country respecting the Marquis de Lafayette." Jefferson's directive stressed preference for "informal solicitations" but also authorized "formal ones" if deemed necessary. These instructions went explicitly beyond the original commission, but Washington approved them nevertheless.[16]

Under pressure from Lafayette and his family, Philadelphia took action that was formal but confidential. Viscount Louis de Noailles, Lafayette's brother-in-law and a veteran of the American war, arrived in May 1793 to press Washington and cabinet members for public gestures. Jefferson then reiterated to Pinckney "to consider [Lafayette's release] as an object of interest in this country, and to let me know what may be expected in the case," especially through Jacobi.[17] A personal plea soon arrived from Lafayette via contacts in Britain.[18] That fall, Washington received another letter from Madame Lafayette. "Can anything be said, or done, respecting the Marquis de la Fayette?" the president implored Jefferson.[19] Jefferson passed the query on to the London embassy, and Pinckney renewed his request to Jacobi "on behalf of our unfortunate friend." This time, however, Pinckney made the petition explicitly "in an authorised stile." Thereafter he addressed both Jacobi and the Berlin court officially, though quietly, at what he deemed appropriate occasions. He also asked the British ministers of war and foreign affairs, William Windham and Lord Grenville, to intervene with Berlin.[20]

In early 1794 Washington decided to address Lafayette's Prussian captor directly, but he still upheld the pretense that it was not an official act. He felt that if he acted as a private citizen through an informal channel, then he could address the king without endangering neutrality or debasing himself as a democratic head of state asking favors of a crowned ruler. At the suggestion of Treasury Secretary Alexander Hamilton, Washington turned to fellow Virginian James Marshall, brother of John Marshall, the future Supreme Court chief justice. James Marshall had recently visited London on real-estate business and planned to sail again from New York City that January. Washington persuaded him to serve as his private courier to Berlin and to solicit Pinckney's advice on his way through London.[21]

In March, during Marshall's sojourn in London,[22] Pinckney handed him written instructions that defined Washington's letter as unofficial, "not written by the President in his official capacity" but as "a private gentleman untinctured by the most distant recollection of his being the President." Marshall was told to keep his mission's object "as secret as circumstances will admit" in order to prevent potential enemies from blocking delivery of the letter. He was to avoid anything jeopardizing American neutrality and to "behave with the greatest reserve on the subject of European Politics, as a subject or object on which we do not permit ourselves publicly to entertain an opinion." Finally Marshall was not to deliver the letter at all unless sure of success, to spare the dignity of president and republic.[23]

Verbally Pinckney told him to seek help from Frederick William's brilliant, politically progressive uncle Prince Henry of Prussia, but to avoid the king's chief minister, Lucchesini. The prince, a hero of the Seven Years' War, had received Lafayette on his 1785 Prussian tour and since then had expressed strong sympathy for him. Experience had proven Lucchesini to be hostile to Lafayette. To avoid alerting Lucchesini, Pinckney kept Jacobi, his Prussian counterpart in London, in the dark about the mission.

Marshall received an enthusiastic reception from Prince Henry at his palatial seat of Rheinsberg, northwest of Berlin. Henry wrote the king and Count Philipp von Alvensleben, state minister for the royal household and member of the Foreign Affairs Department, advocating Washington's petition. Lucchesini was away in Vienna, preparing to accompany the king to Poland, but nonetheless Henry proved to have little influence on his nephew's government, since Frederick William had long been jealous of his uncle's military record and intellectual capacity. Marshall did not succeed in an interview with Alvensleben, who revealed that Prussia had already agreed to extradite Lafayette. Later that day Marshall noted that the minister had not described the captive as being in Austrian hands yet, so he requested a half-hour talk with Lafayette under guard before the transfer. Alvensleben replied that the handover had just occurred.

The claim was false and premeditated. The transfer did not occur until two weeks later. Before the original interview with Marshall, Alvensleben had asked the king if he might use the fabrication to spare his majesty "a useless importunity." Frederick William gave permission, but—perhaps a bit ashamed—pretended that it might be true after all: "I have reason to think Lafayette is already in the hands of the emperor; if not, this will happen at any time." Immediately afterward, in a postscript to his note, the king tried to accelerate plans for Lafayette's extradition: "Send a courier to the commandant of Neisse, telling him to press M. Botta to receive Lafayette if he has not left yet." Taking Alvensleben's argument at face value, Marshall never sought a royal audience and never turned over Washington's letter. He wrote Henry for advice, but Alvensleben and the king had already informed the prince. Henry saw no point in further appeals. Marshall declined his invitation for another visit to Rheinsberg and returned to London empty-handed in June.[24]

Lafayette expressed gratitude for American efforts[25] but was not surprised that they had failed to achieve his release. "America is very far away, and the politics of Europe are very tortuous," he noted. He thought Washington had requested British help and wondered why George III would "do a favor for the two men whom he most detests." The best Lafayette could hope from low-key U.S. initiatives was "to procure modifications in our imprisonment, but not our liberty."[26] It was his best hope, that is, unless the United States was willing to request his release publicly. Lafayette repeatedly encouraged this step in the next months.[27]

In Britain many members of the opposition Whig party sympathized with Lafayette. They were commonly known as "Foxites" after their factional leader, Charles James Fox, in the House of Commons. The news of Lafayette's arrest struck member of Parliament Thomas Erskine "quite prostrate," while Fox's own pity was mixed with relief that Lafayette had escaped the Jacobins. Fox's nephew Henry Richard Fox, Baron Holland, a guest of Lafayette the previous year in Paris, commented after Lafayette's handover to Prussia, "Good God! that after the great and honorable part he has acted in either Hemisphere, he should be at the age of 35 the prisoner of a parcel of unenlightened German Hussars or the Lord knows what."[28]

Whig sympathy turned to action. The great Foxite patron Lady Georgiana, Duchess of Devonshire, cornered James Harris, Baron Malmesbury, whom Foreign Minister Grenville had appointed special envoy to Berlin, and "begged" him to help improve Lafayette's prison conditions. She also suggested an appeal to the Russian tsarina, Catherine II.[29] At the opening of a new parliamentary session on 13 December 1792, Fox attacked the Coalition monarchs for imprisoning "brave but unfortunate" Lafayette "in defiance of the wishes and compassion of us all, and

in a manner that must provoke the indignation of every virtuous man in Europe."
The Alien Bill that came under consideration tightened surveillance of foreign
residents in Britain and simplified their expulsion from the kingdom. In response
George North, Earl of Guilford, asked the House of Lords where French exiles
were then to turn for refuge, given that "the cruel imprisonment of La Fayette
would warn them against approaching any country occupied by a German army."
Charles Grey raised the issue in Commons, pointing to "barbarous treatment"
of French Constitutionals such as Lafayette and Pusy at the hands of the "tyrannic
states" Austria and Prussia. John Mitford, loyal to Prime Minister William Pitt
the Younger, replied that the bill would not deny refuge to Lafayette and other
Constitutionals. However, Fox objected that he had heard "a person of high rank"
advocate deporting Lafayette should he come to Britain. Shortly thereafter Samuel
Whitbread noted in Commons how Lafayette's group was "lingering in the cells of
a German fortress" and voiced outrage at "the slow consuming horrors in which
La Fayette dragged on his existence."[30]

In the course of 1793, a particularly influential Foxite couple rose to promi-
nence among Lafayette's supporters in Britain. Member of Parliament John Barker
Church and his American wife, Angelica, had lots of money and useful ties on
both sides of the Atlantic. As a young man, Church had fled Britain after a duel.
In America he became commissary general of the Continental Army and successfully courted Angelica Schuyler, daughter of Philip Schuyler, distinguished major
general, member of the Continental Congress, and friend of Lafayette. Angelica's
brother-in-law was Alexander Hamilton, Washington's aide-de-camp and later
treasury secretary. After returning to Britain, Church founded a successful trading
business and entered Parliament.[31] During a winter in Paris, Angelica befriended
Lafayette and Jefferson. In England she and her husband had access to the royal
court as well as to Commons. They entertained the powerful, wealthy, and distinguished at their London home on Sackville Street and at their country estate,
Downe Place, just west of Windsor. Guests included U.S. envoys Pinckney and
Morris, French émigrés, and British politicians—both conservative, such as William Pitt and Edmund Burke, and more liberal, such as Fox and the "party of
English Jacobins" that Morris found so "insufferable" one evening at the Church
dinner table.[32] From his Magdeburg prison, Lafayette repeatedly expressed hope
that his friend Angelica could use her influence in American circles.[33]

The Churches did in fact appeal to Washington and Jefferson on Lafayette's
behalf, keep contacts with U.S. officials, and contribute financially to his cause.
Church money went to Adrienne Lafayette and missions to gain Lafayette's release.[34] Angelica promoted, and may have initiated, the idea of compensating
Lafayette for his U.S. service.[35]

Foxite Whigs again brought up Lafayette's plight in Commons while he was
at Neisse. On 6 March 1794, Whitbread moved that Britain end its alliance with

Angelica Church, her son Philip, and a servant. Painting by Jonathan Trumbull, Belvidere Trust, Belvidere Villa, Angelica, New York

Prussia and Austria, calling the treatment of Lafayette "a cold-blooded act of the most malevolent and fruitless cruelty, that ever was perpetrated in the whole history of tyranny." Michael Taylor saw Prussia as "the worst power we could unite with," given how it "had plundered Poland and so barbarously treated that excellent character M. de la Fayette." Fox condemned the incarceration as "that disgrace on civilized society," from which Britain must distance itself. It was hypocritical to support constitutional monarchy in France while looking the other way as "he who loved rational liberty, who loved his country and his king, who had sacrificed, in their defence, all that makes life desirable, was languishing in one of the most loathsome dungeons of a Prussian prison." Pitt responded that Lafayette's "fate was never at the disposal of this country" and that it was vital to maintain the alliance with Prussia and Austria: "The question is, whether we should allow one act of injustice to deprive us of the assistance of those powers in resisting a system of intolerable injustice, not merely existing in France, but attempted to be introduced into every other country." Whitbread's motion went down to defeat, 138 to 26.[36]

Despite their weak numbers, Foxites refused to drop the case. Richard Fitzpatrick announced plans for a motion that George III intercede with Berlin. Some customary Pitt supporters, including General Charles Marquess Cornwallis in Lords, joined the initiative.[37] This was the former General Charles Earl Cornwallis, whom Lafayette had helped to defeat at Yorktown. The motion came up on 13 March, seconded by Colonel Banastre Tarleton, another of Lafayette's battlefield opponents. Fitzpatrick argued that Britain could not simply shirk responsibility by claiming that it had nothing to do with the arrest. "To save the lives of enemies from Austrian and Prussian barbarity" was a matter of basic justice and national pride. Was it not incumbent upon Britain "to notify to our ally, that, as far as this country is concerned, we disclaim all participation in the iniquitous treatment of these unhappy persons?" Lafayette had acted virtuously in promoting constitutionalism and defending his king, as Fitzpatrick could attest from personal acquaintance with the man. Britain was trying to attract the French Constitutionals as allies, and Lafayette was their leader. When Pitt protested that interceding with Prussia would be "setting up ourselves as the guardians of the consciences of foreign states," Fox retorted that failure to interfere would make the British "accomplices of the diabolical cruelty of the Prussian cabinet," and Lafayette's fate would determine many Frenchmen to join the allies or not. He stated that the captives' arrest was "treachery," and their "prisoner of state" status was based on "no law but the law of tyrants." Edmund Burke objected that Lafayette was "the origin and author of all these calamities" of the French Revolution and therefore deserved his fate. Given how so many had suffered, "this extraordinary affectation of sorrow for the lot of one culpable individual was misplaced, ridiculous, and preposterous." After several others spoke, the resolution lost by 153 to 46.[38]

To his nephew Lord Holland, Fox lauded their kinsman Fitzpatrick's performance: "Uncle Dick made one of the best speeches yesterday that I ever heard in Parliament." Even Burke was said to have praised the address, and some Pitt adherents voted for the resolution. Still, Fox conceded, "we made a miserable division, considering the question." The nation was at war; Fox's sympathy for the Revolution and political liberals had lost favor; and his parliamentary faction was shrinking dramatically in size and influence.[39]

Though the motion had failed, sympathy did appear in the press. William Miles, a radical journalist who had met Lafayette during the American war, published a refutation of Burke's arguments in the *Monthly Review,* an article soon available as a pamphlet. The Dutch *Gazette de Leyde* lauded Fitzpatrick's speech and published excerpts. Germany's *Minerva* printed two articles on the debate, both in Lafayette's favor.[40]

Several of Lafayette's London supporters had been his war enemies a decade before. Fitzpatrick and Cornwallis had fought him at Brandywine. Cornwallis and Tarleton had fought him in Virginia. Miles had served in British naval forces along the Atlantic coast. A speaker on Lafayette's behalf in Lords, George North, Earl of Guilford, was son and heir of the prime minister who had directed efforts to quash the American rebellion.[41]

The publicity assured Lafayette that he had not been forgotten. As he faced extradition in May 1794, he wrote of his gratitude: "I feel obliged to both sides for the honor that each does me, to declare itself for or against me." He wrote to London aides, "I cannot express with what feeling, what satisfaction we have heard of the parliamentary debates," concerning not only the role of Foxites but also "the honorable animadversion of Mr. Pitt and his associates." The effect of both parties publicly discussing the case in Parliament, Lafayette believed, was to pressure the British and Prussian governments to avoid blame and leave the emperor standing alone. Now was the time, he suggested, for supporters to "besiege" Vienna. Especially effective, he believed, would be the work of sympathetic publicists: "They are intimidating the men who guard us and encouraging those who help us. Yesterday, again, the commandant of the fortress avowed to me his fears of being treated unfairly by them. The energetic concert of patriotic quills is, under the circumstances, essential to our survival and liberation." Lafayette asked aides to pass his letter to Fox, Fitzpatrick, and others who might address the case again.[42]

Additional aid came from French Constitutionals. They began to form what one of them later called a "holy conspiracy" to deliver Lafayette's party.[43] Among them were former aides arrested with Lafayette at Rochefort, who escaped or gained release from the Antwerp citadel. Notably active were Captains Louis de La Colombe, André Masson, Alexandre and Louis Romeuf; War Commissioner René Pillet; Lieutenant Colonel Charles de Cadignan; and Adjutant General Philippe Charles d'Agrain. By mid-October 1792, three of them had reached Rotterdam, where La Colombe contacted Short to ask of Lafayette's situation. La Colombe then continued on to London.[44] When France declared war on Britain early the next year, La Colombe proposed to the British government that French Constitutionals raise a revolt in the mountainous southern French provinces of the Auvergne,

Cévennes, and Dauphiné, on condition that the Coalition release Lafayette's party and help to reestablish a constitutional monarchy in France.[45] La Colombe also traveled to Philadelphia to provide information and appeal for public action.[46]

Lafayette's family took a special place among those working for his release. Supporters included many in-laws, in a family that had ranked only behind the royals: Viscount Louis de Noailles, Prince Philippe and Princess Anne de Poix, Countess Adrienne de Tessé, and Marquise Anne de Montagu. However, the most active supporter of all was Lafayette's wife, Adrienne de Noailles de Lafayette. She fully shared her husband's political views and supported his work. Jacobin authorities had put her under house arrest after her husband's flight. She wrote to Washington through an English employee, begging public U.S. action on her husband's behalf. In December 1792, she petitioned Frederick William to release his captive. She pointed out that the Jacobins' animosity to Lafayette spoke "eloquently in his favor."[47] She sent new pleas to both president and king early the following year. She complained to Washington about U.S. silence, while she urged Frederick William "that finally your Majesty will be convinced that justice and the interest of your reputation requires that M. de la Fayette be released" or at least that the king would allow the prisoner news from his family.[48] However, Jacobin authorities suspended Madame Lafayette's activities for her husband when they carried her away to prison in November 1793.

A well-connected French couple living in British exile, Princess Adélaïde d' Hénin and Count Trophime de Lally-Tolendal, showed remarkable ability to act on Lafayette's behalf during his Prussian captivity. They approached highly placed British officials to intervene with Berlin and then made appeals directly to the Prussian king.

Princess Hénin was a close friend of Lafayette's, as well as a distant relative by marriage. She had been Marie Antoinette's lady-in-waiting and sister-in-law of the first Constitutional minister of war.[49] In her Paris home Lafayette, Lally, and others had planned Louis XVI's escape. After the Jacobin attack on the Tuileries, wealthy heiress and writer Germaine de Staël sent a Swiss woman to pose as the princess while Hénin took the woman's passport and slipped across the border. Hénin's estranged husband died under the guillotine.[50] She could well appreciate the discomforts and dangers that Lafayette was facing.

Count Lally was a British subject by virtue of Irish ancestry. He also had reason to identify with Lafayette's plight. After the Seven Years' War, the French court had made Lally's father a scapegoat for the loss of India and executed him. Though politically more conservative than Lafayette, Lally had worked closely with him to save France's constitutional order. In the coup of August 1792, the Jacobins imprisoned Lally at the Abbaye in Paris. Influential friends, including Madame de Staël, persuaded city authorities to release him hours before the onset of the city-wide massacre of prison inmates on 2–6 September. This incarceration left Lally with

Princess Adélaïde d' Hénin.
Bibliothèque nationale de
France (68.B.47283)

Count Trophime de Lally-
Tolendal. National Portrait
Gallery, London

lasting anxiety, even after he fled to England. "Poor Lally has been here," said one of his early English hosts, "and he seems better than when he left us, except being somewhat subject to start when the door opens. He is not yet quite sure that the gaoler will not enter."[51] Both his father's fate and his own imprisonment help to explain Lally's energetic engagement for captive Lafayette. Though a British pension came with conditions that prevented Lally from publishing articles openly on Lafayette's behalf, he could and did encourage others.[52]

Lally declared his devotion to Hénin and lived with her in her rented homes in London and nearby Richmond.[53] Here the couple hosted like-minded refugees and quickly evolved into the center of the Constitutional emigrant community.[54] "You seem to me to be the source and the queen of everything," De Staël later wrote the princess.[55]

Lafayette began writing Hénin soon after his arrest,[56] and she became his chief correspondent throughout his Prussian custody. She passed on his news to supporters and relatives and sent him information in return. Lally was her right hand, and together the two became leading advocates of efforts to free Lafayette.[57]

The couple had contacts with many influential people in British government. They were politically inclined to Tories and the royal court, so they initially thought little of the Whig opposition centered on Fox. Lally was on good speaking terms, at least for a time, with George III, cabinet ministers, and members of Parliament favorable to Prime Minister Pitt.[58] These ties even made Lafayette and his fellow prisoners a bit apprehensive.[59]

At first the couple's high-level contacts promised to be useful in aiding Lafayette, but in the end most of them fell short. Lally had spoken with George III on several occasions, both before and after fleeing France,[60] but the king and his court remained prejudiced against Lafayette.[61] Horace Walpole, Earl of Orford, lived near Hénin's Richmond home and originally considered her one of his "chief informers" about French events.[62] Beginning in autumn 1793, however, he avoided returning her visits.[63] John and Abigail Baker-Holroyd, the Baron and Baroness Sheffield, were gracious to many Constitutional refugees, and they particularly welcomed Hénin and Lally to their Downing Street residence in London and their Sussex country home, Sheffield Place.[64] After Lady Sheffield's death in early 1793, however, her husband gradually lost interest in these ties.[65] Lally was related by marriage to Sheffield's parliamentary colleague Alexander Wedderburn, Baron Loughborough. They seemed to be excellent terms even after Lally and his wife became estranged.[66] However, the good relations ended when Loughborough became lord high chancellor in January 1793.[67] Foreign Minister Lord Grenville welcomed intelligence from Lally, but after "two long conferences" about Lafayette's plight, Lally managed to get only Grenville's confidential pledge "to intervene in indirect ways to have [Lafayette's] material treatment improved, whose cruelty he sincerely condemned." Lally recognized that the minister's political reason trumped his humane inclinations, leading him to be "at least indifferent to the effect [of the captivity], and even struck with fear concerning the influence that M. de Lafayette, once set at liberty, could have in the contemporary struggles in which Europe was engaged." Even Lally had to admit that he "could not guarantee the political harmlessness of M. de Lafayette once his shackles were broken."[68]

Politics prevented most Tories, cabinet members, and the court from helping Lafayette. Many had long held him in contempt. Upon hearing of Lafayette's arrest, the queen expressed the hostility succinctly: "Wee see the very man who wonted to crush England, proves the curse to his own country, & I am sure he will meet with his reward."[69] On top of that, in February 1793 France and Britain declared war on one another, an event that weakened ties Hénin and Lally had enjoyed with British notables.

In the course of that year, Hénin, Lally, and associated Constitutionals made their own private appeals to Berlin. One of them occurred through the forceful mediation of Germaine de Staël, another by means of a Hanoverian British courier to the Prussian capital, Justus Erich Bollmann.

During a visit to England, Madame de Staël discussed Lafayette's situation with Hénin and Lally. They met several times: in March at social gatherings in London; in the beginning of April at Juniper Hall, a house De Staël had rented in the Surrey countryside at Mickleham; in mid-April at Hénin's London home; and again shortly before De Staël's return to the Continent in late spring. On the way to her Lake Genevan château, Coppet, in early June, De Staël stopped at Château Löwenberg, near Murten (Morat), to give Adrienne Lafayette's aunt Countess Adrienne de Tessé news from the Hénin-Lally circle. Then De Staël visited fellow writer Isabelle de Charrière in the nearby Prussian province of Neuchâtel to request that she exert her influence with Berlin. Charrière convinced a local man with ties to the Prussian court to make inquiries, but his report of conditions at Magdeburg proved to be inaccurate. De Staël encouraged Charrière to use her prestige as a Prussian writer to gain information, improve conditions, and appeal for the captives' release. Charrière refused, claiming that she carried little weight in Berlin and could find no highly placed Prussian who dared approach the king on the matter.[70]

At the same time, Hénin and Lally sponsored their own, more direct petition to Berlin, one that preceded Washington's attempt through Marshall. At the end of June, Lally wrote an essay praising Lafayette as a chief supporter of constitutional monarchy in France and as protector of Louis XVI and his family.[71] Hénin and Lally sought an appropriate person to deliver the treatise and to argue for release. Justus Erich Bollmann, to whom De Staël introduced Hénin and Lally in early April 1793 at Juniper Hall,[72] seemed a natural choice. He had native knowledge of the German language and culture. As a Hanoverian he was a British subject because George III was also electoral prince of Hanover. Bollmann was a recent

Justus Erich Bollmann. From Friedrich Kapp, *Justus Erich Bollmann* (1880)

medical graduate, who had delayed professional commitments and marital ties to travel. During an extended western European tour, he became fluent in French and English. He also developed wide networks of acquaintances, cosmopolitan manners, and strong political sympathies for Lafayette and the Constitutionals. Above all he proved courageous and resourceful in another rescue: smuggling De Staël's current lover, former French minister of war Count Louis de Narbonne, from Paris to London during the massacres of August 1792. Since then Bollmann had come to know Lafayette's supporters in England and yearned for an exciting political vocation.[73]

By early August 1793, Lally and Hénin had asked Bollmann to take their appeal to Berlin. They hoped to pay his expenses but could offer no additional stipend. Bollmann believed in the cause. The mission flattered him, promised fame, and played into his desire for travel and adventure. It also offered prospects of professional preferment on a successful return. Though French Constitutional émigrés had lost most of their resources and influence, powerful Americans might employ someone who had rescued a national hero. Bollmann accepted the offer.

A key condition was money. Princess Hénin contributed £100 so that Bollmann's trip could begin promptly. As a proxy for Adrienne Lafayette, Lally tried but failed to draw on private funds that Washington had sent her. He also asked

U.S. envoy Thomas Pinckney to urge Gouverneur Morris, his colleague in Paris, to share some of the money that his government had put at her disposal. This effort also failed. Over five months Lally begged and borrowed £674. The money came largely from private sources, but also included £100 in diplomatic funds from Pinckney. Lally planned to pay all the money back from funds at the Lafayettes' disposal. He sent much of it after Bollmann by bank transfer.[74]

Bollmann traveled across the Channel to Brussels; up the Rhine by boat via Düsseldorf, Cologne, Koblenz, and Mainz; then up the Main to Frankfurt. There, in late August, he bought a sturdy new travel coach, with which he drove "day and night" through Thuringia to the Saxon city of Leipzig.[75] Thence he continued north through Prussian Brandenburg to Berlin. When he arrived in early September, Frederick William was off visiting troops in the Rhineland, so Bollmann continued on to the Rheinsberg palace of Prince Henry.

The prince proved to be an enthusiastic host, as he would soon be to James Marshall. He was delighted to welcome a gentleman from England (a place he esteemed for its freedom and enlightenment) and an emissary of Lafayette. Bollmann enjoyed the high-minded company and luxurious surroundings during ten days of discussions, but he suspected that the prince exercised little influence on his royal nephew. Henry described one key royal adviser as particularly unfavorable to Lafayette: the king's chief minister, Lucchesini.[76]

Bollmann retraced his route south and west to catch Frederick William on the western front. When he approached Frankfurt am Main in early October, Bollmann encountered couriers seeking horses for the king. Frederick William had left front lines in the western Palatinate for Poland. His goal was to secure acquisitions that he had agreed on with Russia in a second Polish partition. Then he planned to return to Berlin in a month. If Bollmann wanted to meet the king, he could do little more than reverse course again and wait. Bollmann spent a week in Leipzig translating Lally's defense into German and writing letters. He was convinced that authorities in Saxony were not interested in reading his mail (unlike Austrians in the Netherlands and Prussians in Brandenburg). As a result, he revealed to intimates, including family members and Madame de Staël, the real purpose of the journey. On balance he believed the political situation was in his favor.[77]

When he returned to Berlin, Bollmann approached several officials. Among those who showed sympathy was Count Heinrich von Haugwitz, minister of foreign affairs.[78] Unfortunately Bollmann was unable to get past Lucchesini, about whom Henry had warned him. A Tuscan of brilliant conversational skills, Lucchesini had become a favorite of the aging Frederick II, won recognition by Frederick William II for work in diplomacy, and received a posting as ambassador to Vienna. This post gave him the rank of state minister and effective status as the king's chief minister. Lucchesini had never learned to speak German, so the interview with Bollmann was entirely in French. Deriding Lafayette as an unrepentant fanatic intent on stirring up libertarian ideas that threatened Europe's peace, Lucchesini also revealed plans to extradite the captive to Austria. Bollmann gained the strong impression that Lucchesini spoke for the king. He particularly noted the minister's extreme arrogance and his "hard-hearted aristocratic remarks." Bollmann's impression was confirmed when Lucchesini refused to allow Haugwitz, his nominal superior in diplomatic matters, to hand the king Lally's written defense. Lucchesini claimed that Lafayette was the Coalition's prisoner and that Frederick William was only his custodian; hence the king could not act alone. The chief minister further claimed that a sovereign power could facilitate Lafayette's release by guaranteeing his political inactivity and retirement to America. However, the diplomat added sarcastically, "Lafayette is a madman who would foment disturbances everywhere. Even in America he would incite war on Washington." Bollmann concluded that Lucchesini considered "Lafayette to be a scoundrel because he himself is one." No argument would move the "almighty" minister.[79]

Bollmann was not the only observer to conclude that Lucchesini, not Haugwitz, led the foreign ministry.[80] In truth Haugwitz also enjoyed the king's favor and followed the royal will with what other observers saw as fawning accommodation. Haugwitz and Lucchesini were surely coordinating their responses in what one would later call a "good-cop / bad-cop routine." Haugwitz, known for his friendliness, was playing the role of one who had Lafayette's best interest at heart. It resembled Frederick William's later disingenuous claims that he would have released Lafayette gladly, had the emperor not been the Frenchman's actual warden. Francis later played the same game with Adrienne Lafayette, reversing roles and blaming the king.[81]

Before leaving Berlin, Bollmann had planned to have the captives' treatment "given the greatest possible publicity" regardless of the official response. This included publishing his German translation of Lally's memoir, which Bollmann hoped to give Christian Voss, the Berlin publisher of a new political journal, *Friedens-Präliminarien* (Peace Preliminaries), "as soon as it is time." Bollmann also arranged with the journal's editor, Ludwig Huber, to add two letters that Lafayette sent to Hénin shortly after his arrest.[82] But when he asked Lally's permission, Lally begged him to keep the piece confidential out of concern that it would jeopardize several people in France. Lally particularly feared for his family as well as Lafayette's. He also did not want to anger Lucchesini, which would likely work to Lafayette's disadvantage.[83]

Bollmann gave up his Berlin projects. In mid-November 1793 he directed his carriage northwest, and started back toward London.[84] Lafayette's supporters abroad soon learned of the failure, as did Lafayette himself. Pusy proposed that "in place of abasing his immense talent to make his memoirs for a king who does not read them or does not comprehend them," Lally should simply publicize oppressive Coalition policies, including those directed at Lafayette and company. Lally was baffled that officials intercepted his written defense of Lafayette and kept the king from seeing it. In Switzerland, De Staël lamented that "Lally is eloquent, but he is known in advance" as a Fayettist.[85] She expected Lafayette's jailors to dismiss anything Lally said or wrote.

Lally, however, kept on working for the cause. In February 1794, ten days after seeking an appointment with Jacobi, Lally asked Pinckney to hand Jacobi a letter for Haugwitz that insisted on Lafayette's innocence, objected to officials' refusal to allow the written defense to reach the king, asked in the name of Lafayette's wife that prison conditions improve, and enclosed a note to Lafayette. Lally expected Haugwitz to forward the enclosure. He told Pinckney that Prussia's foreign minister sympathized even if he could not do so openly.[86] Lally also prepared copies of Lafayette's letters and a memoir on strategy for La Colombe, who would travel to America to appeal for public action. Finally, when Lafayette's case came up in Parliament, Lally provided background materials to Tory members of Parliament.[87]

By this time yet another group of Lafayette's supporters had begun to emerge in a place where Bollmann stopped on his way back to Britain, the twin ports of Hamburg and Altona. As a "free imperial city" along the Danish border, Hamburg enjoyed relative political autonomy. The adjacent town of Altona had its own special freedoms, granted by Danish royal charter to help it compete economically with its larger neighbor.[88] The two cities together formed Germany's international trade and publication center and sheltered a linguistically, religiously, and politically diverse population.

Writer and publisher Baron Johann Wilhelm von Archenholz was an especially influential figure, and he became Lafayette's major champion and intermediary on the Continent. A former Prussian army captain, Archenholz spoke several languages, maintained a network of useful relationships, supported the French Constitutionals, secretly corresponded with Lafayette in captivity, and published highly sympathetic essays. He had been released from military duty at the end of the Seven Years' War,[89] and he had traveled extensively in western Europe. In the course of six years in Britain, he had become devoted to that country's culture and constitutional politics. A crippled foot caused him to take up a more sedentary career as author of well-received travel and historical books and as editor-publisher of political and literary journals. He had moved to Hamburg for its relative press freedom, and there he founded what became the most influential German-language journal of current affairs, *Minerva*. The journal was originally planned as a venue to report a variety of international events, but it soon focused on French news from a Constitutionalist point of view.[90]

The Revolution drew Archenholz to Paris, where he developed acquaintances among other German visitors and French notables. He spent months visiting the National Assembly and witnessed the Constitutionals' loss of power to politically less mature, more radical, and violent Jacobins. Full of foreboding about France's

Johann Wilhelm von
Archenholz. Engraving
by Friedrich Groegery,
Bildarchiv Preussischer
Kulturbesitz / Art
Resource, New York

political path, the prospect of invasion, and the danger to which his candid manner exposed him, he returned to Hamburg in summer 1792.

In the February 1793 issue of *Minerva,* Archenholz published a passionate
defense of Lafayette's activities during the Revolution, claiming that he had shown
self-sacrificial devotion to liberty, country, constitution, and constitutional king.
Archenholz condemned Lafayette's incarceration as senseless and illegal; indeed
as "the greatest cruelty that has occurred in this century." He ended the article
with encouragement and praise addressed directly to the captive.[91] After the issue
made its way to Lafayette through a sympathetic Magdeburg officer, Lafayette
wrote to Archenholz to express his gratitude. He also confirmed that Archenholz
had explained accurately Lafayette's reasons for fleeing France.[92]

Archenholz continued to publish sympathetic articles in *Minerva,* which kept
Lafayette's fate in the public eye. One such article, in May 1793, fueled a controversy in the German press. The piece noted how Lafayette's case was drawing
attention especially in England and America, and it castigated prison officials for
holding their prisoner in subterranean cell without access to direct sunlight or
open air and prohibiting correspondence with family and friends. Prussian lieutenant Fritz von Walther und Cronegk objected in a Leipzig journal, *Deutsche
Monatsschrift* (German Monthly). Having guarded the prisoners and personally
spoken with Lafayette, Walther insisted that Lafayette enjoyed good food, his

servants' services, and a daily one-hour walk on the ramparts. The lieutenant had heard Lafayette exclaiming, "I will never forget the generosity of the Prussian officers to me." Archenholz retorted that both reports were correct: *Minerva* had described conditions through April, and Walther's description applied to conditions since that time. Lafayette felt called upon to give his own, more precise version to Hénin.[93]

The report in *Minerva* inspired Baron Friedrich von Oertel of Leipzig, where Walther's rebuttal appeared, to write a pro-Lafayette poem. "La Fayette's Dream" depicted America's guardian angel visiting the "dismal grave" of Magdeburg's Citadel to bless Lafayette with visions of a grateful America, of reunion with his family, and of a happy future for France. Composer Friedrich Baumbach put the poem to music.[94]

Other influential Hamburg residents took up Lafayette's cause. An entire group of democrats centered on the Sieveking-Reimarus family began to establish ties with Lafayette's British supporters, not through Archenholz but through Bollmann and one of their own, Caspar Voght, a Hamburg merchant living in Britain.

A "charming and patriotic circle" surrounded Georg and Johanna Sieveking in Hamburg. Georg was a successful merchant, a major civic leader, and an occasional writer. He shared democratic views with his former business partner Voght. Johanna was daughter of a well-known physician and city reformer, Johann Albert Reimarus, and niece of writer Margarethe "Elise" Reimarus. Christiana "Sophie" Reimarus was wife of Johann Albert, stepmother of Johanna Sieveking, and sister of August Hennings, a democratic Danish publicist and official who admired Lafayette deeply. The extended Sieveking-Reimarus clan welcomed the talented and scholarly, the democratically inclined, and the well-traveled. Their family friends included Piter Poel and Johann Reichardt, editors of *Frankreich,* a democratic Altona monthly dedicated to events of the Revolution. Reichardt, who had met Bollmann in Strasbourg in early 1792, was a well known composer who had lost his job as Prussian court musician because of his prorevolutionary views. Another acquaintance of the Sieveking-Reimarus family was the well-known poet Friedrich Klopstock, who had met Lafayette's close friend La Rochefoucauld and through him corresponded with Lafayette before his flight from France. Klopstock also wrote odes praising the Revolution, received honorary citizenship from the French Republic, and visited Lafayette in prison at Magdeburg.

These notables had sympathized initially with the Revolution, and their views had hurt them politically. In 1790, after celebrating the first anniversary of the Bastille's fall at a "festival of liberty" in Harvestehude, just outside Hamburg's walls, Georg Sieveking and Caspar Voght had been forced to defend themselves before the city senate. Sieveking received anonymous death threats and wrote a public defense while Voght left for a long sojourn in Britain.[95]

Voght's trip was happy for Lafayette's cause because it enabled the Hamburg circle to develop ties with his London supporters. Voght maintained correspondence with Johanna Sieveking, met the Churches, and became privy to Bollmann's activities.[96]

Bollmann arrived in Hamburg in late November 1793 after his failure in Berlin. He looked up Reichardt, who introduced him to the Sievekings. Bollmann met local luminaries at the Sievekings' city home at Neuenwall 149 and their country place at Neumühlen. He found the "brilliant circle" delightful, in particular "intelligent, still unmarried" Christine "Stinchen" Reimarus, Johanna Sieveking's attractive twenty-two-year-old stepsister. The two soon developed a romance, although Christine's parents opposed it because of Bollmann's lack of inherited wealth, a practice, or solid prospects.[97] Still, his interest in Christine kept Bollmann in contact with the clan, to whom he divulged his current mission, when he undertook an even more daring future project on Lafayette's behalf.

Despite the agonies of their Prussian incarceration, all was not dark for Lafayette and his companions. Supporters were cooperating in several countries to give financial aid, maintain communications, defend the captives' role in the Revolution, publicize their plight, and press for release.

3

LOOSENING PRISON BONDS

Even as Lafayette's party arrived at the Magdeburg Citadel on 4 January 1793, the larger political picture was changing in ways that determined the captives' destiny. More than twenty years before, Russia, Prussia, and Austria had jointly attacked Poland, weakened by generations of misgovernment and civil war, and apportioned a third of its population and territory among themselves. Since this partition Russia had been looking to extend its western borders even further, into most or all of the rest of Poland, which Russia had long come to view as its own protectorate. When a democratic-reform movement resisting Russian control established a progressive constitution in Poland on 3 May 1791, Tsarina Catherine II was determined to reassert her control. King Frederick William II of Prussia made note of her decision. When he began plans in January 1792 to attack revolutionary France, he hoped to claim territory in compensation for his expenses. He had his eye in particular on the harbor of Gdańsk and other Polish lands that would better link Prussia's own eastern provinces. In May, Catherine II took advantage of Prussian and Austrian mobilization against France to invade and occupy Poland. The Poles defended themselves nobly. General Tadeusz Kościuszko, formerly Lafayette's comrade in the American war, became a national hero as he successfully took on much larger Russian forces. But within days of the Poles' greatest victory under Kościuszko, at Dubienka in July, the self-occupied, timid, and corrupt King Stanislas II ordered the Polish army to end all resistance.

Prussia wanted its share of the spoils and could prove a useful ally if Russia were willing to settle for less than the whole Polish kingdom. On 23 January 1793, without revealing its plans to Austria, Prussia signed a secret treaty with Russia to share in the second partition of Poland. Prussia received a portion one-fourth the size of Russia's but deemed the new territory of great strategic worth. The justification Prussia and Russia offered for their actions was circular: that they had acted to stop the "contagious" spread of French revolutionary ideas in Poland and that they were thus entitled to an "indemnity" for their costs in warring against the Revolution.[1]

Thereafter Frederick William was increasingly determined to make peace with France in order to release the Prussian forces needed to subdue Polish resistance to his annexations. Poland's partition seemed to offer him much more profit than continued war on France, which to date had brought little more than a string of defeats. When he left the Rhineland front to inspect his new acquisitions in Poland in early October, he ended effective Prussian participation in the war against France. He claimed that the French war had always been Austria's cause with Prussia serving only as a benevolent friend. This statement was ironic because the king had been much more insistent than Austria on going to war against France and much more aggressive in pursuing it.[2] As a result of his new policy, Frederick William lost all interest in holding Lafayette and company. Wriggling out of the yoke of the French war, ridding himself of Lafayette's party, and turning his full attention to Poland became all the more critical when, in March 1794, Kościuszko issued a manifesto in Krakow that sparked a national uprising against Poland's occupiers.

Meanwhile two things helped ease conditions for Lafayette and his fellow captives at Magdeburg: the work of supporters abroad and events within the prison walls. For a time, gaps in security even made it feasible to plan escape. When these gaps closed, new breakout plans developed for Neisse, the next prison site.

Conditions began to improve a few weeks after the Lafayette party's transfer to Magdeburg in January 1793, thanks to Lafayette's supporters, who were sending money and lobbying the Prussian court to improve prison conditions. At the same time contingencies within Magdeburg's Citadel, especially the presence of sympathetic garrison officers, diminished the captives' isolation.

American funds allowed Lafayette to pay for decent, plentiful nutrition. He could request roasted meat, as many servings as he wished, and his choice of wine.[3] Prison authorities allowed him to make other purchases from the account, through people he described as "a galley slave, two orderlies, and a servant on contract." He loaned his fellow captives large sums of money.[4] He, Maubourg, and Pusy bought enough books to assemble considerable personal libraries.[5]

Count Lally's appeals helped to weaken the communications ban. On Adrienne Lafayette's behalf, Lally wrote Lieutenant General Karl von Raumer, commander of a Magdeburg infantry regiment, requesting that Madame Lafayette and her husband be allowed to hear from one another. Raumer soon arranged this, apparently on his own authority, adding his own, underlined cover note to Lally: "Here is the response of the vanquisher of Cornwallis." In February 1793 the king transferred Raumer to Poland. Lally then made another appeal, this one to Berlin through Thomas Pinckney, asking that the Lafayette family be able to correspond on personal matters. Pinckney handed the message to his Prussian counterpart in London, Baron Constanz von Jacobi, who sent it to Counts Philipp von Alvensleben and Heinrich von Haugwitz of the Prussian foreign ministry. They passed on the message to Major General Levin von Geusau, a departmental director in the Prussian Supreme War Collegium. At the personal direction of the king, Geusau instructed Magdeburg fortress commander Hüllesen to allow the correspondence on the condition that Lafayette avoid political references or detailed descriptions of prison conditions. In late April, Lafayette was able to write his wife in the presence of Hüllesen, who censored what he wished. The letter passed through the hands of Geusau, Alvensleben, and Haugwitz in Berlin and then continued through Jacobi, Pinckney, and Hénin in London. Adrienne Lafayette and daughters, Anastasie and Virginie, sent notes to Lafayette via Hénin and Lally, who added words of their own. The other prisoners received the same opportunity to write their families.[6] Correspondence with nonrelatives remained out of bounds, and permitted mail was censored. In one case, according to Lafayette, Hüllesen cut off a note that Lally had added to a letter by Hénin and claimed that Princess Hénin herself must have made the excision. After Lafayette read the preliminarily censored mail, Hüllesen had it copied, translated, and sent to Berlin.[7]

Beyond approved correspondence, the prisoners began to communicate secretly with each other and the outside world. They wrote notes using vinegar, ash, and a toothpick, and folded them into small wads to escape detection. Lafayette and Maubourg were able to communicate confidentially, probably through a shared chimney. Through their rotation, one third of the Citadel garrison came into contact with the captives. Some officers were willing to convey secret correspondence and supply uncensored reading materials. Lafayette alluded to these men as "devoted" people who had been "approachable on the subject of liberty" even within the prison, in a culture that encouraged mutual denunciation. These officers included at least one "lieutenant of this garrison" who served as courier to Hamburg.[8]

Some of these men are identifiable. A Lafayette acquaintance later claimed that an elderly veteran of the Seven Years' War, Captain Johann Müller, brought Lafayette writing materials, newspapers, periodicals, and "a dictionary to enable him to understand them, as they were almost all in the German language."[9] The daughter of another officer, Benyamim von Sievers, recalled decades later that he had often claimed to have risked his life for Lafayette and done so without regrets because "General Lafayette is a man who is worth risking everything for."[10] Two French-speaking lieutenants took similar risks and eventually cooperated in a failed escape plot: Kleist (first name unknown), who came from Baden, along the French border; and an ethnic Frenchman, François Le Blanc de Souville.

To be sure, there were mishaps. In early summer jailers discovered and seized a letter to George Washington that Lafayette had hoped to slip out of the prison.

On some occasions Lafayette was unable to smuggle out secret correspondence promptly and had to destroy it.[11]

Overall the secret activity proved effective. By mid-March, within ten weeks of arriving at Magdeburg, Lafayette had learned through secret notes and oral reports of French victories, Louis de La Rochefoucauld's murder, and Louis XVI's execution. At this time he sent Hénin his first secret note. With the same dispatch, he sent a note to John Parish, U.S. consul in Hamburg, requesting American intervention.[12] Initially Lafayette had received only approved books with blank pages torn out to inhibit secret writing; however, he soon received uncensored books and journals through his officer friends. In March, Lafayette was given the previous month's issue of *Minerva*, with its passionate praise by Archenholz. Lafayette smuggled out a letter of thanks, and a close relationship blossomed.[13] Another work that slipped past authorities was the memoir of a Magdeburg prisoner in 1754–64, Baron Friedrich von der Trenck. Trenck detailed numerous attempts to escape a small fort on the city's south side, a stronghold known after its shape as the Star.[14] The book may have brought Lafayette more pessimism than hope because Trenck was unable to break out on his own.

By autumn Lafayette was reading newspapers from Leyden, Hamburg, and Berlin. Among them were Europe's leading political news journal, the moderate Dutch *Gazette de Leyde*; Hamburg's *Minerva*; and a French-language journal of Berlin, *Mémoires de l'Académie Royale*. Lafayette welcomed the conversation that books and journals offered him, and he often read materials in French, English, and Latin too quickly for his suppliers to keep up.[15]

By autumn "an extremely complicated machine" of surreptitious correspondence existed among Hamburg, London, and Philadelphia. Relying on Archenholz in Hamburg and the cooperative officers in Magdeburg, it also depended on intermediaries between Magdeburg and Hamburg whenever an officer could not serve as personal courier. Hénin's suggestions for go-betweens, though rejected by Lafayette, included an unnamed woman friendly with Countess Angélique de Montrond, a royalist émigré writer in England, and Raumer, currently military governor of Gdańsk. Though for a time the intermediary was Dr. Christoph Girtanner, a Göttingen physician and editor, he lost the position when he thoughtlessly sent the prison administration two secret letters. Happily Lafayette saw that Major Pilsach did not realize what he had received. Lafayette asked to see the letters again, this time unattended, to write a response. He held them over fire to discover a message written in lemon juice on one of them, a practice that Hénin, De Staël, and other Lafayette supporters had adopted for surreptitious correspondence. He promptly burned the letter. He also convinced Pilsach that he, Pilsach, had misplaced it, and that in order to hide his mistake, he had best not send the remaining letter to Berlin. Finally Lafayette slipped out a message to Girtanner through a couple of friendly officers, begging him not to send anything to anyone by public mail.[16]

Berlin also allowed the captives access to their personal attendants. Lafayette was still not able to see his secretary, Pontonnier, isolated for what Lafayette called the young man's crime of being able to write. However, Lafayette's valet, Compte, was able to join him every morning. They enjoyed long chats about home throughout the day.[17]

In June an unexpected visitor ended even the official pretense of a block on political news and prisoner interaction. Infantry General Duke Frederick of Brunswick had been a favorite of his uncle Frederick II, in part for conversational brilliance and literary interests. The general was both first cousin and brother-in-law of the present king and brother of Charles of Brunswick, reigning duke of a substantial north German principality, who had served as supreme commander of Coalition forces. On inheriting the spectacular estate Sibyllenort near Oels (Oleśnica), Silesia, Duke Frederick requested and received permission to surrender command of Prussian troops on the lower Rhine. On his way into literary retirement, he wanted to have a chat with Lafayette, whom he had met at Potsdam in 1785. The visit took Hüllesen completely by surprise, but he could not refuse an officer and noble of this magnitude. Hüllesen arrived at Lafayette's chamber with the duke, Major Pilsach, and two other Prussian officers, all but one of them French speakers.

The group soon expanded. When Duke Frederick asked about Lafayette's health, Lafayette responded that he was doing as well as one could expect, but that Lameth was much sicker from his damp cell and lack of exercise. The duke wondered if Lafayette would mind if the other state prisoners joined them, and Lafayette replied that it would give him great pleasure. The staff opened Maubourg's cell, then fetched the other two chief captives. Lafayette embraced them, explaining to the duke that he had not seen them since their arrival. The visitors were so numerous and the cell was so small, that half the men had to stand outside.

The duke was renowned for his independence of mind, jovial manners, and wit. He freely told Lafayette and company the latest news from the front, including the recent flight of Charles Dumouriez, Lafayette's successor as commander of the French Northern Army, to Coalition forces. The duke described how Dumouriez had been paid to destroy a list of names of key pro-French Dutch. Dumouriez took the money and then gave the list to Coalition officers anyway. Brunswick reported that the Coalition had maintained secret ties with Queen Marie Antoinette and Louis Philippe, sometime Duke d'Orléans, the revolutionary dubbed "Philippe Égalité." Brunswick also reported that Coalition leaders seemed ready to accept constitutional government in France as a necessary starting point for long-range political solutions. Lafayette remarked on the irony that republican Philippe Égalité was now a Coalition ally while he himself, who had repeatedly defended his king, was a Coalition captive.

Brunswick assumed that the talk could not reach beyond prison walls, but he was wrong. Lafayette gave a written report to a garrison officer, who smuggled it to Archenholz in Hamburg. Archenholz passed it on to Hénin near London, who had the U.S. envoy at The Hague informed about the list divulging Dutch patriots' identities. He was to warn Hollanders whom he knew to be closely allied with Lafayette, such as Pieter Paulus of Rotterdam. In case the warning failed to arrive by this route, Lafayette also tried to reach Paulus and other Dutch patriots through U.S. ambassador Pinckney and Lafayette's former aide La Colombe, both in London.[18] Even from a Prussian stronghold, Lafayette was able to protect allies far afield.

The duke's visit appeared to loosen the prohibition against others seeing Lafayette. Friedrich Klopstock was able to visit and chat with Lafayette. Klopstock did not think Lafayette's quarters merited the word *dungeon,* pointing out that the prisoner wrote letters, read, and occasionally received Citadel commander Pilsach for dinner. Klopstock arranged for his friend and fellow writer Friedrich Köpken, a leader of the Magdeburg literary scene, to help supply the captive with books.[19]

The privilege of walking in the open came in late spring of 1793. Lameth seemed close to death, so the prison doctor pleaded with Hüllesen to allow the exercise. The general responded in what Lafayette took to be an abusive manner, but nonetheless referred the matter to Berlin. The Foreign Department, which had received Pinckney's petition for better conditions, gave its support and in mid-May the king gave in, allowing Lameth walks under guard for an hour each day. When Duke Frederick made his visit in early June, Lafayette was convinced that he would report the prisoners' sickly pallor to Berlin. Lafayette came to assume that U.S. pressure also played a role in the king's subsequent decree that not just Lameth but all state captives be allowed to take a one-hour daily walk on the Citadel's southern bastion, each at different times and under continual escort. "Finally, after more than five months, I felt the contact of outside air, not without a shiver," Lafayette wrote. "I saw the sun again, and felt quite well." He noted that being able to walk more than six paces and breathing fresh air strengthened him to withstand the humid chill inside. To be sure guards went to great lengths to hide the prisoners from outsiders' view. For example they arrested the father of a child who had seen a captives' servant at a distance of thirty paces. Still, these walks and the return of warmer weather improved the prisoners' health.[20]

In two cases the authorities even allowed a relative to visit. By September, Lameth's condition had deteriorated to the point that Berlin permitted his mother, Countess Marie de Lameth, to come with her servants, live nearby, and care for him.[21] Maubourg's younger sister, Marie de Maisonneuve, had similar success. Making use of her husband's ties as minister of the Maltese Order in Berlin, she was able to persuade the king to allow her to stay near her brother after his transfer to Glatz in early 1794 and to visit him daily.[22] Though Pinckney inquired whether Adrienne Lafayette might obtain permission to join her husband, her incarceration in November 1793 by the Jacobins voided the petition.[23]

In early 1794 at Fort Prussia in Neisse, his last Prussian prison before extradition to Austria, Lafayette continued to enjoy relatively decent conditions. The food was clean. Jailors spent three imperial florins daily for it, as they did for the food served Maubourg and Pusy when they arrived three months after Lafayette; and thirty crosses (kreuzer), or a half florin, per servant. The cell that Lafayette occupied was roomier than his cell at Magdeburg and surfaced with clean planks. He had access to his valet, Compte, and, for the first time, his secretary, Pontonnier. Soon after arrival, he received permission to write to Princess Hénin. Fort Prussia's commandant, Major Karl von Hanff, watched as he wrote the letter, read the results, and demanded revisions to keep the focus on family rather than political concerns. Hanff had the final versions translated and had copies sent to Berlin. Lafayette wrote similar letters to relatives and to his fellow captive Maubourg, who was temporarily at Glatz. Inspected mail began arriving again for Lafayette, from Simiane, Maubourg, Maisonneuve, and Hénin. Except for Major Hanff, the Neisse prison staff could not speak French, but the staff physician commanded rudimentary Latin, and to speak with him Lafayette was able to draw on his own Latin, which he had excelled in as a youth at the Parisian Collège de Plessis. That, as well as pantomime, enabled him to make desires known. He also began to study German and presumably to apply it in interactions with guards.[24]

Lafayette also enjoyed other improvements. By late January 1794 prison officers were again lending him books and journals, including those he had read in Magdeburg. He met two French speakers, one of whom was a garrison colonel. The other was Hanff's French wife, Caroline, who developed a strong affection for the captive. The escorted daily walks that Lafayette had known at Magdeburg continued at Neisse, albeit in the narrow, wholly enclosed and muddy courtyard. He came to understand that Hanff and other officers showed him as much benevolence as possible, given standing orders from Berlin. Surely at his wife's urging, Major Hanff added a note to one of Lafayette's letters, assuring Princess Hénin that he was trying to care well for her friend.[25]

Evidence of one mailing reveals how complex the provisions could be to send messages to Lafayette and his supporters. Madame Simiane's château of Cirey was conveniently distant from central authorities, some 250 kilometers to the southeast of Paris on the eastern border of Lorraine. There Simiane handed over to a courier a package from friends in Paris and another package addressed to Princess Hénin in London. The courier was a secret agent of De Staël, probably Jacques Tréboux, who had also been involved in smuggling his employer's friends and acquaintances out of France. The agent unsealed and disposed of the envelopes

Neisse fortress city in 1780. The Prussians held Lafayette's party at Fort Preussen, the star-shaped citadel above the city. Staatsbibliothek zu Berlin–Preussischer Kulturbesitz (Kart. N 18 342)

and slid the messages into the pleat of his boot. After passing into Switzerland, he turned the mail over to De Staël at her château at Coppet. She then enclosed the letters in a missive she sent by Prussian Neuchâtel post to Maisonneuve, who had been living near her brother at Glatz since the beginning of February. De Staël hoped that Maisonneuve would be able to pass the message to Lafayette at Neisse, 50 kilometers further east.[26]

The secret communications kept the prisoners hoping for escape. As a former Prussian officer, Archenholz of Hamburg-Altona seemed especially well suited to planning a breakout. In late June a garrison officer brought him Lafayette's plan. Lafayette had concluded that supporters' pleas could bring prison improvements but not release. He felt that, considering matters of time and honor, it was "infinitely better to seize than to receive" freedom. Lafayette asked Hénin to tip him off if a person fluent in German, supplied with money, and skillful in stealth made his way to Magdeburg.[27]

He also sent Pinckney letters of exchange to obtain six thousand French livres (pounds) "for my attempt to emerge from Captivity." One third of the amount was to reward the courier for bringing the rest to Magdeburg. Pinckney paid the agent, sent Lafayette four thousand livres from a diplomatic "contingent fund," and informed Secretary of State Jefferson that the congressionally approved money, administered by Morris, would make up expenses. The United States remained officially neutral, but Philadelphia knew full well that its envoys were plotting Lafayette's escape. Jefferson offered no objection to Pinckney's actions.[28]

In London the Hénin-Lally circle had already directed Bollmann to pursue an escape if his Berlin mission failed. Bollmann confided to editor Ludwig Huber that "there might be means of another (cleverer, more violent) nature, in order to achieve *the same* goal with *certainty.*"[29] Lafayette asked that Bollmann take his orders from Archenholz.[30] Bollmann purported to be on his way home when he stopped in Hamburg, contacted Archenholz, and awaited his signal to start for Magdeburg. Archenholz had already acquired the necessary horses.[31]

Maubourg, a trained engineer, prepared a map of the Citadel and its surroundings. The map showed the known guard posts and a "point where one can easily descend" on the southeastern side of Margrave Bastion. Maubourg traced a path leading northeastward between sheds and a brick oven along walls to the left and a branch of the Elbe to the right, before descending a cofferdam to the island's northeastern point. There the map marked possible places to embark for a trip downriver. The drawing showed that there were no guards en route, although there were some stationed to the west.[32]

The plan had been developing for weeks. In August, Archenholz had sent Lafayette advice drawn from his knowledge of Prussian military protocol and installations and of the territory between Magdeburg and Hamburg. Sievers or Le Blanc carried Lafayette's proposals to Hamburg, likely with Maubourg's map in hand.

The escape would include three phases. The first would take the men downriver to waiting horses. The second would take them to Helmstedt, twenty-nine miles to the northwest, and transfer them to a coach. The third and longest stretch would take them northward by backcountry roads to Hamburg-Altona.[33]

The first phase required them to bribe Captain Friedrich von Münchow, commander of the guard. The captain seemed convinced of the scheme's success and happy at prospect of substantial reward. He hardly seemed to mind violating his duties as Prussian officer and subject. Lafayette foresaw that at 5:00 P.M. on the appointed day, after his afternoon walk, sentinels under Münchow's command would take over. Eventually higher officers would retire to bed, including fortress commandant Hüllesen and vice commandant Pilsach. With any luck Münchow could arrange for his guards to drink a soporific. Around 7:00 P.M., Münchow and Le Blanc would open the prisoners' cells. The officers and the escapees would traverse the fortress walls and, at the north end of the island, pick up a boat to float down the Elbe. Five miles downstream they would disembark on the left bank to continue overland. Le Blanc would be ready with a map, itinerary, arms, passports, and a wig to disguise Lafayette as a gentleman on a normal excursion. The men would find horses waiting in care of a Jewish groom. Lafayette viewed Jews as natural allies because of his support for Jewish political emancipation in France and their communal ties across Europe.[34] Archenholz would pick a time and house in Helmstedt, where he would have a carriage waiting. Lafayette advised that it should be "a six-place post-coach, for which four good horses and a postilion are enough, with a post-boy on horseback." The escapees would then travel north in relays of carriages and horses arranged by the postboy. Archenholz was to specify the route, although there might be necessary detours. The final destination was Altona, a few hundred feet downriver from Hamburg, just across the border in Denmark and out of Frederick William's reach. Münchow would make his way abroad, perhaps moving to France with Lafayette's help, while Le Blanc would accompany the escapees to England.[35]

Difficulties soon appeared. Even before Sievers or Le Blanc left for Hamburg, Lafayette deplored how the officer had been "compromised once more." He questioned whether the man dare ask for leave. Lafayette urged speed within the bounds of necessary caution. If the plan were exposed, Lafayette wanted the officer to flee to Hamburg and from there to Britain.

One key problem was that Captain Münchow had backed out. By late August he had written Lafayette two notes in which he refused participation. The reason he gave was that a brother-in-law had failed to repay a substantial loan. Lafayette suspected that Münchow was holding out for more money. He hoped that a new offer might satisfy him, but if not, Münchow knew only his part of the plan. He had never been told of the correspondence with Archenholz.

Lafayette concluded that there was still hope, but that speed was vital. His most promising strategy was to flee up the chimney of an inner room. The plan's disadvantage was that only Lafayette and Maubourg, in adjoining cells, had access to the chimney. They would have to leave Pusy and Lameth behind. Lafayette regretted the prospect but felt that he owed his supporters an attempt to escape. If successful, he thought, he might be able to accelerate his companions' release.[36]

Three weeks later Lafayette declared that "the most important part [of the project] has been arranged." Countess de Lameth had come to share the incarceration of her ill son, Alexandre, so he would not remain alone. All Lafayette needed was more financial backing from Pinckney for Archenholz to assure ample reward for those whose help Lafayette solicited.[37]

Bollmann posed as a physician seeking to examine Lafayette, and Hénin implored Magdeburg to let him visit.[38] Even when that failed, the captive wrote in code that his situation could not change "except by a *crisis*" (escape). The "old lady who is here" (Lameth's mother) had engaged an aide, perhaps one of her own servants, as courier. Archenholz was "my doctor" and "my Aesculapius" (the god of healing); Bollmann was "your doctor" and "your Aesculapius." The only way to cure Lafayette's "illness" was "to change the regime." Lafayette was sending Hénin a "consultation" on his health requesting "French and American drugs" (money for the breakout). Lafayette asked her to send her doctor, Bollmann, to consult with "the physician who ought not to be far from Hamburg," Archenholz. The goal was "curing me of this nasty illness" for which "your young doctor" had saved Narbonne; that is, rescued him. Lafayette dared to end his letter, "Ah, my dear friends, do not leave me here!"[39]

By the end of October 1793, the plan was set. Lafayette expected his description to Le Blanc would be "for the last time," but he also noted new breaks in confidentiality.[40]

Strategy had come to focus exclusively on Lafayette's escape. The chimney shaft was fourteen inches wide without any grate to prevent a slim person from squeezing through. Lafayette planned to use it as a ruse, by loosening some bricks and placing in the shaft his coat smeared with ashes. The goal was to keep the garrison command from learning the truth: that its own men had let him out. The conspiring officers would use the watch that one of them supervised to bring Lafayette to Le Blanc, who would escort him downriver to the rendezvous with the horses. There would be no reason to think that suspicion had fallen on Le Blanc, so he could return to bed in Magdeburg. Compte would spread the word that Lafayette was ill. Maubourg, for his part, would dress a dummy in Lafayette's night cap and cover it in his bed.

Lafayette also polished his plans for the trip to Hamburg-Altona. He decided to scale down the vehicle sent by Archenholz to a light carriage, since he would be the only escapee. He also moved his rendezvous away from Helmstedt. Although Helmstedt was outside Prussian territory, its sovereign, the reigning duke of Brunswick, was also a Prussian general and was not sympathetic to Lafayette's cause. Lafayette would simply change horses there and continue riding with the Jewish groom to Hanoverian territory. There the men would meet up with a translator, presumably Bollmann, who would help change horses and possibly carriages the rest of the way. Lafayette spoke English, so would pass as an English or American traveler.[41]

Lafayette claimed as late as mid-December that the escape might be possible, but even given "unexpected changes and a happy accident," his window of opportunity had closed. Prison security had increased in early November. Authorities added an additional, fifth inner door and padlocks to two outer gates. Friendly officers had allowed confidential meetings with fellow captives, but that practice ended. The commandant now came armed with pistols and kept door keys on his person at all times. Inspections and other precautionary actions became frequent. Lafayette no longer had access to an intermediary on staff, through whom he could slip messages to Le Blanc and Archenholz. Lafayette had to burn notes for lack of a courier. Still he doubted that the strengthened security was related to the breakout plan. He also did not think it related to his confidential ties to staff members. Instead he assumed that it was owing to his refusal to release his funds for food or to anger at the interest his captivity had drawn.[42]

It is likely, however, that an alleged accomplice had betrayed him. Captain Münchow had declared in October that he would not join Lafayette in flight and would remain in the army. He then petitioned the king to receive an infantry company in another regiment. But he still showed eagerness to know the escape plans, claiming that he could help. Lafayette felt that the captain would do this only "for his own profit" and wanted to appeal to Münchow's greed. He would take the captain aside and accept his decision not to join the flight. If the captain could ensure that Lafayette got out of the Citadel, the freed man would promise to keep Münchow's role confidential, give him handsome remuneration, and enable him to settle abroad.

At the same time, however, Lafayette knew that Münchow's self-interest could unravel the plot. Lafayette kept Münchow isolated from incriminating details and told him that other accomplices had lost interest.[43] Eventually Lafayette lost all trust, but still considered the captain "only slightly dangerous, since he does not know anything." Münchow was more than "only slightly dangerous." Lafayette had every reason to suspect him for betraying confidences and ruining chances for escape, but he refused to believe that the new precautions were "connected with any discovery." He was convinced "that our secrets and our confidants are alike safe, and that the redoubling of inquisitional methods has been occasioned only by stupidity," that the new precautions only "accidentally matched our schemes."[44]

On the eve of transfer to Neisse, he was still convinced that "not one of our intermediaries, not even faithful L. [Le Blanc], has been thus far discovered."[45]

There was a simple and obvious explanation for the tightened security: Münchow had told superiors of Lafayette's determination to escape, though he was not privy to details of the fully matured plan. He may have believed Lafayette's claims that Le Blanc, Sievers, and other officers had withdrawn from participation. He may even have wanted to protect them. If his chief motive was to advance his career, a display of diligence in reporting Lafayette's hopes was quite enough. Münchow did not need to expose fellow officers, and he might not have wanted to put himself at risk. When those officers responded to accusations against them, they might implicate him more deeply than he had suggested to superiors. They might even reveal that he had known of Lafayette's intentions since summer.

Archenholz and Bollmann had ended their cooperation, but this was only subsequent to the project's failure. Relations between the two men had been strained since they had fallen out in Paris. Bollmann described Archenholz by using the anti-Jewish stereotype of a person willing to do anything for money: as "a rough, physically and morally ugly would-be politician, and besides that also a true Jew and absolutely nothing at all besides!" He accused Archenholz of reporting French events only based on the market.[46] Given that Bollmann was impoverished at the time, one wonders if Archenholz had refused him a loan or demanded that he repay one.

Their relations did not improve in Hamburg. Bollmann waited a month for Archenholz's orders to meet Lafayette north of Helmstedt. In truth the delay was caused both by the need for additional funds and by the new security procedures at Magdeburg. However, Archenholz does not seem to have made this clear to Bollmann.[47] At a Christmas party, Bollmann broke his cover by bragging about his intentions to rescue Lafayette. Perhaps he did so to impress the young woman he was wooing, Christine Reimarus. Archenholz told Bollmann that he was unfit to serve as secret agent. He later wrote that Bollmann was "a wind bag and scatterbrain" for having revealed the plot. The project was at an end, and Archenholz sold the horses intended for it. Bollmann admitted that though the mission had ended in failure, he had "presumably warded off great evil and unmasked a useless swindler," apparently Archenholz. Days later in Holland, before he crossed the Channel back to England, Bollmann described his efforts as having been in vain. He blamed unnamed rogues who treated him "as they deserve to be treated themselves." Surely Bollmann was alluding in part to the power broker in the Prussian foreign ministry, Lucchesini, who had refused his appeal in Berlin; but he was also speaking of Archenholz.[48]

Bollmann returned to London frustrated and angry. He later admitted that attracting attention had ruined the plans, but he also claimed that he might have been effective had he remained independent of that "rogue" Archenholz. He blamed the publisher one day for having "tricked" him and eventually for having alerted Austrian authorities.[49] The last version completed his self-justification.

The Prussians sealed the plot's collapse on 4 January 1794, when they transferred Lafayette to Neisse. However, Lafayette did not give up his intention to escape. His secret appeals to supporters in Britain led to two new plans of liberation.

As Lafayette faced the transfer, he noted that Poland, bordering Silesia, might serve as a refuge and escape route from Neisse. He had several ties to the Polish court. Two of his longtime friends, Philip Mazzei and Lewis Littlepage, were advisers to King Stanislas II. The king had expressed admiration for Lafayette, and Lafayette had returned the honor by calling him "the leader of the Polish Revolution."[50] Later events did not substantiate the honorific. Lafayette also knew two prominent brothers, Counts Jan and Seweryn Potocki, who might establish communications with him from Poland. As in Magdeburg he considered the Jewish community useful, and it was particularly large in Poland. Through Mazzei and Littlepage, he requested the aid of Stanislas II. He also asked Hénin, Pinckney, and former aides in Britain to provide money and an intelligent, courageous agent. Meanwhile Lafayette would win over the guard officers at Neisse as he had at Magdeburg.[51]

Polish developments soon drew Lafayette's attention. In March his former comrade Kościuszko called for insurrection against the new partition of his country. Warsaw freed itself of Russian control in April and that summer withstood a siege by Prussian and Russian forces. The national resistance had particular success in western Poland, where rebel forces threatened borderlands of Prussia and Austria as late as September. Lafayette realized that the presence of Polish rebels in eastern Silesia, Moravia, and western Poland could help him.[52]

Unfortunately two key groups of Lafayette supporters divided their efforts. Both were in Britain, and both included French émigrés and Americans. One faction, centered on Hénin and Lally in Richmond, included Lafayette's aide Louis Romeuf and an American fluent in French, Legard Caldwell. The other group centered on the Churches' Downe Place, near Windsor, and their townhouse in London. This circle included U.S. ambassador Pinckney and former Lafayette aides La Colombe and Cadignan.

The division began when Pinckney sent La Colombe and Cadignan to deliver the last secret letters Lafayette sent from Magdeburg. All present discussed Lafayette's plea for another escape attempt and agreed to keep it secret. Within a day, however, a difference of opinion emerged over whom to count as an appropriate insider. To the consternation of Hénin's circle, La Colombe and Cadignan had divulged Lafayette's proposal, "point by point," to other French Constitutionals. The princess erupted in anger, and the two couriers responded in kind.[53]

The Hénin and Church circles began to work on separate rescue projects, each group maintaining its own confidences and oblivious to what the other was doing.

The Church group launched its plan first, probably because it was better funded. John and Angelica Church were wealthy, and Pinckney could contribute sums from the Lafayette accounts he managed. Lally, on the other hand, was surrounded by French émigrés who felt "constantly hindered in their efforts, for they are poor." He appealed to Pinckney, in vain, to help fund the circle's new project.[54]

The Churches and Pinckney picked Bollmann to carry out their operation, offering him the position by early February. He interpreted their words to mean that he would receive a substantial pension even in case of failure.[55] After his Berlin mission, Bollmann had found himself without money or a job. Still he had gained a taste for important, confidential political missions, which prevented him from settling for the less exciting career of a physician. He hoped to become a clandestine agent, mediator for the high born and powerful, or diplomat.[56] Pinckney persuaded him that heroic action for Lafayette would open doors in the young republic.[57] Bollmann also sought marriage to the well-to-do, well-connected Christine Reimarus of Hamburg. A successful rescue of Lafayette or even a glorious failure might enable Bollmann to achieve both his professional and marital goals, a matter he discussed with Voght in London and later with Johanna Sieveking in Hamburg.[58] Bollmann was certainly sympathetic to Lafayette, but his willingness to serve as escape agent would be no selfless act.[59]

Bollmann took a few days to consider the Church offer, but the outcome was never in doubt. Soon he alluded to his confidential project in letters. He spread the story that he was off on a long trip to Ireland and Scotland, but people familiar with his earlier mission could guess what he was doing. He was especially frank with Johanna Sieveking, whom Voght alerted to the new mission: Bollmann foresaw a two-month trip to Vienna, sponsored by a better funded group, of different nationality, than the one that had arranged his mission to Berlin.[60]

It is likely that a few liberal members of Parliament beyond John Church were aware of the expedition and aided it. William Smith, member of Parliament for Camelford and part of the faction voting with Fox, appears to have been a recipient of Bollmann's correspondence during the trip, giving Fox and others reports on the project's progress. Edmund Burke later attributed the escape attempt to "Mr Church, and others of the Fox party."[61]

News of the project reached the highest levels of American government. The Church circle sent La Colombe and Cadignan to Philadelphia to describe the plan to the president and secretary of state. Pinckney introduced the two Frenchmen by letter, referred to the escape plan that Lafayette had proposed, and avowed that "altho' I did not think myself authorized to take an active part in it or to make pecuniary advances for its execution—yet considering it to be attended with a possibility of success I wish to give it what countenance I can without commitment." He also inquired if the president wished him "to give more direct aid to the plan of which the outline is formed or if any other mode should be adopted." At the end of the report, Pinckney wrote a more explicit description of the project in numerical code. The decoded version reads: "This plan consists in sending a confidential person to Silesia[,] to which place Lafayette is removed[,] to try to establish a communication with him by letter and to take advantage of any favorable opportunity to procure his evasion." Two days later, Pinckney reiterated that he supported the project but was using utmost caution to keep his participation secret.[62]

Archenholz, Lafayette's key supporter in Hamburg, later claimed that President Washington "had not the least to do" with the escape project and that only "some careless friends in London had contributed."[63] Washington may have been unaware of what his government was doing, but that is unlikely. It appears that he simply looked the other way while a U.S. envoy kept the secretary of state fully informed.

Unaware of the plans engaging Bollmann, the Hénin-Lally circle began arranging an escape project of its own. They employed Louis Romeuf. "Full of zeal but also of discretion, of candor, always passionate to speak of his general," Romeuf would try to gain the Polish king's aid and slip into Moravia from the east.[64] Hénin notified De Staël in Switzerland, who—in view of uncertain political conditions in Poland—discouraged Hénin from buying some property there as a refuge for Lafayette.[65]

In late spring the Hénin-Lally circle notified the Churches and Pinckney of its interest in arranging another escape attempt. They did not respond, seeming to indicate an unwillingness to participate after the failure of Bollmann's earlier undertaking. Discovering that the Hénin-Lally circle intended to use money left over from Bollmann's mission to Prussia, La Colombe claimed to speak on behalf of the lenders, including the Churches and Pinckney, and insisted that the group was obligated to return the money now that the original mission had failed. Unbeknownst to Hénin and company, the Church circle wanted the money for its own project and hoped to discourage competition.[66]

Early in March, La Colombe and Cadignan announced to the Hénin-Lally circle that they were sailing to Philadelphia to speak with officials about strategy. They did not divulge that they planned to describe an actual escape plan. Unaware of this fact, Lally wrote a memoir for La Colombe to present in Philadelphia, one soliciting funds for his own group's breakout project. To Philadelphia officials, Lally seemed to substantiate Pinckney's proposal.[67]

Only after Bollmann left for the Continent did Pinckney and Church notify Romeuf and Lally that another rescue project was underway. Romeuf wrote Pinckney on 4 July regarding his plans to travel to Poland in Lafayette's cause. In return Church wrote Lally that "Mr P is clearly of Opinion that the project of Mr R's going to Poland will answer to no purpose" because of the Church project already underway. "Every Measure is already taken to make a fair Trial what Industry Activity and Money will effect, and I hope it will be attended with Success," he added.

Pinckney assured Lally in person that the Constitutionalist circle in London "could rely on what he says." He refused to give details, as the Churches "made him promise to keep it secret." Lally protested: "One is charged with a terrible responsibility in forming an enterprise without communicating it to the principal recipients of [Lafayette's] confidence, the representatives of his wife, children, and all his relatives and friends; to those, finally, who are in correspondence with him and to whom he reveals what he intends." If the plan succeeded, however, Lally assured the envoy that "we will be at your feet." Pinckney bowed his head in acknowledgment.[68]

The Hénin-Lally group called off its project and awaited developments. The Church group offered it no role. It also remained silent about the simultaneous American mission of James Marshall to Berlin. Lally never received an answer to packages he sent to Washington, containing letters from Lafayette and appeals for public help. The Hénin-Lally circle soon fell prey to misinformation that fueled resentments. It came to understand, for instance, that Bollmann had left in March. Such an early date created the impression that he "roamed all over Germany in grand style [*au grand seigneur*] until the month of October," when he made his first alleged contact with Lafayette.[69] In fact he left London in May and made initial contact with Lafayette in July. Under the circumstances the Hénin-Lally group would have to congratulate the Church group in event of the project's success, but it would also be ready to blame it for failure.

4

OLMÜTZ

When Prussia transferred Lafayette to Austria in May 1794, the French Revolution in the west and the Polish Partition in the east had entered critical new phases. The previous month Francis II had gone personally to the Austrian Netherlands to command troops attacking the French. Hysteria over the threat of new invasion fueled the Reign of Terror in France, a regime that broadened definitions of political crimes, dispensed with ordinary judicial procedure, and designated immediate execution for the convicted. More than fifteen hundred people died under the guillotine in Paris alone during June and July. But the Coalition offensive had already slowed. Emperor Francis returned to Vienna, and the tides of war reversed. On the very day of Lafayette's transfer, the Battle of Turcoing on the French northern frontier had forced the Austrians and their only remaining effective allies, the British, into retreat. By late July French troops had taken Brussels and Antwerp, forcing Coalition troops to abandon the old Austrian Netherlands. At the beginning of November, French control extended over the entire west bank of the Rhine. As France became more secure against attack, support for the so-called emergency measures of the Terror and its leaders disappeared. In late July the overthrow and execution of Robespierre and other radical Jacobins ushered in a conservative reaction.

A key factor favoring French ascendance on the battlefield was Poland's resistance to the second partition of its territory. In March, Poles rose up against their Prussian and Russian occupiers. In April, Polish forces captured Warsaw and Wilno. Only in the autumn did the uprising succumb to insuperable numbers of Prussian, Russian, and Austrian reinforcements. Disaster for Poland spelled salvation for France as the eastern conflict siphoned off Austrian forces and ended all Prussian contribution to the western Coalition.

In the midst of these events, Lafayette and his companions arrived in Austrian Moravia. Here they faced much stricter security than they had known during recent last months in Prussian Silesia. Authorities seized many personal items and prohibited correspondence, outside exercise, visits from outsiders, and even official use of the prisoners' names. The Frenchmen had to endure heavily fortified surroundings, close supervision, and poor sanitation. At the same time, however, they did have spacious rooms overlooking the countryside, personal belongings that escaped seizure, regular and plentiful food, and access to servants and medical care. Prison security also proved to be looser than it initially seemed, loose enough to enable Lafayette to establish secret communications and in the autumn to begin escorted excursions into the countryside.

On 17 May a Prussian captain and his soldiers escorted Lafayette, Maubourg, Pusy, and their four servants from Neisse. In extraordinary testament to their affection for Lafayette, Neisse commandant Hanff and his French wife, Caroline, followed in their own carriage. The group crossed the border at Ziegenhals (Głuchołazy) and descended into Zuckmantel (Zlaté Hory), the first Austrian Moravian town beyond. Halfway along the town's main street they turned in at the post station. An Austrian unit was waiting. Its captain drew up a report of the seven captives, their luggage, and cash, and gave his Prussian counterpart a copy. Lafayette asked Caroline Hanff to alert a key contact abroad, Princess Hénin in London, of his arrival at Zuckmantel and his next day's destination of Olmütz, where it appeared he was to stay. The Hanffs regretfully left Lafayette, who entrusted Madame Hanff with his last batch of outgoing mail. "M. de Lafayette took with him all our esteem, in the noble fashion in which he has borne his fate," she wrote Hénin in a postscript to Lafayette's message.[1]

The next morning the Austrian escort took Lafayette, Maubourg, Pusy, and servants south through the wooded Altvater mountains (Hruby Jeseník), past fields and villages marked by churches with onion-shaped towers. They stopped briefly at the postal station in Lobnig (Lomnice) and passed through Sternberg (Šternberk).

Toward midnight they arrived at Olmütz (Olomouc),[2] a fortified town[3] of about eight thousand civilians and six thousand soldiers[4] on the imperial highway leading south to the Moravian capital of Brünn (Brno). They crossed two wooden bridges, one about fifty meters long over the Morava River and another, a drawbridge over a smaller tributary serving as moat, the Mittelmarch (Mlýnský Potok). The gate had closed for normal traffic at nine, so the escort had to show special authorization. The carriages entered the white stone Castle Gate,[5] the only eastern vehicular entrance into town and only wide enough for a single wagon at a time. Inside they passed a one-story guardhouse on the right. Behind and above it rose St. Wenceslas Cathedral, seat of the cardinal archbishop. They drove westward

Prison barracks in Olmütz, where Lafayette and his fellow prisoners spent more than three years in a rear wing. Státni okresní archiv v Olomouci, Czech Republic

along Main Street, to a small triangular plaza known as Mary Square. The two baroque towers of the former Jesuit Church of the Virgin Mary of the Snows, now the fortress garrison's chapel,[6] rose on the southwestern side of the square. The carriages turned left into the gate of a long, four-storied baroque building, formerly a Jesuit college. Emperor Joseph II had turned over the college, the church, and related buildings nearby to army use twenty years before.[7] The carriages stopped in an inner courtyard and the prisoners descended.[8] The men had come under Olmütz military command, and remained in its custody for more than three years.[9]

At Olmütz, Lafayette and company were not the first whom Francis II had designated "prisoners of state." By 1793 the term applied to twenty-four persons, twenty French republican and four Polish rebel leaders, held in the Bohemian and Moravian fortresses at Königgrätz (Hradec Králové), Josefstadt (Josefov), Brünn, and Olmütz.[10] Austria soon held others at Kufstein in Tyrol and Eger in Hungary.[11] Lafayette's company of seven joined Bancal, Beurnonville, and Beuronville's valet, Marchand, at Olmütz.

Austrian policy was to isolate state prisoners from each other and from the outside world, to prevent escape or suicide, and to censor reading materials. Its administrators abolished many of the ameliorations granted by the Prussian king.[12] Lafayette's party considered incarceration at Olmütz to be worse than any they had known. Maubourg later confessed that neither the Prussian prisons nor anything he had read or heard about the Bastille and Jacobin jails had prepared the men for Olmütz.[13] Still, because of the Bastille's internationally powerful symbolism, the captives and their partisans later referred to their prison as the Bastille of Olmütz or the Austrian Bastille.[14] One Fayettist declared, "Olmütz, Olmütz: [the tyrants'] condemnation is written there in letters of steel."[15]

Lafayette's company had entered an existence intended to be strict, lonely, and secure. The emperor's orders on state prisoners, issued in July 1793, and subsequent orders by Lieutenant General Count Francesco d'Arco, the Olmütz fortress commandant, made this clear. Arco demanded that prison staff refuse to divulge news or engage in any conversation about a captive's identity or background, observe strict confidentiality, and take every precaution to prevent prisoners' contact with each other or outsiders. The goal was "to treat such a dangerous person as if he had been transferred completely out of the world while retaining only his life, as if he no longer existed and has been forgotten."[16] The instructions became well known to the prison personnel. Arco prided himself on the effort he put into articulating detailed orders in writing and reiterating them regularly to his men. The provost, or prison bailiff, thirty-one-year-old Sergeant Johann Platzer, and his direct supervisor, fifty-three-year-old First Lieutenant Caspar Jacob, kept copies in their separate living quarters.[17]

The strict security ordered by Arco had begun to loosen somewhat even by the time Lafayette's party arrived, and it continued to ease as troop movements brought reductions and changes of garrison personnel. Months before Lafayette's arrival, Arco had requested and received a temporary transfer to a field position in the Rhineland. Lieutenant General Baron Gabriel Splényi von Miháldy became interim commandant.[18] In March 1794, four days after the command change, a front opened in the east and led to a reduction in prison staff.

On the night of 18–19 May, when Lafayette and his men arrived, Jacob and Platzer searched them under Splényi's supervision. The Austrians confiscated some belongings that the Prussians had allowed them to keep. These included cash: in Lafayette's case hard currency equivalent to 652 Vienna florins (gulden) and 55 crosses (kreuzer)—a florin being worth 60 crosses—and increasingly worthless French banknotes (assignats) with a face value of more than 500 French pounds (livres). Also impounded were personal items: jewelry, pocket watches, snuff boxes, mess kits, teapots, padlocks, garters, collars, and buckles; and any sharp-edged or pointed instruments such as spurs, swords, scissors, pincers, saws, files, forks, knives, and razors. The cash and more valuable objects could be used for bribery; other items might enable escape or suicide. All the confiscated items went into storage in a chest at Splényi's quarters on the town's main square.[19]

The removal of sharp instruments seemed no great loss to Lafayette. He later declared that he was not so cooperative as to end his life. At meals he knew how to do without fork and knife. Lieutenant Jacob asked him one day if eating with his fingers were not new to him, and Lafayette responded coolly, "No, I have seen it employed in America among the Iroquois."[20] It must have startled Jacob to recall how his captive was a "hero of two worlds," whose experience had long ago extended beyond European palaces, salons, and officers' quarters.

The prisoners found confiscation of some reading materials more painful. Francis II had imposed strict censorship for the entire Austrian empire. According to his court's first decree on the subject, officials were to confiscate manuscripts and printed works that "contain principles that relate to the currently prevalent doctrine of freedom and to the French Revolution, by supporting or resembling them in any way," and send them "without fail" to the court chancellery in Vienna.[21] Jacob and Platzer seized from the captives all gazettes and books treating the French Revolution and constitutional government. They also impounded works published since the men's arrest. Splényi decided on the spot what had to go. He directed his men to take from the arrivals copies of Jean-Jacques Rousseau's *Du contrat social,* a French translation of Thomas Paine's *Common Sense,* and works of the skeptical philosopher Claude-Adrien Helvétius. Splényi also ordered a late medieval devotional classic, Thomas à Kempis's *Imitatio Christi,* impounded because the edition was recent. Pusy later claimed to have lost twelve books, while his jailors only admitted to having taken two. Pusy also lost several maps, largely of North America. Maubourg lost eight books and Lafayette some maps of Belgium. Maubourg recalled that decisions did not go without protest: "The commandant having opened an abridgement of the history of Greece, fell in the course of a very few lines upon the words 'liberty' and 'republic,' and nothing that I could say, was allowed to save the volume: it was irrevocably lost to us, as well as a number of others, for reasons equally important."[22] Lafayette felt moved to ask "if the Austrian government regarded them as objects of contraband" just because volumes contained such words. The obvious answer was that it did.[23]

Also seized were materials for writing and drawing, including paper, quills, ink, pencils, writing cases, compasses, and other mathematical instruments, along with all correspondence. The captives protested that the Prussians had allowed them to keep these things at Neisse. The Austrian officers "were greatly scandalized, and they bestowed an abundance of contemptuous epithets on the want of intelligence displayed by the Prussians in tormenting their victims."[24] The Austrian jailors did not permit prisoners to correspond with relatives at all, even on nonpolitical topics, hindering knowledge of whether loved ones were still alive.

These restrictions were quite effective for some time to come. When Count Lally wrote Lafayette in June 1794 from London, with an enclosure from Princess Hénin, Splényi passed on the letter to higher authorities. Eventually it reached the Aulic War Council (Hofkriegsrat) in Vienna, as did all recovered correspondence to or from prisoners. Lally's letter never reached Lafayette.[25] In July, Lafayette's request to speak with a cabinet minister about unspecified information of importance failed to elicit a reply.[26] In August, when Maubourg asked to correspond with his family about personal matters, Francis II noted to officials that this was prohibited to state prisoners.[27] That fall, Lally tried to send a letter to Lafayette through the Austrian minister in London, Count Ludwig von Starhemberg. Lally had hoped to tell Lafayette which of his relatives and friends had survived the Terror. Lally also pleaded that Lafayette's wife be able to know if her husband were alive. Starhemberg was personally hostile to Lafayette, Lally, Hénin, and other Constitutionals. He told Lally that the emperor was no less humane than the Prussian king and that the letter would surely reach Lafayette as had several other messages since he had entered Austrian custody. In truth Lafayette never received the letter through the Austrians.[28]

For the foreseeable future, there was also no possibility of exercise outdoors. The three chief captives were confined within the four walls of their rooms. Indeed Maubourg and Pusy never left their rooms until their release.[29]

There were no more visits by outsiders, including relatives offering care. The Austrians rejected the Prussian policy of allowing Marie de Maisonneuve to visit her brother Maubourg. Maisonneuve had followed the prisoners to Olmütz on the strength of a general pass from Neisse commandant Hanff and two handwritten notes of the Prussian king. To avoid attracting attention, Hanff had arranged for her to cross into Austrian Moravia via Troppau (Opava) rather than at Zuckmantel with the prisoners. He reported her presence to Austrian Moravian commander Botta only at the last minute, in a note sent the day the captives left Zuckmantel. Botta was taken by surprise and demanded an explanation. The lady had slipped into the country without proper clearance, he raged, and would publicize "the arrival, names, character of the prisoners, which runs directly against the explicit orders of His Majesty the Emperor." Why had the Prussian Supreme War Council not informed the Austrian envoy at the time it gave him the prisoners' identities? Hanff objected to Botta's aspersions, blaming the Austrians for poor border controls.[30] Maisonneuve appealed to Botta for improvements. They included delivery of an apolitical letter from relatives to her brother and permission to resume sharing his captivity. Botta told her to send the requests to the Aulic War Council, the supreme military body for administrative and legal matters. At the same time, he asked the council for instructions. Archduke Alexander Leopold, substituting for his brother Francis, cleared delivery of the letter but directed the council to enforce standards for state prisoners. Maisonneuve was expelled from the emperor's lands without being able to say goodbye to Lafayette or her brother. She also had to leave behind a letter that Lafayette hoped to send to friends abroad. For travel costs, Splényi let her borrow fifty Prussian louis from Lafayette's impounded cash.[31]

Splényi assigned the prisoners numbers to replace their names. Standard procedure for state prisoners, this practice reduced fraternization, outside contact, and morale. Veteran captives Beurnonville, Marchand, and Bancal were numbers one, three, and four, so Lafayette became prisoner number two, Maubourg number five, and Pusy number six; number seven was assigned to an unoccupied store-room. Lafayette's servants, Pontonnier and Compte, became numbers eight and nine; Maubourg's and Pusy's servants, Grugeon and Jandel, were numbers ten and eleven. Jail attendants and all officials were instructed to use these numbers exclusively, even in communications with the Vienna court.[32]

Each prisoner was assigned a separate room. Grugeon was placed in barracks at the former Clarissan convent. Bancal already resided there, across the square from the former Jesuit college. The others received rooms at the rear of the former college building. The French officers were on the ground floor, where Beurnonville and Marchand lived. Most of the servants were incarcerated upstairs, among soldiers' rooms. Lafayette was lodged next to Beurnonville, almost directly under Pontonnier and sixty meters away from Maubourg and Pusy.[33]

The rooms that Lafayette occupied were quite secure against escape. The top halves of the windows were padlocked and had two sets of iron grilles on the outside. Through the grilles Lafayette looked out onto a narrow yard patrolled by two sentries. Two guardhouses faced out across the prison barracks and terrace. Beyond that, a series of outer fortifications descended past artillery magazines to the city moat, the Mittelmarch, one hundred paces away.[34]

Two units of fifteen guards and a sergeant each alternated patrol of the building. Two soldiers stood outside and one inside a locked door leading to the cells. The men were under orders not to let anyone enter unless authorized by the commandant. The sergeant-provost came by twice a day to see that the guards were at their posts and that doors were locked.

To open Lafayette's rooms, Lieutenant Jacob or, when Jacob was ill, Sergeant Platzer fetched the keys from a cabinet vault at the main guard post at the prison gate. A guard unlocked the two-inch-thick outer cell door, which had a central lock and two padlocks above and below. Then he opened an inner door, which had yet another lock. Anytime the rooms were unlocked, other guards stood in the corridor with sabers drawn. The lieutenant and sergeant kept watch while a private brought meals, cleaned rooms, or barbered the prisoner. The same caution applied when the prison surgeon made a medical visit or fortress commandant Splényi came by. At night the guards patrolled the corridor, reporting any unusual noise, coughing, a signal for assistance, or a candle burning late in a cell. Also the sergeant of the guard carried out unannounced night inspections at times designated by Splényi, taking special care to examine windows from outside.[35]

The prisoners often complained of poor sanitation. The cook at the barracks canteen, a soldier's wife, was alleged to be dirty; soldiers stood around smoking; and the stoneware and mugs remained lying about in the corridor for hours, exposed to misuse by guards, and were only rarely—and then carelessly—cleaned.

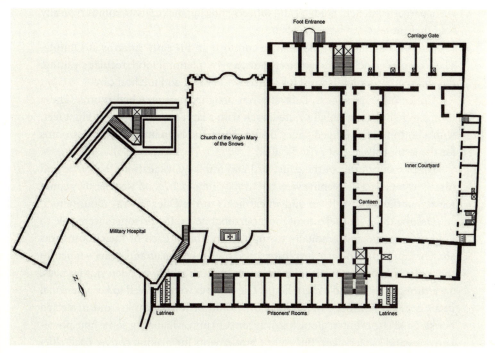

Plan of Olmütz prison. Lafayette occupied the two connected rooms in the southern wing at bottom. Prepared by Eckhart Spalding, Illinois College

Three times a day the provost filled a pitcher with water for the prisoners, typically from a well at the cathedral a short distance away. Those who used the water deemed it hardly drinkable and had two or three lemons on hand to improve its taste. In face of complaints, a later commandant noted that the water was "often cloudy during times of heavy rain," but that it was standard for the town.[36]

Captives found their proximity to sewage particularly objectionable. The soldiers' latrines were at the end of the wing. Directly adjacent were the rooms of Maubourg and Pusy. Fumes seeped into the entire corridor. Poorly covered gutters carried the effluence directly under Lafayette's windows. Similar filth flowed from privies in adjacent courtyards. These belonged to a military hospital to the right or west and to the left, behind a plank fence, cathedral canons' homes and a civil hospital. All of this drainage system emptied into the moat along with sewage from the rest of the town. Buildings formed a semicircle around the rear of the barracks-prison, so "noxious vapours" did not easily dissipate; indeed they seemed sometimes to be funneled into cells. The result, especially in warm weather, was a pervasive stench. Soldiers and officers entering the captives' rooms typically held their noses.[37]

Lafayette did enjoy some relative comforts in his early months at Olmütz. These comforts included spacious rooms, a view, plentiful food, regular cleaning, the ability to order items from town, access to books, and medical care.

Unlike other prisoners, Lafayette was assigned two attached rooms. These rooms were broad and high vaulted, each with a large window, four by eight feet, with a bottom set of hinged panes. These spaces had been intended as classrooms for the Jesuit college, not prison cells.[38]

Despite the clutter of the courtyard and military installations, Lafayette and his fellows enjoyed a sweeping view out from windows. In good weather they could see across the Morava River and wheat fields to the Oder (Odra) mountains.[39]

Despite the initial seizure of most personal items, the prisoners were able to hold on to some and gradually to supplement them. Each of their rooms was already supplied with basic furniture: a bed frame with mats and straw (similar to the soldiers' bedding) two chairs, one or two plank tables, wooden clothes pegs, a wardrobe, a stove, and a night lamp. The captives were allowed to keep personal items deemed harmless, including clothes and bedding, trunks, and inspected books. Lafayette brought along his own copper lamp, Maubourg some blue porcelain cups and saucers, and Pusy a few implements for making coffee. Each chief prisoner used personal funds to buy items such as a bookcase, a plank chest of drawers, and what Maubourg called "a piece of furniture not generally placed in bedchambers": a commode from which the chamber pot could be removed.[40] Occasionally the lieutenant commissioned Sergeant Platzer to buy items requested by the state prisoners, including hair powder, pomade, tooth powder, sugar, and lemons. Besides making the drinking water palatable, the lemons allowed the captives to make lemonade. Prisoners' servants could also run errands outside the prison while under unarmed escort.[41] Captives and captors disagreed about provision of clothing. While Maubourg insisted after more than two years at Olmütz that "everything we brought is in rags, and nothing has been replaced," the authorities recorded that "everything the prisoners ever request and need in the way of clothes and wash is always immediately brought to them without respect of greater or lesser cost."[42] Perhaps jailors and inmates differed as to what was needed or how quickly complaints found satisfaction.

Splényi was not the strictest, most suspicious, or most informed censor of the prisoners' books. He left Maubourg a history of European settlement and commerce by Guillaume Raynal, "a work full of bold passages and liberal reflections"; a racy novel, *Les Liaisons dangereuses* by Pierre de Laclos; and a reformist history of France by Gabriel Mably. Three weeks later, the emperor's police minister ordered the last two books removed from Maubourg's room. Still the captives ended up retaining the bulk of their book collections, which at Olmütz grew to 71 volumes for Lafayette, 65 for Pusy, and 114 for Maubourg.[43]

The prisoners could supplement their libraries through borrowing. Commandant Arco had already initiated the practice for Beurnonville, Marchand, and Bancal, sending Sergeant Platzer to the library of a local cathedral canon. Platzer had the books returned when Arco left for field service prior to Lafayette's arrival. However, interim commandant Splényi quickly gained borrowing privileges from a local imperial library. The collection was housed in the former Clarissan church facing the former Jesuit college on Mary Square, and it contained mostly Latin collections of disbanded monasteries. Splényi sent the catalog to Lafayette, Maubourg, and Pusy a few days after their arrival. He also sent a catalog of German works that a local bookseller was willing to lend. Sergeant Platzer let the prisoners jot down what they wished to order and picked up the books the following day. He laid them on a windowsill in the corridor, taking one to Splényi and reporting on others. When Splényi gave permission, Platzer or Lieutenant Jacob took the books to the prisoners.[44]

Splényi did not honor every book request, but he did show surprising liberality. Maubourg noted that he was never able to get recent books from the bookshop nor, despite putting them at the top of his list, any works by Archenholz. But the prisoners were able to borrow freely many classics of Enlightenment literature from the library, including Pierre Bayle's *Dictionnaire historique et critique,* the entire *Encyclopédie* of Denis Diderot and Jean le Rond d'Alembert, and the complete works of Montesquieu, Voltaire, and Jean-Jacques Rousseau.[45]

The food was varied and plentiful, particularly for the three chief prisoners.[46] For breakfast at 8:00 A.M. a prisoner had a choice of coffee or chocolate and bread and water. Lunch at 11:30 included bread, water, and cheap red Hungarian wine (at first served in its bottle but later reduced to a mug with a half measure). The main courses were soup, precut boiled beef and vegetables in a sauce, hashed meat or fricassé, precut roast meat with a salad, and a small dessert followed by black coffee. Supper, served in summer at 7:30 P.M. and in winter at 5:30, consisted of precut meat with salad, bread, water, and wine. Servants received an abbreviated version of their employers' meals: coffee for breakfast; soup, beef with dressing, vegetables in a sauce, bread, and a quarter measure of red Hungarian wine for lunch; and meat with salad, more bread, and another quarter measure of wine for supper. Authorities drew three florins of Vienna currency daily from military funds to provide for Lafayette, Maubourg, and Pusy, but they spent only twenty-four crosses (a bit more than one-third florin) on each servant.

When a private brought meals, he also fumigated the corridor with a smoldering evergreen branch, opened the bottom panes of windows in warm weather, aired the bed coverings, emptied the chamber pots, and swept. Once a week he collected laundry. The lieutenant or the sergeant inspected and recorded each item. If he deemed it necessary, worn or torn clothing was repaired. On Saturdays the private wiped off the small table where Lafayette ate.

Lafayette received regular medical care. Forty-two-year-old staff surgeon Karl Haberlein's visits began on the captive's arrival and were frequent. Only Beurnonville, languishing next door, received comparable medical attention. The surgeon wrote prescriptions when needed. The surgeon or a soldier carried them to the military pharmacy, usually with a piece of wax paper or blotting paper for wrapping the medicine, while the sergeant returned the writing materials to the storeroom. Sometimes the surgeon wrote his prescription at the pharmacy. Either he administered the medicine immediately on its delivery, or the lieutenant or sergeant laid it on a chest for later use. Eventually Haberlein would apply daily compresses to Lafayette's left arm, wrapping it with spurge laurel, a kind of wood bark, for vitality. A Catholic priest was also available for pastoral care during illness, but Lafayette seems to have never used his services.

On 24 March 1794, before Lafayette arrived at Olmütz, his colleague in the American war, Polish general Tadeusz Kościuszko, had issued his manifesto in Krakow, beginning a national insurrection to regain Poland's independence. The director of the Austrian state chancellery, Baron Francis von Thugut declared that the Polish revolt was a direct consequence of the French Revolution and represented "a battle to the death between sovereignty and anarchy, between legitimate government and the overturning of all order." Thugut wanted "to have sent to Galicia absolutely all the troops from Moravia and Bohemia that would not be indispensably necessary for guarding the fortresses and not risking the internal tranquility of the country."[47] Austria, Russia, and Prussia joined in suppressing the Polish uprising and carrying out a third and final partition that extinguished the remnants of the Polish state. Units in and near Olmütz promptly departed for Galicia. Only a minimal garrison remained, so—just as Lafayette's party arrived—Splényi reduced the number of full officers who directly supervised state prisoners from three to one. Deeming that finding a second capable full officer to be impossible, Splényi decided that "upright and zealous" Lieutenant Jacob could handle the job with the help of "honest" Sergeant Platzer.[48]

Aided by weakened oversight, inmates were able to establish internal prison communications. Six weeks after the group's arrival, Splényi began to allow the servants to see their employers. By fall, Félix Pontonnier was coming with the soldiers every morning to help Lafayette dress, serve his breakfast, and bind his arm with the poultice that the surgeon ordered. Valet Compte came on Thursdays and Sundays. Valet Jandel initially visited Pusy for about an hour every two weeks, then twice weekly, and eventually three hours a day for assistance at meals and bedtime. Presumably valet Grugeon visited Maubourg similarly.[49] Pontonnier's cell was directly above Beurnonville's, so they could secretly speak to one another through the windows. The captives came to share secret messages thanks to Pontonnier and Grugeon's ingenuity. Pontonnier developed signals that were opaque to the authorities—including gestures, facial expressions, and whistling—and employed them especially when walking on the enclosed terrace below the windows. The clearest way to communicate was to whistle French songs because the notes corresponded to words well known to prisoners but unknown to jailers. This secret language began early in their captivity, for Maubourg and Pusy knew when Lafayette began taking escorted drives in fall 1794.[50] Prisoners also found books useful for sending messages on detached pages. At least Pusy ordered German works of piety for this purpose.[51]

Prison surgeon Haberlein opened a potential channel to the outside. Though Lafayette's German was rudimentary, Haberlein spoke adequate French. Thus surgeon and inmate usually spoke that language, unknown to watching soldiers. Still Lafayette preferred speaking when the lieutenant and sergeant had stepped outside momentarily. Lieutenant Jacob claimed that in his presence the surgeon and captive spoke only about medical matters—but Jacob could not understand French. According to Lafayette's later testimony, Haberlein refused to respond to questions about public affairs, but this was probably a white lie to protect the surgeon.[52] Certainly Haberlein's visits offered opportunities, however brief, to converse in relative privacy.

Allowing carriage rides was also an amendment to Arco's original regulations. Emperor Francis approved the new policy and was ultimately responsible for undermining the rules limiting prisoners to their rooms and sealing them off from the outside. Allowing some of the captives to benefit from fresh air outside the prison, eventually outside the town itself, made a rescue feasible.

Francis instituted the excursion policy months before Lafayette's arrival, in response to Haberlein's medical advice that former French war minister Beurnonville and, subsequently, National Convention deputy Bancal needed fresh air. On 7 October 1793, the emperor directed the Olmütz commandant to let Beurnonville take walks into town, escorted by an officer and private, at a time and in a manner that would not excite attention. Arguing that he could not escort a captive through town without arousing curiosity, Arco proposed instead that Beurnonville be taken on walks in the prison keep, which was open to the sky, or be driven about town in a closed carriage under escort. The emperor clarified that the excursions were not to occur on foot but by carriage. Botta's directives stipulated that in case of bad weather, the prisoner could walk for half an hour in the rear yard, escorted by an officer and the sergeant-provost and watched by four sentries.

The walks began four months after the emperor's directive. Arco ordered Lieutenant Jacob and Sergeant Platzer to take every precaution. Several guards were to stand on the perimeter of the garden's lower end, and the sergeant of the guard was to circle the grounds. The lieutenant and sergeant were to stay on either side as Beurnonville walked down the middle. Walks were to occur daily from 2:00 to 3:00 P.M., or if inconvenient, at 11:00 A.M. to noon. At the end of February 1794, Lieutenant Jacob began supervising similar walks for Bancal in a garden of the former Clarissan convent. When Splényi took over command in March, he ordered the walks continued without change.

After Lafayette's party arrived in May, the policy was gradually liberalized. Splényi issued new commands to accommodate the sudden tripling of his state prisoners. The rules did not allow the new captives to see prisoners number one and number four (Beurnonville and Bancal) in the rear courtyard, so Splényi revisited the idea of escorted walks in town. On 14 May he received permission to drive the two men to a place within town fortifications. Sergeant Platzer found a rarely visited spot "in Rampart #15 up to the guard-room" at Castle Gate, and Splényi ordered that Bancal's walk occur there from 4:00 to 5:00 P.M. and Beurnonville's from 5:00 to 6:00 P.M. daily. Splényi continued to emphasize the importance of following customary precautions and being on constant lookout, but the strength of the immediate escort diminished sharply. This was another symptom of the garrison's depletion. From then on, a minimum of a single soldier, either the lieutenant or the sergeant, accompanied prisoner walks, though a private usually came along also. The host of guards at Castle Gate seemed to provide all the additional security necessary.

Meanwhile in Vienna, court physician and counselor Giovanni von Brambilla made a confidential evaluation of Beurnonville's health on the basis of staff surgeon Haberlein's written descriptions and advice. The authorities had put a bathtub in Beurnonville's room and were even considering taking him to mineral baths elsewhere to aid his recovery. But Brambilla concluded that this treatment was insufficient and recommended that Beurnonville should go on the drives that the emperor had approved the previous year.

On 27 July, with clearance by the Moravian General Command, the Aulic War Council, and Emperor Francis, Splényi ordered that Beurnonville's walks be replaced by carriage drives into the country. Splényi explained to the lieutenant and sergeant-provost that the edict had come from the emperor himself and that they must be more responsible and careful than ever, as they would be going outside fortifications. They should try to avoid the imperial highway as much as possible and in good weather turn off onto auxiliary roads. At times they were to drive toward Holitz (Holice) in the southeast and Klein-Wisternitz (Bystrovany) in the east, for instance, or toward Tschernowier (Černovír) in the north. In poor weather, when smaller roads became a morass, they were to drive only a short distance on the main highway.[53]

At first the policy on carriage rides had applied only to Beurnonville, but then Bancal requested the privilege, and in mid-August the emperor approved separate escorted drives for him. Initially Splényi directed that Beurnonville and Bancal go on alternate days at 2:00 P.M., for an hour and a half each. The designated route was through Castle Gate, onto the imperial highway and ancillary roads in all directions except toward Brünn. Jacob or Platzer was to serve as escort.[54]

The emperor also ordered that a close guard take Beurnonville to the sulphuric waters at the village of Slatenitz (Slatinice), a few leagues to the west, on condition that the prisoner not interact with outsiders. Beurnonville promised the escort captain that he would not attempt escape, and thus he was able to spend most of September at the spa.[55]

Finally the excursion policy extended to Lafayette.[56] On 7 September, in response to Haberlein's medical advice, Moravian commander Botta asked the Aulic War Council if Lafayette might also go on occasional drives for his health. The council questioned the need but passed the request on to the emperor, who gave his assent: "What has been granted Beurnonville and Bancal to preserve their health can also be granted Lafayette, if necessary, with the same precautions."[57] On 3 October, three days before concluding his service as Olmütz interim commandant, Splényi received the imperial directive under Thugut's signature. Splényi expressed reservations but noted that "we must comply with the supreme mandate." Then he made three noteworthy departures from a narrowly literal application. Instead of always having the lieutenant accompany excursions, Splényi allowed Platzer, a trusted sergeant, to replace him. He also allowed any captive on a drive to leave the carriage at an appropriate place to walk for a stretch. Then, allegedly to avoid drawing attention, he dispensed with a private on the carriage's rear. Lafayette's outings, every other day, were to be from 2:00 to 4:00 P.M.[58]

The innovation of allowing escorted drives beyond Olmütz and, in Beurnonville's case, an extended stay under guard at a nearby village, was an obvious threat to the security in which the prisoners were held. But since the emperor himself had approved them, the investigative commissions to come never dared criticize these decisions. They had to blame much lesser authorities for allowing things to get out of hand.

5

BOLLMANN'S PREPARATIONS

Bollmann made his rescue preparations in two stages. During his journey from Britain into Prussian Silesia and Austrian Moravia, he curried favor with people who might be useful in locating the prisoner, finding hiding places, and contacting Lafayette. Thereafter he alternated between Olmütz and Vienna, assembling equipment, horses, and aides.

He pretended to be touring central Europe to improve his scientific knowledge, expand his professional network, and sightsee. He had left London in late May 1794 with his Göttingen doctor's diploma, a British pass issued by Lord Grenville, and a crowd of personal references and addresses that would enable him to travel cheaply and gain access to the politically influential.[1] To preserve the appearance of innocent travel, he planned to avoid all political subjects in correspondence. He kept his London supporters informed through what appeared to be harmless travelogues to a friend, Angelica Church.[2]

Bollmann's route initially resembled the one he followed on his 1793 mission to Berlin. He traveled up the Rhine and the Main to Frankfurt by boat, then east by carriage into Saxony. From Dresden the new itinerary departed from the old, and he set off eastward into Prussian Silesia.[3] In late June, Bollmann made his way along the Sudeten Mountains bordering Austrian crown lands. He passed through the spa of Warmbrunn (Cieplice), where the Prussian king had allowed Lameth to convalesce while his fellow prisoners—Lafayette, Maubourg, and Pusy—entered Austrian custody. Bollmann later claimed to have seen Lameth, and Lameth's mother may have alluded to the encounter in a note to his brother Théodore, who was in Switzerland with Madame de Staël.[4] Bollmann continued through Hirschberg (Jelenia Góra) and Schmiedeberg (Kowary), crossing the frontier briefly on what appeared to be a tourist's jaunt to Schneekoppe (Sněžka) Mountain and the highland sources of the Elbe River (the Elbegrund, Labsky dul), but that also served to reconnoiter escape routes from Austrian territory. When he returned to Prussian soil, Bollmann stayed in the home of wealthy textile merchant Johann Alberti at Waldenburg (Wałbrzych) before trying to tour military citadels in the area. The administrative officer at Silberberg (Srebrna Góra) declined his request, but Johann Pohle, the prison chaplain at Glatz (Kłodzko), showed him around the Friedericusfeste, the bastion that had recently held Maubourg and Pusy.

Perhaps through the chaplain, Bollmann learned that the Prussians had extradited Lafayette's party to Austrian Moravia, in the direction of Olmütz. Bollmann concluded that their escort might have even brought them further south, to the infamous Spielberg (Špilberk) fort at Brünn (Brno).[5]

He investigated escape routes and hiding places before continuing in that direction. In early July he snooped about Glatz County, a basin of Prussian territory protruding into Austrian crown lands. He climbed Grosser Heuscheuer (Szczeliniec Wielki) Mountain and visited Silesia's most spectacular waterfall, the Wölfelsfall (Wodospad Wilczki). The mountain overlooked a western pass leading to the Bohemian fortress cities of Josefstadt and Königgrätz, which both held state prisoners. The falls overlooked a southern pass that could lead to or from Olmütz and Brünn.[6] Thereafter he traveled northeast to Breslau (Wrocław), the Silesian capital, where he met the supervisor of Silesian mines, Baron Kaspar von Schuckmann.[7] Bollmann proceeded up the Oder River to the mining center of Tarnowitz (Tarnowskie Góry) just west of the Polish border, where he met other mining officials, particularly the manager, Count Friedrich von Reden.[8] There were extensive caves and many industrial buildings in Tarnowitz. It was also close to Poland. Bollmann deemed the place an excellent hideout. He planned to stay there with Lafayette until the inevitable manhunt had ended. Then they could cross Poland to Gdańsk (Danzig) on the northern coast, to embark for Hamburg and England.[9]

Satisfied that he had established the exit route, Bollmann set off for Brünn. He alleged now that he was on his way to Italy, and he carried an Italian-German dictionary to substantiate his cover.[10] He crossed the frontier at Ratibor (Racibórz) into Austrian Silesia and Moravia.[11] He traveled through majority German-speaking areas until, south of Sternberg, he entered largely Czech-speaking territory. In Olmütz and Brünn, German was the language of administration, power, and most townspeople, while the rural population and a large urban minority preferred Czech.[12]

Bollmann was entering lands where authorities viewed strangers with suspicion, mainly owing to fear of French revolutionary influence. Emperor Joseph II had created an independent police ministry in 1789 to deal with rising internal dissatisfaction, but his short-lived successor Leopold II dismantled it. When twenty-five-year-old Francis II succeeded to the Habsburg thrones in 1792, he began laying foundations for a police state that lasted until the mid–nineteenth century. Soon his Court Chancellery instructed provincial governors to have police inspect passports of all foreigners and keep them under surveillance. A prospective foreign visitor was to obtain a visa from the chancellery or an Austrian envoy. In January 1793 Francis revived the ministry of police and reappointed Joseph's police minister, Count Johann von Pergen, who had built an impressive record for centralizing police work, making it more efficient, giving it autonomy from other ministries, and tightening surveillance of persons and publications. The court then ordered foreigners to obtain a police permit to establish residence, banned secret meetings and private printing presses, strengthened press restrictions, and promised monetary rewards for writing against the French Revolution. In August the court decreed that border guards must more carefully examine passports and keep better records. Before year's end Pergen had shut down Masonic lodges and placed coffeehouses and other social centers under constant watch. When Bollmann arrived in summer 1794, the government was ferreting out what it viewed as a widespread Jacobin plot. The campaign increased censorship and police controls. The court ordered every official down to postmaster, as well as innkeepers, to look out for people passing through, examine their passports and other identifying papers, and report anything untoward.[13] That August the court decreed that a foreigner must obtain a new visa for each trip within the emperor's lands beyond the original destination. On 30 August and 7 October, Count Alois von und zu Ugarte, governor of Austrian Moravia and Silesia, issued new instructions for officials and innkeepers to examine travelers' passports carefully.[14]

Bollmann became aware of the pervasive vigilance. "A strict inquiry is made at every town you pass through, who you are, from whence you come, what your business is, with whom you are acquainted, how long you intend to stay?" he reported.[15] He had all the more reason to keep his own confidences, fit his guise, and avoid making careless inquiries about Lafayette.[16]

In Sternberg the imperial highway took a sharp turn to the south. Soon after that Bollmann caught sight of Olmütz. Level wheat fields stretched out before it, crisscrossed by dirt lanes and drainage ditches. To the east rose the wooded Oder (Odra) Mountains. The domed Visitation of the Virgin Mary Church rose on the slope of Holy Mountain (Heiligenberg, Svatý Kopeček), eight kilometers before Olmütz. On the right, just before Bollmann's carriage crossed the Morava River and drawbridge through Castle Gate, stood the splendid Hradisko seminary. Olmütz itself was often enveloped in haze from marshes. The town rose behind fortifications acquired in the Thirty Years' War, Turkish invasions, and, only a generation before, wars with Prussia over Silesia.[17]

Bollmann's goal was Brünn, which he felt was the likely site of Lafayette's prison. He breakfasted at Olmütz the morning of 19 July and changed horses at Prossnitz. Then a carriage accident bruised him badly and delayed his arrival at Brünn's Three Princes Inn (Zu den drei Fürsten) until the evening of 21 July.[18]

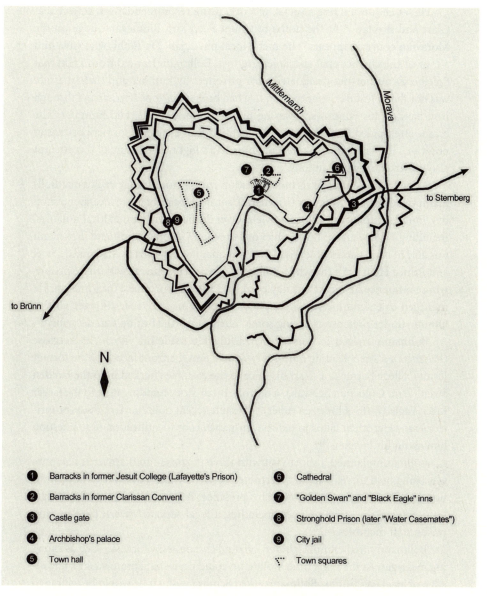

Mittlemarch

Morava

to Sternberg

to Brünn

N

1. Barracks in former Jesuit College (Lafayette's Prison)
2. Barracks in former Clarissan Convent
3. Castle gate
4. Archbishop's palace
5. Town hall

6. Cathedral
7. "Golden Swan" and "Black Eagle" inns
8. Stronghold Prison (later "Water Casemates")
9. City jail
Town squares

Plan of Olmütz fortress city, based on a 1757 map. with key sites of Lafayette's stay there a generation later. Prepared by Eckhart Spalding, Illinois College

He set about building a social network, using recommendations collected at Glatz and Breslau.[19] At the home of Count Peter von Blümegan, judge on the Moravian court of appeals,[20] he met a local physician, Dr. Pfahl, who gave him a tour of the city hospital and Spielberg fort. Bollmann learned from Pfahl that Spielberg's authorities designated state prisoners by number and that Lafayette was not there. Just days before, a captive had broken his foot after sawing through iron bars on his windows, lowering himself by bed sheets, and jumping. The escape attempt led to disclosure of his identity: Jean Drouet, a former postmaster notorious for having helped prevent Louis XVI's flight. The failure of this attempt also provoked new precautions.[21]

Armed with a letter of recommendation from Prince Henry of Prussia, Bollmann visited nearby Kremsier (Kroměříž), summer estate of the prince-archbishop of Olmütz, Anton von Colloredo-Melz. Over dinner there he met local notables, including Field Marshal Botta, chief of Moravian General Command. Bollmann was able to drop names of several famous acquaintances, such as Madame de Staël and Prince Henry. All the while Bollmann deepened contacts with these people, whose influence he might one day need, and listened for useful information. He managed to extend his stay a couple days before making a first longer visit to Olmütz under pretense of seeing some "curiosities" the bishop had described.[22]

Bollmann arrived in Olmütz on 24 July. He made his way to Bäckergasse (Pekařská), a street leading onto Mary Square and the front facade of the former Jesuit College barracks a short distance to the east. He checked in to the Golden Swan (Zum Goldenen Schwan), a narrow, three-story building next to the larger Black Eagle (Zum Schwarzen Adler).[23] Despite recent police orders, Swan proprietor Franz Herbricht failed to request any passport or identification or to question him about his business.[24]

Bollmann planned a short visit with three purposes: to discover if Lafayette was being held there; if so, to determine precisely where and under what conditions; and to let Lafayette know of his presence. Bollmann began constructing a local network of acquaintances, including a local servant, tavern patrons, and prison staff members.[25]

Bollmann hired Olmütz laborer Johann Schramowsky for tasks such as carrying messages. At the same time, Bollmann could draw on Schramowsky's knowledge of local conditions. Bollmann asked Schramowsky if he would be willing to return with him to England. It was a test to see how useful the unsuspecting fellow might prove in the escape project. Bollmann also paid Schramowsky handsomely to keep their talks confidential.[26]

Bollmann frequented local drinking and dining establishments, each with its own clientele, and made a point of conversing with strangers. He began in the Swan's long dining room, eventually turning talk to the subject of where state prisoners were being kept and under what conditions. Bollmann then visited many other inns, taverns, beer halls, and cafés, especially on the Upper Square around the town hall,[27] and quickly pieced together some key facts. No one admitted knowing whether Lafayette was in Olmütz, but it appeared that several French captives were being held at the former Jesuit college.[28] Bollmann also learned that, as at the Spielberg in Brünn, the Olmütz prison staff used numbers to conceal captives' names.[29] When Bollmann asked about Lieutenant General Splényi, he received glowing reports of this senior Hungarian officer's sociable, generous personality and his delight in receiving genteel visitors.[30] Bollmann asked also about the garrison hospital. He presumed that Lafayette would seek treatment for the illnesses he had complained of in previous letters. As a physician, Bollmann hoped to gain quick access to someone on staff with personal contact to Lafayette.[31]

Bollmann walked to Splényi's headquarters-townhouse on Upper Square and presented himself as a young physician from London on study tour. Splényi responded graciously.[32] Granting Bollmann permission to visit the staff surgeon, Haberlein, Splényi even invited Bollmann to join him in his home the next day for lunch. But he refused the visitor's request for a tour of the prison.[33] However generous Splényi felt to the charming man before him, he could not allow a tourist to enter an installation holding secret state prisoners. For his part Bollmann recognized that this high-ranking, sixty-year-old veteran of wars against Prussians and Turks, recently also against the French on the Upper Rhine,[34] would be no easy tool to reach Lafayette.

Surgeon Karl Haberlein was of a different sort. His father and brothers were Viennese glaziers, and his sisters were craftsmen's wives. When Haberlein chose surgery, it was a field still considered a modest craft, which had been associated since the Middle Ages with the barbers' guild. The same people who trimmed one's hair typically also set bones and perform operations, treatments that university-trained physicians could not, or would not, handle. A surgeon traditionally worked without benefit of training outside the guild, training that bore poor comparison with the university education accorded good physicians. The government was trying to change this, expanding the formal preparation of its army surgeons in particular. Haberlein was one of the first to benefit from the policy. On completing a new two-year medical course in Vienna, he had become an assistant surgeon in 1774. He had an unusual intelligence and had acquired a working knowledge of Latin, Italian, and French. In 1786 he won a gold medal in an essay competition sponsored by the new Military Academy for Surgical Medicine (Josephinum). He achieved the rank of staff surgeon and posting to Ofen (Budapest) in 1788 before becoming director of the Olmütz garrison clinic in 1791.[35] He supervised senior and junior surgeons, surgical practitioners, orderlies, invalid soldiers, and soldiers' wives caring for some four hundred patients; made rounds three times daily; and personally performed the most dangerous operations.[36] Still old status traditions persisted. Despite an unblemished twenty-year career, Haberlein held an army rank equivalent only to a junior lieutenant and received one third the pay of a major.[37] Colleagues knew him as unfailingly kind and well intentioned.

The morning after Bollmann's meeting with Splényi, Haberlein returned home from rounds to find a messenger at his door, who informed him that "a foreign gentleman" awaited him in his upstairs room. As Haberlein entered, Bollmann rose, offered a name card, and introduced himself as a London physician who had just come through Prussia on a medical study tour. He was soon to leave for Vienna, after which he would continue to Italy. He asked if the surgeon might guide him through his hospital. Haberlein had no objection. He offered to meet Bollmann there at 10:30 A.M., when the surgeon would be inspecting the patients' noonday meal.

Bollmann appeared a few minutes beyond the appointed time at the hospital gate. The two men entered the facility's wide hallways under high arched ceilings, the walls displaying encouraging maxims. Their tour began of the pharmacy, kitchen, and wards. Bollmann tried to ingratiate himself by showing interest in every detail. He commented on how small the kitchen was and how English practice was to serve patients a more vegetarian diet. He asked to see critical cases and prescribed a medicine not readily available in the military pharmacy for a soldier dying of "putrid fever." He borrowed a new pharmacological work and promised to return it before his lunch engagement.[38]

In Bollmann's eyes Haberlein was "a very weak, good-natured, honest man" whose humanitarian motives could supersede his caution.[39] An official would later agree: "Haberlein appears to be one of those good-hearted people always ready to help, who rely on few ideas and concepts extending beyond their profession, who allow themselves to be led into cooperating and can be easily deceived."[40] Haberlein was especially vulnerable to Bollmann, who had considerable charm and apparent wealth, came from a capital with the highest standards of medical practice, and knew the fortress commander. Also the enthusiastic attention of a physician trained at the leading German medical faculty, Göttingen, must have flattered a mere surgeon lacking a university degree.[41]

The newfound colleagues returned to Haberlein's home to pick up the book that Bollmann wished to borrow. They continued discussing medical topics, and Bollmann mentioned the influence of sorrow or despair on patients' health. He proposed a way to console one of Haberlein's patients in particular. He drew a pamphlet and prepared note from his pocket and announced that the surgeon should give the items to General Lafayette as a gift from a traveler recently come from London. Bollmann noted that "the news will do him better than all your medicine."[42] The pamphlet seems indeed to have been harmless, a ruse to draw attention from the chief contents of the note: a coded list of Lafayette's London supporters. One was Count Narbonne, whom Bollmann described to Haberlein as someone he had healed. The language would reveal to Lafayette that Bollmann, rescuer of Narbonne from the Jacobins, was on the scene to rescue Lafayette as well. Also on the note were Bollmann's name with his title, "doctor of medicine," and his forwarding address for the next weeks: his Vienna banker, Steinmetz and Company.[43]

Haberlein refused to admit that Lafayette was a prisoner, but his confused reaction confirmed it. When he made no move to accept the card, Bollmann laid it on a table and requested that he hand it on. If the information reached Lafayette, Bollmann said, then Lafayette could use the kind surgeon himself to write Bollmann in Vienna.[44]

Haberlein quickly changed the subject, but Bollmann achieved one more goal before leaving for his lunch engagement with Splényi: to gain addresses of medical personnel in Vienna. Haberlein suggested two colleagues at the Military Academy for Surgical Medicine.[45]

In the wake of the interview, Haberlein's concern for his patient's well-being overshadowed the military discipline he was obligated to uphold. Commandant Arco had never given him written guidelines, but he had impressed upon Haberlein the delicacy of his work with state prisoners. Nevertheless Haberlein failed to report Bollmann's attempt to contact Lafayette. In fact he told Lafayette the contents of the note several days after receiving and disposing of it.[46]

Bollmann made his way to Splényi's townhouse for lunch. The men then took a walk with officers and their wives in and around the commandant's garden. The young physician began pumping his new acquaintances for information. He was especially successful with the women. They confirmed that Lafayette was one of the inmates, that two others took escorted walks, and that Lafayette had recently refused the privilege.[47]

Bollmann boldly revealed awareness of Lafayette's presence to Splényi, claiming to know Lafayette's friends in England and describing their compelling interest in his situation. He encouraged Splényi to inform Lafayette of his visit as far as duty would allow.[48] The commandant was undismayed. There was no reason why this English subject of obvious talent and intelligence should not enjoy impressive ties abroad and knowledge of Lafayette's presence in Olmütz. Splényi refused to confirm the rumor, but he graciously encouraged Bollmann to remain a few days so that the commandant could show him the countryside, its estates, and Slavic folk.

Bollmann said that he had urgent mail waiting in Vienna, but he promised to return soon. He had several reasons not to delay departure. First he had told Haberlein that he would leave, and he did not wish to make him too anxious to deliver the note. He also wanted to maintain the charade of a study tour whose next destination was Vienna. In addition he was running out of cash and expected in Vienna a three-hundred-pound letter of credit from London. He also needed the anonymity of a big city in which to collect supplies for a breakout. If he could communicate with Lafayette at a distance, it would arouse much less suspicion than any further attempts Bollmann might make in Olmütz. At the same time, he had gained a pretext to return.[49]

By evening Bollmann had not returned Haberlein's book. The surgeon's wife remarked that she had seen the English doctor in the afternoon, walking with Splényi and scaling fortifications at the city gate abutting the commandant's garden. Haberlein inquired at the Black Eagle, whose proprietor directed him next door to the Swan. Bollmann arrived after half an hour, praised the people he had met, returned the book with apologies for tardiness, bade adieu, and left for his waiting carriage.[50]

Bollmann had accomplished a good deal in his day and a half at Olmütz. He had identified and cultivated local sources of information, confirmed Lafayette's presence and learned of prison conditions, and found someone with access to Lafayette, someone whom he could influence. On the other hand, Haberlein had not agreed to pass a message to Lafayette, and no obvious escape plan had emerged.

When he arrived in Vienna the end of July, Bollmann rented an upstairs room of a small house in the city center.[51] From there he kept supporters apprised of his progress, tried to contact Lafayette again, gathered contacts, and awaited the money transfer to buy supplies.

He sent several progress reports. He brought the Church circle up to date through letters to Angelica. He sent a description of Lafayette's incarceration to his friend Friedrich Heisch in London, information that he surely expected Heisch to pass to designated persons. When he alerted Caspar Voght that things were going well, Voght sent the news to Hamburg via Magdalena Pauli, a merchant's wife in the Sieveking circle. Bollmann also kept Johanna Sieveking up to date.[52] Even to intimates outside the plot, he could not resist hinting at how his work would give a major boost to his career.[53]

He was not able to slip Lafayette further messages through Haberlein. Bollmann asked the surgeon by letter if he had used the "prescription" he had given him, that is, had he slipped Lafayette the message. He offered to send more such prescriptions, but Haberlein did not take the bait. He refused to respond at all to a second letter.[54]

Bollmann struggled to gain useful contacts in Vienna. While Paris was the capital of the Revolution, Vienna was capital of the counterrevolution. The emerging police state of Francis II was tightest here. Police Minister Pergen had inaugurated a policy of issuing special passports to all foreigners residing in the capital and keeping the visitors under surveillance. Vienna notables were open to brilliant, gallant young men,[55] but particularly those with aristocratic rank or at least substantial wealth. A young physician from London might impress the commandant of a provincial town, but he was unlikely to make a splash so quickly in a capital of more than two hundred thousand people, a leading destination of grand tours and foreign study.[56] Bollmann could also not afford the expenditures to present himself as a gentleman to be reckoned with.

Still he found entrance to at least one great house, that of Count Prokop von Lažansky. Lažansky had recently served as governor and supreme burgrave in Bohemia, before accepting office in Vienna as president of the Supreme Office of State Supervision. He had a reputation for being enlightened, having once joined a Free Mason–related group known as the Order of Luminaries and having presided over the Bohemian Academy of Sciences.[57] His home was open to educated and articulate young men, whether or not they were rich. Bollmann came to know the Lažansky family, guests, and staff. He claimed that he "spent many hours, and lived upon an intimate footing" with them. This does not mean that he became close to the statesman himself. It is certain, however, that he successfully cultivated relations with Lažansky's valet Joseph Zudik, who would soon prove quite useful.[58]

Bollmann also looked to medical institutions and physicians' local watering holes as places to make helpful acquaintances. He fit perfectly into what an observer called "a swarm" of young Englishmen studying medicine. He used Haberlein's recommendation to meet colleagues at the Military Academy for Surgical Medicine. He began visiting a coffeehouse frequented by foreign doctors and medical students, a center of talk aided by the coffee, food, complimentary newspapers, and a billiard table in the corner. He became well known and respected there for his intelligence, manners, and fluency in German, French, and English.[59]

Bollmann needed to find a trustworthy assistant among the many young men on a study tour. He soon met John Webb, an Englishman who had served as an assistant military surgeon in the Netherlands under the Duke of York, and Karl Weigel of Leipzig, like Bollmann, a Göttingen graduate and gifted in modern languages.[60] Bollmann kept his plans secret for a time,[61] but he eventually revealed them to Webb and Weigel, asking each to assist in springing Lafayette from prison. Webb refused. Weigel considered it, at least for a while.

In mid or late September at the coffeehouse, probably through Webb, Bollmann met a third candidate for assistant: a twenty-year-old medical student from South Carolina.[62] Francis Kinloch Huger had studied in Britain and volunteered with Webb to join medical staff in the Netherlands.[63] When the military situation there disintegrated,[64] Huger resigned and, probably with Webb, set off on a study tour.[65] At the Vienna café, Bollmann asked Huger about America and spoke of Lafayette's devotion to it. Huger's response was immediate and enthusiastic. His family had produced several leaders in the War of Independence. His father, Major Benjamin Huger, had died in action at Charleston. An uncle had been brigadier general in the American southern army; another South Carolina's first secretary of state; a third a member of the Continental Congress; and a fourth quartermaster

Francis Kinloch Huger.
Bronze-gilt medallion
by R. Tait McKenzie,
1909. Temple University
Libraries, Urban Archives,
Philadelphia

general of the army's southern department. Most astonishing was the personal tie
that Huger and his family had with Lafayette. On Lafayette's first voyage to America in 1777, his ship, *La Victoire,* encountered oyster-gathering slaves outside the
breakers off North Island, South Carolina. The slaves piloted the Frenchmen to the
plantation of their master, Major Benjamin Huger, who became Lafayette's first
host in the infant republic. Lafayette even seems to have held five-year-old Francis on his knees. The major then accompanied the Frenchmen to Charleston and
arranged for them to meet George Washington and the Continental Congress in
Philadelphia.[66]

Bollmann saw Francis Huger "several times" at the coffeehouse and theaters.
It turned out that Huger knew the American circle of Lafayette supporters in
London, including Angelica Church and Thomas Pinckney, a fellow South Caro-
linian.[67]

The coincidences must have dumbfounded Bollmann, but he resisted revealing his mission or drafting Huger into it. Weigel had already seemed open to serving as aide, and Bollmann needed to skirt government surveillance. As a result,
Bollmann felt that he could dispense with a third participant, but he kept Huger
in reserve.

After almost two months, money arrived from London via former Lafayette
aides Charles de Cadignan and Sébastien Baptiste de Boinville, allowing Bollmann
to buy supplies.[68] He collected rope ladders, bundles of hemp cord and twine,
handsaws, iron files and saws, a pickax with a pulley, and iron wire. He also had a
carriage constructed with secret compartments, allegedly to hide valuables during

his return to England. In fact, of course, he needed the hiding places for breakout tools and an escapee.[69] Huger offered to go along, but Bollmann responded that he would first visit Hungary for eight to ten days and from there would write him more definitely about travel plans.[70] Bollmann wrote Splényi in Olmütz that he was ready to take up his invitation to visit the Moravian countryside. To Bollmann's consternation, Splényi replied that he would soon turn over command to Arco and leave for Hungary. He planned to pass through Vienna, and hoped to see Boll-mann there. This meant that Bollmann was losing his most highly placed contact at Olmütz, so there was no point in seeing him again. Perhaps it was best to avoid Splényi altogether, in order not to risk too many questions. Even as Splényi trans-ferred command to Arco on 6 October, Bollmann set out for Olmütz.[71]

Bollmann did this without really knowing how he would gain Lafayette's free-dom. He might have given up if he could not establish contact with the captive on this visit.[72] Weigel may have gone with Bollmann, but he certainly did not play the major part in escape preparations that he claimed decades later. Most likely Boll-mann had concluded that he could not afford the risk, leaving him to go alone.[73]

On 7 October 1794, Bollmann arrived at the Swan for a second stay, this time with his specially constructed carriage and equipment. He aroused little suspicion, as he had been a guest before and had even been received in officers' homes.[74]

Bollmann learned that beyond Haberlein himself, a second weak spot had appeared in the prison's security: Lafayette had begun taking drives. The source of Bollmann's knowledge is unclear, but many locals were aware of the drives.[75] Boll-mann's local hired hand Schramowsky surely knew. Haberlein volunteered the information the morning after Bollmann's arrival. Though Bollmann claimed to have known it even before leaving Vienna, that may have been false: Lafayette's excursions began almost the same time that Bollmann left the capital, and records do not indicate a likely Viennese source.[76] In any event the drives presented a grand opportunity, one that rendered his carefully collected breakout tools super-fluous.[77]

When he arrived in Olmütz, Bollmann prepared a secret message for Lafayette at the bottom of two pieces of white paper, writing it in English, a language un-known to prison staff and using lemon juice. Hénin had taught Bollmann this technique.[78] The secret message dealt with escape and suggested bribing the super-vising sergeant or lieutenant to bring out Lafayette at night under pretense of spe-cial transfer orders and then to take him to a waiting carriage.[79]

Despite Haberlein's wariness, Bollmann knew that his access to Lafayette and his obliging personality continued to make him the obvious mediator. On his first morning back in Olmütz, 8 October, Bollmann sent Schramowsky to announce his return and ask if he might join Haberlein again on rounds. Minutes after Schramowsky returned, Bollmann walked to Haberlein's home. He complained of a sore throat and asked for treatment, to flatter Haberlein and have an excuse to keep in regular contact. He found another excuse when he saw a medical text and asked to borrow it. Haberlein expressed surprise that Bollmann was not on Italian tour. Bollmann replied that he had changed his mind, would stay in Vienna for the carnival season, and return directly to London.[80] He then changed the subject. He got Haberlein to concede that Lafayette was indeed in Olmütz, in good health, and had received permission to go on country drives. Haberlein then returned Bollmann's pamphlet. He said that Lafayette had seen it, heard of the London supporters, and asked about other acquaintances.[81]

Bollmann leaped at the chance to send Lafayette another message. He pulled out the two prepared sheets of paper and wrote an ink message in French on both sides, leaving each page's lower half blank. The message seemed to give harmless but significant news about U.S. diplomacy on Lafayette's behalf. It was too complex for Haberlein to entrust to memory, giving him another reason to hand the actual note to Lafayette.[82] The closing sentence provided a clue to the invisible, English-language message: "Read this with the same warmth as you formerly read the letters of Princess Hénin." That is, Lafayette should hold the pages to a flame.[83]

Bollmann had to use all his charisma to win over the surgeon. Haberlein was well aware of prison policy, but his kind nature and role as caregiver took the upper hand. Bollmann argued that if the surgeon were betrayed, he could slip across the border to Prussia and that Lafayette would reward him when he hand access his fortune again. Haberlein refused emphatically, saying that he wished only "to be able to continue working in peace and above suspicion at his present post, a position with which he was quite satisfied." Finally, however, he convinced himself that he could pass along on an innocuous message.[84] He also agreed to give Lafayette a blue-paper-covered English book, Samuel Richardson's novel *Clarissa*, to hide the note and to use in writing a reply.[85] "Nothing but the good heart of this man and his great guilelessness, from which I tried to draw the greatest possible advantages, let him do what he did,"[86] Bollmann later noted. Still Haberlein refused to assure Lafayette that Bollmann would try to catch sight of him on a drive or to give him "a silver capsule with an English pencil, and two small paper cards." He could not risk having a supervising soldier glimpse them.[87]

Haberlein probably gave Lafayette the note the next day, making it the first of three that he passed from Bollmann and that Lafayette would refer to as "notes from the Messiah": two in October and one on 6 November.[88] At the first opportunity, probably after guards withdrew for the night, the captive held the first message over fire and read the secret words. Then he tore the paper with his teeth, burned it,[89] and wrote a French-language reply on margins of two pages in the book that Bollmann had sent him, using a sharpened toothpick and pale homemade ink of stove ash and water.[90] Lafayette tried to keep the words harmless. He thanked him for news of family and friends, asked questions about them, and carefully conveyed information helpful for the escape. He wrote that his psychological health and physical stamina were good and that he went on his excursions every second day "in a single-color frock coat, with a round hat," accompanied by the sergeant-provost. He had lost faith in negotiations to bring about release, so urged Bollmann to pursue "the means you speak of," a breakout. At the same time, Lafayette stressed concern for Haberlein's safety.[91]

On the pages' reverse sides, Lafayette wrote a secret lemon-juice message in English.[92] He noted that the emperor might execute him before peace negotiations concluded, a comment that would weigh heavily with Bollmann. Prison security was too tight to hope for escape by ordinary means.[93] Bribing the "cowardly" sergeant risked betrayal, as "he may prefer a little reward [for reporting the plot] to a fortune with some risk." Instead Lafayette advocated ambushing the sergeant on a drive. He pointed out how vulnerable the excursions were: the sergeant had a hernia and sometimes had to drive because of the "clumsy" (drunk) hackman's absence; the ride was slow and could take them an entire German mile (6.4 km) from Olmütz. While Bollmann and an aide rode up with an extra horse and halted the carriage, Lafayette would seize the sergeant's sword, force his surrender, mount, receive pocket pistols from his rescuers, and ride off. He, Bollmann, and the aide would be long gone before the commandant was aware of the escape. "The bolder it seems, the more unexpected it is, the better it shall succeed!" Lafayette declared. He then cited poet John Dryden: "Presence of mind and courage in distress / Are more than armies to procure success." From the Tuesday drive on, Lafayette would be ready to flee.[94]

Early on Friday, 10 October, as Haberlein bound his arm with a poultice of spurge laurel, Lafayette slipped the book into the surgeon's jacket pocket. He described it as a reply to Bollmann. Haberlein, startled, wondered how Lafayette even had ink to write with. He felt unable to refuse the book without drawing attention from the sergeant and Lafayette's servant, who were both in the next room. Haberlein examined Lafayette's marginal ink message and deemed it harmless. He agreed to hand it over as soon as Bollmann arrived at his room in the Swan. Bollmann read the ink words, and Haberlein requested the book's return. However, Bollmann insisted that he could see only poorly without glasses, so would need to hold onto it to examine at leisure.[95] The book's marginalia, both explicit and secret, were the only writings that Bollmann received from Lafayette in prison.[96]

Bollmann felt torn over Lafayette's demand to act quickly. He needed at least eight weeks for more extensive preparations. He could return to Prussian Silesia to raise additional money for bribes and buy three to four sets of horses and grooms to wait unobtrusively along the escape route. However, there were advantages to acting much sooner. With the onset of winter, poorer road conditions could prove too much for a weakened Lafayette. Waiting for spring would devour limited funds. There was little chance of a loan from Viennese bankers, who knew that Bollmann had just received a money transfer to cover a winter's medical study. Other events could make escape more difficult or impossible: the reduction of Lafayette's outings as more inmates gained the privilege to go on drives, more vigilant escorts, or a transfer elsewhere. Lafayette had hinted that he feared for his life, and Bollmann feared for his own reputation: "Had I delayed the attempt till the next spring, I had exposed myself to the most unpleasant and most unanswerable of all reproaches, *that of lost opportunity,* and perhaps my zeal and honesty would have been suspected." Above all Lafayette himself had ordered haste. Bollmann concluded that he would have to replace his own expensive plan based on bribery and longer preparation with a relatively cheap, riskier one based on timely attack.[97]

Bollmann knew that he had to observe drives, engage one or two aides to overcome the escort, and obtain some swift saddle horses. Each presented its own problems.

Bollmann was nearsighted, making it hard to time drives and gauge the strength of their escort. He carried eyeglasses, but either they offered inadequate compensation or he avoided wearing them in public. He asked Schramowsky to observe and report on the drives, but Schramowsky balked. This forced Bollmann to observe personally what he could of Lafayette's outing on Thursday, 9 October, and possibly also on Sunday. It is unclear how much Bollmann could see, but he saw enough to agree with Lafayette on the need for an aide to overcome resistance.[98]

Bollmann found no person in Olmütz suited to this task. He had also failed to find adequate mounts. Two horses for sale proved to be "weak and miserable," and there were no horses to rent. Bollmann visited two officers' wives and tried to look up acquaintances on country estates, apparently to elicit tips on other horses. However, all was in vain.[99]

Bollmann tried to alert Lafayette to the delay. Saturday evening, he visited Haberlein under the ruse of returning the surgeon's book. When he did so, he gave Haberlein another book containing a marginal thanks in ink, followed by the real message—that he needed time—in lemon juice. When the book reached Lafayette, he cut the note out and burned it.[100]

Bollmann decided that he had to return to Vienna for both horses and aides, so he prepared a third, seemingly harmless French-language note in ink, followed by the real message, invisible and in English, underneath, saying "that I had neither saddle-horses, nor friend, nor confidential servant; that I did not know where to find all this nearer and sooner than at Vienna, where I should consequently go, but hoped to be back in a fortnight." He turned it over to Haberlein on Monday evening, 13 October, explaining that news just received from England was forcing him to return there after concluding affairs in Vienna and that he would come again to take his final leave. But once Bollmann departed, Haberlein tore up the note, thinking that it contained news already known to Lafayette.[101] In doing so, he destroyed the secret words.

Bollmann arrived in Vienna a little more than twenty-four hours later, and he soon obtained the aides and horses he sought. In wake of Weigel's withdrawal, he knew that the time had come to turn to Huger. He found him packing at the Boeuf d'or inn on Seilergasse, where Huger had moved in anticipation of his departure for England. Huger had not heard from Bollmann for eight days, so he was about to purchase his own carriage for the trip. It was then that Bollmann appeared, had him promise to keep confidential what he was about to say, showed him the book with Lafayette's marginal message, explained the project, and asked him to join.

The young American's response was immediate and passionate. He had to agree to help liberate the man to whom he and his country owed their freedom, the man who had fought in the same cause for which Huger's father had given his life. "When the proposition was first made to me, my feeling was only of gratitude," Huger later said. "I saw an opportunity to free the man who at my age had risked everything for me."[102]

The plan still needed at least one other accomplice, ideally someone whom Bollmann and Huger could initiate into the scheme. Bribery seemed out of the question because they needed their money to pay for other contingencies. Also, if the person were in on the plan, Bollmann and Huger would also be responsible for his escape. Another possibility was to hire a groom to drive the carriage while Bollmann and Huger rode saddle horses and kept the groom in the dark about the trip's real nature. Bringing along a third, riderless saddle horse for Lafayette, especially into a fortress town holding state prisoners, would likely set off alarms. Still Bollmann rejected the idea of a second groom whom he would dismiss abruptly in order to take his horse. The jilted man might resist or alert and help the authorities. Huger offered to give up his own horse and try to escape on foot. He felt that, without knowledge of German or the topography, he was less valuable than Bollmann to guide Lafayette to safety.

Bollmann and Huger then considered yet another, more hopeful alternative. They fancied it possible, while traveling to Olmütz, to train one horse to bear both of them. Once Lafayette was freed, the horse would carry them alongside Lafayette's mount to just short of Hof, almost forty kilometers distant, where the groom and carriage would be waiting. Bollmann would send the groom on an errand, at which point Huger and Lafayette would appear, jump into the carriage with Bollmann, and be off. This could have made for a happy chain of events, but it is hard to imagine that either Bollmann or Huger would think that a horse carrying a double load could ride such a distance, mostly uphill, with the speed and stamina needed to shake pursuers, keep up with Lafayette on the other steed, and reach Hof in good time. At least Bollmann seems to have hoped that the horse might carry them into a wooded area, out of sight of pursuers. Under cover of night, Huger could make his way to the border, a walk approaching one hundred kilometers. He might have as good a chance this way, as Bollmann and Lafayette did by horse and carriage on public roads.[103]

Bollmann decided that Huger should pose as a wealthy Englishman returning home, who had commissioned Bollmann as interpreter-guide and acquired the horses to sightsee along the way. This would explain why they were riding while a groom drove an empty carriage. The men would also spread word in Vienna that they would take the most direct route, northwest through Bohemia to Prague and Dresden rather than north into Moravia.[104]

To obtain saddle horses and a groom, Bollmann turned to a man with extensive connections in the Viennese horse trade, Count Lažansky's valet Joseph Zudik. Zudik arranged for Bollmann to buy a gelding on 31 October and mare on 1 November, and to keep them in the Lažansky stables until their departure.[105] Zudik also found a suitable groom through Lažansky's porter, Bernard Hahn: Joseph Brenda, an unmarried, thirty-nine-year-old Moravian, who had served local officials and nobles over several years. On Saturday evening, 1 November, Zudik arranged for Brenda and Hahn to meet Bollmann at Lažansky's townhouse gate. Bollmann described a route taking them through Breslau to Hamburg. He offered Brenda room, board, three gold sovereigns for return costs, and a very generous salary of four ducats, or eighteen florins. Brenda worried that he might need authorities' permission to serve a foreigner leaving the country, but Hahn assured him that he could cross the border under his master's passport.

That same evening, Bollmann introduced Brenda to Huger. He then sent Brenda ahead with the two saddle horses on the journey's first leg, to Moravian Znaim, and promised that Bollmann and Huger would follow by carriage. Every third day Brenda and the horses were to rest. Brenda secured a cloth sack with a couple changes of clothes, some toiletries, and other items on one of the horses, collected his two pet cats, mounted the other horse, and rode north.[106]

Before departing themselves, Bollmann and Huger completed other tasks. Huger withdrew some two hundred pounds from his Vienna banker, Steinmetz and Company.[107] Bollmann had copies of Lafayette's message sent through a friend, probably Weigel, to Angelica Church in London, to signal that the breakout was imminent.[108] Bollmann stored books and the now useless escape tools in a trunk belonging to Huger at bookseller Johann Stahel's.[109]

In the meantime fortress command had changed at Olmütz, and with it a stricter discipline came to captives' excursions.[110] Returning commandant Arco was critical of changes made since his departure in March. Although there had been three officers supervising five captives in late spring, he noted, now there was only one officer supervising eighteen. He was concerned that these excursions occurred at all, and especially that they occurred under escort of a single officer or sergeant. Splényi explained that since troop withdrawals in May and June, the garrison had been thinly manned. Still Lieutenant Jacob and Sergeant Platzer had proven up to the job, and escort procedures had worked well. Besides the excursion policy had been "approved at a high level."[111] Botta, chief of Moravian General Command, confirmed that the fortress was understaffed and that the emperor had sanctioned excursions. Arco ordered only one change: that a vigilant private stand on the back bumper and always remain with the carriage.[112]

Other security weaknesses remained. The Aulic War Council, which oversaw military justice and discipline, logistics, and planning for Austrian forces, later concluded that to allow a sergeant rather than the lieutenant to escort Lafayette and to let Lafayette walk on foot departed from a strict reading of the emperor's orders. Arco's new directive was largely ineffectual, since the "vigilant" soldier was chosen without regard to experience or intelligence and was sometimes allowed to leave sergeant and prisoner.[113] Beyond this, the driver, fifty-seven-year-old Wenzel Polzel, was habitually drank, even early in the day. Sometimes he was so incapacitated on drives that Sergeant Platzer had to take the reins. The sergeant did not discourage his drinking; on the contrary he sometimes had the private fetch him a beer on the way, or had Polzel and the private drive ahead to a tavern, while Platzer and Lafayette walked.[114]

Bollmann and Huger departed Vienna on 2 November. They kept Brenda at a distance, so the two parties met only at prearranged stations. Sometimes Brenda mounted one of the saddle horses and led the other while Bollmann and Huger drove the carriage. Usually, however, Bollmann and Huger rode while Brenda drove.[115] This strategy accustomed the unsuspecting groom to riding or driving ahead, as they planned for him to do the day of escape; it also allowed Bollmann and Huger to train the mare to carry two riders at once, and by dividing the party, it lowered its visibility. In this manner they traveled six days to Olmütz. Bollmann and Huger arrived by carriage at the Golden Swan on Wednesday afternoon, 5 November. Bollmann was a familiar face, and innkeeper Herbricht never bothered to ask Huger's name. Brenda appeared at noon the next day.[116]

The evening of his arrival, Bollmann visited Haberlein and announced plans to continue the next morning to England. He handed over a final message for Lafayette and requested a message from Lafayette for friends in Britain. The visible, French-language portion contained the usual concocted information of such seeming importance that Haberlein would pass it on. It alleged, for instance, that U.S. envoy John Jay had come to Vienna to seek Lafayette's release. Below the visible lines was the real message written in lemon juice and in English: "*I now have everything ready to carry out the plan, and make an attempt on Thursday or Saturday* [6 or 8 November]."[117] It also named Bollmann's accomplice Huger, whose surname Lafayette would recognize. When the men encountered Lafayette on his drive, Huger and Bollmann were to doff their hats as a signal, and Lafayette was to draw a handkerchief across his forehead in reply. Haberlein reluctantly agreed to deliver the note.[118]

Bollmann had invented the news of Jay's mission to Vienna, but Lafayette believed it the rest of his imprisonment. After he read the secret message of imminent rescue, he burned it as he had previous notes.[119]

Brenda joined Bollmann and Huger at the Swan around noon on Thursday. Bollmann directed Brenda to take the two saddle horses ahead at seven the next day. The groom objected that the horses needed their rest every three days. Bollmann conferred with Huger in English, "a language completely incomprehensible" to Brenda, and agreed to stay a couple days more.[120] While the horses rested, Bollmann and Huger did some sightseeing and attended an evening comedy at the theater on Lower Square.[121] They wanted to look like innocent visitors and to calm themselves by doing something entertaining.

On Friday, Brenda and Bollmann wrote their last letters. To Lažansky's porter in Vienna, Brenda worried about crossing into Prussia without proper papers. Bollmann informed three acquaintances that he would soon visit them: textile merchant Johann Alberti in Waldenburg, pastor Johann Pohle in Glatz, and Johanna Sieveking in Hamburg.[122] This signaled the Hamburg circle that action was imminent. Bollmann also hoped to use the two gentlemen's homes as refuges.

Around 6:30 that evening, Bollmann said goodbye to Haberlein. Bollmann announced that he and Huger would leave the next day at 10:00 A.M., stay a few days in Berlin, and embark in Hamburg for London. He also asked Haberlein to recommend him a last time to Lafayette.[123]

The plans had taken their ultimate form. Brenda would wait with the carriage at Hof's postal station while Bollmann and Huger took Lafayette's escort by surprise on the Saturday drive. Huger would handle the horses while Bollmann freed Lafayette and put him on the gelding. Bollmann would leap behind Huger on the mare, the horse trained to carry two. If necessary, Huger would try to reach Prussia on foot across the wooded Moravian mountains. To help maintain Huger's cover, Bollmann gave him an English passport issued to Bollmann on 27 November 1792, and a German certificate backdated "Brünn, 1 November 1794," identifying the American as his servant. Bollmann also gave him letters to Silesians who might shelter him. Huger copied Bollmann's map into his paper tablet in case they were separated. The map showed two routes: the one that Bollmann intended to follow with Lafayette, leading through Sternberg and Hof to Troppau in the northeast, the other leading through Sternberg and Braunseifen to Neisse. Unfortunately the agents failed to make a similar map for Lafayette.[124]

Bollmann and Huger considered, of course, that circumstances might force a delay. In that case Huger would "wound himself with a stone . . . and pretend his horse had fallen with him" as a pretext to linger in the area until the right moment.[125]

The men assembled their money and guns. They divided the cash into three purses, each containing twenty gold Fredericks, twenty-one half-sovereigns, twelve imperial ducats, and twelve Dutch ducats. Then they split Lafayette's share between them, Bollmann keeping the twenty gold Fredericks and Huger the rest, so that if only one rescuer accompanied Lafayette, he would still have enough. The men depended on surprise and intimidation, not lethal violence, so Bollmann and Huger each packed a pistol loaded only with a paper plug. Lafayette had assured the agents that the escort would offer little resistance, and the men wished to avoid any crime that could bring grave consequences upon themselves. Given dangers he might face several days on foot, however, Huger put two small pistols loaded with lead in another pocket.[126]

The men ate breakfast and paid their bill on Saturday morning, 8 November, then made their last preparations. Bollmann directed Schramowsky to have three postal horses harnessed to the carriage. He told Brenda to drive north to the first postal station, Sternberg, to pick up a fresh complement of three horses and then proceed immediately northeast to the next station, Hof. There he was to harness four horses, since the terrain beyond would be rough and hilly. He would have them ready by 4:30 P.M. for Bollmann and Huger's immediate departure. Bollmann handed over a postal receipt to give the guard at the Olmütz city gate and a card with his own name and Huger's. Around 11:00 A.M. Brenda drove off.[127]

The trip proved relatively routine. Brenda arrived at Sternberg between 12:30 and 1:00 P.M. and had a lunch of soup, brandy, and a half beer. When he requested three new horses, the postmaster insisted that he take four. After "a long protest," Brenda gave in and, around 5:00 P.M., drove off behind two pairs. At Hof, twenty-six kilometers further, Brenda had Postmaster Peregrin Duban lubricate the carriage wheels and harness four fresh horses.[128]

The day of the escape attempt had arrived. With all the preparations finished, Bollmann and Huger needed only to wait for Lafayette's party to exit the city walls and garrison. If all went according to plan, the agents would then attack the escort and spirit him to freedom.

6

ESCAPE

Bollmann and Huger planned to attack Lafayette's escort on Saturday afternoon, 8 November 1794. The men had made all their preparations. All they had to do was to confirm that the carriage had left the town walls behind and reached a suitably distant and vacant location. The events to follow brought Lafayette's fate dramatically to the attention of the reading public.

At lunch hour in Olmütz, Sergeant Platzer received confirmation from Lieutenant Jacob that he was to accompany "state prisoner number 2." Jacob had escorted two prisoners the day before and was happy to delegate Lafayette's drive to Platzer.

Platzer, a thirty-one-year-old bachelor, was unusually alone in the world. A tailor by profession, he was from a Jewish Moravian family. His mother had died three days after his birth while his gin-trading father was away on business. Pious locals promptly baptized the newborn a Catholic. When he reached the age of one, authorities seized him from his grandmother, baptized him a second time, and placed him in the family of a Bohemian paper miller. He stayed there until age ten, then became a tailor journeyman. As a teenager in search of work, he made the mistake of leaving Bohemia without authorization. On his way back, he appeared at the border and could not produce proper papers. Imperial recruiters won him for the army as an alternative to prison. Platzer was now in his thirteenth year of army service, his fifth as sergeant, and had been appointed provost at Olmütz in late August 1793. Platzer had two brothers but kept only loose contact with his family. He had last heard from his father a year ago, and was unsure whether he was even alive.[1]

As the drive was to begin at two o'clock, Corporal Berger of the prison-barracks guard ordered Private Johann Harwich to stand on the rear bumper as escort. Harwich carried a saber but no firearm. He was an illiterate, unmarried, twenty-four-year-old Bohemian with less than two and a half years' service in the army.

His record was unblemished, but army investigators deemed him "to all appearances . . . a dumb, stupid person." Stationed in Olmütz since 1 May, he had accompanied prisoners' drives only three times.[2] Like anyone with rural roots in or near Czech-speaking areas, Harwich must have been used to German-speaking officers and townspeople pushing him around. Factors other than intelligence may have played a role in his behavior that day, including a language barrier, pretense of stupidity in self-defense, and passive resistance.

Carriage driver Wenzl Polzel had been drinking heavily at lunch. He was stupefied by the time the two-horse calash was ready, but his condition seemed manageable. He knew the route that Lafayette preferred: north through Chwalkowitz (Chválkovice), southeast to Klein-Wisternitz (Bystrovany), and back west through Bleich (Bělidla).

After lunch at the Swan, Bollmann readied his saddle horses. Huger loitered near Castle Gate and watched for Lafayette's carriage. Around 1:15–1:30 Huger saw what he mistook to be the vehicle. He hurried back to Bollmann, and the men rode out in pursuit. Unbeknownst to them, however, Lafayette's carriage had not yet left town.

At 2:00 P.M. Polzel picked up his passenger and escort at the barracks' gate. Sergeant Platzer carried a sword but was dressed in civilian clothes: a long-sleeved undershirt and gray hooded riding coat under an overcoat, white breeches, hat, and boots. Lafayette appeared more official: his hair was powdered, and he wore a blue greatcoat typical of the Prussian military, probably acquired before his extradition to Olmütz.

The carriage headed down the main street and then turned left into an alley leading to Castle Gate. Along the way Sergeant Platzer pulled the calash bonnet halfway up, so that Harwich could not eavesdrop. As drunk as Polzel was, he had the presence of mind to confirm the day's route with Platzer. The sergeant replied that the driver already knew the route that "this gentleman" liked. Once through the gate, the calash crossed a bridge spanning the Mittelmarch, another over the Morava, kept to the right at a fork beyond, and drove onto the imperial highway northeast toward the villages of Pawlowitz (Pavlovičky) and Chwalkowitz.[3]

Conditions seemed to favor escape. As Bollmann and Huger had hoped, the escort was weak, and the route would take the carriage well beyond the town.[4] But Bollmann and Huger had left Olmütz prematurely. They trotted ahead of Lafayette's carriage for most of an hour. Saturday was market day, so there were more travelers. The two men had ridden a distance toward Sternberg before they surmised a mistake. Perhaps Lafayette had taken a different route. The men retraced their path through Chwalkowitz and debated how they might explain their return.

Suddenly, just south of the village, the two-horse calash appeared. The would-be rescuers doffed their hats as they passed on the right. Lafayette and the sergeant saluted, and, as agreed, Lafayette wiped his handkerchief across his forehead.

Bollmann and Huger were close enough that the near-sighted Bollmann was able to confirm Lafayette's presence. Bollmann and Huger continued riding a short distance toward Olmütz, then turned about and began their pursuit.

By then the carriage was passing through Chwalkowitz. Bollmann was impatient and urged immediate attack. However, his poor eyesight forced him to rely on Huger, who cautioned patience until the calash had left town. When Huger said that it had disappeared momentarily, Bollmann exclaimed that they must attack or lose every chance. Then the carriage reappeared. It drove out into open fields and stopped at a large statue of an angel, a marker on a pilgrim trail leading to the church on Holy Mountain.[5]

Shortly before the stop, Sergeant Platzer had asked Lafayette if he wished to take a walk. Lafayette replied, "Yes, the weather is nice." Platzer directed Polzel to leave the highway by veering to the right onto an empty dirt lane. The angel statue lay two hundred yards ahead, where another lane branched off toward the village of Klein-Wisternitz. The sergeant said that they would now begin their walk. The way was pretty, Platzer noted, and exercise would give Lafayette appetite and thirst to enjoy the tavern stop. Platzer climbed out of the carriage, helped Lafayette descend, and ordered Private Harwich to take the rear seat. Polzel and Harwich drove ahead to await Lafayette and Platzer at the inn of Klein-Wisternitz. He started the carriage forward as Platzer and Lafayette strolled behind arm in arm, soon following by forty paces.[6]

In these promising circumstances, the attack began around 3:00 P.M.[7] Huger reported that sergeant and captive were alighting, and Bollmann exclaimed, "Let's lose no more time!" They spurred their mounts, galloped up, and yelled, "Halt!"

Platzer, on Lafayette's left, turned in surprise. Bollmann shouted to Lafayette in English to seize the sergeant's sword. Lafayette was able to draw it halfway out of its scabbard before Platzer grabbed it and asked what he thought he was doing. Bollmann leaped to the ground, pointed his pistol at Platzer, shouted, "Give us the man!" and tried to give his rein to Huger. The horses reared up, so Huger was unable to grab the rein. Bollmann's horse bounded off. After calming his own animal, Huger dismounted, held the rein over one arm, and pointed his pistol at Platzer. Huger quickly saw that intimidation did not work, so he pocketed his weapon and tried to help Bollmann subdue the sergeant. Platzer held his sword in his left hand and grabbed Lafayette's cravat with his right. Platzer held on so tightly that Lafayette gasped, "Il m'étrangle" (He's strangling me). Huger tore the men apart. Lafayette shouted in English, "Kill him! Kill him!" but the rescuers refused.

When Lafayette tried to mount the mare, Platzer grabbed his coat from behind, pulled him backward, and held on. Bollmann, Platzer, and Lafayette ended up in a heap. The horse fell on top of them, spraining Lafayette's arm. Then the mare stepped on the sergeant's right thigh before righting itself.

Platzer screamed for help, but the peasants working the fields did not respond. Their knowledge of German may have been shaky, since they came from Czech-speaking villages.[8] They were also confused about the nature of the fight because Platzer was not in uniform.

It took great effort to subdue Platzer. Lafayette tried to hush him by offering money. Huger cried, "Gag him! Gag him!" When Lafayette tried to stuff a glove in his mouth, Platzer bit down on his finger and spit out the glove. Bollmann immobilized the sergeant with a knee to his chest, as Huger crammed a handkerchief down his throat. Bollmann also held a pistol to the sergeant's head and ordered him to release Lafayette. Both rescuers, one of them wielding a riding crop, pummeled Platzer's arm. The pain forced the sergeant to loosen his fist. Lafayette broke free and rolled away. As Platzer reached out to grab him again, Huger kneeled quickly on his arm while Bollmann shouted a warning: "Take care of his sword, Sir, take care of his sword!" Bollmann managed to draw the weapon, cutting Platzer's left thumb in the process, and hurl it away. Platzer wounded his right hand as he tore away Bollmann's pistol and pitched it.

Huger and Bollmann told a badly shaken Lafayette to mount the remaining horse. Once astride, Lafayette turned about and asked how he could help. Bollmann and apparently also Huger shouted, "Go to Hof!" but Lafayette heard the English words as "Get off!" Lafayette cantered slowly up to the highway. He had never heard of a town named "Hof." Neither rescuer managed to hand him map or purse.

Meanwhile an attentive peasant had caught the gelding two or three hundred meters away. Huger saw this, but nearsighted Bollmann did not. In fact Bollmann had not realized that his horse was gone. Huger released Platzer and started off to fetch the animal. Bollmann asked him where in the world he was going. At Huger's reply Bollmann left Platzer and hurried after. He fished out a gold piece, and the peasant helped the men mount: Huger on the saddle, Bollmann behind on the rump. Huger saw Lafayette near the highway, but for Bollmann, he was out of sight.

Platzer tore the gag from his mouth, ran after Lafayette, and screamed for help. He begged drivers to unhitch horses and ride after the escapee. He promised munificent rewards, but no one paid heed. Lafayette, muddy and bloodstained, saw the sergeant in pursuit. Travelers began to stare. Lafayette galloped a short distance up the highway, then turned back for a second look. He saw his rescuers reaching the other horse, and assumed that they would follow. With that, he took off toward Sternberg. His kidneys had been painfully bruised in his fall, so he could only hope that his rescuers would meet him before Sternberg. At least he had a general idea that Silesia lay north.[9]

Bollmann later claimed to have given Lafayette more detailed instructions in English.[10] But in the midst of the fight, Lafayette did not understand the directions he heard. He could not have known which road to take beyond the fork at Stern-berg.

Platzer continued north on foot until he reached Teiniczek (Týneček), a ham-let consisting of little more than a two-story inn. He rushed into the building, only to find the owner gone and rooms empty. He convinced a nearby peasant to har-ness a pasturing horse and give chase. Only now did the sergeant turn and run back south toward Olmütz. At the edge of Pawlowitz, he ran into two peasants, Martin Fokal and Franz Runtak, as they drove by an inn. Bloody and hysterical, he cried out that French prisoners (plural) had escaped, begged the peasants to pur-sue them, and promised a generous award. Platzer rushed into the inn to raise the alarm, and customers poured out onto the road to give chase. Two of them, Nor-bert Teymer and Johann Karner, joined Fokal and Runtak in their foot chase. They saw Bollmann riding in full gallop toward Sternberg and Huger running toward Holy Mountain. The pursuers chose Huger as the only feasible target. Teymer yelled to a fifth peasant plowing nearby, Franz Reiczeck, to unharness his horse and give chase. Reiczeck did so immediately.[11]

Platzer ran up to Castle Gate at Olmütz. He reported the escape to the first guard post, then repeated the message to the sentry within and to commandant Arco. The commandant ordered Lieutenant Jacob to incarcerate the sergeant in the staff stockade on the city moat.[12] He also issued orders to sound the cannon, mount a pursuit, and alert authorities. He sent staff officers to border towns Trop-pau (Opava) in the northeast and Teschen (Těšin; Polish Cieszyn) in the east. He notified his civil counterpart, Circle Captain Baron Vinzenz von Dubsky, who ordered all local authorities to pursue instantly "a young man, a Frenchman, with white [powdered] hair and a blue coat," who had fled an hour before, to arrest him on sight, and return him under heavy guard. The posted reward was twenty-four florins.[13]

Private Harwich later reported his own versions of events. Back in Lafayette's erstwhile carriage, he supposedly heard a noise after he and Polzel left sergeant and captive. He turned to see a horse running off but assumed it had escaped a peasant. He told Polzel to halt and climbed out to investigate. A besotted Polzel waited a bit, then set the two horses in motion again, driving slowly away "in com-fortable stupidity."[14] He focused his attention on the tavern ahead. Harwich saw a fight but took it to be peasants brawling over the escaped horse. As he walked some ten paces toward the struggle, he saw a man (Lafayette) riding off toward Chwalkowitz. Two other strangers seemed as if they were leaving for Pawlowitz, but disappeared. Only when the private saw Sergeant Platzer running after the rider did he realize something was wrong. He followed Platzer and rider into Chwalkowitz but lost sight of them. Onlookers there told him that someone had throttled the sergeant. Harwich returned to the site, where he found the sergeant's unsheathed saber and hat, a right-hand leather glove, a small copper-sheathed staff, and a riding crop.[15]

Bollmann's rendition of events is more likely. He wrote that the brawl progressed in full view of Harwich; that Platzer called for help, but the private was "so frightened" and "ran towards town [Chwalkowitz], as fast as he could." Bollmann knew that they could not prevent Harwich or Platzer from raising an alarm.[16] Harwich would have waited until the field was clear and then returned to collect evidence.

Once on their own, Bollmann and Huger rode toward Holy Mountain with the helpful peasant following behind. Their horse bucked several times, likely because of Bollmann's spurs or the unfamiliar weight of two riders. Bollmann fell from the horse, and followed a few hundred yards on foot. Then he remounted, only to be thrown again. He suggested trading positions. With the peasant's help, Huger mounted ahead. After several paces at a trot, Bollmann and Huger tried galloping, but the gelding stumbled at a drainage channel and pitched both men. The fall bruised Huger and stunned Bollmann, injuring his left eye and wrist. Once more, the horse bounded away, but it was quickly recaptured. Huger insisted that Bollmann ride on alone to help Lafayette. They had aroused attention, cannons were booming, and further delay risked capture of both. Bollmann was the more valuable aide, they had agreed, and Huger had volunteered to go on foot if necessary. The men embraced and parted. Bollmann mounted and galloped after Lafayette. But as it turned out, the South Carolinian was not as expendable as they thought, for only Huger could see Lafayette from afar.[17]

Huger realized that his situation was desperate. He turned and ran toward the wooded, generally overgrown Holy Mountain. He hoped to hide in the forest until nightfall. At first he saw no pursuers. Then he caught sight of a mounted peasant closing quickly, with others right behind. Huger threw away the two loaded pistols and the purse intended for Lafayette. He climbed the hillside and managed to reach the forest edge. Huger was exhausted. He considered hiding behind a tree, fighting the pursuing rider, or bribing him for his horse. Finally he deemed escape impossible, so he dug a hole under a tree, threw in the pistol loaded with paper, covered it with earth, and sat down on the grass to await the inevitable. The rider arrived, followed by four men on foot. Huger did not resist as they grabbed him and searched for weapons. He offered his pocketknife, the only potential weapon still on him. Reiczeck returned to his plowing while the other four peasants took Huger to Castle Gate.

An escort of four soldiers, bayonets fixed, took Huger into custody. Sometime after 4:00 P.M., they delivered him to a holding cell. That evening, they led him to the town hall for an initial hearing.[18] Thereafter they escorted him to a communal cell in the Stronghold (Fronfeste), a damp, gloomy state prison at the moat. After

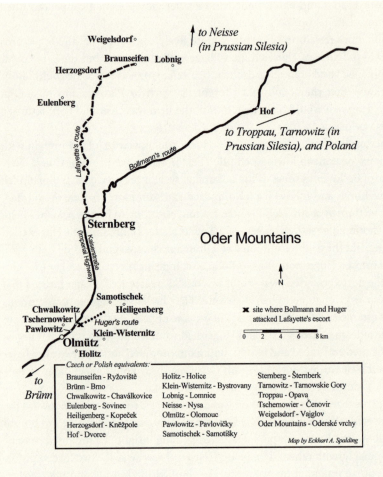

Escape routes taken by Lafayette, Huger, and Bollmann in 1794. Prepared by Eckhart Spalding, Illinois College

a strip search, he was chained by a wrist and ankle to an iron bar on the wall. Soon he was transferred into isolation, a small cell lit by a slit near the ceiling.[19]

In the meantime a peasant had approached Harwich, handed over Bollmann's small pistol, and asked who the gentlemen were. Harwich explained that a state prisoner was trying to escape. The peasant then informed him that two men were being chased toward Holy Mountain. Harwich continued down the lane and asked a plowman if he had seen two riders. The man replied that he had, but that they were long gone. It dawned on the private that he was in big trouble. He turned toward the Klein-Wisternitz inn, where he found Polzel and told him the story, interjecting repeatedly a cry from the heart: "What's going to happen to me?"

Polzel took Harwich back to Olmütz and dropped him off at the barracks-prison gate. As Polzel drove home, he noted a general hubbub in the city. Meanwhile Harwich reported to the sergeant of the guard and handed over objects he had collected. He was taken immediately into custody.[20] Soon thereafter, Circle Captain Dubsky summoned Polzel for interrogation.[21] The investigation moved swiftly. The same evening, two sets of inquiries began, one under army command and the other moderated by the leading civil magistrate.

By order of Commandant Arco, the military hearing interrogated Lafayette's escort. Presiding was Johann Teich, regimental staff auditor or lawyer, assisted by two other officers. They took testimony first from Sergeant Platzer, who concluded dramatically by displaying his bloody hands, and then from Private Harwich, who brought out Lafayette's glove. The witnesses were then returned to custody. Authorities carefully collected, searched, and listed Platzer's personal effects, including the straw sack he slept on.[22]

The civilian hearing took place at the town hall before Dubsky and Arco. Dubsky and Arco interrogated the four peasants who had brought Huger into town, as well as Polzel and Huger. Habsburg law did not allow Huger to retain an attorney before criminal charges were filed. The young, articulate, and educated representative of the new American republic was a most exotic creature in Moravia. The panel recorded his South Carolinian hometown as "Charlsthom," and the city council later called it "Karlstown in South America." Huger knew little German, so he testified in French. His translator, who soon grew in importance for Huger, was Christoph von Passy, political science professor at the town lyceum.

Huger was quite open. He identified himself and the fugitive Bollmann, described how they had met in Vienna and arrived at Olmütz, and detailed their escape plans. When the panel showed him the pistol found in the field, he identified it as Bollmann's. In response to concluding questions, Huger brought the hearing to an emotional climax. When Dubsky asked, "How could you do such a thing in the very country of the sovereign who held M. La Fayette prisoner?" Huger replied, "When the proposition was first made to me, I could only feel gratitude. I saw an opportunity to liberate the man who, at my age, had risked everything for me." He noted that he had not intended any harm, and that Lafayette had hoped to retire from European politics to America. To the question, "Do you have a particular acquaintance with La Fayette?" Huger replied, "That which every American has. But beyond that, my father knew him and fought in the same cause." "Do you have anything to say in your defense?" was the final query. Huger responded, "I hope that what I have already said will be my defense." Huger had given powerful, succinct expression to his idealism, love of country and liberty, and personal devotion to a comrade in arms of his fallen father. It touched his hearers. Their reports spread admiration in the right places. A couple of those present that evening became Huger's active counselors and supporters.

At hearing's end Dubsky agreed to transfer Huger to the city prison, where he was treated there as a violent criminal, cut off from visitors, and locked up in irons, to await further examination and sentencing by the town judiciary. Dubsky confiscated Huger's money, gold pocket watch, letter book, pencil, and pocketknife.[23]

News of the escape and interrogations spread along two lines of Austrian imperial authority, one military and the other civil. Dubsky reported the escape and first examinations by special courier to Count Alois von und zu Ugarte, governor of Austrian Moravia and Silesia, then to Field Marshal Botta, the province's commanding general. Botta and, in the governor's absence, Ugarte's assistant, Baronet Joseph von Platzer conferred, then alerted their respective superiors in Vienna: the president of the Aulic War Council and the minister of police. They notified the emperor.[24]

Francis II was shocked. "It goes without saying how irregularly things were carried out on Lafayette's drive. . . . How could it be possible for these foreigners to carry out such a bold operation, for which they had to make trips and rehearsals?" he scribbled on the military report. He ordered the army to work with police to ferret out a wider conspiracy.[25]

Brünn quickly sent orders to Olmütz. On 8 November at 6:45 P.M., Baronet Platzer dispatched a courier to Dubsky, approving Huger's transfer to civil authorities and urging continued interrogation. Platzer also ordered Dubsky to examine the postmaster at Hof and the innkeeper at the Swan in Olmütz, to send many of Huger's effects under seal with the first post, and to report developments in detail every postal day. Should Lafayette and Bollmann be captured, a thorough search was to be carried out of all their belongings, especially Bollmann's papers.[26]

Meanwhile Bollmann was galloping north after Lafayette. He managed to control a fast but skittish horse, and he soon caught up with the mounted peasant pursuing Lafayette. Bollmann convinced the man to give up the chase: "I am pursuing the escaped man also; my horse is better than yours; I soon shall overtake him; spare your trouble." At other places people on the road shouted, "Are you following the other rider? You soon will reach him; he is not far."[27] Bollmann had good reason to anticipate seeing Lafayette at any moment.

Bollmann reached the highway fork in Sternberg only ten minutes after Lafayette had passed. From there he followed the imperial highway northeast to Hof. He soon noticed that travelers had stopped shouting encouragement. Then, almost an hour beyond Sternberg, Bollmann asked travelers whether a rider had passed by in the last minutes. When they said no, he concluded that Lafayette must have taken a left branch off the main highway. Bollmann decided against returning and seeking the right road, since he was unlikely to overtake a man with a stronger horse and a long lead. Bollmann also risked falling into the hands of trackers and tipping them off to Lafayette's trail. Bollmann determined instead to continue through Hof and lead them away from Lafayette.[28]

The intersection in Sternberg where the imperial highway takes a ninety-degree turn
to the right. Lafayette continued straight ahead, exited the wrong gate, and rode into
a maze of hilly country roads. Author's photograph

Lafayette had indeed pursued another route. As soon as he entered Sternberg,
he saw a northern gate straight ahead that seemed to mark the main road. But the
imperial highway actually turned sharply right just before that gate, and exited at
a quite different opening in the eastern wall of the town. Because of his panic and
his poor German, Lafayette never saw a signpost. He also assumed that the northward route would be the shortest way to the border. So straight ahead he trotted,
onto a side road that led up a steep and winding incline into a confusing network
of minor country trails.[29] In retrospect the mistake seemed almost inevitable. But
when Bollmann planned the route, he had not seen how easily an unescorted rider
proceeding through Sternberg could leave the main road.

When Bollmann and Huger failed to appear, Lafayette thought that they may
have fallen prey to pursuers or passed him by another way. He also knew that it
would be hard to cross the border without being recognized and that he would
have to do it without his rescuers. If the others had been captured, he reasoned, he
could negotiate their release once he was safely away. There was no point in riding
back to Olmütz, so he continued northward.[30]

Between 6:00 and 7:00 P.M., thirty-year-old master tanner Joseph Dröxler was
walking home alone when he heard a rider approaching from behind. He turned
and saw a man mounted on a splendid chestnut thoroughbred mare. Dröxler
clicked his tongue and called out to the horse. The rider trotted up, and the tanner bade him a good evening. In "very harsh and corrupt German," the stranger
thanked him and asked the name of the town ahead. "Braunseifen," Dröxler

replied. The rider asked if he was on the imperial highway, and Dröxler said he was not. He asked for the nearest postal station, and Dröxler directed him to Lobnig (Lomnice), just east of Braunseifen. He added, "You must be a Romanic [*Welscher:* Frenchman, Italian, Spaniard]." "No," the rider objected, "I am from England." Dröxler thought otherwise: "We have a Romanic among us too, who works for a merchant." "Are you a merchant?" the rider asked. "No," replied Dröxler. "What then?" "A tanner [*Rotgerber*]." Lafayette had no idea of the German word's meaning, but he did not seek clarification. Instead, he asked how far it was to Olmütz, Troppau, and Neisse. Dröxler gave him an accurate distance south to Olmütz, but less accurate distances to Troppau in the east and Neisse in the north "because he sensed already that something might not be right with this person."[31]

Dröxler had reason to be suspicious. A fine thoroughbred rarely appeared on this minor country road. Lafayette's clothes were muddy, bloodstained, and torn, but Dröxler seems not to have noticed in the deepening dusk. What definitely sent up red flags, however, was Lafayette's ungrammatical, strongly accented German. Authorities had instructed all subjects in the area to watch for foreigners able to speak only French or broken German.[32]

Lafayette found Dröxler "quite obliging," even though he was unsure how much the tanner understood. He asked Dröxler to show him the way to Neisse, even to ride along as guide. Dröxler declined because of domestic duties but offered a trusted hired man. Lafayette asked how many ducats the tanner would demand. Dröxler replied, "Surely you'll give me no more than one." "It is too little; I give you as much as I have," Lafayette declared, making a sweeping gesture to indicate the money he carried, without ever showing any. Lafayette soon offered large amounts of money to others, trusting that he could find means to pay when beyond the frontier.[33]

Dröxler led Lafayette down a footpath toward Braunseifen. They crossed a field and entered a thick forest of firs, beeches, and birches. For most of an hour, they followed the trail, twice crossing a brook, encountering little more than the field mice scuttling underfoot. When Lafayette's horse began to tire, Dröxler climbed a birch, cut a branch, and gave it to Lafayette to use as a switch. Lafayette "accepted it as if [Dröxler] had given him his heart."

When they emerged onto an open field, Lafayette began to grow nervous. He had not understood Dröxler's offer of a hired man to accompany him, so he asked the tanner to fetch his horse. As they continued down a slope, Braunseifen appeared dimly below. The scene was remarkably similar to Lafayette's fateful evening approach to Rochefort two years before, and Lafayette had every reason to be on guard because Dröxler had determined to turn him in. The tanner began to ask for more money. He persuaded Lafayette to proceed down the hill, even as Lafayette begged the tanner to keep silent. They reached a barn at village outskirts, where Dröxler told Lafayette he could wait.[34]

Dröxler dashed into Braunseifen to alert Joseph Richter, the thirty-eight-year-old mayor and hereditary bailiff. At Richter's large, two-story house, Dröxler reported that an "Englishman" with a magnificent thoroughbred was seeking to cross into Prussia and offering all the ducats he had. Richter did not want to risk delay by sending for law-court beadles or other local citizens for help, so he called together his own seven hired hands: Franz Langer, Franz Letzel, Johann Schub, Anton Jakobi, Joseph Wanke, Johann Frömel, and Melchior Tillich. Initially Richter proposed that Dröxler lead the man to the village infirmary, where the men would be waiting. Dröxler objected because that would arouse the stranger's suspicions. Instead he proposed an ambush at a woodpile on the town's northern edge. Richter agreed. Armed with clubs, he and his men accompanied Dröxler to his house. The tanner ducked into his stable and emerged with hired hand Carl Hatwicher astride a horse. Richter's group headed for the north end of town.

Dröxler led Hatwicher west to the barn, only to find it empty. Perhaps the suspicious foreigner had fled in the dark. But when Dröxler's horse whinnied, Lafayette's replied from a nearby field. The two villagers spun about, followed the noise, and, under a full moon, found Lafayette. He made ready to dismount, but Dröxler told him to stay saddled while he took the bridle in hand. As Hatwicher rode before, Dröxler went on foot, leading Lafayette through a village alley and onto the road leading north. As they passed a row of outlying barns, Lafayette felt misgivings. But his escort seemed so calm that he dismissed his concerns.[35]

At the woodpile Dröxler stopped, let Lafayette join Hatwicher, and wished him a safe journey. At that moment one of Richter's men stepped out from behind the woodpile and asked Lafayette where he was riding. Lafayette retorted indignantly, "What right have you to ask?"

At this response a second hired hand appeared and then Richter and the others grabbed the mare's bridle. Richter ordered Lafayette to dismount, asking him who he was and whether he had a pass. Lafayette refused to respond. Richter directed two men to hold him under his arms to prevent escape. Lafayette, desperate, began thinking furiously of a way out. All returned into the village, entered Richter's house, and ascended to the upper floor.[36]

The men arrived upstairs to find Richter's business secretary, Giovanni Buricelli, eating supper by the fireplace. A native of Milan, Buricelli was the local "Romanic" whom Dröxler had mentioned to Lafayette. Richter addressed the stranger in German and Latin but failed to get a response. Then he told Buricelli to ask him in Italian who he was. Richter wanted to know where he was headed and whether he could present a passport or written instruction verifying identity and status. Lafayette did not answer; instead he asked Richter in broken German if he were mayor. Richter confirmed that he was. With that Lafayette grabbed him by the hand and pulled him into an adjoining bedroom. Buricelli tugged Richter by the other sleeve and murmured that the stranger was Lafayette. Buricelli

Richter's house in Braunseifen, where the town bailiff held Lafayette under arrest on the night of 8–9 November 1794. Author's photograph

had been at the inn of the nearby Lobnig postal station the day Lafayette's escort brought him to Olmütz. A guard had divulged the prisoner's identity. Buricelli even appeared to have exchanged words with the famous man. The memories came back quickly as Buricelli saw Lafayette again and heard his voice.[37]

Once alone with Richter, Lafayette confirmed Buricelli's identification. He asked if Richter had read about him in the newspapers, and the mayor replied that he held Lafayette in esteem. Lafayette told him of the escape. Richter noted evidence of violence, including Lafayette's injured finger and bloody clothes. Lafayette, however, insisted that he had neither killed nor shot at his guard. If the mayor would let him flee, he was prepared to pay him one thousand ducats. Richter saw no sign of the money. In any event he politely refused the offer. Richter had orders to stop and report any traveler without a passport, and he would be shirking his duty if he failed to do so. Besides his aide had already recognized Lafayette.

The remark about Buricelli startled Lafayette. He insisted on speaking with him. Richter stepped back into the central room, elicited details from Buricelli about how he had recognized Lafayette, and led him into the bedroom. After confirming that Buricelli was single, Lafayette asked if would like to flee with him. Buricelli protested that he owned a house in Milan, under Austrian Habsburg sovereignty. When Lafayette asked what it was worth, Buricelli estimated three thousand to four thousand florins. "This is a trifle," Lafayette responded. He was still used to having been one of the richest men in France. He said he would keep

Buricelli in princely splendor the rest of his life. Eventually Lafayette offered twenty-five hundred ducats and generous lifetime pensions to any children Buricelli might one day have.[38] But Buricelli proved obstinate.

Lafayette turned to Richter again. He promised Richter two thousand ducats, twice the original offer, to look the other way. Richter said that it was impossible now that Dröxler had turned him in. Lafayette pointed out that the tanner did not know his identity, so Richter could claim that Lafayette was someone else and carried a correct passport. Richter replied that no matter what the offer, his duty prevailed. Lafayette proposed that Richter leave Buricelli in the room as his guard. With his cooperation Lafayette could climb through the window and get away on foot. No one would blame Richter, since Braunseifen lacked any soldiers, and Lafayette had managed to escape all the troops in Olmütz. But all Lafayette's pleas proved futile. The mayor tried to reassure him that peace was only a few months off, at which time he would be freed to return to Paris. Lafayette responded, "Not Paris, but London!"[39]

Lafayette kept asking questions. Several times he inquired about an American envoy in Vienna. Richter said that he had neither heard nor read about it. Lafayette also asked whether an accomplice had made it away. Again Richter knew nothing.

Richter provided Lafayette with food, drink, and newspapers, and set a guard detail in and around the house. He stationed Langer, Frömel, and Tillich inside the upper bedroom where Lafayette could sleep. He put Letzel, Schub, Jakobi, and Wanke in the adjoining rooms. Two night watchmen stood outside, one man in the alley directly under Lafayette's window.

Richter returned downstairs to write to the senior district magistrate, Anton Krömer, in nearby Eulenberg (Sovinec). He promised to bring Lafayette in a guarded calash. Richter asked whether the prisoner need be in irons and suggested that Krömer immediately report the capture to the Olmütz commandant. Richter dispatched his courier at 11:00 P.M.[40]

Around midnight Tillich left to warm himself at the central room's fireplace. Meanwhile in the bedroom, Langer washed the mud from Lafayette's hooded coat and breeches. Lafayette begged the two remaining guards to let him exit by the window for one thousand ducats. The men answered that they would not and could not, even if he gave them a roomful of ducats. They would not risk a life sentence in Brünn's Spielberg fortress. Lafayette finally realized that it was futile. He fell silent and began reading the newspapers that Richter had provided.[41]

Richter's courier arrived at Eulenberg around 12:30 and awakened Krömer. The magistrate was astounded at the news of Lafayette's arrest, immediately called for his carriage, and drove off into the night. He arrived in Braunseifen around 2:00 A.M. to find Lafayette asleep. As soon as the captive stirred, Krömer had him led from the bedroom and announced that Lafayette was now Krömer's prisoner and had to come with him immediately. The men climbed into the magistrate's calash sometime after 4:00 A.M. An escort of two riflemen and three other men came along, one of them leading Lafayette's exhausted mare. They drove first to Eulenberg, then to Olmütz. Along the way Lafayette asked about his two rescuers and was told they had also been arrested. (This was untrue in Bollmann's case.) During a brief stop at Eulenberg, Krömer's daughter bandaged Lafayette's finger. At that point the captive remarked that "we tried, but it was all for nothing." The ride continued south into Olmütz. When Krömer arrived at the prison-barracks, he turned his captive over to Arco, who had Lafayette strip-searched "as diamond miners are said to be," and returned to his rooms. Circle Captain Dubsky took possession of the mare, heard Krömer's report, and ordered him to keep Lafayette's name strictly confidential.[42]

Lafayette occupied the same rooms as before, but this time the conditions were grimmer. Carriage drives and library privileges were no more. Much of the furniture was removed. His servants could no longer wait on him. For a time he received no candles. Prison authorities stored his room keys at the commandant's home on the main square. Only after a long delay, could Lafayette receive any help during the fourteen to sixteen hours of lockdown at night. Almost a year of "the most absolute solitude" began. The experience later led Lafayette to declare that such punishment can drive a man insane.[43] He avoided being chained only by warning his jailor that it would exceed the emperor's orders and invite his displeasure.[44]

Lafayette soon fell ill from his injuries. His arm and side, which had been bruised by Sergeant Platzer, started swelling. The finger Platzer had almost bitten off became infected, resulting in a fever that soaked both Lafayette's shirts. Only after four days, did Haberlein attend to Lafayette. The surgeon hardly dared speak and ended up dismissing his illness as minor while Lieutenant Jacob urged Haberlein to hurry and leave. Jacob himself seems to have taken over much of the prisoner's care for a time. It was an especially cold winter; the guards were stingy with wood for the stove; and Lafayette rarely received a fresh shirt. Early in 1795 surgeon Andreas Axter transferred from Ofen (later Budapest) to take Haberlein's job. When he first saw Lafayette, the prisoner was emaciated, feverish, congested, and prematurely aged. Axter judged him near death. Lafayette had worsened his condition considerably by trying to escape.[45]

Staff changes also contributed to worsening conditions. Unlike Haberlein, Axter could speak no French and relied on his poor Latin to communicate with Lafayette. Arriving to supervise the prison "by express order of the court," was a Major Czernak, who proved to be unnecessarily cruel.[46]

Lafayette suffered anxiety about his rescuers' fate. When he asked about them, the guards answered only, "How do you know that they are here?" Commandant Arco taunted him with the notion that Bollmann and Huger would die: "The rogues, who were so bold as to carry you off, are arrested. They shall be hanged. It shall be under your window; and, if there is no executioner, I will do that office myself."[47]

Though untrue,[48] Arco's remarks showed how bitter he was that the escape had blotted a family history of service to the Austrian throne, as well as his own long, honorable military career and his solid record of administering the army base of Olmütz.[49] He was so humiliated that he pleaded with Field Marshal Botta not to lose trust in him.[50] The escape may also have shortened his life. By winter's end he had fallen ill, and on 5 April 1795 he died of dysentery.[51]

News of Lafayette's capture sped through official channels. Dubsky sent a special courier to Brünn to relay the news with a copy of Krömer's deposition. The Olmütz courier arrived in Brünn at 5:00 A.M. on 10 November. Baronet Platzer had just signed his report of the escape, and a rider made ready to speed to the capital. Platzer added news of the capture in a postscript, promising to fill in details with next day's post. He also sent news of the latest developments to Field Marshal Botta, who notified Count Michael von Wallis, president of the Aulic War Council, and to Count Johann von Pergen, the police minister. Both Wallis and Pergen passed the news to the emperor. Francis II ordered drives for all prisoners halted: "Since this incident confirms once again that these state prisoners only think of cunning and deceit, to abuse the good manner in which they are being treated, it is quite right to suspend all the driving that until now has been allowed them for their health. Francis." The note was superfluous; military authorities had already stopped all prisoner drives and walks in Moravia.[52] No state prisoners would ever again get carriage rides.

At 6:30 P.M. on 8 November 1794, as Lafayette encountered Dröxler west of Braunseifen, Bollmann was riding into Hof, where Brenda waited at the postal station in the gathering dusk. He began to see that something was wrong. Bollmann was alone, and the gelding was soaked in sweat. When Brenda asked where their companion and second horse had gone, Bollmann replied, "The other gentleman [Huger] remained behind in Olmütz with the mare, will be staying there for some days to come, and will follow after with a groom." Brenda was told to have the gelding watered and fed overnight, then to follow Bollmann in the morning and meet him in Breslau. When the groom asked for money to cover expenses, Bollmann handed him such an exorbitant sum that Brenda protested it might invite robbery. Bollmann replied that it did not hurt to have plenty but agreed to take most of it back. He left Brenda three gold sovereigns, the amount promised for the return from Hamburg. He also gave Brenda a card with the address of Baron Schuckmann, a contact in Breslau. Less than fifteen minutes later, just before 6:45, Bollmann drove off.[53]

Brenda took care of the gelding and fell asleep in a bed of straw. Shortly after that Cavalry Major von Simich and a posse arrived in the stable. Apparently they had learned from the innkeeper that Brenda had hitched fresh horses to his carriage for two men in a hurry. "When I was in my first phase of sleep, I was awakened," Brenda later recalled. "I opened my eyes to see several people accompanied by an officer, with lanterns around me."

Simich asked "where the gentlemen were." Brenda could only say that one had remained in Olmütz while the other had driven to Troppau. The major had Brenda taken to a nearby house and placed him in irons. The next morning Brenda was taken back to Olmütz by postal wagon under armed escort, with a peasant leading the gelding. That evening Circle Captain Dubsky arrived in Olmütz from Brünn and confiscated Brenda's effects, including fifty-one shillings and fifty-three crosses, a pocketbook containing address cards, and a silver pocket watch. A rumor circulated that Simich had caught Bollmann beyond Troppau. Dubsky could only hope that the story was true, "for this villain would not deserve to escape the criminal laws."[54]

Civil authorities investigated and tried to correct the breakdown in surveillance. They also rewarded those involved in capturing Huger and Lafayette. Within a day of the breakout, Baronet Platzer ordered Huger to be isolated from all visitors. Platzer also had materials found on Huger sent to Brünn and demanded swift reports of all developments. From the army Platzer requisitioned a transcript of Lafayette's initial testimony, to compare it with Huger's "in investigating the further circumstances and relationships" of the men.[55] At the town hall, Dubsky interviewed the civilians involved, and he collected and listed effects found on those arrested.[56] The governor's office noted that Hof postmaster Duban had failed to demand Bollmann's identification, and Duban was soon relieved of his job.[57] At the same time, authorities recommended a reward of three ducats for each of five peasants involved in capturing Huger since customarily "the state has offered payments for bringing in a deserter or thief."[58] Noting the "advantage for the state . . . that bonds of love and loyalty to their prince are strengthened,"[59] the office also rewarded those who captured and returned Lafayette. It deemed Dröxler and Richter particularly deserving, suggesting a reward of four ducats for Dröxler and a gold medal "of the larger sort" for Richter and announcing the awards in the *Brünner Zeitung* for undefined patriotic acts. The governor's office advised ten ducats total for Richter's men and a special public decree of praise for Krömer. When Dröxler protested that he was the one who had reported Lafayette originally, the emperor raised his reward to a gold medal "of the smaller sort," worth twelve and a half ducats, rather than a large one worth twenty ducats like Richter's, perhaps because of Dröxler's lower estate.[60]

Bollmann, however, was still a free man. As Brenda had told Simich, Bollmann was indeed passing the border town of Troppau. Soon after 10:00 P.M., he crossed into Prussian Silesia, entering the first Prussian town, Ratibor (Racibórz), three or four hours later.[61]

Bollmann had intended to hide with Lafayette and Huger at Tarnowitz, which lay sixty kilometers beyond Ratibor.[62] After searches subsided, they would have crossed into Poland in a surveyor's carriage, traveled north to Gdańsk, and embarked for Hamburg and England. But political and military turmoil was blocking the way. An overwhelming force of Russian and Austrian troops had routed the Polish insurrection and captured its leader, Kościuszko, at Maciejowice on 10 October. Warsaw had fallen to the Russians on 4–9 November, just as Bollmann and Huger were rescuing Lafayette. The Polish king signed his abdication on 24 November. Austria and Russia were moving in to partition Poland for the third and last time with Prussia demanding its share. Troops were everywhere, and bands of Poles were marauding along the frontier. All travelers trying to cross from Prussia to Poland were facing delays of three to four hours, and travel within Poland was rife with peril.[63] A plan to escape this way would almost surely have failed even if, as Bollmann claimed, "we could easily have reached the frontier of Poland."[64]

Had he thought only of his own safety, Bollmann might have continued to Tarnowitz. But he still hoped that Lafayette would reach Prussia on his own and they could reunite. "I imagined that he might be concealed somewhere in a Silesian village, helpless, or ride about in great distress, uncertain which road to take, and how to get on further!" he later stated. "I thought it my duty not to leave him, but to endeavour to give him farther assistance if possible!"[65]

Bollmann turned west to search for Lafayette along the border. For six days he hid under the alias of "Folkmann" at a friend's home in Neisse, then drove over eighty kilometers of poor, stony roads along the foothills of the Giant Mountains to Waldenburg. At that point he hoped for asylum, a saddle horse, and an assistant from Johann Alberti, with whom he had stayed in July.[66]

Just as Bollmann stepped from his carriage at the Waldenburg post station on the evening of 16 November, men surrounded him. A low-ranking officer from nearby Schweidnitz (Świdnice) announced that he was under arrest by personal order of the Prussian king. Apparently Prussian authorities had tracked him along the postal route west and sent men just ahead of him. Had Bollmann arrived and departed only a half hour earlier, he later claimed, he might have escaped.[67] But surely it would only have delayed, not prevented his capture. He received astonishingly liberal treatment. He was able to send for Alberti, see him alone, tell him what happened, dictate a message for Lafayette, turn over money and a passport, and ask Alberti to engage a trusted man to seek and help Lafayette.[68]

After Bollmann gave a deposition in Schweidnitz for Berlin, local officials sent a courier to the Austrian brigade command at Troppau. They reported his capture and offered to turn over Bollmann and his effects. All they asked in return was reimbursement of thirteen or fourteen Thaler, which they could discount from the money he carried. Troppau military commissar Baronet von Demel carried the news to Olmütz and Brünn, and from there it reached Vienna. Botta's attaché and interim replacement at Brünn, Major General Baron Joseph von Rechbach, sent emphatic orders by express courier to Troppau brigade commander Colonel Baron Anton Duverger to thank Schweidnitz officials and reimburse them for all documented costs. Rechbach asked for Bollmann to be escorted quickly and securely to Troppau, where an Austrian unit would take over and bring him to Olmütz.[69]

Bollmann spent ten days in loose confinement at Schweidnitz. Dignitaries and acquaintances from as far as Breslau visited him, including Count Karl von Hoym, governor of Prussian Silesia. Bollmann was able to accept invitations to dine at important local homes, albeit under guard. His hosts and other guests openly admired his attempt and regretted its failure. Bollmann wrote to Hamburg, reporting developments and requesting 150 ducats.[70] He also learned that the Austrians had captured Huger and Lafayette. "It was all the less uncomfortable for me to experience the same fate," he later testified, "as my freedom would hardly have been welcome to me while leaving both my friends in the lurch."[71]

On 26 November a courier arrived with Frederick William's authorization for Bollmann's extradition. An officer and two privates escorted Bollmann in his own carriage to Neisse. The captive was still free of shackles and still carried valuable possessions on his own person, including five imperial ducats and change, a gold watch, and a pocketknife. At Neisse he ate at the table of commandant Hanff, who promised to seek his timely release. The next day another escort took Bollmann to the Austrian border town of Troppau and handed him over with his carriage and its contents, including a large sum of money beyond the cash in Bollmann's pockets: twenty-one golden half sovereigns and nine golden Fredericks. In bidding farewell to his Prussian escort officer, Ensign Bosswel, Bollmann thanked him for his kindness.

The prisoner experienced a different kind of treatment in Austrian hands. A sergeant and three privates under Lieutenant Andreas Kovits took Bollmann to the Troppau town hall, where they undressed him "down to his shirt" and searched him, confiscating the rest of his money and valuables, even his eyeglasses. Then they chained him to a twenty-pound ball of iron. Bollmann was appalled, muttering repeatedly, "Fine, the whole world will learn of this treatment." He asked to speak with his earlier Prussian escort officer. Though the new captors could allow it only in their presence, Bollmann thanked Bosswel again and asked him to report the shackling to Hanff and encourage quick action on his behalf. That night he slept in his chains with two hussars standing guard, one near his bed, the other at the door, curved swords drawn.

At 5:30 A.M. Kovitz and his men set out for Olmütz with their shackled prisoner. After driving through Dorfteschen (Deštné), Hof, and Sternberg, they arrived in Olmütz at 6:00–7:00 P.M. There they transferred Bollmann and his effects to Circle Captain Dubsky. Dubsky waived detailed interrogation, sent the captive to the town jailor, and ordered him kept in isolation until summoned. No one beyond prison staff, regardless of position, was to see him.[72] Bollmann remained there, in the same jail that held Huger, for the next two months. In the dim light and without his glasses, Bollmann could see little. The hygiene was dismal. Bed-bugs swarmed over him when he tried to rest. Weakened from lack of sleep, he developed a sore throat, becoming so hoarse that his inquisitors had to abbreviate sessions with him.[73]

News of the escape and its immediate consequences rippled across the Continent. On 1 and 3 December, the Dutch *Langestaate* reported Lafayette's flight. On 2 December, the *Gazette de Leyde* announced his recapture. Berlin letters that still assumed Lafayette to be on the run and perhaps already in Hamburg reached a French agent in Switzerland. On 4 December, he informed Paris.[74] The same week, Hamburg partisans heard of the escape. Sophie Reimarus told her brother August Hennings, a Danish official, that "Bollmann, a worthy, noble young man, openly wanted to transform his self-interest into a noble act, and rescue Lafayette." He acted on "commissions from America, and with as much money as he needed," but all had failed. Still, she put his fate in context by pointing out "how insignificant that is, compared to 18,000 Poles who have just died in Warsaw's suburbs, struggling for national freedom."

Soon Johanna Sieveking would write that "poor B is arrested because he had freed LF. LF has been caught, so all is for nothing." Even so, she added, "We are still suspended in uncertainty about it, with only a spark of hope glimmering."[75] News of the escape, recapture, and arrests reached Madame Lafayette at year's end. Unlike most political captives after Robespierre's fall in July, she still remained in a Parisian prison.[76]

Lafayette's British supporters heard news of the escape by late November.[77] Angelica Church broke the news to Princess Hénin and Count Lally at their Richmond home and apologized for having kept the plans secret. She also assured them that she had not tried to compete for the honor of having saved Lafayette; that "the issue was only success, and not to whom one should credit the success." Hénin worried about Lafayette's fate: "He's escaped prison, but is he all right?" she asked repeatedly.

Two days later, news arrived that Lafayette and Bollmann had been captured. Several of Hénin's friends were furious at having been excluded from the project. They were convinced that they could have helped it succeed and attacked Bollmann as wasteful and foolish. Voght found their criticisms unfair, calling Hénin's circle "thoughtless and basely unjust toward Bollmann."[78]

For some time London journalists reported that Lafayette was still free. By Christmas, however, Charles Fox was inclined to believe those who claimed that Lafayette had been recaptured. When confirmations came, he rose in Commons to denounce "the gross outrage and breach of all laws of nations, honor or honest, in the confining of M. Lafayette; a transaction . . . which has damned their names who did it to perpetual infamy, and excited the indignation of every honest heart."[79]

News typically took a month and a half to cross the Atlantic, so contradictory reports kept arriving in America for some time. Since adolescence, John Quincy Adams, who had just been accredited American resident minister to the Batavian (Dutch) Republic, had known Lafayette personally. Adams reported from The Hague on 24 November about a dependable message from Breslau to "a gentleman in Amsterdam" that "La Fayette has made his escape from prison, together with two companions one of whom however was retaken."[80] From London, American envoy Thomas Pinckney reported Lafayette's escape and recapture to Secretary of State Edmund Randolph on 10 December. Pinckney asked permission to request Lafayette's release.[81] On 4 February 1795, Philadelphia's *Gazette of the United States* published a garbled report from Troppau that Bollmann and a servant had jumped an officer escorting Lafayette and Maubourg on a drive, and provided the Frenchmen with money and horses to reach a waiting carriage.[82] On Washington's birthday, 22 February, a toast was made in Philadelphia wishing Lafayette's successful escape and arrival in America.[83]

The reality of course was that Lafayette's breakout had failed. The very attempt, however, brought new attention to his incarceration.

7

INQUEST

In the wake of Lafayette's escape attempt, the military and civilian commissions investigated what went wrong, defined culpability, and recommended remedial action. Though they found that no subject of the emperor had cooperated knowingly in the escape, the army panel noted a series of failures by garrison staff, and the civil panel reported foreign involvement. The findings led to punishments of military personnel and the transfer of civilians Bollmann and Huger to criminal court. The former rescue agents put up a noble defense and received help from sympathizers, leading to increasingly indulgent treatment and, after six months, release and expulsion from the emperor's territories. Meanwhile Lafayette's fellow prisoners suffered few official consequences from the escape. Soon they and Lafayette were engaging again in secret correspondence with each other and the outside world.

Field Marshal Botta planned an inquest as soon as he heard of the escape. The Aulic War Council, the army's main administrative and judicial body, quickly allowed it to proceed. On 20 November 1794, Botta ordered the "Lafayette investigative commission" to start work.[1]

The commission first convened at 9:00 A.M. on 24 November. The commission moderator, Lieutenant Colonel Menrat Geppert, and three other officers began to assemble the evidence.[2] In addition to what was already on hand, they added a list of Bollmann's effects[3] and information on breakout tools found in Huger's trunk at Johann Stahel's Viennese bookstore.[4] When suspicion fell on Haberlein, they searched his quarters.[5] They took testimony from Lieutenant Jacob, Sergeant Platzer, tanner Dröxler, Braunseifen mayor Richter and his hired men, prison guards, Private Harwich, surgeon Haberlein, and finally Lafayette. The commission also received transcripts of depositions to the civil panel, including those of Huger, innkeeper Herbricht, and Bollmann.[6]

Baronet Platzer of the governor's office appointed the province's leading constable, Brünn chief of police Johann von Okacz, to preside at the three-person civil panel, "the Dr. Bollmann investigative commission."[7] Platzer was convinced that Bollmann "must have maintained understandings with various persons in Vienna and other places."[8] In this belief the baronet echoed Francis II, who emphasized the importance of "proceeding *with great precision* to discover the intrigues that must have been at work in this affair."[9]

Those under investigation had no legal counsel. The second day of interrogation, Bollmann asked Police Chief Okacz, moderator of the civil inquest, to explain the law he had violated. Okacz refused, answering cryptically "that this, his question, came four months too late."[10] Huger faced threats of physical abuse despite his forthright testimony. At a chance encounter, Arco told him that his crime could carry the death penalty. Huger's warden teased him by showing off a tiny punishment cell, torture instruments, and an execution sword.[11] In truth Empress Maria Theresia had abolished legal torture in 1776, and the Universal Penal Code that her son Joseph II introduced in 1787 limited capital punishment to martial law. However, the young American lacked any knowledge of Habsburg criminal law, so he must have felt extremely vulnerable.[12]

Even in absence of formal charges, there was no right to a writ of habeas corpus. The circle captain and governor's office concluded almost immediately that Bollmann's groom, Brenda, "seems not to have had any conscious part in the entire escape project," and he did not face criminal charges. However, they only eased conditions of his captivity rather than ending it. On 11 November they released Brenda from shackles. Twelve days later they began giving him more food than the daily minimum. They still barred visitors. Brenda remained "on call" for the civil panel's convenience and in case evidence against him appeared in course of other interrogations. The panel never again called him to testify. After Okacz sent in the commission's report in mid-December, he reported to superiors that Brenda's innocence was certain. Finally, on the morning of 27 December, after deducting the cost of Brenda's incarceration from the cash he had carried, Okacz returned to him his effects, gave him a new passport, and ordered him to go directly to his hometown for proper identification papers.[13]

The commissions worked symbiotically, their goals encouraging cooperation. What the army panel learned could help track civilian conspirators, and what the civil panel learned could help clarify the breach of prison security. Each board commonly shared information it thought relevant to the other's work or for which it received a request. Higher authorities in Brünn and Vienna also mandated this cooperation.[14]

The process, however, was not always smooth. Sometimes a panel withheld intelligence that it believed relevant only in its own sphere. The civil board agreed, for example, that it would turn over only those excerpts of Bollmann's testimony that it deemed relevant to the army inquiry.[15] Since copying by hand went slowly, sometimes a panel sent only an excerpt.[16] There were bureaucratic oversights and misunderstandings. In a couple instances, the civil panel expressed frustration at what it viewed as recalcitrance by its military counterpart, though in at least one of those cases the information was already on its way.[17]

The commissions' general strategy was to collect and share testimony initially from more peripheral persons in order to ensnare those most culpable and to use testimony of the principal agents against each other.[18] The strategy was quite effective in interrogating the three key witnesses, Bollmann, Haberlein, and Lafayette, all of whom resisted divulging what they knew.

In testimony Huger and Lieutenant Jacob had drawn attention to Haberlein as the only possible mediator between Bollmann and Lafayette.[19] The military panel treated the surgeon's case gingerly, however, because he was the only officer directly implicated. The panel asked Arco to arrest Haberlein "without exciting attention" and to have him escorted to the staff auditory.[20]

In his opening description of contacts with Bollmann, Haberlein completely ignored his own role as messenger. The panel asked him directly about information that Bollmann had sought, but Haberlein outright lied. The panel kept pressing, weakening his resistence. He admitted that Bollmann had told him in July that he knew Lafayette to be in the prison and in October that there were drives. Haberlein also admitted how he had initially given Lafayette personal news from Bollmann. After insisting that he had refused to pass on writing materials, he admitted that he had finally passed written notes back and forth. But he had seen no harm in a selfless favor.

Then the commission revealed how Bollmann and Lafayette arranged the escape through the message exchange. Haberlein was "extremely shocked, lamented, and wept at the unanticipated disaster that his good intentions had caused." Only then did he learn of the lemon juice messages and realize how Bollmann had duped him. He begged "that this, his first mistake during twenty years of loyal, zealous service, be overlooked" and noted that it would remain "a reproach for the rest of his life."

Haberlein appeared to be genuinely remorseful. His well-intentioned gesture had turned out to be aiding and abetting criminal activity. It threatened to end his professional career and to spell disaster for his wife and child. It quickly worsened his confinement. The panel ordered Arco to shackle the surgeon and isolate him in a fortress cell from all outside contact. Only later, after the military inquiry ended, did army authorities request the Aulic War Council's permission to remove the chains.[21]

When the civil panel interviewed Bollmann, it had the benefit of letters found on Bollmann and in Vienna and of testimony by Huger and Bollmann's Viennese acquaintances.[22] It did not challenge Bollmann's story that his search for Lafayette was part of a scholarly tour. Still it doubted Bollmann's claim that he used Haberlein only to send harmless messages to Lafayette and that Lafayette had initiated escape plans by dropping a note from his carriage. Bollmann was, of course, trying to protect Haberlein.[23] Police Chief Okacz made sure to record the testimony personally, sometimes suspending it to consider implications and prepare further questions. He took it to be "full of merry tales"[24] and objected to Bollmann's lack of cooperation.[25]

Okacz and his panel drove Bollmann to ever greater admissions by warning him that every falsehood would increase his culpability, revealing that they already knew more than Bollmann had suspected, and offering improvement of his abysmal prison conditions. Bollmann conceded that he had indeed given Lafayette a message through Haberlein though its true contents were invisible to the surgeon; that Lafayette answered not by dropping a message from his carriage but through Haberlein; and that there had been not one but several notes that Bollmann sent Lafayette through the surgeon. At the same time, Bollmann stressed Haberlein's laudable intentions: his reluctance to cooperate, his refusal to be bribed, and his overriding concern for his patient.[26] A breakthrough came on 8 December, when Bollmann negotiated for better prison conditions in exchange for cooperation that resulted in "very important statements." Some of these statements dealt with "matters of state": foreign accomplices and high Austrian contacts, intelligence so sensitive that Okacz preferred to report it orally. By the end of the hearings, he was satisfied that all the key witnesses had given consistent testimony.[27]

The army panel turned to Lafayette only after Haberlein and Bollmann had finished their testimony. It ordered Arco to select a room near Lafayette's but not abutting another prisoner's, to provide it with five overstuffed chairs around a large table, and to have a fire going in the hearth. No one was to forewarn Lafayette, and the hearing was to remain confidential.[28] At 2:30 on the afternoon of 9 December, the panel began questioning Austria's most famous captive. Lafayette offered to cooperate for the sake of men whom he dubbed divine rescuers, his "two messiahs."[29]

He began with what the panel considered an irrelevant outburst, that "no power is authorized to hold him captive, because he is a citizen of the United States of America and not a prisoner of war." The commission responded that it "had no authorization to accept his protests here. Rather, it was to ask him questions and he to answer." Lafayette repeated that, though "born in France," he was now "a citizen of the United States of America."[30] He returned to this theme repeatedly in his testimony. Even in his closing statement at his last hearing, he demanded that commissioners give a testimony transcript to "an ambassador or minister of the United States of America."[31] Army authorities never complied.[32]

Lafayette kept downplaying his rescuers' guilt and stressing his own. He testified that he had planned the escape with friends abroad before the transfer to

Olmütz. He said he had seized the sergeant's saber, forcing the foreigners to join in, and he had stuffed the glove in the soldier's mouth. In the midst of the struggle in the wheat field, he claimed, the two foreigners purposely avoided harming the sergeant. One of them may have waved a small pistol, but never used it. He concluded, "I must be regarded as the first author of abduction projects."[33]

Lafayette also did his best to protect Haberlein. He claimed not to know the surgeon's name; he could not recall ever speaking to him about Bollmann; Haberlein brought him "nothing" from Bollmann. When commissioners asked whether Haberlein passed him three notes from Bollmann, Lafayette replied, "I keep to the previous response, namely, nothing!" Panelists cited others' testimony and showed Lafayette the signed transcripts. In the process Lafayette learned of Bollmann's capture and the extensive admissions that he and Haberlein had already made.[34] After each new revelation, Lafayette balked: "I refer to my previous responses. . . . I refer to previous responses, without pretending to exonerate myself from possible criticism, since I have declared I was author of the project! . . . I must keep to the same response. . . . I must make the same negative response."[35]

Eventually he reconsidered, as commissioners had hoped. When the next morning's session began, he declared himself ready to talk. But even as he admitted his helpers' complicity, he kept trying to exonerate them. He maintained that the surgeon was a well-meaning man who was very reluctant to transgress regulations, unable to withstand appeals to his humanity, and ignorant of escape plans. Only Lafayette's insistence had brought Bollmann to cooperate: "I knew that Mr. Bollmann was extremely generous and sensitive. I abused these two feelings by all arguments that a spirit like his is unable to resist." Lafayette's attempts to draw the wrath of jailors from his rescuers would continue even into the closing statement of his final hearing.[36]

By mid-December both commissions had finished their investigations. The war council and police minister summarized their conclusions, added recommendations, and reported to the emperor in mid-January.[37]

The war council noted that of the three people most responsible, Bollmann and Huger fell under civilian jurisdiction, so the council restricted its analysis to Lafayette. Even in his case, it expressed legal uncertainty. It admitted having jurisdiction only "insofar as one wishes to consider him a real prisoner of war." Lafayette had claimed not to be one, and the council knew that status as a prisoner of state ought to have put him under civil authority, not military.

The throne had pressured the council to act, so it simply put the legal problem aside, accepted Lafayette as a prisoner of war, and proceeded to consider his guilt and punishment. Perhaps surprisingly, it seemed unable to condemn him for having attempted the escape and even praised his efforts: "It cannot really be considered a crime that Lafayette tried to cooperate in escaping his captivity. . . . The inner drive for freedom is a natural impulse that is perfectly justified in a prisoner of war who has not made any pledge [to resist escaping]." His only real crime was to have used force to disarm and incapacitate the sergeant-provost. The council noted that Lafayette would be captive anyway and without further excursions. The only additional punishment that it could foresee was to put him in chains for three months. However, it recommended against this measure indirectly by adding the telling phrase, "unless His Majesty is prevailed upon by other political considerations that have an influence on future circumstances, not to go through with this and merely to let the more restricted captivity suffice."

The council then described careless breaches of prison security. None of the breaches was decisive by itself, nor did any reveal evil intent. Together, however, they had made the escape possible. The council attributed several mistakes to the two recent commandants. Splényi and Arco should have avoided visiting Lafayette. They should have supervised the sergeant-provost better. They should not have given him access to the keys at any time. They should not have brought inmates writing materials, nor should they have given the surgeon such unfettered access to prisoners. Each commandant made errors uniquely his. On his own authority, Splényi had modified the emperor's order that a full officer and private escort the prisoners' drives: he had eliminated the private and allowed the officer to alternate with a mere sergeant. Arco had reinstated a private on excursions but allowed the sergeant to continue replacing the full officer. He had also failed to choose an experienced, responsible, and intelligent private to go along.

The prison's administrative officer, Lieutenant Jacob, shared responsibility for the inadequate supervision. He had failed to secure cell keys and access properly. He had allowed Lafayette and Haberlein to talk alone. He had overlooked ink hidden by Lafayette and allowed the writing materials for book requests and prescriptions.

Sergeant Platzer's interactions with Lafayette were, in the war council's view, so careless "that they have the initial appearance of collusion among him, Lafayette, and his aides." Like the commandants and Jacob, Platzer had failed to supervise medical visits and excursions properly. On the other hand, all testimony, including the reports of his heroic struggle in the wheat fields, redeemed him from any suspicion of collusion.

Of all Austrian subjects, the council judged, Haberlein seemed most involved in the escape plot. He had, after all, enabled the prisoner's correspondence with Bollmann. However, all the witnesses said that he knew nothing of the plot. "He seems to be one of those good-hearted and willing people who are easily convinced to do things going beyond the concepts and ideas of their competence, very seldom suspect anything bad, and in this way are most easily defrauded," the council explained. His guilt lay in involving himself in nonmedical matters and smuggling secret notes.

Finally Private Harwich failed to exercise the most basic sense in executing orders. "May he be ever so dumb and stupid a man, it should and must have been obvious to him even with the slight degree of human understanding he possesses, that he was ordered to drive along for the security of the state prisoner." His defense—that he thought the noise and violence was only a peasant squabble—was implausible. He must have seen clearly that it involved the captive. Had he done his duty, to run to the scene with side weapon drawn and help the sergeant, he surely could have prevented the escape. The council concluded that "in these circumstances, his natural stupidity can procure him mitigation but not a complete suspension of punishment."[38]

For each soldier deemed guilty, the council recommended a specific penalty. Arco and Splényi were to receive written censure; Lieutenant Jacob a two-week arrest and removal from garrison administration; Sergeant Platzer degradation to private's rank for six months and replacement as prison provost; Staff Surgeon Haberlein arrest in irons another four weeks, followed by transfer to another post at his own expense; and Private Harwich two weeks' confinement.[39]

The severity of punishments tended to increase down the chain of command, though higher authorities bore a full share of responsibility for Lafayette's escape. In armies of later times, Sergeant Platzer might have received a medal for heroism in single-handedly fighting three attackers, suffering wounds in the process, and sending out the alarm so quickly. Instead he suffered stockade arrest and was reduced to weeping for mercy at the end of a hearing three weeks later. Then, after another month and a half of incarceration, he faced six months of degradation.[40] He had done his best, but "higher ups" needed a scapegoat. The emperor received not a word of criticism, even though he had sanctioned the drives that allowed the escape.

The emperor agreed with most of the council's recommendations, but did make two amendments in the margins of the report: "the suggested laying of irons on Lafayette for three months should be dropped," and Lieutenant Jacob was to be retired from the service.[41] The latter directive would have been a severe blow for a man of fifty-three years with a wife and four children, who had never learned a trade beyond military service.[42] Though the emperor surely had an eye on the poor publicity he would receive if he were to treat Lafayette harshly, he had no such inhibition in the case of an obscure officer in his army.

Arco received only a written reprimand. He certainly felt the penalty sorely, however, if the concern he expressed about his standing with his superior, Botta, is any indication.[43] Although Arco soon died in disgrace, at least two others were eventually able to overcome the ordeal.

Haberlein eventually returned to his old post as staff surgeon at Hungarian General Command headquarters in Ofen (Budapest). In some ways Ofen was a less desirable post, further from German-speaking parts of the empire, particularly Haberlein's hometown of Vienna. Yet it seems to have been a relatively mild demotion. Haberlein spend the rest of his career in Ofen, achieving success there that surely assuaged his Olmütz wounds.[44]

Splényi was outraged at the written rebuke he received. He protested through Hungarian General Command that the escape did not occur under his watch, but a full month after he had turned over command. He refuted every charge. His occasional visits were systematic personal inspections for the sake of security. His policy for storing keys had followed Arco's precedent and proved reliable. He had followed existing regulations by letting Haberlein visit prisoners with health complaints, and since he lacked medical training of his own, Splényi took seriously the surgeon's advice. He had seen to it that the provost did not bring Lafayette writing material. He had never ordered an officer or provost to escort prisoner drives alone nor had he heard of such an order under his command. Splényi also alluded to the responsibility of war council and emperor: they had approved Lafayette's drives and received regular reports about policies that they could have corrected at any time.[45]

Splényi's protests gained him an additional reprimand. The implication that council and emperor might share in blame was, in the council president's view, an outrageous impudence.[46] It could also not have helped Splényi's application shortly afterward to succeed Arco. Splényi failed, and the post went instead to Baron Wilhelm Schröder von Lilienhof.[47]

Still the censures did not affect Splényi's reputation for long. Within a few months the emperor named him a privy counselor, and the following year called him out of retirement to command recruitment among Hungarian nobility. The uproar about his culpability in Lafayette's escape was already disappearing and would continue to do so.[48]

Vienna had good reason to leave the incident behind. Haberlein did not face dismissal almost surely because the army lacked skilled army surgeons.[49] Likewise the empire could not afford to deal harshly with such a loyal and experienced Hungarian officer as Splényi. Hungary had always had tense relations with the Habsburg ruling house. Only recently Hungarians had been prominent among so-called Jacobins in the empire. Francis II had made brutal examples of them in showcase trials ending in long prison terms and executions. The empire had entered into a mortal struggle with France and needed all useful and loyal subjects.

While the army report focused on Lafayette's guilt and the military's failings, its civil counterpart tried to ferret out conspirators in the escape and determine the degree of their guilt. It concluded that no Habsburg subjects had knowingly taken part but did note considerable evidence of foreign involvement. Bollmann had drawn several people into the project unawares, including Brenda,[50] Count Lažansky's servants Zudik and Hahn,[51] Schramowsky,[52] personnel of Stahel's

Vienna bookstore,[53] and Splényi, even though Bollmann had been only his dinner guest.[54] The civil investigation also found nothing to incriminate a Brünn resident who had visited Olmütz and showed interest in the hearings, a man whom Okacz dubbed "M."[55] The police chief seemed concerned not to reveal the identity of "M" because of his high estate. The obvious candidate for "M" is Count Nepomuk von Mitrovsky, an enlightened Moravian noble[56] to whom Huger's interpreter, Passy, had conveyed the captives' noble intentions.[57]

In the eyes of Vienna police, Karl Weigel, the young Leipzig physician whom Bollmann had tried to recruit, was at least guilty of not reporting the plot. Weigel saved himself from further investigation by quickly acquiring diplomatic immunity as physician to the Portuguese ambassador, and leaving for Italy with his new employer.[58] Other foreigners whom the authorities identified as supporters of Bollmann's project had always been beyond reach of prosecution. They included Bollmann's contacts in the Prussian cities of Waldenburg, Glatz, and Breslau; the free imperial city of Hamburg; and London.[59]

Bollmann and Huger were the only conspirators to whom the Austrian government had access. Baronet Platzer pointed out to the police minister that assaulting a military guard deserved criminal prosecution. But he argued against giving the case to criminal court: the investigative commissions had already confirmed the case facts exhaustively and exposing details in open court would embarrass the government and persons of rank. Instead Platzer proposed that the emperor forego a trial and set a punishment by executive order. He recommended holding the agents in relatively mild conditions until war's end. Huger should be released from chains, given a good room, and granted reading privileges. Because Bollmann was guiltier, however, Platzer advised keeping the chains on him.[60]

The emperor decided that general law should apply and ordered Bollmann and Huger "turned over to the regular criminal judge for sentencing."[61] Two city counselors presided at criminal proceedings that lasted from 30 January until 1 May 1795 in the Olmütz town hall.[62]

Huger and Bollmann were "at first greatly mortified" at news that they would be tried for assaulting a fortress guard, the possible sentence ranging anywhere from a month's confinement to four or five years.[63] They put up a noble defense and received increasingly sympathetic treatment and help.

At trial Bollmann and Huger spoke of selfless idealism without criminal intent.[64] Bollmann claimed that he was trying to help an innocent, virtuous man. "If Lafayette is a criminal, then I am too; if he is a dangerous man, then I must be one too; all the more so, since I consider his principles to be mine," he declared. Bollmann praised Lafayette as an active opponent of Jacobins and loyal supporter of Louis XVI, the French constitution, and good government. By political conviction Bollmann had felt compelled to undertake the mission. Once he had started it, he felt he had to carry it out. "Whatever punishment one may give me, it will be much more bearable than the justified reproach would have been, that I used Lafayette's money for my own enjoyment." Bollmann claimed not to have known that he would jeopardize innocent people.[65] Huger claimed youthful enthusiasm, good intent, a spotless previous record, and the impossibility of recurrence, all of which were extenuating circumstances under Habsburg law. He had sought only "to render service to a man who did so much to establish the liberty I enjoy in my native land." He pointed out that a severe sentence would have little deterrent value, since Americans rarely came to this part of the world. He even appealed to his judges' paternal instincts: "If there is any one of my judges who has a son, I ask him only to imagine him in my situation, in a foreign country, unable to benefit from [his father's] help or advice."[66]

The men's daring actions on Lafayette's behalf and their impressive defense were engendering sympathy in Olmütz, Vienna, and abroad. Although Huger and Bollmann referred to new friends they acquired locally without citing them by name,[67] some are identifiable. During the investigative hearings, Bollmann and Huger had developed good relations with the warden's young wife and then with the warden himself. Handsome Huger gave his jailor's young wife polite, playful attention, practicing his primitive German and teaching her some English words. Through her, Bollmann and Huger learned of one another's presence in the same building and established communication. She was able to pass a simple message orally and another, written by Bollmann with wall mortar, wrapped in a black silk scarf. Huger then wrote Pinckney a note in ink, presumably from the jailor's wife, folded it into a 1½-inch square, placed it in a walnut shell, and lowered it from his window to Bollmann. In turn Bollmann bribed the warden with gold pieces he had hidden in his gloves during the initial strip search to smuggle the note out.[68] He sent a second note a few weeks later.[69]

Huger developed an unexpected friendship with Arco, the man whose professional reputation had been ruined by the escape. At one point the old soldier complimented Huger for what he had done, saying "if he had a friend he would wish him to be an American." In addition to Huger's idealistic testimony, other factors may have aroused the commandant's sympathy: the death of Huger's father in battle, Arco's lack of a son, and Huger's service in a British medical unit alongside an Olmütz-based infantry regiment in the Netherlands.[70]

Huger's translator, lyceum professor Christoph von Passy, often interpreted Huger's responses in hearings diplomatically, so as to protect the young man's interests. Passy sought moments to assure Huger and Bollmann that unnamed friends were exercising influence on their behalf.

One friend was Count Nepomuk von Mitrovsky, almost surely the "M" showing such interest in the captives. Passy tutored Mitrovsky's family and described the situation of Bollmann and Huger so movingly that the count provided Passy with unlimited funds, some of them for bribes. Bollmann and Huger attributed prison improvements to this powerful man's kindness and zeal. Mitrovsky seems also to have made representations to influential people in Vienna.[71]

Some of Bollmann's acquaintances in the imperial capital, including nobles, showed what Minister of Police Pergen called "a lively interest" in Bollmann's fate. "Rosenfels," an old friend of Bollmann's who was visiting Vienna, followed the story closely. He may have visited Brünn and Olmütz, and he later notified Bollmann's aunt in Karlsruhe of his eventual release.[72]

There was also support coming from outside Habsburg crown lands. Authorities intercepted a Prussian merchant's inquiry about Lafayette and his rescuers[73] and an international money transfer to Bollmann, probably from John Church.[74]

Unknown to the authorities, members of the Sieveking-Reimarus circle in Hamburg tried to send Bollmann aid. Writing from Britain, trader Caspar Voght assumed that his former partner, Georg Sieveking, would help Bollmann and cautioned Sieveking's wife, Johanna, to keep the activity confidential. Perhaps acting as her husband's intermediary, Johanna sent Voght news that Bollmann had smuggled out.[75] Voght encouraged sending Bollmann funds secretly through trader colleague Heinrich Burmester.[76] Conrad Matthiessen, yet another associated merchant, worked closely on Bollmann's case with William Hanbury, British consul in Hamburg. Hanbury's wife, Caroline, was a close friend of Johanna Sieveking's.[77]

From Hanoverian Hoya, Georg Bollmann worked energetically to secure his son's release. This notably well-educated trader in rural produce enjoyed many connections with regionally influential people. He had raised Justus in a house full of books, provided him the best of educations, and encouraged him to see the world after completing his university degree. In turn Justus had written his father often, alerting him to grand projects underway. Their relationship seemed to be most sympathetic. As soon as news of the arrest arrived, Georg Bollmann appealed to his home government, which turned to Karl von Hardenberg, former Hanoverian official and now Prussian envoy in Vienna. Georg Bollmann also wrote directly to Austrian authorities. Voght attributed ameliorations in the son's treatment to this "wonderful" father, "who with all his paternal love stormed the government of Hanover and every single member of the Aulic War Council."[78]

London supporters helped where they could. Voght cited Count Lally, Bollmann's friend Friedrich Heisch, and former Lafayette aides as people "ardently" trying to gain Bollmann's release.[79] In April 1795 Pinckney had Huger's banker send funds to Bollmann's South Carolinian accomplice.[80] A few weeks later, Pinckney asked his Austrian counterpart, Count Starhemberg, to seek ameliorations and release for Huger, stressing how "infinitely" he was interested in the matter.[81] It was almost surely Pinckney who got word to the Huger clan, whose chief, Francis Huger's uncle Francis Kinloch, asked the president to intervene.[82]

The groundswell of sympathy brought Bollmann and Huger improved conditions. This began even before the criminal proceedings as civil authorities found the two men to be cooperative and innocent of any plot to undermine the state. Within days of the escape, Dubsky asked permission to purchase clothes for Huger from the captive's funds. Baronet Platzer allowed it on condition that "all unnecessary expense is to be avoided, and the clothing limited only to what is necessary to maintain cleanliness." He also allowed Dubsky an addition of fifteen to twenty crosses daily from Huger's money to improve the prison fare. Soon Huger had his own clothes.[83] When the case went to criminal court, authorities moved the prisoners into cleaner, better-lit quarters, lengthened their chains, served them higher quality food, and allowed them books.[84] One judge let Bollmann read a couple letters from the woman he hoped to marry, Christine Reimarus,[85] though the formal ban on correspondence continued.[86] On 1 April authorities moved Bollmann and Huger to another prison, where they enjoyed larger apartments linked to one another. They could talk for the first time since the breakout.[87]

Olmütz criminal court reported its findings to the full city council, six members under moderation of Mayor Franz Josef Willperth, on 15 May. Bollmann and Huger were sentenced to one-month of captivity in light chains, during which they would perform public work. Each was to pay his own confinement costs and half the expense of capturing Lafayette. Bollmann was to go without food Wednesdays and Saturdays. On release, both were to receive their remaining assets and proceed under escort to the Prussian border to be expelled from Austrian crown lands.[88] In private acquaintances told Bollmann and Huger that their sentence was quite lenient. The prison term was the minimum required by law. The men could have gotten up to five years for aiding a prisoner's escape and the same for committing injurious assault. Huger even looked forward to the labor as relief from boredom.[89] The incarceration counted legally as "temporary" rather than "continuous" or "protracted," and jail conditions would be "lenient" rather than "harsh" or "most severe." The men could also have faced confiscation of all their assets and even beatings. Though Joseph II had eliminated capital punishment for civil crimes, he had clarified that "punishments must be substituted for it, ones that are much more dreadful and painful than death itself."[90] Bollmann and Huger could consider themselves fortunate.

Soon better food and more privileges appeared. On Sundays and occasionally another weekday, the two captives began receiving a piece of meat beyond the daily dry bread, water, soup, and (thrice weekly) peas or beans. They were able to walk twice a week in a courtyard.[91]

The sentence was to go into effect only after review by the Moravian-Silesian appeals court in Brünn. That body found grounds for additional clemency in the fact that Bollmann and Huger had already suffered seven months' detention.[92] Another factor was surely that Count Nepomuk von Mitrovsky's uncle, Count

Baptist von Mitrovsky, was the presiding appeals judge.[93] On 5 June the appeals court announced that Huger and Bollmann were to serve only fourteen more days and be relieved of public work and that Bollmann was to do without food only on Wednesdays rather than twice a week. At the end of the two weeks, the city council was to arrange return of personal effects and escort the men to the border. The verdict went into effect with its publication on 10 June, with no further review by the emperor or the high court in Vienna.[94]

Baronet Platzer was not so well disposed to Bollmann and Huger. He asked the emperor for an additional decree expelling them permanently and having them pay all costs. He was even willing to hold the men "in decent custody" after their sentence had run out, until the emperor's decision arrived. On 12 June, Francis II issued the decree that Platzer sought.[95] It confirmed past practice of dipping into the agents' funds[96] for all expenses associated with the escape.[97]

During their last two weeks of custody, Bollmann and Huger were able to receive friends and make departure arrangements. "Many flattering marks of kindness and good will" came from local sympathizers. Fearing a change of policy, Passy advised the men to leave as soon as they were released.[98] Huger wrote his banker to send money and correspondence to Hamburg.[99] Bollmann wrote a five-line note to London supporters, celebrating their upcoming rendezvous.[100]

Bollmann and Huger were released the evening of 24 June 1795. The men signed a pledge that they would "never again enter the royal and imperial hereditary lands, on pain of arrest and harsh punishment."[101] Huger wrote his grandmother in South Carolina that "tomorrow morning we are to be escorted to the Frontier."[102]

Early on 25 June, authorities sent Passy to see off Huger and Bollmann. Their baggage was loaded into Bollmann's carriage. Passy reportedly went with them to a brief breakfast at the home of "their unknown but generous friend," Count Nepomuk Mitrovsky. At 5:15 A.M. the erstwhile rescuers left Olmütz under escort of a local police sergeant and city chancery clerk.[103] After more than seven months of incarceration for Bollmann and nearly eight months for Huger, Bollmann wrote, "Our delivery . . . pretty nearly resembles a miracle."[104]

The route was similar to that planned for Lafayette's escape. The men must have found this journey to freedom all the more gripping for that reason, providing ample opportunity to discuss how their plot might have succeeded after all. They passed through Sternberg, Hof, and Dorfteschen, arriving at Troppau, the last post before the border, at 3:30 P.M. They later left Troppau for Ratibor in Prussian Silesia, where they arrived at midnight. At 5:00 the next morning they started out for Leobschütz in the northwest.[105]

Lafayette, Maubourg, and Pusy remained in the dark for some time about the release. They had heard after the mid-May sentencing that it would soon occur, but they did not get confirmation until more than a month after the event.[106] At least one captor claimed that just at the time Bollmann and Huger left, Vienna sent orders for a new trial likely to have ended in their execution. Lafayette believed it.[107] But there was no basis in Habsburg law for a new trial, much less a sentence of death, and there is no evidence of any such orders.

News of the release spread quickly. An unnamed Olmütz inhabitant, possibly Passy, notified Bollmann's stepmother in Karlsruhe, who sent the news on to relatives in Bremen. A report appeared in a Hamburg newspaper on 21 July, in both the South Carolina *State Gazette* and the *Massachusetts Magazine* in October, and in the *New York Magazine* in November.[108] Francis Kinloch sent an excerpt of a letter from his released nephew to Secretary of State Timothy Pickering, who gave it to President Washington.[109]

Meanwhile, although official policy was to deprive Lafayette of drives, servants, and news,[110] treatment of the other prisoners of state hardly changed. If anything, it improved in the course of 1795. Maubourg later claimed that the escape attempt did not affect his prison conditions, as one could hardly have made them more rigorous. Authorities did confiscate a small computational table from Pusy, but he and Maubourg retained use of their servants a couple of times a week and, within a year, three hours a day. Interim commandant Major General Stanislaus Mikovényi von Breznobánya returned the computational table that summer. Beurnonville regained some exercise privileges. The war council rejected his initial request that he be allowed to go on walks within fortress works, but granted the privilege in early June. In September authorities moved Bancal to a room with fresher air.[111]

Most important, authorities allowed all state prisoners except Lafayette to resume limited correspondence early in 1795. The French secretary of mission in Basel, Switzerland, asked Field Marshal Duke Albert of Saxe-Teschen for help in contacting state prisoner François Lamarque at Brünn's Spielberg citadel. Teschen enclosed the letter with his own recommendation to the citadel's commandant, Cavalry Captain Clemens Gresselsberg. Gresselsberg sent the request and enclosure to the war council, which laid them before the emperor. Although Francis and Thugut had rejected earlier petitions of the kind, they found themselves unable to refuse Teschen, a royal Polish and Saxon prince, the husband of an Austrian imperial princess, and an uncle of Francis himself. Thugut returned the council report with instructions that state prisoners could now correspond, on two conditions: that they not reveal their place of incarceration and write only on family matters.[112]

State prisoners at Olmütz seized the opportunity. On 10 March, Thugut gave the war council a letter he had received through Lucchesini, Prussian envoy in Vienna, from Marie de Maisonneuve to her brother Maubourg. The council notified Botta that the letter had cleared. In early April, a few weeks before his death, commandant Arco allowed Maubourg to read it in his presence. Soon Botta passed a letter of response. Maubourg considered every letter to come "a kind of miracle."

In June Vienna cleared a letter for prisoner Bancal and his response. In July it passed another letter for Maubourg from Maisonneuve and Maubourg's reply. By the end of August, Maubourg had received a third letter from his sister. He replied in September.[113]

By summer Lafayette was again able to engage in "absolutely confidential" communication through unnamed helpers. Maubourg told his sister that he dare not reveal the means of the secret network "because if they slipped out, a number of persons . . . would be compromised." The captives had several methods of spreading news, including the encoded whistling that Pontonnier had invented. Around the beginning of June, Lafayette learned that Bollmann and Huger would soon be free. He also received a note from outside friends via Maubourg and replied with a message he wrote in his own blood on a handkerchief. In late July, Maubourg smuggled out a copy of Lafayette's note enclosed in one of his own. By summer's end, a letter announced the survival of Lafayette's family. Maubourg's servant Grugeon apparently whistled the news to Pontonnier, who did so in turn to Lafayette. By the same method, Lafayette could exchange messages at times with Beurnonville, until the latter's release on 3 November. The authorities did eventually catch Pontonnier and Grugeon in the act, padlocking their windows and putting them on a diet of bread and water for three months.[114]

The key message had reached Lafayette, however: his wife, daughters, and son were alive. Though Adrienne was still in prison, the threat of execution had ended for her at last, and she could hope for release. She looked forward to seeing her children again, and she was also determined to do whatever it took to see her husband.

8

ADRIENNE

Lafayette saw an end to months of isolation on the morning of 15 October 1795, when, unexpectedly, his wife and daughters, eighteen-year-old Anastasie and thirteen-year-old Virginie, walked into his cell. Adrienne Lafayette had miraculously escaped the Jacobins' guillotine. In November 1793 French authorities had arrested her at home in the Auvergne and imprisoned her at Brioude. They held her under the new Law of Suspects, which allowed them to arrest former nobles and their relatives.

In June of the following year, in the midst of the Reign of Terror, they transferred her to prison in Paris, holding her first at La Petite-Force and then at Lafayette's former school, the Collège du Plessis, to face the blade that would take her grandmother, mother, sister, and other relatives in July. U.S. resident minister Gouverneur Morris acted incessantly to save her, telling authorities that her execution would damage relations between the American and French republics.[1]

The mortal danger ended with Robespierre's fall in late July 1794, but Madame Lafayette remained imprisoned. Morris's successor, James Monroe, appealed to the Committee of Public Safety and visited her at her last prison, the Maison Delmas, rue Notre-Dame-des-Champs.[2]

Madame Lafayette was released the morning of 2 February 1795, after almost fifteen months of continual incarceration, and immediately set about to join her husband. She collected what money she could. Monroe advanced her some and informed her of more available from funds voted by Congress for her husband. From Warsaw, Lewis Littlepage sent letters of credit.[3] La Colombe and Cadignan mediated funds with which she sent her son, George Washington Lafayette, in April to stay with his namesake in America. She obtained passports from the Committee of Public Safety and gathered up her daughters. On 18 August, the women left Paris for the port of Dunkirk, armed with letters of introduction from Monroe.

Adrienne de Noailles de Lafayette. Bibliothèque nationale de France (67.B.41689)

U.S. Consul Francis Coffyn served as their host. He volunteered to mediate future communications with their Paris executor, an official in the French ministry of finance. On 5 September the women boarded an American ship, the *Little Cherub*, which sailed northeast to the Danish border town of Altona, within a few hundred meters of the Free Imperial City of Hamburg.[4]

Adrienne Lafayette's sister Pauline de Montagu-Beaune and their aunt Adrienne de Tessé had been living in Altona and were about to move north to an estate near Plön. Princess Hénin alerted them to the visit. Adrienne and her relatives had an emotional reunion on the morning of 9 September, minutes after the *Little Cherub* entered the Altona harbor.[5]

Two hours later, the Lafayette women visited Baron Johann von Archenholz. "I could hardly believe my eyes," he confessed. Adrienne revealed her intention to travel to Olmütz, but Archenholz tried to dissuade her. "In this my decision is firm, and nothing in the world can bring me from it," she replied. He offered to ask Danish ministers for help with Vienna.[6]

The visitors' presence soon became more widely known. Lafayette partisans flocked to their inn. André Masson, just returned from Britain, brought letters from Hénin and Bollmann. An associate of British member of Parliament Richard Sheridan conferred with Madame Lafayette on his way back to London. Local American merchants offered to undertake a joint appeal, but Madame Lafayette asked them to put it off. She did not want it to jeopardize her own petition.[7]

Archenholz took the women to the home of Friedrich Klopstock, hoping to persuade the famous writer to take an active role on the family's behalf. "I've never seen pain that was deeper or endured in a more manly [*sic*] way," Klopstock declared of Adrienne Lafayette. He promised to write powerful acquaintances on behalf of the family. Months later he reported its situation to an unnamed minister, but he refused to treat the subject of the family's struggles in an ode, despite urging by Fayettists. He claimed it beneath his dignity as a poet. Writing such a poem also carried risks. The French Revolution and its apostles had become increasingly unpopular among the powerful in Germany. Holding two state pensions, one from the king of Denmark and another from the margrave of Baden, Klopstock must have considered how overtly lobbying for Lafayette could jeopardize them. He also knew that both Hamburg and Denmark struggled to remain neutral in the revolutionary wars.[8]

Adrienne Lafayette planned for a personal audience with the emperor. She hoped to convince him either to release her husband or allow her and her daughters to join him in jail. The emperor had barred French citizens from his dynastic lands unless they had a special visa,[9] so Madame Lafayette obtained a new passport as an American. With help of John Parish, U.S. consul in Hamburg,[10] she assumed the identity of Mrs. Motier from Hartford, Connecticut. The city had, after all, awarded her husband its citizenship. She arranged for Parish to forward correspondence after she left Hamburg-Altona and for Masson to handle her business affairs. She wrote her son, recently arrived in Boston, describing her intentions. She also encouraged him to press President Washington to ask Francis II to release Lafayette. She bought a carriage and hired a young Swiss-born servant fluent in French and German, Jean Depuit. She began the journey on 21 September with her daughters and servant. Captains competed for the honor of carrying the party across the Elbe. The trip took the better part of a month.[11]

The Lafayette women arrived in Vienna between 4:00 and 5:00 A.M. on 3 October. They passed through inspection at the city gates and quietly moved into an inn. That same day, armed with letters of introduction and her clout as a Noailles, Adrienne Lafayette visited Countess Caroline von Rumbeck, sister of an Austrian ambassador and cousin of a recent foreign minister. She did not share Madame Lafayette's democratic sentiments but did receive her "with a touching goodness and sensitivity." The countess claimed that her brother, a cathedral canon living near the former Jesuit college in Olmütz, had seen Lafayette on a drive only fifteen days before. In fact drives were a thing of the past, but the alleged sighting indicated that Olmütz residents talked of Lafayette's presence. Countess Rumbeck considered how best to help Madame Lafayette meet the emperor. Applying to chief minister Thugut was pointless. The empress also seemed an unpromising channel. Instead Rumbeck arranged a next-day appointment for "Mme. de Motiers née Noailles" with the grand chamberlain, Prince Franz Orsini-Rosenberg.

Rosenberg was familiar with the Noailles family but had never heard of a Madame Motier. At first he feared that he was dealing with an adventuress and was delighted when she revealed her true identity. Rosenberg was grateful for the reception her relatives had shown him in France. He knew her uncle particularly well: Marquis Emmanuel de Noailles, who had served as French ambassador to Vienna in 1783–92. On the other hand, Rosenberg felt no sympathy for her husband's political ideals and politely warned her that the emperor would not release him before a general peace. Still he supported her proposal to join her husband, and he arranged for her to meet Francis II on Saturday morning, 10 October.

The emperor was surprised at the identity of his visitor. Madame Lafayette gave an eloquent plea for her husband's relief. Francis responded that he "would have done the same in [her] place" but that he could not grant release since "his hands were tied" and "it was a complicated matter." She had the gumption to reply "that nothing was less complicated than to return [Lafayette] to his wife and children." Francis did allow her and her daughters to join Lafayette in prison, assuring her "that it was all that he could do, but that he would grant me this permission with great pleasure, that M. Lafayette is well treated, and that my presence with him would be one more satisfaction for him." When Madame Lafayette asked about the other prisoners, Francis admitted that he didn't know exactly who they were. Documents referred to them merely by number. But he promised to grant their wives the same privilege as he had Madame Lafayette, should they ask. Then she made one more request: to be able to write the emperor from prison through Rosenberg. Francis assured her that this would present no problem, but that she could always find satisfaction from the local commandant.[12]

To many Lafayette partisans, the young emperor seemed humane. They would claim that nasty advisers promoted injustice behind his back, particularly blaming his chief minister Thugut, Empress Maria Theresa of the Two Sicilies, and acting police minister Franz Joseph, Count von Saurau—whom the Lafayettes collectively called "the triumvirate."[13] While the emperor wanted to look good and have subordinates take the blame, praising his motives also served the aims of Lafayette supporters. It might convince Francis that to free his captives could only redound to his credit.

In fact he had refused similar requests before and would do so again. Earlier that year, the sister of state prisoner François Lamarque had asked to share his cell at the Spielberg in Brünn. She had enclosed recommendations from the French Commission on Exterior Relations and François Barthélemy, French ambassador in Switzerland, and sent her petition through Duke Albert of Saxe-Teschen. With the emperor's blessing, Thugut told Teschen that such an arrangement "would cause too many problems."[14]

It was quite exceptional when Francis made his concession to Adrienne Lafayette. The families of Pusy and Maubourg tried in vain to follow her example. Pusy's wife, Julienne de Bureaux-Pusy, and her mother, Marie Poivre du Pont, hoped to enter Vienna with Swiss passports or, with John Parish's help, American ones. Once there they could ask Francis to fulfill his promise to let them join their husbands. Perhaps Madame du Pont could enter the prison disguised as her daughter's chambermaid, so that Pusy would have even the pleasure of his mother-in-law's constant presence. Maubourg's sister Marie de Maisonneuve considered entering Vienna on a Swiss or Polish passport and using her husband's many diplomatic connections to press the case.[15] Early in 1796 Maisonneuve wrote Field Marshal Botta to express concern for Maubourg's health and request permission to join him.[16] At the beginning of July, Pusy's wife petitioned the Aulic War Council to be allowed to come with her child and appeal to Francis for her husband's release or at least the privilege of sharing his cell.[17] A year later the wives and children of Maubourg and Pusy traveled across Germany to Dresden, where they applied—again fruitlessly—for visas to Vienna.[18]

Adrienne Lafayette enjoyed special advantages. She gained court access through her substantial family rank and connections. She showed up unexpectedly and argued skillfully. Francis may also have been swayed by a sense of chivalry, his youth, the presence of two girls, and the absence of his steely chief minister. In the surprise of the moment, Francis may have felt that he could not deny the request. Once Thugut learned what happened, he vowed to block similar appeals.

Francis notified Aulic War Council president Wallis "to arrange everything necessary" to reunite the Lafayette women with their husband and father. The entire matter was to remain strictly confidential. The women were to enter Lafayette's confinement under regulations applying to state prisoners, except that they were to fund themselves.[19]

Adrienne Lafayette notified Lally and her aunt Tessé and approached several powerful people. In doing so she gained the impression that the Austrian elite was better disposed toward her husband than she had thought. She spoke with women who proved quite sympathetic, including sisters-in-law of her close friend Countess Marie Ursule d'Arenberg de La Marck: Countess Françoise von Windisch-Graetz and Duchess Marie d'Ursel, both born princesses d'Arenberg. Adrienne Lafayette also met a "very aimiable" second-rank minister named Hagendorf or Heygendorff at the Windisch-Graetz home. Said to be a secret admirer of her husband, he predicted that release was imminent. Countess Windisch-Graetz did not want her husband, Josef, to be embroiled in a suspect affair. However, she and Duchess Ursel expressed confidence that their brother, Count Auguste d'Arenberg de La Marck, could sway the court and do so without personal risk.[20]

On 12 October, Adrienne Lafayette visited chief minister Thugut, whom she soon deemed "the coldest and most impenetrable of men." She pointed out strong reasons to release her husband, including peace prospects and favor to a family that had already suffered so much. She expressed conviction that the emperor had liberty to act on his good inclinations and that his allies would not raise serious objections. Thugut treated her politely but showed hostility to her husband. "As I observed to him that the Coalition governments were attributing too much importance to a single man," she recalled, "he repeated, 'Too much importance!' several times, with a tone and a grimace that showed how much importance he attributed to him." She suggested that the French princes should not tell the emperor what to do, but he replied that the Austrian court did owe them some regard. When she asked that he consider all that she had endured, he claimed that the emperor had suffered misfortunes too. Thugut then launched into a litany of woes that the Revolution had brought the entire continent.

Adrienne Lafayette visited the war council vice president, Infantry General Count Joseph von Ferraris, to obtain papers to enter Olmütz and its prison. Ferraris told her that she would share difficult conditions. She took to heart his warning that the authorities would inspect her letters. He advised her to seal those that she intended for the emperor. Her health had already deteriorated during her long incarcerations, and returning to prison threatened it further. She bluntly remarked later that "my separation from M. Lafayette was to me more painful than death."[21]

The necessary papers arrived the evening of 13 October, and the women and their servant promptly set out. At Prossnitz (Prostejov), the last postal station before Olmütz, Madame Lafayette sent off reports to Archenholz in Hamburg with enclosures for her son in America and for Princess Hénin in Britain. Confident of the emperor's generosity, she promised her son that she would write again soon.

Lafayette's wife and daughters greeting him in his prison cell. This engraving appeared in *Captivité de La Fayette* (1797), a poem by Lafayette's former aide Philippe Charles d'Agrain. Marquis de Lafayette Prints Collection, Special Collections and College Archives, Skillman Library, Lafayette College

The women glimpsed the church towers of Olmütz on the morning of 15 October, and Madame Lafayette sang a canticle from the biblical book of Tobit (13.1–3): "Blessed be God who lives forever. . . . For he afflicts, and he shows mercy; he leads down to Hades in the lowest regions of the earth, and he brings up from the great abyss."

The women found their way to the stately home of fortress commandant Schröder on the Upper Square. Instead of receiving them directly, Schröder delegated the task to Major Czernak, who led them into the prison to Lafayette's rooms.[22] With that, the captive's year-long isolation was suddenly over.

Lafayette's encounter with his loved ones was a shock on both sides. No one had told him that they were coming. The women tearfully beheld and embraced an emaciated figure in tattered clothes. "I will tell you only," Adrienne Lafayette wrote to Thomas Pinckney "that we found him in the most absolute solitude, not knowing our frightful misfortunes; that it had been expressly prohibited to tell him if we existed, his children and I, that his wasting away is frightful, his chest a source of horrible suffering."[23]

Despite his poor health and a physical appearance that "frightened" her, Adrienne Lafayette found her husband harboring the same spirit and opinions as ever. "He is morally as you left him," she wrote to former aides. "You know the force and sweetness of his soul, and despite the moral and physical tortures that [his captors] have chosen to heap upon him, there is not the least alteration in his character, nor the least imbalance in his temper."[24]

In the meantime staff members searched the women's luggage and confiscated three silver forks, a gilt silver fork and spoon, a small silver coffeepot, a packet of papers, a violet silk purse, and French and Dutch currency amounting to 1218 Vienna florins 4 crosses, but they did allow the women to keep a pocket watch. They readied a room for their servant, Jean Depuit, and another, Beurnonville's former quarters next to Lafayette's, for the daughters.

Lafayette had to assure himself that he wasn't going mad and that his loved ones had really come. Once he had regained his bearings, he spent the day learning what had happened in the outside world. That evening, after guards had taken the daughters to their room and no one could overhear, his wife told him the most painful details of her own long incarcerations and the executions of so many relatives and acquaintances.[25]

Despite the news, the reunion brought Lafayette immense comfort. Prison surgeon Axter noted improvements in his physical health and emotional outlook. Lafayette remained emaciated and subject to occasional fevers and asthma, but Axter concluded that his patient was out of mortal danger.[26]

Adrienne Lafayette and Jean Depuit agreed that Depuit should return home, with payment of 147 florins 20 crosses. But Axter determined that Depuit had caught "the Venetian [venereal] disease" and needed a month of recovery before he could safely travel. Madame Lafayette promptly deemed Depuit an "imbecilic hired lackey." He spent long hours strolling the prison corridor and talking with soldiers, the expense of his upkeep still being paid by his erstwhile employer. Finally, in late November, a policeman escorted him to Troppau, where he crossed the border that evening.[27]

Once Adrienne Lafayette had seen her husband's living conditions, the emperor's remark about Lafayette's "satisfactions" began to rankle. It became a bitter running joke among the captives. In January 1796 she wrote of how, "besides the other satisfactions of our regime," the inmates suffered a "remarkable assemblage" of unhealthy conditions. Soon thereafter she sarcastically wrote supporters, "We don't have need to detail all the *satisfactions* of this sojourn to be assured of your zeal to bring us out." "This stay is really hardly a satisfaction, regardless of what the Emperor said," she remarked; "there's nothing here but insects, stench, and dirt."[28] She hated the rituals of army discipline that she witnessed in the inner keep, such as the practice of forcing soldiers to run the gauntlet. She found appalling that some guards even pointed out these sights to the Lafayette girls.[29] She deemed the prison supervisor, Major Czernak, particularly nasty, agreeing with Maubourg that the major was "a born jailer, as Voltaire was a born poet." When Czernak noticed Pontonnier cultivating a few plants on his windowsill, for instance, he waited until the blossoms had just opened, then pushed the little garden off the sill into the courtyard below. When he discovered that Pusy's old servant Jandel could climb to a window by means of grooves in the walls, he had the window walled up and forced Jandel to live in gloom for six months. He released another captive's pet birds and refused to let Maubourg's dearly loved dog leave his servant's room.[30]

At times the Lafayette family found the emotional distance to make fun of the harsh procedures. Adrienne Lafayette described how Major Czernak and "a fat sergeant-provost holding his bunch of keys in his hand" arrived at their cells, accompanied by a contingent of armed guards: "You would laugh to see my two daughters, Anastasie blushing to the ears, Virginie making a face so proud, as well as comical, pass under the crossed sabers over the doors of our cells that are shut again immediately." When the guards brought food and led the young ladies back and forth from their room, Madame Lafayette later reported, they did so with "ridiculous ceremonies," acting as if they were guiding panthers to and from their lairs.[31]

The Lafayettes, Maubourg, and Pusy could feel only outrage when they learned of the release of other French state prisoners at the end of 1795. The freed men included Pierre de Beurnonville and Henri Bancal at Olmütz; François Lamarque, Nicolas Marie Quinette, and Jean Drouet at Brünn; Armand Gaston Camus at Königgrätz; and Charles Louis Huguet de Semonville, and Hugues Bernard Maret at Kufstein. In midsummer 1795 news reached the captives that Francis II had proposed a prisoner exchange. He would trade Beurnonville's group of state prisoners for the eldest child of the deceased French king and queen, sixteen-year-old Marie de France. France agreed, and Austria transferred the eight men to Basel, where the exchange took place on 26 December.[32]

Efforts to include Lafayette's group proved vain. Émigré journalist Joseph Masclet made a public appeal in London. The sympathetic French envoy to Switzerland, Barthélemy, tried to intervene with his government. But it was to no avail. Adrienne Lafayette had learned of the prisoner exchange while still in Vienna and hoped that her husband might benefit. She asked her father to meet French deputies in Switzerland and to lobby for expanding the group due to be freed.[33] The Lafayette party noted that the Beurnonville group had supported the throne's overthrow and even voted for the king's execution, whereas the three chief state captives remaining in Olmütz had defended the king and a constitution that gave the monarchy a central role. Maubourg muttered that the released men had been "either Jacobin chiefs or murderers of the king." Lafayette remarked that "arbitrary governments . . . must really detest the honest friends of liberty more than the Robespierres, Marats, and all the others who have soiled its name."[34]

Adrienne Lafayette's hope for imminent release proved groundless. Her husband teased her for such naiveté. "Gilbert mocked me, and he has reason," she conceded.[35] She set about trying to improve conditions, only to find that Francis's other assurances were empty. Three days after arrival, she asked to see commandant Schröder but was rebuffed. She received permission only to write him with materials provided by Czernak as the major stood watching. She asked that the Lafayette women be allowed to attend Mass on Sundays and holy days at the adjacent garrison Church of the Virgin Mary of the Snows. She requested that the family have the services of Lafayette's secretary, Pontonnier, since Beurnonville and former members of the Convention had enjoyed the help of their servants. She wanted a soldier's wife rather than a soldier to clean her daughters' room. Schröder refused either to respond or to allow Madame Lafayette to write the emperor. He did forward her requests to Field Marshal Botta, who sent them on to the Aulic War Council, where President Wallis conferred with Thugut, who obtained the emperor's written instruction: "Madame Lafayette and her daughters are to submit themselves to everything in state arrest that is prescribed and to be observed for her husband as well as for all state prisoners." In other words, he denied her requests.[36]

No one hastened to inform Adrienne Lafayette. The authorities did not feel that they had to enlighten prisoners on the making of an administrative decision, when the decision occurred, or if a decision had occurred at all. Unaware of the refusal, Madame Lafayette tried again on 14 December. This time she wrote to General Ferraris via Countess Windisch-Graetz, expressing hope that she might be able to attend Mass by Christmas. She added another request, that she have access to Maubourg and Pusy. Ferraris replied that he could not grant her wishes: "I have not myself the means of complying with your desire, notwithstanding my wish to do so. I can only observe that, as you have consented to share your husband's lot, it will not be possible for you to obtain any change in your situation." Adrienne Lafayette received this response a month after she had written.[37] She assumed that the emperor played a role in the decision, and she was furious. Ferraris's letter revealed, she claimed, "what has come of the polite remarks of Vienna, by virtue of which I had the stupidity to cultivate some hopes; . . . and that in the system of these gentlemen here against us, all the nice words that aren't accompanied by a passport are made only to fool and sedate our friends."[38]

Her anger notwithstanding, she replied to Ferraris that "we all three repeat with all our heart that we are happier with M. de Lafayette, even in this prison, than anywhere else without him"; that prison authorities had prevented her from writing the emperor through Prince Rosenberg, as Francis II had promised she could; and that her health had deteriorated to the point where she felt constrained to ask leave for several days to consult physicians in Vienna. Ferraris allowed her to write the emperor and Rosenberg.[39]

Rosenberg did not respond as she had hoped. He wrote that he was willing to help, but "affairs of state are not my responsibility." He assured her, "The heart of the emperor does not need to be animated to do acts of benevolence; thus I flatter myself that the obstacles will not be insurmountable." But while Francis II gave her permission to leave Olmütz, he demanded a condition that she could never accept. "I am not disinclined to issue her permission to leave the prison," he wrote Wallis, "but she's to be told that as soon as she will have left the prison, she can no more be allowed to return to her husband; and she is never to be permitted to travel here to Vienna." Wallis ordered Moravian commander Botta to have the Olmütz commandant deliver the message in person, and to have Adrienne Lafayette respond in writing. Schröder did so the beginning of April. It was the first time she had ever seen him, two months after she had made her request.[40]

Adrienne Lafayette's reply was emphatic, that she would never accept the conditions. "They will not tear me away from here except with M. Lafayette, unless, perhaps, they drag me away dead," she remarked.[41] Schröder's visit ended her attempts to correspond directly with the court.[42]

She and the other captives avoided blaming their predicament on the emperor, whom they deemed ill-informed. Rather, they blamed authorities farther afield: the Vienna cabinet, particularly Thugut, and British prime minister William Pitt. They claimed that Thugut often carried out his prison policies without informing Francis and that, if the emperor had known, he would surely have put a stop to them. The captives also claimed that Pitt paid prison costs and encouraged Vienna to reject demands for release, while he was impudently claiming in Parliament to have no responsibility for the captivity or influence on it.[43] Adrienne Lafayette called Pitt "our principal enemy," "our common adversary," even "the prime minister of *anti-liberty*." Her husband broke into foul language when speaking about him.[44] At the same time, she claimed that the emperor "did not appear to be any more than a little fool whom I think is neither good nor bad."[45] Though she judged him harshly, she did not accuse him of intentional malice.

The reality was that Francis kept himself well informed. "Until now, everything having to do with our French state prisoners, and especially their treatment, was to be brought to the knowledge of the Emperor," Wallis noted.[46] On the other hand, there is no evidence that Pitt subsidized or otherwise encouraged Lafayette's captivity. It drew only brief, infrequent attention from the British Foreign Office.[47]

Adrienne Lafayette also made a modest request to have knives and forks at meals. Schröder referred it to Botta in Brünn, who sent it to Vienna. The court denied the petition; the privilege would violate regulations governing state prisoners and would have to be extended to Maubourg and Pusy; the canteen cut all food into small pieces before delivering it to prisoners, and if they were given utensils instead, additional supervision would be necessary during meals.[48]

Madame Lafayette kept on raising objections. She reiterated that a woman should replace the soldier cleaning the girls' room; asked for a second pallet to allow the girls to sleep apart, especially in case of illness; and condemned separation from Maubourg and Pusy as "a barbarity without pretext." Prison officers did offer hope for a second pallet, but even that request failed to find Vienna's approval.[49]

Eventually Adrienne Lafayette adopted her husband's way of describing captivity as a living death. She wrote often of the Olmütz prison as a "tomb" or "tombs."[50] Similarly she spoke of "the vaults of the Inquisition of Olmütz" in which "one is redoubling all the precautions that can prevent communication between Lafayette and the rest of the living."[51]

The captives' supporters picked up the metaphor of burial. Archenholz wrote in *Minerva*, "I consider [Lafayette] buried alive," and called the prison "a true grave." In a long poem he published in Paris in early 1797, Agrain described the prison as a "tomb" and "sepulcher."[52] Others who wrote of the Olmütz prison as a "tomb" were the Lafayettes' son, George, as well as Mathieu Dumas, Germaine de Staël, and Louis Romeuf. On the floor of Parliament, Fox painted a gripping picture of the family's fate: the Lafayettes were living in a "dungeon," he cried, where "they remain together, the living, and yet buried."[53]

The presence and energy of the Lafayette women, however, improved prison conditions. Lafayette's isolation gave way to the happiest kind of companionship. His wife called it a "resurrection" for them both. They were able to enjoy an intimate family life. Anastasie made shoes for her father, robes for Virginie, and corsets for her mother. The women hung curtains and bought furniture. Anastasie drew likenesses of her executed grandmother and aunt with contraband Italian chalk.[54] Adrienne wrote a biography of her martyred mother in the margins of a volume of Count Leclerc de Buffon's *Histoire naturelle*.[55] The girls practiced English by reading popular novels by Samuel Richardson and Fanny Burney d'Arblay.[56] After the women arrived, the authorities allowed Maubourg and Pusy access to their servants three hours a day, apparently for reasons of equity. The women thus "dissipated the shadows" for all the prisoners.[57]

Better clothing became available. Prison authorities judged Lafayette's clothing indecent in the presence of women. They supplied cloth for his wife, at Lafayette's cost, to make homespun flannel breeches and a waistcoat. The material was rough, but supervising officers deemed a better quality too extravagant for a prisoner. Pusy claimed that he had resented wearing little more than rags, but he had brought up the subject once with "brutal" Major Czernak and vowed not to do so again, "firstly because my clothing spoke for itself, and because I preferred doing without rather than entering into the humiliating discussion that would have been necessary." The authorities eventually did offer Pusy and Maubourg new clothing, but Maubourg took pleasure in refusing it, continuing to wear rags as a point of honor. He proclaimed sarcastically that he did not want to put His Majesty to any expense, and that, when he regained his freedom, he would only regret "not being able to return his wonderful attire."[58]

Adrienne Lafayette helped to assure better treatment by giving regular tips to soldiers serving her family. She also gave "extraordinary gratuities" to staff, including eighteen florins to mark the women's first anniversary in the prison and twenty-two and a half florins for New Year's Day.[59] This generosity did more than simply engender gratitude; it also helped remind staff of the Lafayettes' rank and create the pretense that they were clients rather than inmates.

The army budget covered only the costs of holding Lafayette, Maubourg, and Pusy, whereas Madame Lafayette needed a minimum of 15 louis or about 130 Vienna florins per month, 100 florins for food alone, to maintain herself and her daughters. When her funds threatened to run out, Botta asked the war council whether he might draw on her husband's money. Vienna denied the request and asked Madame Lafayette how she intended to pay in the future. When the money ran out in May, the military arranged loans on her credit from local merchant-bankers Michael Sassati and Wolfgang Karl Hirsch. Hirsch, who became her most important local financial agent, was ironically the son-in-law of Anton Krömer, the official who had driven Lafayette back to Olmütz after the failure of his escape attempt. In June, John Parish, U.S. consul in Hamburg, gave Madame Lafayette an unlimited line of credit; that fall he placed 200 ducats at her disposal. Parish asked for documentation, so Vienna directed that Schröder inform Madame Lafayette personally and send in quarterly reports. After having sent 600 ducats through Hirsch by February 1797, Parish requested receipts in her own hand. The authorities agreed to let Madame. Lafayette send receipts and notes to Parish. Overall she took out loans from Hirsch amounting to 1,100 ducats or 5,000 Vienna florins. Added to other loans from Parish, the amount she owed the U.S. consul was around £1900.[60]

The prisoners suffered from incarceration in various ways. Lafayette inclined to congestion and fevers and became emaciated. Axter could offer only the palliatives that others had given Lafayette: balsamic pills, bracing drinks, compresses, Peruvian bark (for nerves), and laxatives. His condition improved in the first months with his family, not only from his loved ones' companionship and care but also from a relatively mild winter. Lafayette suffered a rough period of congestion in May 1796, but the following summer went well for him. In autumn, however, his wife noted that he suffered occasional cold-related fevers and other physical complaints. Prison staff remarked on his skeletal appearance to Maubourg, who began to imagine the ancient mummies that he had once seen in the crypt of a Franciscan convent in Toulouse. "If this continues," he remarked, "the court of Vienna will learn to its regret that one fine morning he will evaporate through the narrow squares of the double wire grating on his window."[61] Lafayette was not nearly so far gone, but his health was indeed poor and did not improve significantly until his release.

The elder Lafayette daughter, Anastasie, withstood the rigors better than the younger, Virginie. Only in 1797 did Anastasie begin to fall ill, developing a skin outbreak much like one that afflicted her mother. Virginie could be so full of energy that she skipped about the rooms, but eventually she suffered what Axter described as feverish paroxysms.

Maubourg and Pusy remained out of sight, but by spring of 1796 Adrienne Lafayette gathered that the two Frenchmen had aged dramatically. Pusy suffered from rheumatism and Maubourg from scurvy-related ailments in his stomach, eyes, teeth, and legs.

Axter, on the other hand, deemed both of Lafayette's former comrades in arms fundamentally robust men. He was confident that they would recover fully after release. Pusy did not even call for the surgeon until early spring 1797 and then only for stomachaches that Axter soon cleared up. However, Pusy was quite emaciated, a far cry from the stout man he had been even in Prussian prisons. For three months Axter treated him for hemorrhoids. Pusy began to worry about his physical deterioration. Axter judged his greatest problem to be emotional, the result of being deprived of his wife and friends.

Maubourg also enjoyed a rugged constitution. He confided to the surgeon that he had hardly ever been sick before confinement. At Olmütz, however, he developed scurvy, stomach and chest pains, severe headaches, and general lassitude. From the summer of 1795, Axter treated him with various medicines to no avail.

The surgeon noted that at least Maubourg did not suffer significant further decline. At the beginning of 1797, Maubourg was sure that he would only need a month of freedom, some herbs, and regular exercise to return to his old self.

The prisoners' servants showed varying degrees of physical and emotional stamina. The two youngest—Maubourg's valet, Grugeon, and Lafayette's secretary, Pontonnier—held up best of all through 1796. Still they both became pallid and thin, suffering congestion, heart palpitations, and trembling in limbs. "All that's left to us is our bones," Pontonnier wrote in a secret note. Maubourg attributed Grugeon's nervous condition to side effects of a medicine. The valet had a hard time making it through the winter of 1796–97, at the end of which Adrienne Lafayette described him in stark terms: "Jules is no longer well, he has chest problems, often mouth sores, at this moment he's unable to digest anything, but these habitual torments come from problems of nerves that cause him at 25 years of age to tremble like an old man." In contrast Pontonnier displayed impressive powers of resistance. He had a sunny disposition, intelligence, and skill in communicating with fellow prisoners. He read voraciously, teaching himself English and German. Pusy's valet, Jandel, old and illiterate, found few compensations in his solitude.

Among the servants, Lafayette's valet, Jean Pierre Compte (whom Axter called "Peter") did worst of all. He arrived with constipation and eventually developed congestion and depression. Axter concluded that isolation and lack of exercise were especially devastating to this young man accustomed to physical labor, who commanded only rudimentary literacy and showed no interest in educating himself after Pontonnier's model. "What have I done to these kings that they're holding me prisoner?" Compte asked. His case became serious enough that Axter began to fear the worst. On Axter's recommendation, Schröder petitioned Vienna for several months to release Compte. In autumn 1796, when he developed dire intestinal inflammation, Vienna allowed him to be transferred to the adjacent army hospital, with a sentry standing before his door. An observer, probably Passy, reported "alarming signs" to Lafayette supporters abroad, including a heightened prison guard, more frequent visits from the physician, and more visits to the pharmacy by guards, leading to the inference that "one or several prisoners are dangerously sick." Gradually, after three months, Compte's condition improved. Axter knew that full recovery was impossible in prison.[62]

The most grievously affected person of all was Adrienne Lafayette. She seemed healthy on arrival, but she had noticed early symptoms of disease during her previous incarceration in France. It drove her in February 1796 to request a medical consultation in Vienna. By April she was complaining of stomachaches and rheumatoid arthritis. She began to suffer persistent rashes and migraines. Her consumption of medications rose. By October 1796 outbreaks had appeared on her arms, skin peeled off, and both arms and hands swelled to the point that she was unable to close her fist or write. She suffered nervous twitching, evening fevers, headaches, stomachaches, and swollen eyes. Axter asked persistently that she be able to take walks or carriage rides, but his requests were denied. Axter routinely saw all captives twice a week, but he visited her more often, even daily. He was confused about her condition's progress. He tried to reason according to the traditional medical paradigm based on humors, fluxions, and blood qualities. He diagnosed "a deposition [on limbs and joints] of an acrid matter generated in the blood," prescribed "blood purifying and sweat inducing decoctions," and even pronounced her skin outbreaks to be *helpful* by diverting the disease from internal organs. He regularly applied ointments and poultices. He may well have encouraged wine consumption in mid-1796, but she gave it up abruptly when her condition worsened sharply in the fall. At that time Axter was able to obtain permission for her pallet to be moved to her daughters' neighboring cell, where she could enjoy warm herbal baths in a tub that Beurnonville had used. The bathing did bring relief, and she returned to her husband's room, at least temporarily, on 24 November. Her consumption of medications peaked in December, and she claimed to be improving in January 1797. In February she wrote her sister of having mouth sores that she attributed to bad water and dirty crockery and of teeth gradually crumbling away. By early spring the swelling in her arms had declined, but a leg had begun to swell and develop a rash. By later in May, skin eruptions had appeared in several places. Axter blamed them on prison air, lack of physical exercise, and predisposition to scurvy. He prescribed continuing herbal baths, relaxing, and walks in the countryside. The authorities again refused the walks.[63]

Adrienne Lafayette appreciated Axter's efforts. Beginning in summer 1796, she gave him a regular monthly *douceur* of nine florins. Early the next year, she presented him with a small silver coffeepot and a gilded silverware set. Schröder had the gift reviewed by the Aulic War Council, whose president conferred with Thugut. The authorities finally gave clearance, but Axter chose the way of caution and refused to accept this gift.[64]

Adrienne Lafayette was only the most spectacular of several women who played key roles in the support of Lafayette during his prison years and eventual rescue. Princess Adélaïde d'Hénin was Lafayette's most important single correspondent during his prison years and a sponsor of Bollmann's appeal to Berlin in 1793. Angelica Church sponsored his rescue attempt in 1794. Germaine de Staël introduced Bollmann to Hénin and used her high connections in Paris and elsewhere on Lafayette's behalf. During the rescue operation of 1794, Johanna Sieveking of Hamburg served as chief correspondent with Bollmann, who wrote her information on his whereabouts and prospects under the guise of innocent travel accounts. Marie de Maisonneuve served as another important mediator of both secret and open mail. Georgiana Cavendish, Duchess of Devonshire, a leading Foxite, addressed British officials on Lafayette's behalf. Henriette de Latour-Maubourg and Julienne de Bureaux-Pusy, wives of Lafayette's fellow prisoners, moved from petitioning government officials in Paris to traveling toward Vienna to make appeals after the model of Madame Lafayette.

Many men saw such political activity by women as exceptional, even objectionable. Thomas Jefferson caught himself writing Angelica Church of political matters in New York and added, "But that need not agitate you. The tender breasts of ladies were not formed for political convulsion." He then criticized openly those women who, like Madame de Staël, played such important roles in public affairs of the day: "The French ladies miscalculate much their own happiness when they wander from the true field of their influence into that of politicks."[65]

Such attitudes did not prevent these women from maintaining contact with Lafayette, addressing officials, planning strategy, and patronizing efforts directed at his release. Indeed male dismissal of women as politically irrelevant seems to have contributed to their political effectiveness. They were often able to operate under the charade of political harmlessness since Lafayette's captors did not examine their correspondence or other activities so carefully. The reality was that women formed key links in increasingly powerful networks working on Lafayette's behalf.[66]

Beyond any previous action, Lafayette's escape attempt had drawn international attention to his fate and inspired calls for his release. His wife's initiative to join him in prison had a similar impact on world opinion. Arguably that impact was even greater.

9

SECRET COMMUNICATIONS

Austrian authorities tried to limit the Lafayette family's contacts with the outside world and to cut them off entirely from fellow captives. But local and foreign supporters helped the family develop extensive secret communications within the Olmütz prison and beyond.

Vienna banned Lafayette from writing but did allow his wife limited correspondence. She had to restrict "open" mail to family and to private and financial matters. It was not to describe prison conditions or address political matters. The supervising major brought writing materials and watched Adrienne Lafayette write, sometimes with other guards looking on.[1] Authorities did not allow her to contact her son, currently in care of his namesake in America, but they did permit her to correspond with her father in Switzerland, her sister and aunt in Danish Holstein, her "cousin" Princess Hénin in London, war council vice president General Ferraris, Countess Windisch-Graetz, and Prince Rosenberg in Vienna.[2]

Adrienne Lafayette was also able to correspond openly with John Parish, U.S. consul in Hamburg. At first Parish tried sending her several letters care of Olmütz merchant Wolfgang Hirsch. Hirsch found no means to get them into her hands, so he ended up burning them. Parish and André Masson, now a Hamburg merchant, persuaded James Monroe's courier, Bartholomew Terrasson, to deposit mail for her with Parish until conditions improved. Parish then sent an unsealed letter through Olmütz commandant Schröder, requesting permission to write her about private affairs. The request was granted. By late February 1796, Madame Lafayette had received and responded to a letter from Parish and also to an apparent enclosure in it from Princess Hénin and Count Lally.[3]

Like outgoing mail, incoming letters were subject to inspection and seizure. Some were intercepted at the post office while others were received care of

Schröder in Olmütz or Botta in Brünn. All went to Vienna for examination by the war council and chief minister Thugut. Only a fraction of the incoming mail ever arrived and then a month to three months late.[4]

Authorities returned inmate letters complaining of treatment. In mid-March 1797 Schröder had four letters returned to Madame Lafayette, with reproof and warning that future notes of the sort would be returned as well.

The officer who brought this message was the new, sympathetic prison supervisor, Captain Baron Peter Karl von MacElligot. The captain led Madame Lafayette through the corridor to her husband's room. When she asked why Vienna had stopped her outgoing letters, he told her that he had received orders to say only that the messages contained falsehoods. When they entered the room, the Lafayettes asked why Schröder was not bringing this news in person. The captain muttered that poor weather had stranded him. Lafayette accused the government of cowardice. MacElligot protested, but Lafayette replied that "you do not have to get upset, Monsieur. It is not you to whom [these words] apply, by any means, nor to any of your commanders—who are, like you, only passive instruments. . . . The Austrian officers and generals have never done anything to me but show pity. It is for their government that I have reserved contempt." Madame Lafayette began to read the letters and, at each passage, asked if it were not true. She asked precisely what she could write and suggested that Vienna prohibited the commandant from telling her. MacElligot agreed but tried to defend the general. Lafayette assured him that he knew people "much higher" than the captain were responsible. "But what do we have to write?" Lafayette exclaimed. "That the Vienna court is a government of humanity and liberty, and that I love it with all my heart? That they are charming men?" Then he went on, charging MacElligot to tell the person who claimed Madame Lafayette's letters contained falsities "that I send him to —. I cannot say it before ladies, but you know the French compliment." He dismissed the idea of giving up writing altogether; to do so, he said, "We'd have to be even more imbecilic than your court." Madame Lafayette proposed writing a protest to Thugut. Her husband suggested making "the donkey the emissary." The goodnatured MacElligot pantomimed long ears and smiled.[5]

Madame Lafayette wrote Thugut that her letters had softened the truth. She demanded clarification of what seemed to be new restrictions. The war council president returned the letter, ordering Schröder to inform her, this time in person, that Thugut would not respond and that Vienna would accept no further letters in this tone. Schröder visited the Lafayettes in early May. It was only the second time they had seen him. "M. Lafayette countered with a compliment for the minister that you will excuse me from writing you here," Madame Lafayette wrote.

Other prisoners also had mail returned. Maubourg, who had "for some time been making his custody every day less palatable" for MacElligot and other jailors, sent his sister complaints about lack of cleanliness, exercise, and fresh air; deterioration of clothing; limitations on correspondence; and lack of control over heating. His letter mocked Schröder, who had recently refused Maubourg money to tip guards for walking his dog. The satire pushed the commandant to his limits. He declared to Marshal Botta that this "extremely surly" prisoner opposed the staff closing windows and lighting his stove even while complaining that his cell was "like an ice pit," refused replacements of his rags, and would surely reject food itself if he could live without it. Botta passed the letter on to the interim president of the war council, Count Ferdinand von Tige, who deemed Maubourg's language to be "in an even freer tone" than Madame Lafayette's, "bordering on impudence" and full of "satanic expressions against the fortress commandant." Tige had the letter returned and ordered Schröder personally to set the inmate straight.

Madame Lafayette and Maubourg both tried to slip out messages to their respective sons in a letter to Parish. In that instance Vienna authorities excised the objectionable passages and sent the rest on. In early June, Schröder made a third personal visit to the Lafayettes and Maubourg to return the excisions. He carried out his commission with chagrin and made little comment.[6]

Schröder's duty and self-interest motivated him to isolate the captives. In 1796 a guard suffered fifty lashes for having responded to a comment that Pusy made from his window. That fall an unnamed Olmütz source reported tightening security, and the Lafayettes temporarily lost contact with Pusy. Early in 1797, after Czernak's transfer elsewhere, Schröder notified the war council that Maubourg was keeping his dog with him again. The council urged special precautions to prevent Maubourg from passing messages through his pet.[7]

Prisoners still circumvented these measures. Beyond secretary Pontonnier's code of whistles, inmates were sometimes able to talk directly to each other. Pontonnier's cell was above the Lafayettes' rooms. When sentries were not watching, Adrienne Lafayette spoke with him through her daughters' windows. She gave Pontonnier news that she gleaned from incoming mail.[8] Some soldiers cooperated. At night the Lafayette women would prepare a parcel with a message for fellow prisoners. Including part of their supper to bribe the sentry in the courtyard below, they would lower the parcel through the window with string; the sentry would take the food and pass the rest of the parcel through Pusy and Maubourg's windows.[9] Occasionally staff described to captives their companions and brought secret notes with the meals.[10]

These internal communications enabled unsupervised correspondence with the outside world. Just two weeks after the Lafayette women arrived, Maubourg surreptitiously wrote to his sister that Adrienne Lafayette had sent him notes from his family by means of "our secret means of correspondence."[11] When authorities released Beurnonville in early November 1795, Maubourg slipped him a note

The rear of the Olmütz prison, where Lafayette's family occupied rooms on the bottom floor, at the present drain pipe and beyond. On the left was the military hospital. Author's photograph, with thanks to Colonel Mojmír Sklenovský, director of the Czech Army Administrative Archive in Olomouc

for the Hamburg and London circles. Late that same month, October messages from Masson, Romeuf, Boinville, and Lally arrived "as if from heaven." Prisoners sent responses through the same channel. A staff member smuggled out messages written on margins of German-language books.[12] Maubourg addressed supporters in America and Danish Holstein. Lafayette also wrote a few lines in his own hand "only to certify his existence." He dictated "a kind of manifesto" to John Quincy Adams, U.S. envoy at The Hague, encouraging official American action. In late November, Adrienne Lafayette sent other secret messages through "friends" to Masson and Romeuf. She sent thanks to supporters in Hamburg and London. She also pressed her sister Madame de Montagu, her father, Jean Louis de Noailles, Duke d'Ayen, and her friend Hénin to open up new lines of correspondence through Rosenberg in Vienna. In the new year she hoped that Littlepage's letters of exchange at Vienna would provide her with money to help "loosen the imperial talons." Presumably this meant payments or bribes to soldiers and other aides. She also mentioned how a "voyager friend" took the messages to Masson in Hamburg.[13]

The "voyager friend" whom Adrienne Lafayette mentioned repeatedly[14] could hide his role behind legitimate business taking him to and from Hamburg. This person may have been Olmütz banker and trader Hirsch. Parish was already using him as middleman for money transfers.

Madame Lafayette also spoke of "friends from here [Olmütz]," "the generous friends who take charge of our letters," and the like.[15] She credited them for "the most difficult and perilous of the correspondence": bringing it in and out of town and prison, and across the border.[16] She emphasized the importance of keeping their work confidential.[17] One former Lafayette aide in Hamburg, René Pillet offered to carry prisoner news to Paris. Adrienne asked him to take only his notes, confide exclusively in her brother-in-law Marquis Alexandre de Grammont, and refer to her husband by the code name "noisy bitch"! When she sent off a letter for Fox in early 1797, she asked go-betweens that they remind him and his parliamentary colleague Fitzpatrick to keep the means of correspondence confidential as a necessity "for our generous friends' security."[18] She often stressed this last point.[19]

But who, beyond Hirsch, were the "devoted," "generous" friends who smuggled messages in and out of the prison, and in and out of Olmütz and Moravia? There is a remarkable degree of certainty about who some of them were.

Staff surgeon Axter was one intermediary working within the prison. His willingness to divulge prisoner news to outsiders and serve as intermediary took great courage, given what had happened to his predecessor, Haberlein. He surely weighed carefully the risks he took. He was well aware that after months of strict security following Lafayette's attempted escape, prison routine had once again loosened enough to allow secret communications. Axter was on close terms with the provost and guards, and "the officer did not generally think it necessary to make a note of his visits" in daily reports to Schröder.

Professor Passy, who had interpreted for Huger during civil hearings, served as an Olmütz middleman beyond the prison walls. Passy worked for several months to detect and exploit weaknesses in prison security in order to send Adrienne Lafayette's messages abroad. Once Passy received the letters, another "friend" carried them across the border.[20] Lafayette referred almost surely to Passy when he later wrote that "an inhabitant of Olmütz, of a very noble character and of a very great merit" had provided the prisoner's wife with "some means of correspondence." Passy wrote an addendum to an October 1796 letter by Madame Lafayette, in which he promised to send Hamburg a new communications plan. He was surely the mysterious aide who smuggled in a note the summer of 1797, a man whom Lafayette referred to as "my brother who has taken all risks to get through to me some hopes." As a precaution, Lafayette crossed out and replaced "my brother" with the vaguer expression "dear and devoted persons," and changed the originally singular verbs and personal adjectives to plural. However, he forgot to make the changes in a postscript where he stated, "My brother believed he ought to keep the notes of which you speak to me in his possession. It is as if I had them myself."[21]

Passy's pseudonym was "Cant." It probably derived from the most famous German philosopher of the time, Immanuel Kant, an appropriate source for an academic. The name appeared on mail to and from the prisoners and in their testimony. Passy signed himself as "Cant" on marginal notes to Adrienne Lafayette's outgoing mail. She praised him to Masson and Pillet: "One day you will know all that M. Cant has meant to us. Doubtlessly you imagine quite a lot about him, but the reality surpasses that." Lafayette agreed: "There is no one to whom we owe as much."[22] By prior arrangement, the prisoners glimpsed "Cant" through their window grills before midsummer 1797.[23] He almost certainly presented himself by entering the courtyard behind the military hospital, which was easily visible from the captives' rooms.

Count Nepomuk Mitrovsky also helped outside the prison walls. In a marginal note of April 1796, "Cant" notified Masson how he had received his latest message via "Count M." In June, Adrienne Lafayette noted how prisoners were awaiting newspapers addressed to "M" and how his social skills and contacts in Vienna would prove useful to Mesdames Maubourg and Pusy in reaching their husbands. In October, Madame Lafayette reported how an American supporter had sent a letter of credit to "our friend M" and acknowledged having received secret intelligence from Vienna. The next month she expressed hope that "Count M." could serve as middleman once the money arrived. "Cant" added, however, that "our good Count M: had the unhappiness of losing his amiable daughter, and he is consequently inconsolable. He writes me nothing!" Mitrovsky was back in action with the new year. In February 1797, Madame Lafayette promised Pillet and Masson that "the friend M" would bring up possible Russian intervention. Soon after she wrote that "M. Cant and the other friend, M" would seek information in Vienna and plan how France could gain the captives' release.[24]

It is unlikely that prison supervisor Captain MacElligot played a role. An eventual agent sent from Hamburg, Henri Ducoudray-Holstein later claimed that MacElligot was "one of the secret friends of General Lafayette, and rendered me, during my mission to Olmutz, very important services."[25] It is true that MacElligot sympathized, but Ducoudray's words do not indicate that the captain cooperated in or knew about the secret mail.

Outgoing secret mail went through several stations. Hamburg served as the central exchange. Occasionally Pusy was able to smuggle notes to Maubourg. Maubourg slipped them in some of his own messages to the Lafayettes. After reading them, the Lafayettes sometimes erased lines that they deemed impolitic.[26] They sent such notes with their own, which were in Adrienne Lafayette's handwriting, to their Hamburg contact Masson or, in his absence, Archenholz. Madame Lafayette wrote Masson how satisfied the prisoners were with the arrangement, "that the central point of all our affairs is [in Hamburg], and that all which deals with us will pass through you."[27] After other Hamburg supporters (such as Parish and Sieveking) read the messages, copies went to destinations further afield, including Denmark and Britain, via Britain to France, America, Switzerland, and Holland.

Pusy's notes ultimately reached his wife and mother in Paris. Maubourg intended some mail for Hamburg or London recipients. Other mail went to his sister Marie de Maisonneuve in Romainmôtiers, Switzerland. She forwarded some of it to family and friends in Paris. The Lafayettes' letters landed in even more widely dispersed locations. Recipients included Hennings or "Hennel," Tessé and Montagu at Plön, Denmark; De Staël at Coppet on Lake Geneva; Madame Chavaniac in the Auvergne; Simiane at Cirey in the Haute-Marne; Adams in The Hague; Cadignan, Boinville, Pillet, Pinckney, Masclet, Fox, Fitzpatrick, and the Churches in London; Hénin and Lally in Richmond; Poix, Grammont, Ségur, Beauchet, the Maubourgs, and later Pillet in Paris; and Bollmann and George Washington Lafayette in Philadelphia. Copies spread further through private, diplomatic, and press channels.

Early on, the "voyager friend" brought letters from Hamburg to Olmütz via Hanover and Dresden.[28] The system became more efficient over time. Eventually the Lafayettes hoped for twice monthly delivery, though they sometimes experienced "a full month of fasting" without mail.[29] Hamburg letters reached them one and a half to three weeks after being written.[30] Letters for Maubourg or Pusy came first to the Lafayettes. After reading the letters, they often had to wait a few days for a cooperative staff member to take them down the corridor.[31]

In at least one instance, Passy used Trieste, Austria's Italian harbor on the Adriatic, as a relay station. An envelope addressed to "M. Cant, merchant in Trieste" reached the prisoners with handwritten versions of Masclet's articles for the *Morning Chronicle* of London. Charles Moré de Pontigaud, a Lafayette aide in the American war, a close friend of La Colombe, and an itinerant among Philadelphia, Hamburg, and Paris, considered Trieste "a second home." His brother had become a successful local trader and patron of refugees. It is possible that Moré arranged for mail from Hamburg to travel via Trieste to Passy in Olmütz. Ducoudray also claimed that Passy was "a native of Trieste."[32] Whatever the connections, Trieste seems, at least temporarily, to have served as yet another hub in the secret network.

The system did have its mishaps. Cadignan sent a package from London in early 1796, but it seems never to have arrived. In May an unspecified project failed, and the Lafayettes had to destroy outgoing letters. An incoming letter might be missing a page. Maubourg became alarmed that an investigative team would be visiting the prison in January 1797; he feared that the team would search the cells, so he burned several notes from abroad.[33]

Other factors beyond the work of local sympathizers enabled secret correspondence. One was that Adrienne Lafayette took her husband's dictation. His familiar handwriting could be recognized beyond the prison walls. "He will not write," she explained, "for his prohibited writing is too dangerous to risk beyond this place, and we must not, above all, abuse the devotion of our friends."[34] It is often impossible to distinguish Madame Lafayette's words from those that Lafayette dictated to her. At times the couple dictated to daughter Anastasie or expected Masson to copy letters to keep the source secret.[35] This surreptitious correspondence meant that the circle of those familiar with its operation remained small. Olmütz "friends" initially stipulated that there be only one contact person in Hamburg. However, the responsibility soon extended to include Masson, Romeuf, and Archenholz in Hamburg; and Hénin, Lally, and Cadignan in London.[36] Eventually Pillet and "Hennel" (Hennings) joined the Hamburg group.[37]

In spring of 1796, Ducoudray replaced the "voyager friend" as Lafayette's primary middleman between Olmütz and Hamburg. He came from Hamburg specifically to help develop and maintain contact with the captives and to seek new opportunities for escape. Much later he published details of the secret communications system. Though he remained quite confused about events at Olmütz before his arrival,[38] he described the evolving situation thereafter with the accuracy of personal experience.

Like Bollmann, Ducoudray came from a background that gave him skills useful to establish links with Lafayette in prison. Born to a Huguenot family in Danish Holstein, he grew up speaking French, German, and perhaps Danish. He also picked up some Swedish and English. After attending the Prussian university of Halle, he entered the French army as a volunteer. In 1795 he went on medical leave and moved to Hamburg-Altona near his childhood home. Free of demanding professional or family responsibilities, he enjoyed associating with journalists and refugees.

Archenholz approached Ducoudray with a request to establish contact with the captives. "In December, 1795, I was at Hamburg, at the house of Captain d'Archenholz," Ducoudray later recalled. "He spoke to me, with great warmth and feeling, respecting the melancholy situation of the prisoners, and asked me if I was inclined to do anything to assist them." Ducoudray jumped to the challenge. That evening the men visited Masson, who told them of others working for Lafayette's release, including Masclet and Cadignan in Britain. Masson said that the United States had provided generous funds that Parish and he could release. Ducoudray conferred on several subsequent occasions with Archenholz, Masson, Parish, and Georg Sieveking, receiving their unanimous support. He asked the French minister of war for an extension of leave for pressing family matters. Sieveking and Archenholz advised him to assume the identity of a wealthy Swedish merchant, Peter Feldmann. Archenholz took him to Carl Nordenskiöld, the local Swedish mission secretary, who obtained a Swedish passport for Ducoudray complete with the signature of resident minister Claes Peyron.

In March 1796 Ducoudray left the city in "a very elegant berlin," a carriage with secret compartments and a team of four horses. He took with him a longtime German servant named Johann, a packet of letters from America and France, and two hundred thousand Austrian florins in cash and credit.[39] Ducoudray traveled through Leipzig, Dresden, Prague, Hohenmauth (Vysoké Mýto), and Leutomis-chl (Lytomysl). When he arrived in Olmütz, he rented a suite at a local inn, sent for banker Wolfgang Hirsch. Pretending to onlookers that he and Hirsch were old acquaintances, Ducoudray led Hirsch to a private inner room, where they made plans to contact Lafayette. Hirsch reported that the captives were in relatively good health, but that Madame Lafayette was morose over lack of news. Hirsch identified Axter and Passy as key local supporters, and then offered to smuggle a short note through Axter. "An old and true friend of your family, my dear general, and of your companions in misfortune, is just arrived within the walls of Olmutz," Ducoudray wrote to Lafayette. Assuring the captive that his son and friends abroad were well, Ducoudray signed his assumed name and folded the note into a tiny square.

The following morning, Axter carried the message on his prison rounds. He slipped it to Adrienne Lafayette, "who was not as closely watched as her husband." She was overjoyed and composed a short thank-you while Axter lingered with her husband. She then alerted Pontonnier, who whistled the news to Maubourg and Pusy.[40]

All concerned continued the exchange. Later that day Axter took Madame Lafayette's reply to Hirsch. Ducoudray gave Hirsch a purse of a hundred ducats for Axter. Hirsch was to hand this reward and retainer to Axter when he had successfully delivered the first, most important of three packets of mail. Ducoudray enclosed writing materials and a long cover letter in which he offered to assist Lafayette's escape. Axter went back to the prisoners at lunchtime under the pretense of checking their diet. He feigned that he had discovered signs of unhealthy humidity in Lafayette's quarters, and requested access to the nearby women's room to inspect it for the problem. Here, when alone, he placed the delivery under a straw mattress. He alerted the Lafayettes by gesturing behind the backs of the provost and guards. A few days later, Ducoudray received a response. The family expressed thanks, but refused his offer to aid a breakout. Now that his wife and daughters were with him, Lafayette was no longer willing to take the risk.[41]

Before Ducoudray had finished his first visit to Olmütz, Adrienne Lafayette wrote him an introduction to Passy. The men spoke on several evenings. Hirsch also took Ducoudray to see the sites of Lafayette's escape and capture, including the barn outside Braunseifen where Lafayette had waited in the dark. Hirsch was allegedly godfather and friend of Joseph Richter, who had arrested Lafayette on his way through the village. Richter happened to be director of local linen production, so Hirsch presented Ducoudray as a Swedish linen merchant. Ducoudray spent two days at Richter's home and heard many stories of Lafayette's recapture.

Ducoudray then left Olmütz and established a line of private couriers, which connected Archenholz and Masson in Hamburg to Hirsch and Axter in Olmütz. Ducoudray also collected introductions to important people in the emperor's territories and adjacent lands. He took on the identity that Hirsch had suggested, using the pseudonym Peter Feldmann and pretending to seek local trade, especially in linen. He also began using the aristocratic "von" or "de," and the title "baron." Servant Johann and Hirsch himself had been calling him this to expand his influence. Ducoudray moved about the borderlands of Prussian Silesia, especially the Schweidnitz area, and kept Hirsch abreast of his movements. He came to Olmütz four times after his first visit. He often reduced incoming mail to key extracts for easier delivery and claimed later to have received a total of "more than thirty [outgoing] letters from Madame de Lafayette."[42]

For her part Adrienne Lafayette may have taken time to adjust to the new courier. She wrote to Masson in July 1796 that one more "friend" in Olmütz was useless. But a few days later, she expressed gratitude for the "excellent and quite charming courier." She must have changed her mind after seeing the results. Early the next month, she wrote Masson that she was awaiting his news "by Prussian post from Silesia," joking code for Ducoudray's clandestine delivery system via Schweidnitz.[43] Masson referred to Ducoudray in private letters as "my German" and at least once as "my correspondent from Germany."[44]

The new lines of communication worked to astonishing effect. Madame Lafayette's report on prison conditions in May 1796 soon reached the *Morning Chronicle* in London and British opposition leader Fox.[45] In mid-June, John Quincy Adams wrote that a note had arrived from her through Lally and presumably Hamburg. Adams sent his reply along the reverse route.[46] In July "the friend" (surely Ducoudray) brought Masson a list of writings that the Lafayettes wanted him to compile for publication. In late summer and early fall, Adrienne Lafayette smuggled out a message to her son in America and received news from him.[47] In October she also received a packet of letters from Masson, "Hennel" (Hennings), Boinville, and Pillet, and the Parisian paper *Journal de Perlet*. She wrote Masson that "you can well imagine that we have been very satisfied with our courier."[48]

By November 1796 a more reliable system had formed, thanks to someone whom Adrienne Lafayette called "the friend from here": Passy or Ducoudray. She did note that the Austrian stretch of this system was less secure than the Prussian. On 14 November a message from Lafayette was on its way from "Schweid[nit]z" to Hamburg "according to our new manner." The next day a package of Hamburg letters and newspapers arrived at Schweidnitz en route to Olmütz. On 23 November Madame Lafayette cited a recent article of the republican *Gazette de Hambourg* "that our friends managed to slip into this country." She asked Masson to pass on news to Hénin in Britain and enclosed a note for Maisonneuve in Switzerland. She instructed Masson to send a large package of "volumes, letters, news, excerpts of public papers, pamphlets" every eight days to "the friend of Swed– [Schweidnitz]" and to deliver it in plenty of time for "the hour of the post." The package would then "pass the perilous place," presumably the Prussian-Austrian border. Masson was also to address each package to a particular local "friend of liberty, very zealous for us." The captives expected to send off messages every fifteen days to Hamburg, with travel time of about eight days. In the course of a delivery, Ducoudray's servant, Johann, seems to have stolen a short conversation with Pontonnier through his cell door.[49]

Versions of this system lasted until captivity's end. Since Lafayette dictated messages to his wife and since she incorporated other prisoners' notes, she served as what she called "the interpreter of the prisoner triumvirate," the inmates' common voice.[50] Thus in communications a triumvirate of captives (the Lafayettes and Maubourg) successfully countered Vienna's alleged triumvirate of captors (chief minister Thugut, police minister Saurau, and the empress).

Supporters considered various cover explanations to disperse secret information. They could claim for instance that they learned the news from open letters, including at least one message that Adrienne Lafayette sent war council vice president Count Ferraris, which was published in Reichardt's *Frankreich,* a German-language Altona journal covering the French Revolution. But this risked losing her the privilege of limited correspondence. A safer cover was to claim that intelligence came from the commandant or prison staff. By summer 1796 Olmütz had had a succession of four regular commandants at the rank of general and for shorter periods a couple of interim commandants at colonel's rank. From the more than thirty soldiers and officers originally forming the prison guard, seven had left by advancement and transfer. When guards were off duty, they walked about town and divulged details of their charges to fellow soldiers and townspeople, or so the allegation went. In theory news might have come from anyone in the garrison, which numbered hundreds of soldiers. Other alleged sources could be former Olmütz prisoners Beurnonville and his companions; Madame Lafayette's former servant Depuit, who had lived in the prison several weeks; and the countless travelers passing through Olmütz.[51]

Authorities first learned of secret mailings in early 1797. The revelation occurred when a twenty-six-year-old postal driver, Niklas Sauermann, reported some suspicious deliveries. Sauermann had driven for the post in Vienna and Prague for four years before coming to Olmütz in 1792. He followed a regular route north across the border to Preussisch-Neustadt (today Prudnik, Poland) and back into Austrian Moravia-Silesia through Jägerndorf (Krnov) and Troppau. Around New Year's Day, a gentleman just off the coach from Schweidnitz (Ducoudray as "Baron Feldmann") approached him at the Black Eagle inn (Zum Schwarzen Adler) in Preussisch-Neustadt. The man asked Sauermann if he were the postal driver from Olmütz and if he would be willing to deliver a package to the postmaster there. The postmaster was Sauermann's boss, so the driver assented. The stranger said that he had no package this time, but would send one to innkeeper Valentin, who would give it to Sauermann when he returned. Sauermann learned from others in the inn that the mysterious gentleman was a Schweidnitz commercial counselor. Before he drove off, he confirmed the arrangement with Valentin.

Shortly thereafter, Sauermann happened to be at the Blue Star inn (Zum Blauen Stern) in Olmütz when Professor Passy approached him and asked if he had brought anything for the postmaster. When the coachman said no, Passy replied, "Perhaps you'll bring something along another time." Sauermann concluded that Passy had some inside knowledge.

When he left Olmütz next, Sauermann had received word from the postmaster, Paul Batka, to expect a package in Neustadt. Sauermann picked it up from the innkeeper, who said little about it. It turned out that a servant (Ducoudray's skillful and clever Johann) had brought it from Schweidnitz. The package was addressed to Valentin, but inside the outer wrapping were five seals and Sauermann's name with no further address. On arrival in Olmütz, Sauermann handed the package to Batka, who acknowledged it with a substantial tip.

In mid-February, Sauermann received a similar package at Neustadt's Black Eagle inn. When he turned it over in Olmütz, Batka gave him an even greater tip and told him that he should bring such packages to him directly, without letting anyone else know. The remark struck Sauermann as unusual and began to raise his suspicions.

On 9 March, Sauermann picked up a third package in Neustadt. It carried only one seal, so he managed to lift a corner of the cardboard wrapping. Inside, he saw material written in French, surely contraband. When he crossed back into Austrian territory, he confided in an archpriest named Marschhofer. Like other imperial subjects, priests were legally obliged to report criminal activity.[52] Sauermann was tempted to send the package directly to the emperor. However, Marschhofer suggested that he send it to the governor in Brünn, and he offered to write an accompanying report. Sauermann protested that this would betray his superior and risk his own job. They decided to pursue a third strategy. Troppau was Sauermann's next major stop, so Marschhofer would alert the police chief by special courier and ask the chief to pretend to find the package in a routine inspection. This would remove all suspicions from Sauermann and bring the package to authorities' attention quickly.

In the end Troppau police chief Dherbel blew the scheme. He made known at the postal office that he was awaiting the coach. As soon as Sauermann arrived, Dherbel asked him to come to his office. When Sauermann expressed dismay, Dherbel tried to make up for his clumsiness by returning the package and having a police commissioner pretend to find it. By that point the entire post office was in on the plot. Sauermann tried to contain the damage by going to Batka as soon as he arrived in Olmütz, reporting the inspection and seizure in Troppau and offering the notion that a Prussian sergeant-major had denounced him. Batka was quite upset and claimed no knowledge of the delivery's contents. Word spread through the post office. Batka tried to avert suspicion by writing the postmaster in Breslau, capital of Prussian Silesia, alerting him of the seizure and asking him to interrogate the coachman who drove from Breslau to Neustadt. The Breslau postmaster did so, with predictably absent results.

Troppau police chief Dherbel sent the contraband to Governor Ugarte in Brünn. An associate named Martin notified Moravian commander Botta on the governor's behalf. He also alerted police chief Okacz of Brünn and directed him to visit Olmütz to investigate. Okacz was to interrogate Sauermann under guarantee of protection from recrimination by the postmaster. He was also to ask Batka what he knew of other persons involved. This was a delicate situation because the only evidence against Batka thus far was the coachman's testimony.

Okacz took depositions on 29 March. Batka kept feigning ignorance, but he did admit that the previous two deliveries had been last year's issues of the forbidden Danish Altona journal *Frankreich*. He alleged that a Hamburg acquaintance named Maier had sent them.

Batka may have offered this common name as a ruse. However, he may have meant Friedrich Meyer, who was close to Georg Sieveking and Carl Voght and was deeply involved in the book and journal world. Meyer had been living off a sinecure as Hamburg's last cathedral canon. He frequented the newspaper stalls of Hamburg's Great New Market (Grossneumarkt), founded private reading societies that subscribed to German and foreign journals, and cultivated relationships with local authors, publishers, and journal editors.[53] He would have been an excellent source for a subscription to a progressive Hamburg-area paper.

Okacz could do little to investigate this "Maier" of Hamburg, but Sauermann's testimony also led the police chief to suspect Passy's involvement. When Okacz questioned Passy on 1 April, Passy claimed that he knew only generally of Batka's access to foreign journals, the only one of which he had requested was *Minerva*. Passy had become familiar with the journal a couple years before, he explained, when it was still a legal import, and he kept up a purely scholarly interest. Otherwise Batka and Passy spoke only of literary matters, and Passy never knew if Batka had received other journals.[54]

The investigation dissipated as authorities turned their attention to the postmaster's dereliction of duty. The governor's aide Martin censured Batka in writing for receiving foreign journals against postal regulations and gave notice that he would lose his position if he committed any further violation. Martin also asked the police ministry in Vienna whether this penalty was sufficient. The police did not respond for a couple weeks, so Martin wrote the emperor directly. The Vienna court stripped Batka of his post that autumn. By then, however, the court was not as concerned with this security breach because it had begun to make final arrangements to release Lafayette's party.[55]

Beyond those active at Neustadt and Schweidnitz, at least one other mediator may have helped the captives correspond. Reinhold Forster lived in the university town of Halle, directly on the road between Prussian Silesia and Hamburg. He was a well-known professor of natural history and mineralogy who had founded the academic discipline of ethnology. He had lived for years in England with his son and colleague Georg. They had served as naturalists on James Cook's second voyage around the world in 1772–75, and both had gained appreciation for Anglo-Saxon freedoms. In 1790 Reinhold Forster wrote a flattering introduction to the translation of a French biography of Lafayette. Bollmann had stayed in Mainz from August to October 1791, where Georg Forster had become university librarian and soon emerged as a leading German supporter of the French Revolution. The two men had grown close because they shared scientific and political interests. "My best company is in Forster's home," Bollmann wrote his father at the time. "I spend every evening in this family, where several clever and interesting people have free access." Reinhold Forster taught at the University of Halle and had personal ties to the Sieveking circle. Bollmann could have easily introduced himself when he stayed in nearby Leipzig, which he had done when he was lobbying the Prussian king to release Lafayette. Bollmann or a Sieveking circle member could have later approached Forster to solicit his help.[56] Lafayette later wrote that Forster did play a role and thanked him not only for writings that helped in "easing our captivity" but also for other undefined "efforts."[57]

The Sauermann incident strongly suggests that these mailings depended on the local complicity of Passy, Batka, and a soldier or officer at the prison in the former Jesuit compound. Passy was the one who oversaw local deliveries and had the surest knowledge of their contents.

At least in the early months of 1797, the secret mail route began in Hamburg-Altona under Masson's or Archenholz's oversight. It may have run through the hands of Forster in Halle before it reached Ducoudray in Schweidnitz. From there Ducoudray's servant Johann took each delivery to the Black Eagle inn in Neustadt. That correspondence came at least twice by postal coach to Olmütz. Passy likely told the Olmütz postmaster that the expected packages were of an illegal German journal needed for professional study, for which he was willing to pay a generous bribe. In turn Passy would have paid a soldier stationed at Lafayette's prison to smuggle the two arriving packages, perhaps in portions, to the Lafayette women. The soldier may well have tied each delivery to the bundle that the women lowered when he was on nighttime courtyard guard. A similar route in reverse brought messages to the outside.

It seems likely that Batka was the one whom Adrienne Lafayette described to Masson in her first, November 1796, letter about the initial version of the new system as the person to whom he should address mail. Passy would be "the friend here" who mapped out the sequence of delivery drops and Ducoudray "the friend of Swed—[Schweidnitz]."[58]

Olmütz authorities kept trying to prevent contacts from abroad, especially those portending a new escape attempt. Their challenge was to know where to look.

One visitor who drew attention was Friedrich Winckelmann, a miniature painter from Hanover who had come to Brünn late in April 1797. He made known that he was headed for west Galicia. Around the beginning of June, he continued to Olmütz, where he stayed at the home of a master mason. The librarian of the lyceum, Nepomuk Hanke von Hankenstein—a scholar of Slavic literature and a colleague of Passy—took notice of the visitor's foreign accent and language, the company he kept, and his general activities. Late in June, Hankenstein wrote the Moravian governor that he deemed it his duty to point the man out as a potential threat. Indeed, he asserted, "I consider him to be an American—a second *Bollmann*, who seems to be hammering out new plots here for the violent or surreptitious escape of Lafayette, and, under the cover of painting, is trying to gain the time necessary to carry out his plan."

Hankenstein offered several reasons for his suspicions. At times Winckelmann claimed to be the son of the famous, deceased Saxon classicist Joachim Winckelmann, whom Hankenstein believed never to have married or had progeny. Indeed the renowned Winckelmann had died at the hands of a homosexual lover. Alternatively Hankenstein heard that the artist claimed to be the classicist's nephew. Friedrich Winckelmann was a skillful painter, to be sure, but his abilities would have found a far richer market in a world-class city. He offered portraits for only two florins, whereas a more appropriate price for work of such virtuosity would be twelve. His general attitude and manner were unusual: "He has more the air of a free American, an English lord, than an artist wanting to seek his fortune in Olmütz. He lacks timidity and modesty." The painter had quickly gotten to know Axter and taken an outing with him to the nearby Slatenitz spa. It was there, Hankenstein had heard, that authorities were considering bringing Lafayette for recuperation. Winckelmann was strikingly well informed about local conditions. He also seemed to avoid persons who might expose him.

Hankenstein invited the governor to burn the letter if he found it unimportant. However, the governor's associate Martin took it quite seriously. He notified Circle Captain Dubsky of Olmütz to investigate quietly. Nothing incriminating emerged over the next few weeks, but on 1 August Martin instructed Dubsky to expel Winckelmann from Olmütz.

The expulsion order took Winckelmann by surprise. He petitioned Dubsky for an eight-day delay in order to receive an expected delivery of art materials from Vienna. He substantiated his story by post-office receipts, but Martin insisted on immediate departure. The next morning, 10 August, Winckelmann was on his way to Krakow.[59]

There is no evidence that Winckelmann intended to contact Lafayette or arrange his escape. However, the case illustrates how authorities still took precautions three years after Lafayette's escape. It is a tribute to Ducoudray's acting ability that he seems not to have come under any suspicion at all.

In the end the communication system worked. It kept the prisoners informed about each other and the outside world. It also produced solid intelligence about their situation for supporters abroad, who put it to good use.

10

NODES IN THE NET

In 1795–96 the ancient Polish kingdom disappeared in the East, while the young French republic rose triumphant in the West. Prussia, Austria, and Russia carried out a third and final partition of Poland. Stanislas II abdicated and became a Russian state pensioner. When Tsar Paul I succeeded his mother, Catherine, late in 1796, he released Kościuszko from the Peter and Paul Fortress in St. Petersburg for an exile in America and western Europe. Meanwhile France achieved internal stability with the return of more moderate political leaders. A new constitution strengthened the trend, providing for the five-member Executive Directory and two legislative chambers, the Council of Five Hundred and the Council of Elders. France also solidified its international position by making peace with Prussia and establishing outright alliances with Spain and the new Dutch state, the Batavian Republic. The only serious remaining contenders of France were Austria on land and Britain on sea. France annexed Belgium and Germany west of the Rhine. A young general, Napoléon Bonaparte, crushed a royalist revolt against the Directory, which led to his appointment as commander of the French Army of Italy. In the early spring of 1796, he launched an invasion of Italy, many of whose northern states were Austrian possessions. The campaign proved astonishingly successful in bringing Austria to terms. Britain tried to keep Austria fighting by loaning it large sums. While the United States tried its best to remain neutral, France began to seize American ships, alleging that Jay's Treaty with Britain (1794) had broken the French-American alliance of 1778. At the end of 1796, the Directory refused to receive the new American ambassador.

During this time Philadelphia, London, and Hamburg-Altona remained the centers of Lafayette's network of support. Radical Jacobin sentiment was declining in France, so Paris soon joined those centers and grew in importance. The work of the pro-Lafayette circles in these cities provoked little diplomatic action, but it did inspire widespread publicity.

If one could speak of a Lafayette circle in Philadelphia, it was diffuse. Philadelphia was then the young American republic's capital and largest city. The broader public gave Lafayette a lot of credit for the nation's birth, and traders and visitors in Europe showed interest in his release. Lafayette's U.S. acquaintances and former comrades in arms tried to aid him by using quiet persuasion, sending money, and keeping in contact.

President Washington was working to protect the country from entanglement in European wars. As a result he avoided public appeals while encouraging private efforts. French veterans of the American war called for more forceful action. They included Duke François de La Rochefoucauld, now a refugee in Philadelphia; Count Mathieu de Dumas, member of the French Council of Elders; and Count Louis de Ségur, Lafayette's uncle by marriage. Washington told Ségur how he looked ardently toward his protégé's release: "Everything in my power, as a private man (and in a public character I could not commit myself, or rather the government entrusted to me) has been essayed to effect his enlargement." He expressed hope that the efforts of others would soon have more effect.[1]

Some Lafayette supporters still wanted Washington to take official action. Among them were Lafayette's would-be rescuer Bollmann and Lafayette's own son. Bollmann and Huger had traveled leisurely for several weeks after their expulsion. They passed along the length of Prussian Silesia and arrived at Saxon Dresden. There, on 1 August 1795, Bollmann wrote Angelica Church a description of the escape and custody, which the Churches then published in London. Bollmann and Huger turned north through Leipzig, where Bollmann sent a similar missive to his aunt.[2] They continued through Dessau, Braunschweig, and Hanover to Bollmann's hometown of Hoya; then they went to Hamburg to sail for England. Everywhere sympathizers praised them for their daring action. Yet it was hard to see it as a real victory parade, since the ultimate prize was missing: Lafayette's liberty.[3]

Bollmann had two overlapping goals. In Hamburg he expected to harvest one of the first fruits of his heroism by engaging Christine Reimarus in marriage. Thereafter he would pursue a career in America. He could build on his new fame and draw on Lafayette's own plea that he arrange a public American approach to Vienna.[4]

The first goal slipped from his grasp. When he arrived in Hamburg at the beginning of September, he found Christine's family solidly opposed to the marriage. As established merchants, they were not impressed with his claims of extraordinary opportunities in America. Christine gave in to her parents but insisted on saying goodbye to Bollmann in person.[5]

The second goal remained in sight for some time. However, members of the Lally-Hénin circle were furious at Bollmann's report. They blamed the escape's failure not only on his inadequacies and mistakes as an agent but also on their having been excluded from the project. They believed that their knowledge and experience could have made all the difference. Eventually even the Olmütz captives got wind of the split between the two key groups of supporters in England.[6] But Lafayette continued to set his hopes on Bollmann, expecting for months that the rescue agent would not only reach America but would return to Europe with diplomatic credentials. Lafayette wrote a secret message to Hamburg in November 1795, supporting Bollmann's involvement in Philadelphia's negotiations with Vienna.[7]

In London, Bollmann prepared for his transatlantic trip, hoping that it would bring him fortune. He left as his European forwarding address the banking firm Boyd, Benfield and Company, where his friend Friedrich Heisch worked. He had used the same address when he wrote the London circle from Moravia.[8] Angelica Church gave Bollmann a letter for her sister Elizabeth Hamilton, along with an introduction to brother-in-law, Alexander Hamilton.[9] Thomas Pinckney was still in Madrid, but Cadignan released one hundred pounds to Bollmann from funds Pinckney had provided in August.[10]

On 24 October, the eve of his departure, Bollmann wrote a final letter to his aunt. He said he hoped to meet "the most distinguished persons," to learn much, and to further his career with help from his new reputation and the Churches' recommendations, in "a beautiful, promising land that unites great advantages; that has no prejudices to fight against, no defective institutions." He was confident that "the force of circumstances will soon free Lafayette," circumstances in which Bollmann planned to play a part.[11]

Bollmann and Huger landed in New York City on 1 January 1796.[12] They made their way to Hamilton's home and law office at 28 Broadway. Hamilton welcomed the travelers and gave the aid that Angelica Church had requested.[13] His recommendations opened many doors into the homes and offices of Philadelphia's leading citizens.[14] Washington received the agents for dinner, heard details of the escape, and expressed disappointment at its failure.[15]

Huger gave up on efforts to free Lafayette and returned to medical studies. However, Bollmann kept promoting diplomatic initiatives in conversations with the president. Washington was skeptical. By the second week of February, he said that Bollmann could continue the talks through Secretary of State Timothy Pickering. Weeks passed without an appointment.[16] The president was tiring of his importunate, freeloading visitor. By May, Washington was saying that he feared Bollmann "will be found a troublesome guest among us." He gathered "that the Doctor is without funds," noting that "no mention . . . has come to my knowledge of his going away."[17]

In the meantime a man with greater influence than Bollmann had arrived: the president's namesake, Lafayette's son. The landing of George Washington Lafayette and his tutor, Félix Frestel, in Boston in late August 1795 took the president by surprise. Young George Lafayette wrote the president to say that "I will owe this yet to you: to see also my father happy and free." The teenager was seeking asylum, having just escaped Jacobin France under the name "Motier." However, Washington took him to be primarily the envoy of a Fayettist lobby and feared the teenager's arrival could upset French resident minister Pierre Adet, perhaps leading to a deeper rift with France. On the other hand, Washington felt a greater connection than ever with the captive and pledged "to become a friend and father" to his son.[18]

After a few weeks' silence from the president and intense interest from Bostonians, George Lafayette and Frestel traveled to New York City, where they met Hamilton and then sought out a private refuge between Hackensack and Ramapo, New Jersey.[19] Both Washington and Hamilton were inclined to bring the Frenchmen to Philadelphia, but their New York colleagues warned of political consequences. Washington agreed to keep his patronage secret. In a first letter to young Lafayette, he offered personal and financial support but asked him to remain incognito. Hamilton would keep the president informed.[20]

At winter's end Washington could no longer stand to keep the young man away. Secretary of War James McHenry, a former Lafayette aide, warned the president that Adrienne Lafayette had surely sent her son as the person "best fitted to act impressively on your feelings, and thereby remove any political obstacle to a diplomatic application." All the same Washington invited George and his tutor to visit his Philadelphia home. His sense of urgency increased when political opponent Edward Livingston initiated a House resolution "to inquire whether the son of Major General Lafayette be within the United States, and also whether any, and what, provision may be necessary for his support." The Frenchmen arrived in Philadelphia the second week of April.[21]

Washington quickly determined that young Lafayette was indeed a refugee, not just a lobbyist. Still the young man did lobby, encouraged by Bollmann and others, with the persistence and persuasive power that McHenry had feared. Washington soon wrote Pinckney, "The visible distress of the Son, who is now with me, grieving for the unhappy fate of his parents . . . [is] giving a poignancy to my own feelings."[22]

The president reviewed his options. He had already asked Pinckney to make known his unofficial concern for Lafayette to the imperial resident in London.[23] He proceeded to ask Pickering that he have Bollmann draw up a memorandum on strategy.[24] Bollmann wrote his plan over the weekend of 9–10 April. He suggested that the United States send a secret envoy to Prince Henry of Prussia and Danish foreign minister Count Andreas von Bernstorff, to solicit their governments' intervention with Vienna for Lafayette. Even if they failed, Bollmann reasoned, the attempt would bring honor to America, raise Lafayette's public profile in Europe, and assure him he was not forgotten. Bollmann wrote a job description for the agent that fit himself perfectly. The agent should be familiar with the principle actors, the language, and the territory. He admitted to Hamilton that "it was impossible not to have myself in view."[25]

But Bollmann failed to convince the president that the plan complied with America's neutrality policy. Also, "while in Public Office," Washington was unwilling to send Bollmann on another secret mission into lands that he had pledged never to re-enter. The president certainly would not provide money to save Bollmann from the possible consequences.[26] Washington hoped that funds for another rescue attempt might come from someone else, but they never appeared. Bollmann gave up and turned to a business career in Philadelphia.[27]

On Hamilton's advice, the president wrote a note in his own hand, "*as a private person,*" to Francis II. He requested that Lafayette "be permitted to come to this country, on such conditions and under such restrictions, as your Majesty may think it expedient to prescribe."[28]

Like Washington's prior letters, the appeal proved fruitless. When the note arrived in London, Ambassador Rufus King was to have passed it on to Starhemberg, his Austrian counterpart. By fall Cadignan had notified the Lafayettes that the emperor ought to have received it. The letter, however, had vanished. In Hamburg, Masson complained that King had not sent the letter by personal courier. Masclet sought a copy from King, to entrust to a dependable messenger. King admitted having a duplicate but refused to hand it over. Apparently he was following the president's instruction not to send the letter if it appeared that the effort would fail.[29]

Washington's final "private" effort on Lafayette's behalf was to commission his new ambassador to Paris, Thomas Pinckney's older brother, Charles Cotesworth Pinckney, with a special plea for aid. He was to state, Washington wrote, "my ardent desire that no favourable occasion might be omitted, by you, of signifying how much it was my wish, and the wishes of the People of this country, that that friend to it, Mr. de la Fayette, could be liberated from his confinement."[30] But again nothing came of it. Angry over Jay's Treaty, the Directory refused to receive Pinckney at all and ordered his expulsion.

Other Americans were also at work. Gouverneur Morris had turned over the post of American minister in France to James Monroe and left Paris on 12 October 1794. Morris had then begun a European tour that eventually took him to London and Vienna. Along the way Lafayette supporters had pushed him to use his influence. These people included Mesdames de Staël and Tessé, whom he visited in Switzerland in fall 1794; John Parish, with whom Morris developed a friendship in Hamburg from December 1794 to spring 1795; Morris's old friends the Churches, whom he saw in and near London in summer and fall 1795; and Masson, who approached Morris at his lodgings in Altona on 20 June 1796 to describe "projects to get [Lafayette] out of prison."[31]

When Madame de Staël heard that Morris was visiting Vienna, she pressed him to exercise influence with the court: "Open for M. de Lafayette the doors of his prison. . . . You have saved his wife from death. Well then, be the savior of the whole family: pay the debt of your country." Morris replied that he shared her concerns but did not have the power she attributed to him. He also did not think that a confrontational approach would work. When supporters accused Lafayette's captors of injustice, he claimed, they only angered them. He emphasized how deeply the Vienna court hated Lafayette; how, though it would not increase his miseries, it could still prevent his release; and how Austria's chief minister Thugut was likely to reject advice on the subject.[32]

In fact Morris put in a good word for Lafayette to both British and Austrian officials. On 12 December 1795, he told British foreign minister Grenville "that it would be a pleasing thing to America if he procured the release of Lafayette." Grenville replied that "the prejudices here are so strong against him." At this, Morris opined that the king would be too reasonable still to be upset over the past (the American war). Once released, Lafayette would feel so obliged to Britain as to avoid acting against its interests. Also the release would undercut the parliamentary opposition. A year later Morris wrote Grenville that Vienna seemed willing to release the captive if London requested it. It would bring Britain much good will in America and France, Morris wrote, and it might even engage Lafayette as an ally to Britain.[33]

In Vienna, Morris suggested that Lafayette's release would be politically prudent. At an elite gathering where Thugut was present, the hostess addressed the subject. Morris commented "that it is a piece of folly keeping [Lafayette] prisoner." Morris was shocked at the furious reaction. It underlined difficulties of convincing the court and brought him, despite his own political conservatism, momentarily to see Europe's old regimes through the eyes of revolutionaries.[34] Morris brought up Lafayette's detention to Sir Morton Eden, British minister in Vienna and younger brother of Lord Auckland, but Eden replied "that there is not much likelihood that he will be liberated."[35]

As he prepared to leave the city, Morris received a letter from Madame de Montagu, asking that he intervene on the captives' behalf. He made an appointment with Thugut for the morning of 18 December, under the pretense of a diplomatic talk upon departure, and showed him the letter. Thugut expressed regret that the Austrians had ever "had anything to do" with Lafayette and denied that they had mistreated him. He declared that Adrienne Lafayette could leave prison at any time but then not return, while Lafayette's release would have to await a general peace; that is, unless Britain was willing to take him earlier, in which case "they may, if they please, turn him loose in London."[36]

The talk aroused new suspicions about the reason Morris had come to Vienna. He had claimed to an inquiring baron that he was there merely for his own edification, but now it appeared to local observers that he had come specifically to seek Lafayette's release. The talk certainly showed Morris's concern for the prisoner. He wrote to Adrienne Lafayette care of Thugut, repeating Thugut's assurances that conditions were as lenient as possible within security requirements and that release would come in time. Morris asked her to point out instances of ill treatment. He also asked Thugut to allow a note for Lafayette, or, better yet, to release him out of political prudence and Christian forgiveness. At the same time, Morris wrote Grenville, reporting Thugut's words and encouraging Britain to grant Lafayette asylum.[37]

On the same day that Morris wrote Grenville, another dignitary temporarily in Vienna did so as well: British diplomat James Harris, Baron Malmesbury. He too had just spoken with Thugut for release, and he had used arguments similar to Morris's.' It is likely that Morris had engaged Malmesbury to help him move the Austrian and British foreign ministers.[38]

Under Masson's coordination, U.S. merchants on the north European coast solicited their envoys in Hamburg-Altona (John Parish), Copenhagen (Hans Saabye), and The Hague (John Quincy Adams) to engage the Danish court in pushing Vienna to release the prisoners.[39] The Lafayettes strongly supported the idea of American diplomatic pressure on Vienna, either via Paris or by means of a special envoy, and they were delighted with the petitions. They thanked Masson, encouraged the translation and publication of the petitions, and asked for copies.[40]

In Paris a group of U.S. merchants hosted a sumptuous Fourth of July 1796 celebration at the Hôtel de Maillebois in Faubourg Saint Germain. They seated some two hundred male guests, including French officials and generals, U.S. resident minister James Monroe, and Consul General Fulwar Skipwith, at a huge horseshoe-shaped table in the garden. They left one chair empty. A card lay on the place setting, reserving the seat for "General La Fayette, Commander of American Light Infantry." The merchants likely did this with connivance of Monroe and Skipwith, who could not openly sponsor it. Paris papers reported on the event, and August Hennings, publisher of the Danish Altona journal *Genius der Zeit,* spread the news to Germany.[41]

In early 1797 René Pillet of Hamburg, an American citizen, asked John Quincy Adams that he press London to mediate with Vienna. Adams took the occasion to write his father, U.S. president-elect John Adams, about how Pinckney and he had received many such appeals. The president's son sympathized with Lafayette, but he had not addressed other governments for two reasons: he had never received clearance from Philadelphia, and he doubted that the action would bring results.[42]

Concern for Lafayette eventually found its way into the U.S. House of Representatives. On 3 March 1797, Robert Harper, a South Carolinian Federalist and veteran of the War of Independence, made a motion encouraging the new president,

John Adams, to take "any measures which he may deem expedient" to bring about Lafayette's release. Edward Livingston suggested that Congress might appropriate funds to the cause. Thomas Hartley, another veteran, noted that "if any of the soldiers of 1781 were here. . . , there would not be a dissenting voice to using every exertion." Supporters demanded immediate action, and were confident that the new president would take a safe, effective approach. The attempt would silence rebukes that the nation had failed in its duty to Lafayette. But several men spoke against the motion. They argued that it did not belong in Congress because it involved only an individual. They also felt that any action would involve dangerous and ineffective negotiation with Vienna, that it should be a matter of presidential discretion, and that it could damage American ties with France. Finally the motion went down to defeat, as did a second, similar motion by Livingston. Perhaps, as the session report had it, the late hour was the chief reason for failure, given that "all were agreed as to the merits and the misfortunes of the man."[43]

The fact remained that the United States had little influence and was vigilant to avoid war. Adams's new administration followed Washington's neutrality policy. As a result, U.S. officials continued to offer covert aid to Lafayette but avoided public overtures.[44] In London former Lafayette aide Cadignan distributed money that he and another aide, Boinville, received from Thomas Pinckney.[45] In Hamburg, Masson received substantial payments "on account of M. La Fayette." They included 3,225.14 Dutch guilders (equivalent to $1,290.28 at the time) from Pinckney via Cadignan and Boinville; and £650 ($2,888.89) from Monroe, the U.S. envoy in Paris.[46] Monroe was also able to send directly to Maubourg a total of 3,600 livres ($653.40) in January and March 1797 to improve Lafayette's food and clothing.[47]

The public reticence of U.S. officials frustrated some Fayettists. Philippe Charles d'Agrain chided America, particularly Congress, for its "cowardly silence,"[48] though he applauded Washington's private efforts and Dumas's demonstration on Lafayette's behalf at a Fourth of July celebration.[49]

London's Fayettist leadership shifted with time. Princess Hénin and Count Lally kept mediating information and political influence.[50] The Church family's involvement faded, then ended altogether when they returned to the United States in spring 1797.[51] Former Lafayette aides Cadignan and Boinville took over administering communications and coordinating activities on the prisoners' behalf. Pillet joined them after returning from America at the beginning of 1796. In the eyes of the captives, these men composed "a very dear triumvirate," the "excellent triumvirate" in London.[52] Perhaps most important of all, the London-based partisans publicized Lafayette's cause. The story of his imprisonment appeared in journal articles, parliamentary debates, and debating societies.[53]

Joseph Masclet emerged as chief writer for Lafayette's cause in Britain. He used the pseudonym *Eleuthère* (freeman) to avoid prosecution under the Alien Law.

Masclet had fled the French Army of the Rhine when Jacobin enemies came to power after the coup of 10 August 1792. He had gone first to Switzerland and then to Britain, where he had acquired lasting political and financial security by marrying a wealthy English widow of Swiss parentage. Lafayette's plight came to his attention at the weekly Saturday meeting of a London-area democratic discussion group in early summer 1793. Masclet promptly wrote to the *Morning Chronicle,* the leading Whig paper. He followed up with many similar letters, often in response to such Tory papers as the *Times* and The *True Briton.*[54] In the summer of 1796, he sent examples of his published letters to George Lafayette and Congressman Livingston in Philadelphia, with news of prospects for more parliamentary debate. He sent similar materials to Masson in Hamburg for the Lafayettes. He kept in contact with other Fayettists on the Continent, including Pillet, who traveled among London, Hamburg, Holland, and Paris.[55]

Charles Fox rose in the House of Commons on 10 May 1796, to criticize the British ministry. It had failed, he said, to engage French Constitutionals by demanding Lafayette's release. It could have required the Prussian king to surrender him in return for the vast subsidies with which Britain had underwritten the Prussian war effort against France, but instead the ministry had allowed his transfer to Austria, there to be "kept in the same scandalous and inhuman bondage." Fox emphasized the brave suffering of Lafayette's wife; how after release from Jacobin prisons, she "flew, on the wings of duty and affection, to Vienna, to solicit the Emperor" and ended up sharing "all the horrors of his captivity." At this point the reporter of the speech wrote that "a burst of indignation and sorrow broke from every part of the House." Fox continued: "This, however, had no terrors for her affectionate heart; she plunged into his dungeon, and there they remain together, the living, and yet buried, victims of this inhuman power." However, Prime Minister Pitt responded that the British government had no part in Lafayette's treatment, nor was it "warranted in interfering with the allies upon the subject." In the end only 42 out of 216 supported Fox's motion to change British policy.[56]

News of the debate spread quickly. Pillet lauded the Foxite position in an open letter to the *Morning Chronicle* and other London papers. Archenholz quoted and praised the debate in his Hamburg journal *Minerva.*[57] The prisoners thanked Masson and Archenholz for their anonymous commentaries in journals of Hamburg, London, and Paris and asked for more publicity to "torment our jailors, of whatever kind, by all imaginable means." They claimed that it had contributed recently to better prison treatment.[58] Adrienne Lafayette acknowledged that Foxites could not get London to pressure Vienna, but they might get Paris to do so.[59]

Partisans prepared for a whole new battle. Masclet met with Foxite Richard Fitzpatrick about strategy. Granville Sharp asked Tory member of Parliament and fellow abolitionist William Wilberforce to intervene with his friend Pitt. Boinville gave Fox letters from the captives, and Masclet told him of prison conditions.

Masclet also claimed that bringing the case before Parliament might fail again to move Pitt, but it would exercise a positive influence on public opinion and authorities in Paris. The captives agreed and sent language that Foxites could use.[60]

Partisans tried but failed to get American traders in London to make a public appeal. The new U.S. ambassador, Rufus King, had known Lafayette in the war but was now bound to neutrality. Masclet found him immovable. Masclet brought U.S. merchants a template for their address, but they made various excuses. They finally cited their chargé d'affaires, William Deas, who had advised them to clear any address with King. Masclet called the traders "Dutchmen of the New World" who "carry their souls in their bags of dollars." As far as he was concerned, they could "go to the devil," and he wrote a scathing note to the *Morning Chronicle*.[61]

On 7 December, the British ministry praised the Austrian emperor for his courageous stand against revolutionary France. Fox remarked that "his Imperial Majesty by no means possessed all the concomitants of valour or heroism while he lay under the foul disgrace of still keeping M. de La Fayette in cruel captivity." Fitzpatrick announced that he would soon address the subject.[62]

The prospect infuriated Edmund Burke, who had retired from the House. "A fine business this of La Fayette," he wrote a friendly member of Parliament. "Good God—among all the imprisonments[,] confiscations, murders and exiles to find no one object for a British House of Commons to take up but Citizen de la Fayette." To another acquaintance, he pointed out "the innumerable victims of La Fayette[']s rebellion, of which this Country is full and who are scattered all over Europe," and he asked why Fox did not call for aiding them. To a third correspondent, Burke complained that Fox's remarks concerning "this poor puppy de La Fayette" were "indecent, unparliamentary, unpolitick."[63] Lord Chancellor Loughborough agreed, telling Burke "that this Fayettism ought to be driven out of the House with indignation and scorn."[64]

Lafayette's friends prepared for Fitzpatrick's address. When Fitzpatrick's earlier motion failed in March 1794, publicist William Miles had produced a pamphlet refuting his opponents' positions. Miles was now working on another pamphlet justifying Lafayette in the Revolution, and he lent Fitzpatrick the manuscript. He also asked member of Parliament Thomas Erskine to give Fox a copy and to support Fitzpatrick. Miles provided Richard Sheridan with his *Morning Chronicle* articles and details of the captives' situation. Miles suggested emphasizing the Lafayette women's heroic devotion, to put "the hypocrite vizier" Pitt on the defensive. Masclet sent Masson the Whig *Morning Post*'s announcement of the debate, asked for French and German translation and publication, and offered information and support to Foxites likely to participate. On the morning of debate, to "prepare the spirits," he published a pro-Lafayette article by Pillet in the *Morning Chronicle*. He also helped Fitzpatrick reply to a recent article in *L'Éclair*, which disputed claims of inhumane treatment.[65]

Fitzpatrick's address on 16 December 1796 reiterated his 1794 motion that George III request the captives' release. Fitzpatrick's key change was to update the jailer, replacing "king of Prussia" and "Berlin" with "emperor of Germany" and "Vienna."[66]

Pitt and war minister William Windham stood by their opposing views. The former questioned the accuracy of Fitzpatrick's description and insisted again that Britain's monarch had no part in the imprisonment or authority to interfere. He asked how the British would feel if another country objected to their immoral yet still legal slave traffic.[67] Windham claimed that the emperor had solid political reasons for holding Lafayette. His words recalled the Luxembourg tribunal: "It was well known that there were persons, both in France and out of it, who . . . might be able to cabal with him, to raise a new standard, and to bring about new revolutions in France and elsewhere." Windham also wondered why Lafayette should be an object of sympathy when he had spurred the revolution bringing ruin on Europe. The war minister claimed that "he would not be sorry—indeed he should rejoice,—to see such men drink deep of the cup of calamity which they had prepared for the lips of others." It was a most vengeful conclusion.

Fox maintained that Fitzpatrick's account was true, that there were exceptions to the principle that one state should not interfere in another, and that a freed Lafayette would threaten the Jacobins' republic. Surely, he said, Windham was not now an ally of that cruel regime. He added cuttingly, "If [Lafayette] was not to be pardoned because thousands had fallen by his means, what must become of the right hon. gentleman himself, and of the minister of England [Pitt], who had caused rivers of blood to flow by their wild and horrid enterprises?"[68]

Like Fitzpatrick's earlier motion, this one went down to lopsided defeat, 132 to 50. Pitt sent the king a report that evening from Downing Street, and George III replied from Windsor Castle how happy he was with the results: "Besides the very objectionable conduct of that gentleman [Lafayette] towards this country, which would be reason enough for not appearing in his favour, I cannot see any right this or any country has to meddle with the Executive Administration of any foreign one."[69]

The government had good reason to be satisfied. The day after the debate, the *Sun* spread Windham's rebuttal over four columns. The *True Briton* attacked Lafayette in an open letter to Fitzpatrick. Burke praised Windham, who expressed surprise at his speech's impact.[70]

Masclet found the coverage dismaying. He joined other Lafayette partisans to collect debate transcripts, publicize them, and rebut Tory claims. He wrote a sarcastic letter to Pitt and colleagues for the *Morning Chronicle,* thanking them for provoking French opinion in Lafayette's favor. Masclet sent Masson several articles to publish in Germany. He encouraged Pillet to publish others in France, while Lally sent translations to Paris. Masclet finished another pamphlet defending

Lafayette, and disseminated copies to Lally, leading Foxites, London reviewers, the *Morning Chronicle,* and Masson in Hamburg.[71]

Another, more radical forum was that of the popular London debating societies. Their constituency came largely from the working classes and sought wider suffrage. The British administration associated them with the Jacobin Club of Paris. They faced official pressure under a royal edict and parliamentary laws directed against treasonous activities and seditious meetings. Two such societies, the London and Westminster Forums, were active at the time of Parliament's autumn 1796 debate on Lafayette's incarceration. In a lower-class echo of the ruling-class debate, both forums argued over Lafayette's imprisonment.[72]

Until well into 1797, Hamburg and Altona remained the Continental hub of Fayettist activities. These twin cities formed Germany's center of journalism and international trade.[73] They were the home to publisher Archenholz, the Sieveking-Reimarus circle, and John Parish, the only U.S. envoy stationed in German-speaking Europe.

Lafayette's former aide, André Masson, also lived here. After his release from captivity in Belgium, he had established himself in Hamburg trade. In April 1796 he registered his merchant banking firm, "Andrew Masson & Comp.," with the city's Commercial Bureau (Kämmerei). His home served as his business address: Catharinenstrasse 86, just off the plaza surrounding St. Catherine's Church, a short distance from the harbor by foot or canal boat.[74] He discussed aid to Lafayette with Archenholz and Charles de Talleyrand. Masson corresponded about it with Masclet and Lally in London, Pillet in Paris, Julienne de Bureaux-Pusy in Basel,[75] Mesdames de Tessé and Montagu at their Wittmold estate, and August Hennings in Plön.[76] Masson was also able to maintain secret communications with Lafayette himself.[77]

Publicity was a chief weapon in the Hamburg-Altona campaign. Archenholz's articles in *Minerva* kept the captives' fates in the public eye. Besides defending Lafayette, Archenholz reported such events as toasts to the prisoner at a local American Fourth of July celebration in 1793.[78] Hennings praised Lafayette in his Altona journal, *Genius der Zeit.* An article in January 1796 defended him; another in August lamented his family's incarceration.[79] In spring 1796 Masson and others collected a wide selection of Lafayette's letters and other writings, including "four small notebooks" from Olmütz, to publish in Britain. They soon expanded this to include a second collection, published in Holland.[80]

Supporters disguised the origins of prison reports. That summer Masson received an enclosure from Adrienne Lafayette, with instructions to make copies and burn the original with its distinctive handwriting. Masson had it translated into English, sent it to Masclet in London, where it was published in the *Morning Chronicle* as a letter by an Englishman traveling on the Continent, and then sent to Pillet in Paris. In the meantime Masson sent Pillet a copy in the original French.

With the English version in hand, Pillet could publish the French version in Paris, claiming it to be a translation of already published material. Finally Masson could send the English version to Hennings ("Hennel"), to translate and cite for Germans in *Genius der Zeit*.[81]

Accomplices also targeted their publicity elsewhere. The Lafayettes directed Masson to send articles throughout the United States and slip them into Vienna.[82] They proposed that he convince bankers in Hamburg, Holland, and London to write Vienna colleagues and complain that the detention was bad for business.[83]

In fall 1796 Madame de Staël sounded out a Hamburg contact about possible help from Sweden, her husband's employer. She asked Jonas von Hess, a well-connected Swedish author, for any information and help he could find for the Lafayettes. However, she soon admitted to another Hamburg contact that she could do "very little" for Lafayette.[84]

The Lafayettes hoped that the Hamburg partisans could convince the Danish court to send an envoy or commission to Vienna on their behalf. Those in or near Hamburg who might have influence on Copenhagen were Archenholz, Tessé, and Klopstock, the last of whom held Danish court rank. These hopes seemed dashed by autumn 1796.[85]

The death of Tsarina Catherine II on 17 November 1796 inspired Hamburg-Altona partisans to lobby the new Russian regime. Her idealistic son and successor, Paul I, released many of the Poles arrested during the insurrection of 1794, including Kościuszko. When Masson and Pillet heard of this magnanimous act, they asked Kościuszko to ask Paul for help in getting Lafayette released. Other Hamburg Fayettists wrote Ludwig von Nicolay, writer and official at the imperial court in St. Petersburg, to the same end.[86]

Masson sought relevant articles from both London and Paris for translation and publication in *Genius der Zeit*. In December 1796 he invited August Hennings to cooperate more closely. Masson explained how he had agreed with Archenholz to send Hennings British and French publications, such as two enclosed *Morning Chronicle* articles and how he would pay postal costs for Hennings's correspondence on the subject.[87] At Masson's urging Pillet visited Hennings and his wife in Plön. Masson then commissioned Pillet to write the Danish official about current French journals that favored Lafayette's cause. Pillet enclosed a pro-Lafayette excerpt from the Parisian *Nouvelles politiques* and asked Hennings to use it in his paper. Masson sent Hennings an excerpt of parliamentary debates and a translated note he thought appropriate for Hennings's journal *Genius*.[88] Hennings printed some of the material and added his own articles.[89]

During this time the Lafayette circle in Paris was also coming back to life. It included both civilians and soldiers of considerable influence. Pro-Lafayette voices tried to convince the National Convention to demand the captives' release in exchange for important Austrians in French hands. However, they were unable to overcome opponents led by deputy Emmanuel Sieyès. Then, in September 1795, a bicameral legislature succeeded the Convention. Moderate pro-Lafayette deputies peppered both the lower house (the Council of Five Hundred) and the upper house (the Council of Elders) with calls for release. The deputies persevered against still strong Jacobin sentiment.[90] Many formed a caucus known as the Club de Clichy, which met at the elegant home of Jean Gibert-Desmolières, on the rue de Clichy near the Tivoli Gardens. While still in Swiss exile, Mathieu Dumas had joined others to offer Britain an alliance with French moderates in exchange for Lafayette's release. Now he took the leading role in the Club de Clichy on Lafayette's behalf.[91]

Prorelease sentiment appeared among high officials. In the five-member Directory heading the executive branch, politically moderate Lazare Carnot had known Pusy in engineering school and remained close to Dumas and Pusy's wife, Julienne. François Barthélemy, ambassador in Switzerland and soon a director, felt that the captives' release would be the best assurance that Austria was serious about peace.[92] Charles de Talleyrand had been in exile for four years. During that time, he had developed ties with Angelica Church in London, U.S. officials in Philadelphia, and Hamburg's Voght and Masson. On the evening of 1 September 1796, Masson accompanied Talleyrand to Hamburg's harbor for his departure to Holland and Paris. Masson encouraged Talleyrand to help Lafayette's cause, and Talleyrand agreed.[93] By the following summer, Talleyrand was the French minister of foreign relations.

Other well-connected Fayettists in, or tied closely to, Paris lobbied for the cause. The prisoners' relatives included Maubourg's wife, Henriette, and sister Marie de Maisonneuve; Pusy's wife, Julienne; Lafayette's uncle by marriage and longtime friend, Ségur; Adrienne Lafayette's brother-in-law Grammont and cousin by marriage, Princess Poix.[94] Lafayette's friends included Countess Simiane, former commander of the Army of the Center Pierre de Montesquiou-Fézensac, and finance official Philippe Beauchet. Other supporters included friends and aides of Germaine de Staël, including Frédéric Gouvernet, Mathieu Montmorency, and journal editors Jean Lacretelle, Pierre Roederer, and Pierre du Pont de Nemours. Most effective of all was De Staël herself, a woman of great wealth, daunting intellect, supreme social and persuasive powers, iron persistence, and extensive experience in rescue. She had been banned from France in October 1795, but she kept exercising influence from her Swiss château at Coppet. She returned to the Paris area in early 1797. Fayettists often met in two salons: those of Princess Poix at the Hôtel Beauvau on the rue du Faubourg St. Honoré, and of Madame de Staël in the old Swedish embassy, Hôtel de Suède on the rue du Bac.

Beyond pro-Lafayette civilians, several army generals showed sympathy to the cause. They included Jean Moreau, from 1795 commander of the Army of the Rhine-and-Moselle; Louis Lazare Hoche, from early 1797 commander of the Army of the Sambre-and-Meuse; François Lefebvre, Hoche's adjutant; Pierre du Pont de l'Étang, director of military correspondence between Paris and the Army of Italy; and Michel de Regnauld, the Army of Italy's hospital administrator.

Most important was the young Corsican Napoleone Buonaparte, who had been named to command the Army of Italy in February 1796 and soon gallicized his name to "Napoléon Bonaparte." His aides and colleagues also proved critical, including Alexandre Berthier, his chief of staff; and Henri Clarke, who served alongside Bonaparte as French plenipotentiary in peace negotiations of 1797.[95]

French partisans publicized Lafayette's cause. An apocryphal letter from Washington to Lafayette appeared in Paris as a pamphlet in 1796.[96] That summer Pillet collected Lafayette's correspondence for publication.[97] Prominent Parisian publicists began to speak and write more openly for Lafayette's release. They included Jean Charles de Lacretelle, editor of *Nouvelles politiques;* Pierre Roederer, editor of *Journal de Paris* and writer for the *Journal d'économie publique;* Pierre Denis-Lagarde, editor of *Journal de Perlet;* Pierre du Pont de Nemours, editor of *L'Historien* and a deputy; and Jean Suard, editor of *Gazette de France* and *L'Éclair.*[98]

With the emergence of a freer press in France,[99] public opinion there began to swing in Lafayette's favor. Masson observed this from Hamburg in August 1796, and John Quincy Adams from Holland in February 1797. Soon Hennings did so from Danish Holstein and Jacques Mallet du Pan from Switzerland.[100]

In 1796 American Fourth of July celebrations in Paris displayed support for Lafayette and enjoyed wide publicity. Pierre Roederer and Olivier Corancez of the *Journal de Paris* faced criticism for not reporting them. They had believed a public declaration of sympathy for Lafayette impossible, given the still valid French warrant for Lafayette's arrest, but they noted that apparently enough time had passed to put his flight in perspective. Lafayette's incarceration proved that he had never plotted with the Coalition, they wrote: "Now there is no longer anyone of loyalty and honesty who does not recognize him to be an upright friend of liberty and his country."

Such publications reached far beyond France and the French-reading elite. Masson emphasized how important it was for Paris papers to offer detailed coverage, so that journals in Hamburg could translate, cite, and discuss those reports with less risk of censorship.[101]

Lafayette circles cooperated in international debate over prison conditions in the fall of 1796. Masson recast a letter from prisoner Maubourg, describing harsh treatment of Lafayette and company, as an alleged report by an Austrian officer recently stationed at Olmütz to his brother. Masson sent the letter to Masclet in London, who gave Fox a copy in English and published the text in the *Morning Chronicle*. This spurred a private retort by a government minister and a public one by the *True Briton*. Masclet responded in the *Morning Chronicle* and the *Morning Post* with new insistence that Austria was abusing its captives.[102]

The text then reappeared on the Continent. *L'Éclair* described the grim picture given by the "Austrian officer." The report appeared soon as a pamphlet. Jacques Mallet, imperial agent in Bern, complained to *L'Éclair*'s editor that the alleged officer's letter was a fraud to arouse public opinion. He argued that the affair would only fan jailers' fury and delay release and that Lafayette's custodians treated him and his family better than the French jailors of "the holy Revolution" treated people in their "prisons of freedom." Mallet did not know why the emperor was holding Lafayette, but he trusted that the reason would come out in time.[103]

Lafayette sympathizers in England were appalled. They took up their cause with new insistence. The uproar took Mallet's son Jean by surprise when he arrived in London at the beginning of December. On 12 December, Baron Pierre de Malouet took Jean Mallet to visit Princess Hénin in Richmond, at her request. After a half hour of silently enduring "all the fire of her vivacity," the young Mallet expressed surprise at the note and pointed out that his father had "often spoken at the Vienna court in favor of Lafayette and his companions." Hénin accepted this statement, but she lamented seeing "the cry of public opinion on behalf of these unfortunate men [being] suddenly suffocated." She described Adrienne Lafayette's sufferings, showed young Mallet her letters, and convinced him to write his father. Young Mallet was embarrassed and concerned that "all Mme d'Hénin's society" had taken the *Éclair* letter to be an attack on Lafayette; also that it would prevent public opinion from forcing ameliorations in his prison. Malouet and Prince Poix, Madame Lafayette's cousin, admonished the elder Mallet.[104] Masclet and Hénin alerted Fitzpatrick to the *Éclair* letter and asked him to refute it. On the House floor, Fitzpatrick treated the elder Mallet as Lafayette's enemy, angering Mallet the younger, who asked Hénin to set Fitzpatrick straight. Soon Charles Saladin, a Genevan émigré with British aristocratic ties, told Fitzpatrick that, having long known Jacques Mallet, he could not believe that he had justified Lafayette's harsh custody.[105]

On the Continent, Lacretelle and Perlet—writing in *Nouvelles politiques* and *Journal de Perlet,* respectively—criticized Mallet's position. Mallet replied that readers had completely misunderstood him, that he had always criticized the imprisonment and supported release. Lacretelle declared that while this was all to the good, Lafayette's enemies had benefited from the report of mild prison conditions. An example, he reported, was how War Minister Windham cited it in Commons.[106]

The debate persisted into the new year. Adrienne Lafayette wrote of "the project of the Vienna court to diminish interest for the prisoners by maintaining they are quite well off here." Maubourg tried to refute the *Éclair* article by painting inmates' health and treatment in alarming terms. He encouraged supporters to make use of his open correspondence even at the risk that Vienna might end it. An anonymous note appeared in the *Times* on 4 February 1797, claiming that Austria was treating the captives well and that the harshest treatment was justified in light of Lafayette's role in the Revolution. Emphatic rebuttals appeared in the *Morning Chronicle*. Poix emphasized the severity of Adrienne Lafayette's suffering. Masclet attacked the note in the *Times* as "a work of our nasty [French émigré] aristocrats." He cleared his letter to the editor with Fitzpatrick and timed its publication for Parliament's opening on 14 February. He also sent copies to Masson in Hamburg and Pillet in Paris.[107]

The debate entered the German-language press at Hamburg-Altona. *Frankreich* translated Lacretelle's letter to *L'Éclair*. In *Minerva*, Archenholz alerted readers to the *Morning Chronicle* translation of the "Austrian officer's" letter, declaring it too sensitive to publish in German. At the same time, he protested Lafayette's cruel treatment, his companions' long, "Inquisitional" incarceration, and the Lafayette women's sad existence "in an unhealthy dungeon . . . ; a true grave." He confided to his friend, writer Johann Gleim, that "what is behind this is no secret: it is the lowest form of revenge." Gleim replied that there must be good, if still secret, reasons for holding the captives, but Archenholz told him flatly he was "in error." Besides, he remarked, "What then did the servants of these men do, who are also being treated cannibalistically in Olmütz?"[108] In *Genius der Zeit*, Hennings published the entire letter of the "Austrian officer" in German, along with a corroborating letter by "a friend to distressed patriots," Masclet. Hennings alleged both to be translations from the *Morning Chronicle*. Later he published Mallet's letter to *L'Éclair* and rebuttals, including his own.[109]

Francis II and his court were alarmed by the publicity. They sponsored several rebuttals justifying incarceration, which appeared in the late 1796 and early 1797 in such loyalist journals as Vienna's *Magazin der Kunst und Litteratur* and Leipzig's *Eudämonia*. A paid announcement in Jena's *Allgemeine Literatur-Zeitung*, one of the key review journals in Germany, called for Hennings and Archenholz to respond. Hennings refused to dignify them with a response. Archenholz also questioned the loyalist journals' importance.[110]

To refute claims of harsh conditions at Olmütz, Austrian authorities simultaneously launched prison investigations and improved conditions. In January 1797 Schröder removed the latrines and outside sewage channel that had made the prisoners' wing so smelly. The drinking water had been coming from a well that Axter deemed of low quality, so Schröder sought out a better source.[111] Police minister Pergen asked for "precise and trustworthy information" concerning conditions "in the strictest confidentiality." Army authorities instructed city commandant Schröder to have the captives' chambers measured, apparently to substantiate claims of expansive quarters, and to take statements from prison staff. The council ordered that Axter evaluate each captive, including servants and women, and send monthly updates.[112]

The government printed the results in a pamphlet titled *A Reliable Report of the Treatment of Lafayette and His Family in the Prison at Olmütz*, which combined a short commentary by Lorenz Haschka with Schröder's report. The pamphlet was published in Vienna on 8 March 1797 and distributed to German papers at the government's own cost.

Government patronage suited Haschka. A former Jesuit who had once collaborated with Archenholz on journal projects in Saxony, Haschka attacked Lafayette in the loyalist *Magazin der Kunst und Litteratur.* At the behest of acting police minister Saurau, he also produced lyrics in honor of Francis II; set to music by Franz Joseph Haydn, they became Austria's national anthem. Haschka offered to promote the emperor's position once again. It is likely that Pergen had concocted the scheme, given that Vienna paid for Haschka's pamphlet and supplied him with the greater part of it in the form of Schröder's report.

Haschka's pamphlet insisted that conditions were not at all awful. Prison rooms were spacious, dry, light, well ventilated, carefully heated, regularly cleaned, and thoughtfully furnished; food was fresh, abundant, and diverse; clothing and linens were washed and replaced regularly and on demand; captives had daily access to their servants, twice-weekly visits from the staff surgeon, and, in case of illness, constant attendance by servants or responsible garrison soldiers. None of the men had ever really been sick, except for a servant with "a weak chest." Madame Lafayette had suffered a painful arthritic condition but was now "completely healed."[113] One might have thought the inmates to be the emperor's honored guests.

Around the end of May 1797, north German journals received Haschka's pamphlet from the Lower Austrian administration. Jena's *Allgemeine Literatur-Zeitung* and the *Berliner Archiv* printed Haschka's piece in full. Christoph Wieland of Weimar announced in his *Neue Teutsche Merkur* that Haschka's work seemed trustworthy. Privately, however, he admitted that he did not want to appear partisan or incite the emperor's wrath by failing to advertise the pamphlet. He also trusted that Lafayette would correct the record on his release. Archenholz noted in *Minerva* that Haschka's treatise contradicted the accounts of prisoners, officers, and other witnesses. He tried to undermine Haschka's credibility by accusing him of having written antiroyalist poems in the 1780s and by claiming to have these poems in original manuscript form. In Altona's *Annalen der leidenden Menschheit,* Hennings repeated Archenholz's arguments. Maubourg's sister wrote a letter to the newspapers denying the pamphlet's veracity. Masson advised Mesdames Maubourg and Pusy to send Archenholz a refutation and gave Masclet material to use against Haschka in Paris.[114]

In 1797 two lengthy poems appeared, one British, the other French. Both asserted that Lafayette and company suffered harsh conditions. *The Castle of Olmutz* came out anonymously in London as a pamphlet to laud "the captive Knight" whom it described as having been "bound with triple chains, / And triple bars secur'd" after his escape attempt. It also professed confidence that "the hour shall come, nor distant far the day / That makes thee free."[115] The poem offered much sympathy, but little dependable detail.

Captivité de La Fayette, on the other hand, provided many accurate notes about Lafayette's flight, incarceration, escape attempt, and family reunion in prison; it was the first extensive and reliable published account of Lafayette's prison years. The author was Philippe Charles d'Agrain, who had been captured with Lafayette at Rochefort. He had read inmates' letters and interviewed reliable informants, including Bollmann.

To be sure Agrain's poem and its accompanying plates aimed more at arousing sympathy than establishing accuracy. A frontispiece showing the Lafayette women embracing the famous prisoner for the first time has them standing under the slogan, "Suffer and Die" (*Souffrir et Mourir*). In truth, however, that sign was located in the prison at Magdeburg. The picture also showed chains hanging from stones, chains that Lafayette never wore. A plate at the poem's end shows Lafayette sitting alone, looking up into a small grated aperture high in a wall, to all appearances his only source of light. In neither picture is there any sign of furniture or books.

The poem's first lines strike its tone: "In these somber dungeons, image of hell, / Bent down now for five years under the weight of my chains, / Dead to all humanity, entirely so to the natural world, / In this abyss where light barely descends, / Must I, in my wrenching pains without relief, / Die by intervals in the sight of my oppressors?"

A guard sees in "this great man" a peer of classical heroes and senses that "his soul is in the heavens, he is no longer captive." Suddenly, after musing about sacrifice for liberty and yearning to see his family, Lafayette hears doors open and finds himself embraced by wife and daughters. On that note, the poem ends.[116]

Both poems made strong emotional appeals. They drew a gripping picture of unpleasant conditions in Olmütz.

Vienna's sensitivity to criticisms in western European journals may have led the Austrian government to replace the despised Major Czernak as prison supervisor with Captain Baron MacElligot at the end of 1796. MacElligot, a man of Irish background, spoke fluent English and French, and was, in captives' view, "personally replete with courtesy and even kindness." He deplored conditions and improved them as far as he could. Prisoners praised his humaneness.[117]

The chief result of efforts by Lafayette's supporters on both sides of the Channel and the Atlantic was indeed to publicize his plight and that of his company. A critical mass of pro-Lafayette sentiment developed to the point that finally it moved French government policy in Lafayette's favor. A chief tool of the government was Bonaparte, its most successful general. He was also an actor with a will of his own.

11

BONAPARTE

The triumphs of the French Army of Italy and its young commander, Napoléon Bonaparte, captivated observers. An opening, furious ten-day campaign in April 1796 gave Bonaparte control of the Kingdom of Piedmont-Sardinia on France's southeast border. His forces entered Milan on 15 May, then took Verona and invested Mantua. They managed to frustrate repeated Austrian counteroffensives in the coming months, culminating in a smashing French victory at the Battle of Rivoli in mid-January 1797 and the capitulation of Mantua on 2 February. As Archduke Charles, Austria's finest general, arrived from the Army of the Rhine to take command of imperial forces in northeast Italy and the Tyrol, Bonaparte launched a preemptive strike into the Alps. Its trajectory was toward the imperial capital itself.

Lafayette and his supporters followed the French campaign closely and concluded that France must be the instrument of his redemption. Indeed France would insist on the release of the Olmütz prisoners in subsequent peace negotiations. But there were many delays. In the meantime Lafayette's supporters assailed Paris and Vienna alike, determined that he not be forgotten by powers haggling over the fate of the Continent.

By late summer 1796, Lafayette had decided that "only France has the power to tear us from the talons of all these governments."[1] His hopes fit well the sonnet "La Fayette" that Samuel Taylor Coleridge had published months before in the *Morning Chronicle:* "Within his cage the imprisoned matin bird / Swells the full chorus with a generous song: / . . . Thou, FAYETTE! who didst wake with startling voice / Life's better sun from that long wintry night, / Thus in thy Country's triumphs shalt rejoice / And mock with raptures high the dungeon's might."[2]

Urged on secretly from Olmütz, Lafayette's supporters fought to convince Paris to force the captive's release. Masclet told Fox that since efforts in England had

had little effect, supporters ought to focus on shaping French opinion instead. He hoped particularly to influence the Directory. The goal was to reach agreement after the model of prisoner-of-war exchanges already occurring in Germany and Italy. Masclet asked Fox for more vocal support to provide ammunition for Lafayette's influential friends in France. In autumn 1796 imperial agent Mallet told Vienna that the prisoners' supporters were counting on French power.[3]

On orders from presiding director François Reubell,[4] Major General Henri Clarke, French plenipotentiary in peace talks, asked his counterparts to ease conditions in Olmütz.[5] This request foreshadowed formal demands for release.

Lafayette and his party became pawns or hostages only at this time, when the French government made its first appeal to the Austrian court. Vienna realized that finally Lafayette had become valuable property, something negotiable as Beurnonville and his party had been two years before. The original motive for holding the Frenchmen was to stop the contagious spread of their ideas and to keep them for a restored French king to deal with. That motive had long since lost its foundation with the victories of the French republican armies; yet the prisoners remained in custody because of a new reason for holding them: to use them for leverage with France.

Bonaparte broke into the central Austrian provinces, taking Klagenfurt, capital of Carinthia, and arranging an armistice with Archduke Charles. Peace talks opened on 13 April in Leoben, only 120 kilometers from Vienna, even before the Directory agreed to authorize Bonaparte to pursue them. Five days later, without awaiting Clarke, Bonaparte signed preliminaries with Austrian representatives Major General Count Maximilian von Merveldt and Marchese Marzio di Gallo, Neapolitan ambassador to Vienna and friend of the empress, also from Naples. The ninth article stipulated that "after ratification of the preliminaries, prisoners of war will be turned over at the different places, respectively, that will be designated by each side."[6] However, the emperor deemed Lafayette and companions to be prisoners of state rather than of war, so the article did not mandate their release. Bonaparte's private secretary, Louis Bourrienne, claimed that the captives became the object of negotiations only weeks after Leoben.[7] But Bourrienne did not arrive until the day after signing, so he missed Bonaparte's discussions with Gallo. Later Bonaparte noted how they had included his demand for release of Lafayette's party. Lafayette was convinced that "from the first day of the negotiations of Leoben, Bonaparte spoke of us" and acted before the Directory did.[8]

The Directory also included the release of Lafayette and his fellow prisoners in the ongoing negotiations. On 24 April it instructed Bonaparte to draw up secret articles for release, including a provision stating that Lafayette's group could sail to America if it wished. Bonaparte had already signed secret articles that made no mention of the prisoners; however, the Directory's charge moved him to present his counterparts with a note on the subject. Eventually he had messages from

Mesdames Maubourg and Pusy forwarded to their husbands.[9] By early May, Austrian chief minister Thugut addressed his colleagues on Lafayette's case.[10] He told his envoy, Gallo, that release would only occur with a final peace agreement.[11] The prisoners assumed that Thugut felt so vengeful toward Lafayette that he would seek every occasion to delay and hope to avoid compliance altogether.[12]

The Directory's instructions contained an important provision: that once released, Lafayette's party could not return directly to France. Bonaparte also stressed this. Lafayette remained an important political rival. In Paris his partisan Pierre du Pont de Nemours made assurances that Lafayette would stay away. Du Pont was a prominent deputy in the French lower chamber, editor of *L'Historien,* and husband of captive Pusy's mother-in-law. He explained the commitment in a note he gave César de Latour-Maubourg's brother Victor to carry to Hamburg and Vienna. Other supporters, including deputies Jean Étienne Portalis and Jean Louis Emmery, hoped for a time that Lafayette might be able to return soon after all, perhaps via Dresden and Frankfurt, under some form of amnesty. However, most supporters came to accept that Lafayette's continued exile from France was politically necessary. Masson even came to blame the Directory's failure to pursue release more vigorously on Fayettists seeking their hero's immediate return. He proposed that Du Pont reassure Paris and that Romeuf reassure Bonaparte, that Lafayette would remain abroad.[13]

The question became where Lafayette should spend that exile. Supporters rejected several places close to French borders as too dangerous. French troops under Major General Louis Lazare Hoche had occupied the free imperial city of Cologne on the Rhine's west bank. Hanoverian territory, subject to the British crown, surrounded the free imperial city of Bremen on three sides, and British-Hanoverian troops had occupied the city in the past. The free imperial city of Frankfurt am Main was vulnerable to Austrian occupation. In the southwest, across the Rhine from French Alsace, the margraviate of Baden hosted émigré forces of Prince Louis de Condé. Swiss cantonal authorities were too deferential to France. By process of elimination, supporters chose the neutral Danish province of Holstein, which bordered Hamburg on three sides. It offered the right combination of distance from danger and unwanted visits and proximity to lines of transportation and communication. Supporters could secretly rent a house near Plön, "eighteen large leagues in the sands" (more than seventy kilometers) northeast of Hamburg. Lafayette, friends, and family might stay there until political circumstances allowed them to move first to Holland and then to France.[14] Plön was, of course, the seat of Lafayette supporter August Hennings, within sight of the Wittmold estate of Lafayette's aunt Tessé.

In the following weeks, the Directory continued to assume that the peace would include release. In early May the director supervising foreign affairs, Lazare Carnot, sent instructions to General Clarke: "Obtain provisionally, if possible, the liberty of Lafayette, Bureaux-Pusy, and Latour-Maubourg. It is a matter of national honor that they leave behind the dungeons where they are kept because they began the Revolution." Carnot directed Clarke to show Bonaparte the letter. Clarke and Bonaparte gave Gallo a note on the subject. Lafayette sympathizer François Barthélemy, who had just entered the Directory days before, added his support. He sent Bonaparte a note repeating the Directory's insistence on release, which the *Annales politiques et littéraires* reported.[15]

Everything seemed ready. In May, Masson asked Ducoudray to travel to Olmütz for the great event. Early the next month, Masson sent a Parisian Fayettist a superficially innocent business message reporting Ducoudray's secret activities: "The traveling salesman I sent just wrote me that one morning he had caught sight of the merchandise for which he was making the visit." Ducoudray had seen an inmate at a prison window. Masson was convinced that "our expedition can occur" soon because "my salesman alerts me that the commandant, who was supposed to go on leave for a pleasure trip, has received the official order not to leave because the expedition and departure of all the seized merchandise is going to occur in a short while." As for the goods themselves (the prisoners), "they are in good condition, and even better than one could or ought to have expected." Masson asked his Paris contact to pass the news to interested colleagues there. He promised to send notice when the "expedition" began and to finish arrangements for routing and provisioning. He reported plans to ask Maubourg's brother Victor, newly arrived in Hamburg, to bring "the merchandise" from Olmütz via Dresden.[16]

But the plans were premature. As peace talks continued, Lafayette's case stalled. Bonaparte occupied Villa Crivelli at Mombello (Montebello) on 5 May 1797 to pursue final agreement. At the end of June, negotiators announced that talks would shift eastward to the Venetian town of Udine for swifter communication with Vienna.[17] On 27 July, Bonaparte took up lodgings in another magnificent palace, that of the last Venetian doge, the Villa Manin in Passariano near Udine. The young general enjoyed the princely lifestyle and power. He knew that at the end of talks, he would return to subordinate roles in less luxurious conditions. Lafayette was not his highest priority, as major territorial exchanges came under discussion. Bonaparte probably also considered that Lafayette's future career might rival his own. At the same time, Vienna hoped to avoid an unfavorable peace by drawing out talks and awaiting favorable developments.[18] French elections in the spring had brought into the legislative councils more conservative deputies. Barthélemy's legislative election to the Directory gave the moderate Carnot an ally, leaving the three more radical directors holding a bare majority.

Fayettists began to worry. They feared that the incarceration might continue indefinitely. Masson thought that the usually belligerent Bonaparte had been too polite about Lafayette's release. The general's behavior must have led Vienna to conclude that Paris gave the release little priority. He also assumed that London played a role in the delay.[19] He wrote of his concerns to Roederer and joined Masclet and Victor Maubourg in writing a joint letter to Bonaparte. They suggested that British envoy George Hammond had visited Vienna with secret instructions to keep the prisoners.[20] Emmery, deputy in the French lower chamber, began to suspect that neither Bonaparte nor the Directory were any more trustworthy than Emperor Francis.[21]

Supporters used several strategies to persuade the Directory to apply greater pressure on Vienna. They praised it for having demanded release. A one-act play opened in Paris on 20 May, celebrating Adrienne's Lafayette's devotion to her husband and calling for intervention to free them. A letter in *Journal de Paris* declared Lafayette innocent of past charges and encouraged the directors to orient themselves to the British opposition and French public opinion. Partisans cast Lafayette, Maubourg, and Pusy as prisoners of war and promoted their release as a national cause. They noted that France had shown good faith by releasing Austrian war prisoners shortly after signing the armistice. Bonaparte had freed some at Genoa, and the Directory had released Austrian major general Franz Lusignan from Temple Prison. Lafayette supporters pointed out that by delaying release Austria showed bad faith; perhaps it betrayed its intention to reopen hostilities. They circulated a story illustrating Franco-Austrian differences over the release. On his way home, they claimed, Lusignan complained to Bonaparte of treatment in French custody. In response Bonaparte angrily cited Austria's inhumanity toward Lafayette's party.[22] Partisans floated the idea of sending special envoys to Vienna. Masson and Pillet volunteered to serve in this capacity. Each claimed special competence as a former aide and fellow prisoner of Lafayette.[23] Masson also proposed sending an agent to Lille, where France had been negotiating peace with Britain since autumn 1796. He hoped to push release as a condition of peace; that is, the Directory could exchange the Olmütz inmates for Captain Sir William Smith, who was being held at the Temple.[24]

On 9 April 1797 moderate majorities won election to the upper and lower French legislative chambers, the Council of Elders and the Council of Five Hundred. Fayettists sought to convince these bodies to ask the Directory for more forceful action. At the Hôtel Beauvau in early May, upper-chamber deputy Portalis declared that a decree of the sort was quite likely. Lower chamber deputy Du Pont de Nemours emphasized the importance of guaranteeing the captives' temporary exile in order to strike a deal. Others who supported a legislative appeal to the Directory included Emmery; Vincent Marie, Count de Vaublanc; Joseph Vincent Dumolard; and Claude Emmanuel Pastoret in the Council of Five Hundred; and Claude Louis Petiet and Mathieu Dumas in the Council of Elders. In Hamburg, Masson asked Parisian colleagues about the decree. He wondered if the

Germaine de Staël.
National Portrait
Gallery, London

lower chamber, which initiated all legislation, had begun discussing it; and if the chamber's new president, Jean Pichegru, would add his authority to it.[25]

Several Fayettists founded an antiroyalist, pro-Directory "Constitutional Circle" that shared information about the captives and promoted their cause. Founders included Germaine de Staël, returned to Paris after months of exile; her lover, Benjamin Constant, who had recently written a pamphlet defending the Directory; and Madame Simiane's cousin, Charles de Talleyrand, aspirant for the post of foreign minister. Others soon added their support, including publicist Masclet, who had moved to Paris after writing extensively on Lafayette's behalf in London; and prisoner Pusy's mother-in-law, Marie Poivre du Pont.[26]

De Staël played a particularly energetic role in keeping Lafayette's case alive. She knew that at least one of the five directors, Reubell, despised her. She had known Director Jean Nicolas, Viscount de Barras, for some time, but did not feel that she enjoyed influence with him anymore. She asked Pichegru to mediate, but he refused.[27] On 16 July she interceded to get Talleyrand appointed minister of foreign affairs. This appointment soon proved useful for Lafayette's cause.

At the end of July, Masclet shared with the Constitutional Circle an electrifying report in which Adrienne Lafayette wrote that the captives were in decline and that Vienna's cabinet was toying with the Directory. The group considered how much support they had for more decisive official action. Only two directors clearly favored immediate release, Carnot and Barthélemy. The remaining directors—Reubell, Louis Marie de La Revellière-Lépeaux, and Barras—considered Lafayette a political rival. The two French legislative chambers were so anxious to ratify a peace that they would not insist on the captives' liberty as a condition. This would allow "the interests of individuals [to] disappear before the grand interest of France and Europe." The Constitutional Circle assumed that Austrian chief minister Thugut was aware of the French political constellation and that it might allow him to "to close again, forever, this dungeon that he was prepared for an instant to open." The thought made circle members "shiver."

The Constitutional Circle's strategy focused on Barras. Together, De Staël, Constant, and Talleyrand might influence him. In turn Barras exercised persuasive power over Reubell and Bonaparte. Perhaps Barras could get the Directory to issue a more emphatic order to Bonaparte, that he demand the captives' release. Talleyrand claimed that he could not gauge Directory sentiment on the matter, but he promised to work on Barras, Reubell, and Bonaparte. De Staël and Constant planned to solicit Barras's help and to arrange for Masclet to do the same. If Barras appeared anxious at the prospect of Lafayette's return, De Staël would promise that Lafayette would remain abroad for up to six months.[28]

On the morning of 2 August, accompanied by Constant, Madame de Staël addressed Barras. "Barras, dear Barras, citizen Director, I think I know better than anyone the nobility of your spirit, the generosity of your heart," she told him. She assured Barras that—in contrast to Pichegru's icy personality—he had "a soul of Provence," his warm ancestral province in the south. She swore that Lafayette had always been and would continue to be "a very good Republican" and that, after release, he "would remain outside of France for an appropriate term." She also asked Barras to send an urgent missive to Bonaparte.

Barras felt that he was already "a convert" to Lafayette's cause and had never needed convincing. He assured De Staël that he had already intervened on Madame Maubourg's appeal, and would willingly write Bonaparte. He agreed that Lafayette should not return to Paris but perhaps should retire to his home province of the Auvergne. De Staël wanted to avoid irritating the councils and Directory with her own lobbying, so she proposed "a very good Republican" to represent Lafayette's cause. Barras readily agreed. Constant offered to present Masclet, recently arrived from Hamburg, for this role the next morning. Masclet vowed to see that Barras would carry through his promise to write Bonaparte.

The two directors whom Barras had thought least sympathetic, radical republicans Reubell and La Revellière, vigorously supported release. They lamented that exchange of state prisoners for the king's daughter at the end of 1795 had not included Lafayette and company. Reubell admitted that he and others had harbored grievances at Lafayette's support of monarchy; however, he said, those feelings had dissipated. It was time to recognize Lafayette's incarceration "as an injustice and even a crime of our enemies." Masclet noted that the Directory's position turned Lafayette's case into a national cause.[29] The Directory used a plea from Madame du Pont as reason to act. It asked the War Ministry to draw up a letter to Bonaparte, demanding Vienna release the captives. On 1 August, the Directory received the draft, approved it, and sent it off under President Carnot's signature. The letter referred to "the new requests that people are making to the Directory about the prisoners of Olmütz" and then reiterated its early position: "Citizen General, the Directory reminds you of the desire it has expressed to you to see that their captivity ends as soon as possible. It doubts not that you share the concern their misfortune inspires."[30] The proviso that Lafayette not return to France remained.

In addition Talleyrand had just used his new position as foreign minister to write his own letter to Bonaparte and Clarke. They should ask if Vienna was prepared to conclude negotiations based on the terms established at Leoben. If so, Vienna ought to show its "amicable dispositions" by releasing the captives as it had promised. Not to do so "must naturally raise concerns that it anticipates or desires a renewal of hostilities."[31]

Supporters also identified several generals stationed in Paris or Germany, whom they might approach. They included General Jean Moreau, commander of the Army of the Rhine-and-Moselle; General Louis Lazare Hoche, commander of the Army of the Sambre-and-Meuse (and from July, minister of war); Major General François Lefebvre, Hoche's adjutant; and Major General Pierre du Pont de l'Étang, director of the military's topography office and military correspondence between Paris and Italy.[32] Fayettists also looked to officers and administrators of the Army of Italy. They included Bonaparte's chief of staff, formerly Lafayette's, Major General Alexandre Berthier; Berthier's aide-de-camp, Colonel Adrien du Tallis, also a close friend of Louis Romeuf; administrator of army hospitals Michel de Regnauld; and Major General Clarke, Directory liaison and plenipotentiary in peace negotiations. During imprisonment in Paris, Adrienne Lafayette had become acquainted with fellow captive General Charles Kilmaine, who had proven sympathetic to her husband. After his release, Kilmaine had become one of Bonaparte's key officers. In September 1796, he became commander of French forces in northern Italy.

Above all, Lafayette's partisans pinned their hopes on Bonaparte himself. He was the person who, more than anyone, set the course of negotiations. "He alone can save the friends from the imperial talons," Masson wrote.[33]

Madame de Staël again took a leading role. She wrote Bonaparte some "long and numerous letters" that he remembered as "full of spirit, of fire, of metaphysics."[34] Most important, she sent Louis Romeuf, former Lafayette aide and fellow prisoner in Belgium, to Italy. Her knowledge of efforts to free Lafayette became so comprehensive that Lafayette compared it to Bonaparte's knowledge of the peace negotiations.[35]

Romeuf left Paris during the latter half of June, just after Mesdames Maubourg and Pusy had commenced their own voyage eastward. Unconfirmed reports held that release was imminent. Accompanying Romeuf was his brother Jacques, who had also fled France with Lafayette. The Romeufs carried money from De Staël and letters from Director Barthélemy. De Staël kept supplying help in the coming weeks. She sent French journals favorable to the captives, especially those containing articles by Masclet, for Louis Romeuf to show Bonaparte. The Romeufs arrived at Bonaparte's Mombello headquarters on 2 July 1797. De Staël had already alerted Hamburg supporters. Masson proposed that she have Louis Romeuf seek military commissions for partisans. The plan was to give them staff positions throughout the army, so that they could gather information and exercise influence. Masson advised her to always send Romeuf an extra four or five copies of each favorable French journal to share with Bonaparte's staff.[36]

Romeuf soon learned that release was hardly imminent, nor was it as high a priority for French negotiators as supporters had hoped. He wrote De Staël the day after reaching Milan, "I believe that according to what I have heard, we have reposed much too much upon those who have had your confidence, though I do not want to accuse anyone before having more certain data." He later noted, "Those who are acting here are far from bringing to [the goal of release] the passion we have desired. They need to be pushed." He regretted that the French had not demanded liberation "when they were all-powerful," immediately after their victories.[37]

Romeuf's initial "cold" encounter with Bonaparte confirmed his impression that Lafayette's fate was not central to the general's concerns. It also opened a window onto Bonaparte's motives. "He seems indignant at the Vienna court's perfidies perhaps more because of the [exhalted] idea that he has of his own power than because of any interest he has in the prisoners," Romeuf noted. Bonaparte informed him of his Austrian counterparts' claims that Vienna had long sought a pretext to get rid of the captives and that a formal request of Tsarina Catherine II had kept them in jail. But Bonaparte and Romeuf agreed that Prime Minister Pitt had used the Russian empress as his agent. Bonaparte asked about Lafayette's future place of exile. When Romeuf hesitated, Bonaparte suggested America and France as the only countries Lafayette would consider seriously. Romeuf answered that he could not be sure of the captives' wishes. He knew that Bonaparte had handed the Austrians a Directory note requesting that Lafayette not return to France, but concluded from Bonaparte's remark that the condition no longer applied. He assumed that the freed party would want first to come to Bonaparte, who could direct it, circumstances and health permitting, to go where it wished. Bonaparte said he regarded the prisoners as émigrés who would be allowed eventually to return to France. He promised to introduce Romeuf to Gallo and support his petition.[38]

Romeuf had a long second talk with Bonaparte on the evening of 17 July. He was "satisfied by his dispositions in what interests us, but without finding him showing the enthusiasm we would desire." To be sure, Romeuf conceded, "on this matter my attachment to my misfortunate general renders me difficult to please."

Romeuf did find sympathizers at Mombello. They included Lafayette's old friend Major General Berthier and his aide, Romeuf's friend Colonel Tallis. Berthier had introduced Romeuf to Bonaparte. To allow Romeuf to deal directly with Austrian authorities, Berthier recommissioned him a lieutenant colonel. Bonaparte's wife, Joséphine, also encouraged Romeuf's mission.[39]

Romeuf started out for Udine and resumed discussions with Bonaparte's fellow plenipotentiary Clarke. He found Clarke to be much more enthusiastic about release than he had assumed. In a long conversation the evening of 24 July, Clarke filled in Romeuf on recent developments. Clarke had complained to his counterparts about delays of the release and presented a second official note on the topic on 17 July. Romeuf described Major General Count Merveldt as "a harsh and inflexible man, extremely limited by Thugut's instructions, and unwilling to take any personal initiative." Merveldt told Clarke that Francis II had sent emissaries to Olmütz to investigate foreign journal reports about alleged mistreatment. Clarke spoke to the much more sympathetic Austrian envoy Gallo, who was about to depart for Vienna. Clarke voiced fear that the captives might have to deny the journal reports as a condition of release. Gallo found his superiors' conduct embarrassing and assured Clarke that he would do everything possible to bring about quick release. To keep the issue alive even after Gallo's departure, Clarke promised Romeuf to mention the captives in another diplomatic note. Romeuf remarked about the Austrian envoys, "I believe that the best manner to succeed with these men is to harass them continually; in the end they will have to respond or act."

Romeuf spent the morning of 26 July at Clarke's quarters. The general showed him the second note he had passed to the Austrians. It included the stipulation that Lafayette's party not return directly to France. Clarke commented, "This [condition] is not my style; it comes from Bonaparte. In any case, I do not think it is obligatory. The essential thing for our friends is that they be free, and in fact they will decide then on what they wish. As for me, I have never doubted they will return to France." The general declared that it would be senseless to retreat into any German state, given the emperor's influence. Clarke did criticize Lafayette's past behavior, but Romeuf felt he was able to refute him. The two men parted as friends, and Romeuf was convinced that Clarke would do all he could.

Romeuf made his way to Merveldt's quarters for his first talk as a French representative with an Austrian official. Merveldt assured him that the captives would go free as soon as they had agreed to leave Austrian crown lands forever and avoid returning to France. His Majesty would provide funds for the departure. Merveldt claimed that the prisoners had never lacked any necessity during their sojourn in Olmütz. Romeuf asked why, then, Lafayette had no decent clothes when his family arrived. "Our discussion of this topic was rather lengthy," Romeuf noted, "and the fear to harm those still in prison imposed on me a reserve that I do not reproach myself about, but that was quite painful for me to maintain." Romeuf had hoped that Merveldt might issue him a visa to Vienna. Merveldt said that he first needed cabinet clearance.

Despite Romeuf's initial frustration, that clearance came a few days later. He set off immediately for Vienna with Clarke's personal secretary and a note from Clarke.[40]

While Romeuf traveled to Mombello, Udine, and Vienna, family members of the captives were also on the road. They hoped to appeal to Francis II, either in person or through Bonaparte.

Henriette de Latour-Maubourg and Julienne de Bureaux-Pusy received guarantees of support from Director Barthélemy and assurances from both Austrian envoy Gallo and an unnamed leader of the Army of Italy that release was imminent. Clarke also wrote Madame du Pont, Pusy's mother-in-law, of Gallo's promises. However, after months of not having heard from their husbands, Mesdames Pusy and Maubourg decided to travel to Vienna or Mombello. Their first object was to seek an audience with Francis II, ask permission to visit their husbands, and either bring them away or share their incarceration. Failing that, they would turn to Bonaparte.

Henriette de Latour-Maubourg left Paris in mid-June 1797. Julienne de Bureaux-Pusy delayed her own departure a few days in hopes that she could accompany Bonaparte's chief of staff Berthier, or Florimond or Victor de Latour-Maubourg. When the plan fell through, she found Lafayette's former aide Pillet, who was willing to serve as escort. Pillet also learned that the director supervising foreign affairs, Reubell, had a strong personal interest in Lafayette's fate. Pillet and Madame Pusy left for Basel early on 20 June. They carried a letter for Lafayette from De Staël and her close friend Montmorency. The travelers also carried official papers, including a passport from Minister of War Petiet; his request to General Moreau, commander of the Army of the Rhine-and-Moselle, to help Pillet obtain a visa from the emperor's brother Archduke Charles for travel to Vienna or Olmütz; and a similar letter of Director Carnot to General Moreau. "We can only applaud the duty you are carrying out," a note from the Directory read. "We put into your hands execution of the demand that General Bonaparte made at Montebello. You can have confidence in the Emperor's generosity: in learning of the release of General Lusignan, he will want to give France a reciprocal act of goodwill."[41]

However, the route did not lead Pillet and the captives' wives either to Vienna or northern Italy. After journeying through the night, Pillet and Madame Pusy arrived in Basel at noon on 21 June. They found that Madame Maubourg had impatiently left some days before to seek a visa from Archduke Charles. The following morning Pusy and Pillet drove to Strasbourg and then to Stuttgart, where they picked up additional travel documents from ducal Württemberg. They continued on to Bavarian Augsburg and Landshut. Along the way they caught up with Madame Maubourg and visited the headquarters of Austria's Rhine Army, where Archduke Charles received them. Charles expressed his hopes for peace with France, and promised to obtain visas. Pillet spoke to Charles's top aide, Major General Prince Johannes von Liechtenstein, who also advocated peace. In Landshut, Pillet asked the Austrian chargé d'affaires to send a visa request to Count Saurau, acting Austrian minister of police. On 5 July Pillet and the captives' wives arrived in Regensburg, seat of the German imperial diet, where they awaited visas and received mail under the pseudonym "Smith," care of the local prince-archbishop's privy counselor. They informed the Olmütz inmates of their progress. After several days, they told their Hamburg colleagues that Vienna showed little inclination to provide the necessary papers. Pillet became convinced that Thugut had conspired with Saurau to keep them far from Vienna. Against the wishes of Francis II and his army, Thugut was not seriously negotiating peace. Pillet noted how many diplomats in Regensburg dismissed the practicality of peace and promoted renewed war to stop the Revolution. After three weeks, Pillet's party gave up and proceeded to Saxony's capital of Dresden. It was the major city closest to the western borders of the emperor's Bohemian crown lands. It was also along the captives' probable exit route, and had good communication links to Vienna and Hamburg.[42]

Pillet, Henriette de Latour-Maubourg, and Julienne de Bureaux-Pusy spent several more weeks petitioning and waiting. They were anxious, bored, homesick, and thirsty for news. Pillet wrote to the Hamburg and Paris circles. He received information from Olmütz and passed it on. Among supporters he reported to in Paris were upper-house deputy Pierre du Pont de Nemours; Director Barthélemy; lower-house deputy Emmery; publicist Masclet; Madame Simiane; and foreign minister Talleyrand. Pillet petitioned Talleyrand and the Directory that they send a special commissioner to Vienna to demand release. Mesdames Pusy and Maubourg, as well as their children, wrote Thugut an appeal claiming "that what we have suffered for five years gives us some right to solicit from His Imperial Majesty either release of our husbands and fathers, or favor to go to give them our attention in order to reestablish their ruined health." Every French citizen, they asserted, "the army general as well as the soldier, the chief of the Directory as well as the last magistrate," identified with the captives.[43]

The Dresden party received a great deal of advice. From Paris, Masclet, Madame du Pont, and Emmery recommended that they go to Bonaparte's headquarters to shame him into action. "I think and dream only of Italy, as the sole means of salvation," Masson declared in Hamburg. He urged Madame Pusy and Pillet to go there to press Bonaparte. Meanwhile Madame Maubourg could stay in Dresden to receive and pass on letters from the French armies in Italy and the Rhineland. She could proceed to Vienna only if and when visas arrived.[44]

Meanwhile prisoner César de Latour-Maubourg's brother Victor was leading a second family initiative. He left England soon after Leoben in hopes of meeting Lafayette's party returning from captivity. To this purpose he received 150 louis from Cadignan, likely from funds managed by U.S. envoy King. However, Victor Maubourg soon reached Paris and learned that the party had still not been released. He then received 3,600 livres from Monroe. He also conferred with Dumas, the powerful pro-Lafayette leader of the Club de Clichy.[45]

Victor Maubourg left Paris in mid-May with his younger brother Charles, sister Amélie, and nephew Florimond, César's eldest son. He planned to reach the Rhine frontier, learn what he could of Vienna's intentions, and proceed to northern Italy or Vienna. He carried a letter from Du Pont to Lafayette that described Du Pont's guarantee to the Directory that Lafayette would remain abroad after release. The Maubourgs reached Strasbourg and visited the army at the upper Rhine headquarters of General Pierre Antoine du Pont-Chaumont. They spoke with officers responsible for communications with Vienna, and, since Victor Maubourg was fluent in German, they read local German newspapers. Maubourg found the papers poor sources of the news he wanted. He changed his plans and traveled north to Germany's publication center. He arrived in Hamburg the morning of 11 June, conferred with Masson and other Fayettists, and learned that the captives may have just been freed. Masson hoped to send Victor Maubourg to meet them. In code he was told "to convey the merchandise, that will probably come here from Dresden."

When the release news proved to be false, Victor Maubourg decided to travel south to lobby Bonaparte. At the same time, Masson wanted to reestablish recently interrupted communication with Olmütz. The men decided to combine their goals. On 28 June, Maubourg, Masson, and Masclet wrote a joint letter that Victor was to bring Bonaparte. They asked him to add to his victories by conquering "the Bastille of Olmütz."[46] On the way to Mombello, Victor would join the one whom Masson identified as "my German," Ducoudray, and visit Olmütz.[47]

The plan went smoothly. Victor wrote Ducoudray, and asked to join him. Ducoudray received the letter while staying at Warmbrunn as guest of a wealthy, generous, and oblivious aristocrat hostile to Lafayette, Count Leopold von Schaffgotsch. Ducoudray asked Victor to come. While his younger brother, Charles, and sister Amélie stayed behind, Victor left Hamburg on 1 July with César's son Florimond. He hoped to arrive soon "at the door" of Olmütz. Count Schaffgotsch extended his hospitality to the new visitors, and then Ducoudray led the two Maubourgs across the border.[48]

They successfully entered Olmütz with help of local "powerful friends." On the evening of 18 July, Adrienne Lafayette addressed a secret message to "our dear friends and, as we suppose, the travelers with you or near here." "The good courier" brought them her note, and returned with a response that evening. Presumably the "dear friends" included Christoph von Passy, "the travelers" Victor and Florimond de Latour-Maubourg, and the "good courier" Ducoudray. A soldier or officer of the prison must also have cooperated. The next day Madame Lafayette smuggled a long note to Victor, which celebrated the men's visit: "I cannot express the joy that your arrival is causing, not only to your brother and Lafayette. You know how dear you are to both, but also to the entire prison of Olmütz, where one is doubly happy to hope for deliverance and the pleasure of having you as liberator." A week later she wrote Victor, "It is with great joy that we have learned of your detour, Monsieur. We were quite afraid that the trip to Italy would retard the moment when we would have the happiness to see you again. Here you are, happily, in the same town as we. Nothing remains but to put us in the same carriage." She referred to the Maubourgs and Ducoudray as "the three merchants of Hamburg," and Passy as "M. Cant." She even requested that the visitors give the inmates "an inexpressible pleasure" by walking under their windows.

The visitors planned to leave the second week of August. In the meantime Madame Lafayette smuggled them messages and advice. She offered letters for Francis II, Vienna contacts, and generals Bonaparte and Berthier.[49] She, or rather her husband through her, advised the travelers to obtain visas for Vienna, contact her friends there, and arrange an imperial audience. If the plan failed, Ducoudray ("Feldmann") should return to Olmütz while the Maubourgs continued to Italy. They could travel via Schweidnitz and Dresden, to meet Pillet and Mesdames Maubourg and Pusy. The Lafayettes' emissaries could show the Pillet party various letters and bring news from across the border. Perhaps Pillet himself had already left for Italy, which could save the travelers a detour. Once Pillet had received the latest news, he could notify Director Barthélemy and other Paris supporters. Berthier could also do so. In any event, the prisoners depended on "Cant" to supply news and smuggle out notes.[50]

Both Passy ("Cant") and Mitrovsky ("M") offered helpful information about Vienna. Passy was friends with a sympathetic Vienna official "whose situation puts him very much in a position to be informed" and also with "a man of letters who gave us many signs of his own zeal and friendship for us." Both contacts knew Saurau. Apparently the "man of letters" had loaned Saurau some money that Adrienne Lafayette controlled.[51]

Ducoudray and the Maubourgs managed to visit Vienna at the end of July. However, they found it impossible to approach the emperor. They blamed this on the security that Empress Maria Theresa, Thugut, and Saurau had thrown up around him. As planned, Ducoudray returned to Olmütz, where he received word that Pillet and the families of Maubourg and Pusy had stopped in Dresden. With the Lafayettes' encouragement, Ducoudray rode to Dresden, reported that nothing in the prison regime had changed, and returned to Olmütz. Victor and Florimond Maubourg traveled to Italy.[52]

The Maubourgs arrived at Mombello to find Romeuf already there. Berthier introduced them to Bonaparte, and Victor handed over Adrienne Lafayette's note. According to Ducoudray's secondhand account, Bonaparte responded enthusiastically: "What a woman! How eloquent in a few words! Well, well, Monsieur de Maubourg, assure her, on my part, I will do my best to relieve them soon from all their long and undeserved sufferings!" Bonaparte spoke of the injustice done to these most distinguished men, for whom he felt the sincerest esteem. He added that "if my request is not attended to, I shall find the proper means to force the emperor to grant it." Bonaparte supposedly sent a note on the subject to Archduke Charles, who forwarded it to Vienna. When no response came, Berthier got Bonaparte to send Romeuf as personal envoy. He carried several important papers, including letters by Directors Barthélemy and Carnot to substantiate France's position and similar notes from Clarke to Gallo and Thugut. Two missives came straight from Bonaparte: one requesting Archduke Charles to help Romeuf reach Vienna and the other threatening Francis II with new hostilities if he failed to release the captives.[53]

Lafayette's supporters had kept his cause alive in the negotiations between France and Austria. Madame de Staël had lobbied the Directory personally and sent Louis Romeuf to work similarly on Bonaparte and Clarke. Both strategies had proved successful. The Directory had made Lafayette's release official policy. Romeuf was on his way to Vienna, invested with credentials from Bonaparte and Clarke to speak for France.

12

RELEASE

Throughout the summer of 1797, the French continued peace negotiations with the British at Lille in northern France and with the Austrians, first in the Duchy of Milan and then at Udine and Passariano in the Venetian Republic. The Lille talks failed when the British found themselves unable to accept French claims on Belgium and the left bank of the Rhine. Those in northern Italy reached stasis for a time, as three of the five French directors dealt with internal challenges to their power from more conservative forces; Bonaparte enjoyed his princely status in Italy; and the Vienna court awaited more favorable events. The most favorable event turned out to be Bonaparte's offer of generous territorial compensation, including much of the Venetian Republic, for Austria's losses in a permanent peace agreement.

Emperor Francis II knew that, as part of the agreement, he would have to release Lafayette and company soon. He tried to save face by getting the captives to say that they had enjoyed decent treatment while in his custody and would never return to his territories. Failing that, Francis could at least release them to the Americans rather than the French, as if it were an act of grace. He could also hold the U.S. consul responsible for seeing that they leave the German Empire. Thanks particularly to John Parish, cheerfully coming out of retirement to play the role of grateful and respectful American envoy, the release was able to proceed.

All summer the Austrian court had been preparing for release. In June negotiators notified the French Army of Italy that the emperor had agreed in principle.[1] At the same time, Olmütz commandant Schröder received orders to delay a planned leave. Lafayette's supporters took this to mean that release was imminent.[2] Prussia's conclusion of a defense pact with France in the mid-July spurred Austria to conclude its own agreement.[3] Late that month Francis had Thugut direct Major General Chasteler, quartermaster general of the Austrian Army of Italy, to visit the captives and persuade them to sign documents that would help Francis preserve some dignity. Chasteler was the very officer who, as lieutenant colonel, had commanded Namur, where Lafayette was first imprisoned. The emperor probably did not choose Chasteler with a sense of irony, though the upcoming meeting could not help but be weighty with it.

Chasteler's mission was twofold. First he had to investigate prisoner complaints and prison conditions to verify that the incarceration was humane. The general was supposed to report any conditions contradicting imperial orders. Second Chasteler was to advise the inmates that Francis II was prepared graciously to release them with passports and directions. The only conditions would be that they leave for America and never return to the emperor's lands without his permission.[4]

In truth, of course, Bonaparte had forced Francis's hand. The emperor had given much attention to holding state captives and had drawn large sums from the military budget for this purpose. For the Olmütz prisoners alone, the amount would soon total more than twenty-six thousand florins in the midst of a financially ruinous war.[5] For Francis the captives' imprisonment was an important engagement of the war; their release was one more lost battle.

Chasteler's mission was to control damage to the emperor's reputation and pride. This meant whitewashing a legally questionable incarceration that had gone on at Olmütz for three years. He also had to define the release as an act of imperial benevolence. He carried out the task with great care.

Thugut issued his directives on 21 July. However, the corresponding orders of the Aulic War Council to Schröder did not reach Chasteler until two days later. He left Vienna at once and arrived in Olmütz the following evening. Schröder had left to visit the sulphuric waters at Trentchin (Trenčín), Slovakia, but Chasteler managed to convince interim commandant Mikovényi to unseal and read the orders. Since it was already 9:00 P.M., Chasteler agreed to begin questioning the captives the following morning with the help of prison supervisor MacElligot.

Captain MacElligot appeared at Chasteler's quarters at 7:00 A.M. on 25 July. The general ordered that, when the captain entered the cells to bring breakfast at 8:00, he was to take along a note announcing Chasteler's visit at 10:00 and its importance for Lafayette, his wife, Maubourg, and Pusy. The note would inspire exuberant hope among inmates.

Chasteler entered Lafayette's rooms, and the prisoner approached "in a very friendly manner." Chasteler declared it a pleasure that the emperor had chosen him for such an agreeable commission. Lafayette assured Chasteler that he would be as obliging as when they had last conversed at Namur.

Chasteler turned to his commission's first point: the emperor assumed that the allegations of mistreatment were false but wished to ascertain the truth. Chasteler asked if Lafayette had complaints about persons or conditions. Lafayette replied "with fire" that he had not suffered mistreatment from prison staff, but other conditions could not have been worse. He stated that no published complaints about them could have been exaggerated. Chasteler asked him to elaborate, and Lafayette launched into what Chasteler took to be "an immense detail of small inconveniences." He complained about the prison's location between infirmaries whose staffs carried out corpses "almost under his windows," the "disgusting" sewage nearby, the lack of fresh air in his rooms, the lack of news about family members for two years "while they were under the knives of the Jacobins," and his isolation from Maubourg and Pusy. Chasteler pointed out that the prison "was situated on the highest elevation in town," that the Jesuits "would not have built such a magnificent building in an unhealthy place," and that aristocratic cathedral canons lived right next door. Lafayette offered a litany of objections "too long to report."

Chasteler proceeded to his commission's second point: His Majesty's requirement that Lafayette go to America on release. Lafayette responded, again "with warmth," that the Austrians had arrested him "on neutral territory in violation of international law"; that he owed the emperor no explanation for his behavior or plans; that he did not intend "to make any commitment to him that seems to give him rights over my person"; that though he had always seen America as his destination, he would have to test the waters there after release. Chasteler admitted that His Majesty could be flexible on the matter.

Chasteler finally tackled his commission's third point: to explain that the emperor was ready to release Lafayette "without further delay," but that the captive would have to promise never to return to the emperor's lands. Lafayette remained a threat to the Austrian empire because he proclaimed a doctrine that encouraged the overthrow of governments. As soon as Lafayette made the required commitment, "the orders for release, as well as the passports and directions for the further voyage would be delivered."

At first Lafayette seemed to agree "with all possible joy." However, he was surprised that Austria still saw him as a threat. After all, his ideas were now everywhere, and he hardly spoke a word of German. But then Lafayette had second thoughts, and he replied with his own conditions. He would not return unless in the military or diplomatic service of America or France. Chasteler stressed that His Majesty wanted an unconditional commitment. Besides, it was unlikely that Lafayette would reenter the French army, or that Vienna would receive him as an envoy. He argued that setting conditions would only delay release. However, Lafayette insisted that he would name these exceptions even in promising the emperor of China not to enter his lands; and that Chasteler would have done the same for his sovereign.

The talk came to an end. Lafayette offered to write up as full a commitment as he could, along with a statement on his treatment. Chasteler ordered that Lafayette be supplied with quill, ink, and paper, and promised to return at 5:00 P.M.

Lafayette asked that his fellow prisoners join him, but Chasteler declared "the moment had not come for this" and took his leave.

The Austrian general entered the adjacent room to a polite reception from the Lafayette women. Adrienne's arm was bandaged, and she limped from her leg wound. Chasteler explained to her that critical remarks about prison conditions had appeared in foreign journals and had reached the ears of Francis II. The general also noted that she had requested to enter prison with her husband and received permission "as a grace of the Emperor." Chasteler then asked her if, in that light, she might have any complaints. She had several. The authorities had refused her request for an additional bed so that each daughter could have her own. They had refused her any news about her son. General Schröder had returned a note she had written her son two months before, and Thugut had not responded when she protested to him. "A dirty, clumsy, and most sullen soldier" served the meals, and the women had had to eat with their fingers. Madame Lafayette was particularly indignant that, when physicians prescribed medical consultation in Vienna as "the only means to cure a scorbutic malady," the court insisted that any departure would mean no return. In other words she would have to choose between abandoning her husband or facing death. Finally she criticized the lack of "savoir vivre" by former prison supervisor Czernak. Chasteler reminded her that she had agreed to share her husband's incarceration under the same standards as he; that in a prison "it was impossible to find there all the attentions in the world that the beautiful sex has a right to expect"; and that Chasteler would repair any "real shortcomings" in treatment.

Chasteler then visited Maubourg and Pusy in their separate rooms. Maubourg answered the general's questions on treatment "about the same" as the Lafayettes but with "his characteristic passion." The responses of Pusy, whose changed appearance took Chasteler by surprise, were "more measured" but "no less energetic." The wishes of his future homeland, whether France or America, would override any commitment he made to Austria. Chasteler left writing materials, and promised to return at 5:00.

When Chasteler reentered the prison that evening, Lafayette handed him two statements. The longer one opened with explicit refusal to recognize "any legitimate right of the Austrian government to my person" and "what it arrogated to itself concerning disarmed Frenchmen, and strangers to the affairs of the provinces that recognize its domination." It then addressed each point that Chasteler had brought up. Chasteler glanced over the complaints. His embarrassment grew, especially when he looked up to see the Lafayette girls stifling laughter. The parents joined in the hilarity. But Chasteler claimed to already know the details. He diverted the conversation as the Lafayettes brought up more grievances. He deemed "one as frivolous as the other" and explained to Lafayette why he did not find them persuasive: they "all conformed to his status as a state prisoner."

The other statement was "a short, very exalted note": "I the undersigned engage myself to His Majesty the Emperor and King not to enter his hereditary provinces at any time without having obtained his special permission, apart from the rights that my homeland has to my person." Chasteler objected "that since [Lafayette] wanted to go to America as he said himself, I only wanted to facilitate the means, and that finally the conditions he put to the commitment not to return into the hereditary states rendered it, so to speak, null and void." Lafayette responded, "Far be it from me to have feelings of revenge. I would be quite happy to be away from here as soon as possible, but I cannot abase myself." He suggested that Chasteler allow him to meet his fellow inmates in order to establish a common position. It would expedite matters more than eight days of separate meetings. Chasteler promised to consider and respond that evening.[6] He also vowed to immediately send Vienna a courier with Lafayette's unsatisfactory response. This would prove to be an empty threat. Lafayette did not budge, and Chasteler found pretexts to delay the courier till early the next morning, then until noon.[7]

After Chasteler left, Lafayette wrote a fuller statement to hand over the following day. He refused to detail his prison conditions; instead, he referred the general to his wife's letters to Vienna. Lafayette withheld any guarantee to leave for America, as "an assurance to this effect would seem to recognize a right to impose this condition on me." He stressed, "It is my fixed determination never again to set my foot in any country that yields obedience to His Imperial Majesty, the King of Bohemia and Hungary," unless he was bound by patriotic duty to do so.[8]

After he met with Lafayette, Chasteler visited Maubourg and Pusy. They handed him similarly noncommittal notes. The Austrian general realized that the three Frenchmen had somehow been consulting among themselves, and none of them wanted to risk saying too much. He announced that he would have Maubourg, Pusy, and Madame Lafayette brought the following morning to Lafayette's rooms to meet before MacElligot and himself. Chasteler wanted to reach an agreement about prison conditions and a commitment not to return; he believed it was the only way to bring the matter to conclusion.

That evening, as the Austrian general recorded the day's events, Adrienne Lafayette wrote her own account for friends outside. She and her husband assumed that Chasteler would paint as rosy a picture as possible about treatment; however, the Lafayettes refused to sign anything undermining their supporters' claims. They also suspected that Vienna sought a scapegoat for the alleged poor treatment, and they refused to cooperate. Lafayette still felt flattered by this approach from an imperial envoy. He noted "the honor that the Emperor was showing him, to treat with him as one power to another, and to believe that this simple individual threatened such a vast monarchy whose armies were numerous and whose subjects so devoted to their master." Adrienne Lafayette asked that "the good courier" return with local Olmütz friends' views and news the same evening.

The next morning, as promised, Chasteler and MacElligot brought the prisoners together. The ensuing scene became very dramatic. Only "after having left some time for the outpouring of joy by these persons to see each other for the first time in thirty-eight months," could Chasteler proceed to business. Security had been so tight that the Frenchmen had not glimpsed each other in three years even though they lived in close proximity. They all criticized their treatment, but Chasteler claimed that almost everything they described was consistent with the standards for state incarceration. Adrienne Lafayette claimed that Chasteler refused to record anything that reflected poorly on Vienna. After much debate, Chasteler drew up a report that the chief prisoners were willing to sign. It discussed their room and board, access to help by servants and soldiers, medical care, and the succession of prison staff members and commandants. Chasteler wanted to include comments that the care was decent, but he left them out in face of the prisoners' objections.

The Lafayettes were able to pocket the original draft and later compare it to the final version. They concluded from erasures and interlinear notes that the general tried to soften harsh descriptions, but that he also avoided straying far from truth. They smuggled the draft to Ducoudray, to keep in a collection of materials the Lafayettes referred to as "our little archives."

The most difficult object of negotiation was still the commitment not to return to Austrian lands. Chasteler warned that the emperor could refuse any conditions the captives added. Lafayette reminded Chasteler how, five years before, Lafayette had refused political concessions that might have led to his release. Each side made proposals that the other side deemed inadmissible. Finally, after twenty drafts, Chasteler agreed to include separate statements by each of the three men. Each man agreed, with slight variations, not to return unless their homeland required them to do so. However, Maubourg made sure to add that he did not recognize any authority that Vienna claimed to have over them. Chasteler was amiable throughout; he even joked that Germans no longer needed Lafayette, since there were now so many apostles of his doctrine of the rights of man.

Once the main business was finished, the inmates asked to see their servants. Chasteler agreed. Lafayette had not seen either of his, Pontonnier and Compte ("Chavaniac"), for more than twenty months. When the men appeared, Chasteler seemed embarrassed at their haggard condition. Pusy's old servant Jandel later called the Austrian general's scrupulous courtesy "the manners of the devil.'" Chasteler refused the captives' request for future access to each other although he did allow them to stay and dine together that night.

Chasteler returned at 7:00 P.M., allegedly to oversee return of the captives to their cells, but perhaps he wanted to see if they had changed their minds after all. Though their written statements varied from his proposed wording, he thought that they might satisfy Thugut and the emperor. He hoped to deliver the statements that weekend and write the captives on Monday that their passports were on their way. A few days after that, he could arrange carriages and other necessities for departure. He bantered a bit with the captives, and again he told Lafayette, "You are no longer a dangerous man. Your principles are now in the mouth of the entire world." Lafayette answered how delighted he was that the world had become so enlightened. The Austrian general made final preparations to leave at 5:00 the next morning.[9] He left word that Lafayette could resume limited correspondence.[10]

In truth, of course, the captives were already carrying on their own secret correspondence. During and after Chasteler's visit, they slipped notes out to "M. Cant" (Passy) and "the three merchants of Hamburg" (Ducoudray and Victor and Florimond Maubourg). The "three merchants" were passing through Olmütz on the way to Bonaparte's headquarters. One note enclosed a letter from Lafayette to Alexandre de Lameth, written in the margins of a German-language book. In turn the prisoners received notes from local supporters every morning.[11]

The Austrian general's visit caused the prison staff to expect imminent release. The female cook received permission to bid the prisoners goodbye.[12]

But prisoners' obstinacy led to delay. It certainly gave the Austrian cabinet another reason to put off release. It was a grand late example of how Lafayette refused to compromise what he believed to be principles of liberty and justice. His defiance in this matter had long since struck his aunt Tessé as "puerile pride," but it only deepened his supporters' admiration.[13]

Even without the concessions, Austria had little choice but to surrender its captives. On the same day the Directory sent its letter to Bonaparte, Austrian envoy Merveldt informed Thugut that General Clarke, Director Barthélemy, and Minister Talleyrand all wanted to hear that the release had finally occurred.[14] On the same day, Romeuf arrived in Vienna as special envoy to press the issue.

Romeuf traveled under tight security. A Major Auernhammer of the Staff Regiment of Dragoons escorted him everywhere until he left the emperor's lands. The court housed him in Marchese di Gallo's townhouse, which had bars on the windows. Allegedly a French barber shaved Romeuf every morning and, in the process, slipped him notes from supporters.

Romeuf spoke with Gallo and another official, Count Philipp von Cobenzl. When Gallo reported Lafayette's refusal to accept the emperor's offer, Romeuf was shaken. "I admired your unwavering character," the envoy wrote Lafayette, "but I admit that concerning the way in which [Gallo] spoke to me of the emperor's determination, I trembled that this circumstance would greatly retard the day we await with such great impatience." Romeuf tried his best to smooth the court's ruffled feathers. He also sought permission to visit the prisoners and even stay with them, but officials claimed to be unable to give it. Gallo advised Romeuf to go to Hamburg to await the outcome.

Though he could not see Francis II, Romeuf had a long talk with Thugut, a man whom he would soon call "the grand vizier of Austria." Thugut furiously attacked Lafayette's ideology and his refusal to accept conditions for release but also acknowledged that His Majesty would release him anyway. In fact Thugut claimed that the only remaining holdup had been determining where to set the men free, but the court had finally reached a decision. An Austrian escort would take the captives to Hamburg, where it would turn them over to the American consul. However, Francis demanded a new condition, this one for the consul: to promise that Lafayette would leave all German states east of the Rhine within twelve days of arrival in Hamburg.[15]

Thus Francis had decided to make someone other than Lafayette responsible and to surrender him not to the French but the Americans. It was a neat trick to preserve the emperor's pride even in face of Lafayette's intransigence. Pillet had already expected this trick when he wrote John Quincy Adams. In turn Adams notified his father, the U.S. president-elect: "The Emperor by giving [Lafayette] up now to the application of the American government, will only be spared the mortification of being compelled to yield him to the claims of France."[16]

Thugut refused Romeuf's request to take the offer to Olmütz. However, he did suggest that Romeuf write Lafayette. He promised that Lafayette could write Romeuf in Hamburg and, through him, Lafayette's aunt Chauvaniac in the Auvergne. On 9 August, before he left imperial Austrian territory, Romeuf sent Lafayette a letter. It arrived as promised. Lafayette informed his fellow captives, and all agreed to accept the offer. Lafayette could not hide his gratification when he wrote Romeuf: "As anxious as I am to leave here, I am all the more inspired to tell you how sweet it is for me to owe you so much." He also thanked Barthélemy, Bonaparte, Clarke, and even Gallo, enclosing notes to Chauvaniac.[17]

The day after Romeuf left for Hamburg, Bonaparte and Clarke met Gallo and reiterated that the Directory wanted Lafayette's party released.[18] Thugut responded by describing his talk with Romeuf. He assured Clarke that the choice of Hamburg "will solve your difficulties and ours" and expressed confidence that Romeuf was helping Parish to arrange the transfer. Clarke sent the note to Talleyrand and wrote Thugut of his satisfaction and hope that Romeuf could receive the prisoners "at the moment they will be freed."[19]

The arrival of Romeuf's letter in the Olmütz prison set off a series of communications. Through secret offices, presumably those of Passy and Ducoudray, the inmates informed supporters in Dresden. Maubourg composed a note for his wife, Henriette, and smuggled it down to Adrienne Lafayette, who added words of her own. She also enclosed a note for Pillet that included a description of Chasteler's visit in late July, transcripts of his report, and Lafayette's written declaration. Romeuf may have had the letters in hand when he passed through Dresden, where he reported to Pillet and Mesdames Maubourg and Pusy. Pillet then sent dispatches to Paris supporters, including Director Barthélemy, Minister Talleyrand, Deputy Emmery, and publicist Masclet. He requested that Paris authorize him to visit Vienna as a special envoy.[20]

Romeuf arrived in Hamburg on the evening of 18 August. He rushed with the latest news to André Masson in the Catharinenstrasse. The next morning, Masson took him to Parish's country home at Nienstedten. Parish wrote the emperor's representative at Hamburg, Baron Rudolf von Buol zu Schauenstein, that he had a "pressing desire to satisfy" the emperor's conditions. He gave Buol his personal thanks and the gratitude of the United States. He also asked permission for Romeuf to bring the consent to Vienna. Masson and Romeuf returned to Hamburg to have a scribe make a formal copy, which they sent back to Parish by special courier for signing. Then, with Parish's teenage son David in tow, they set out for Buol's home.[21]

Buol had received a dispatch that morning explaining the new conditions. Thugut had written that His Majesty saw fit to free the prisoners, and he asked Parish to see that they left German territory within eight days of arrival (not twelve days, as Francis had specified). The freed men should proceed to Holland or America since the Directory barred them from entering France. Thugut asked Buol to work with Parish and Romeuf to make a plan for receiving Lafayette's party and sending it on its way. As soon as Thugut received the plan, he would send the release and extradition orders.[22]

At 6:00 P.M. Romeuf, Masson, and Parish appeared at Buol's door. They explained their business and turned over an explanatory note from Marchese Gallo. Buol reported that the dispatch had just arrived from Vienna, and he said he was ready to serve them. They pulled out Parish's freshly composed commitment. Buol agreed that it fulfilled all conditions, and proposed informing Vienna immediately. The visitors asked that since Parish had commissioned Romeuf to offer all necessary aid in the name of the United States, he could serve as Buol's courier. Romeuf hoped dearly to have the "incomparable joy of opening the padlocks of Olmütz myself." Although Buol wanted to oblige, he said, His Majesty had prohibited him from issuing passports, and Thugut had barred Romeuf from returning to Vienna. Romeuf stressed that they had no time to waste. The visitors asked Buol to write one or two friends in the foreign ministry to expedite the matter. Buol mentioned a few influential candidates, one of whom Romeuf recalled from his recent visit. The Austrian envoy composed his letter on the spot and sent it by ordinary post that evening.[23]

Oddly enough, despite what Thugut and Romeuf thought, Parish was no longer American consul in Hamburg. The previous year President Washington had appointed a replacement, a merchant named Samuel Williams.[24] Parish and Buol both knew this, of course. The day after their talk, Parish approached Williams to gain his support for the arrangement with Vienna. Williams claimed that he had not received official authorization, but he agreed to cooperate as a private American citizen. He decided to simplify matters by letting Parish continue to represent the United States in correspondence on the matter.

Meanwhile Williams conferred with two American merchants in Hamburg-Altona, George Joy and Francis Childs, who offered to transport the Lafayette family to America. On the morning of 21 August, Williams, Parish, and Masson visited Buol to confirm the agreement and discuss details. One matter was where Lafayette's party should proceed once released. Masson thought the group should avoid Hamburg altogether. He recommended embarking at a place further up the Elbe and sailing to Holland. Each Frenchman could then slip into neighboring France. Buol wanted to ask Vienna for guidance, but Masson proposed that it was better to reserve any imperial decree on the matter until after Lafayette's party had left Olmütz. Buol conceded that going even to Altona would fulfill the demand that the party leave Hamburg.

Word of the agreement spread quickly among Lafayette's supporters. On 22 August, Masson and Romeuf sent the news to De Staël, Masclet, and Simiane in Paris. Williams sent it to colleagues William Vans Murray, who had succeeded John Quincy Adams as U.S. consul at The Hague, and Rufus King, American minister in London. Williams and King then reported the arrangements to Secretary of State Timothy Pickering. Murray and King also notified George Washington, who had retired to Mount Vernon.[25]

Masson was surely the "correspondent in Hamburg" who sent the news via Paris contacts to George Lafayette. When La Colombe visited Mount Vernon on 7 October to report it, the young Lafayette insisted on returning to Europe. Washington supplied him and his tutor with money and letters. On 12 October, the former president drove them to Georgetown to catch the postal coach for New York City. The two young men visited Hamilton a final time, and on 25 October they embarked on the brig *Clio* for Le Havre de Grâce.[26]

Masson made sure to send the news to a select few. He did not want to jeopardize the agreement through premature publicity, so he dared not announce anything publicly until the captives had left prison.[27]

Parish was happy to play the part that the Austrians, French, and Americans desired of him. He asked that Thugut allow Romeuf to come and offer the prisoners "help in my name and that of the United States, that may be necessary at the moment of their release." Such aid would include arranging the party's departure for America. Armed with the letter and a U.S. passport, Romeuf left Hamburg at dawn on 26 August. He carried American funds and mail for Lafayette from De Staël and other supporters. Charles Maubourg, younger brother of the prisoner, also came along. However, the men were unable to proceed beyond Dresden because of Austrian refusals to receive them. Thugut informed Buol that Romeuf's offer of money was unnecessary. The imperial treasury was covering the costs of extradition. In any case Parish had authorized Olmütz merchant Hirsch to provide the Lafayettes any necessary funds.[28]

The day of release seemed at hand. Lafayette supporters in Hamburg debated where Lafayette should live before conditions allowed return to France. They discussed and rejected such preliminary destinations as Switzerland and Bremen. Masson consulted Balthasar Abbema, minister plenipotentiary of the Batavian Republic in Hamburg, and set hopes on Holland. He did not recommend going directly there. The Batavian Republic was now a French satellite state, so going there could be almost as provocative as entering France. Masson wanted Lafayette's company to avoid Hamburg, given the emperor's influence there, and even neighboring Danish Altona, as it was so accessible to the curious. He planned to find them a few days' lodgings two-three leagues down the Elbe. After that the party could take up quarters elsewhere in Danish Holstein: the area of Plön, where Mesdames de Tessé and Montagu lived, or perhaps Itzehoe in the west. It would be prudent to avoid the British electorate of Hanover bordering Hamburg and Danish Holstein on the south. With the passage of time, the attention of the public and Directory would turn elsewhere, and the Lafayettes could slip quietly into the Batavian Republic. As a cover, supporters would spread the word that they were on their way to America. Once Lafayette was at a suitable house near Utrecht, Romeuf or Pillet would visit the Paris circle and confer with its members about how to persuade French authorities to allow his return. It would not be to Paris, but to a provincial spot such as Auvergne, his native region. The judgment of Pierre du Pont de Nemours on timing and strategy would be particularly valuable. Perhaps the legislative councils would be willing to issue a suitable decree when they ratified a peace treaty.[29]

The French government kept pushing for release, and opinion in Paris seemed ever more strongly on Lafayette's side. Masclet carried Lafayette's 25 July declaration to the foreign ministry and read it to Talleyrand. The minister was "enchanted." Talleyrand had Masclet read it out loud a second time, then read it himself to three officials happening by. All found it "admirable." Masclet wanted to take it immediately to Director Barras but feared that Lafayette had written perhaps too nobly. The declaration might cause the Directory again to worry about Lafayette's potential as a rival. Talleyrand disagreed. He could not resist going to Luxembourg Palace to read the declaration to the entire Directory. He advised Masclet to publish it, but Masclet objected that this might jeopardize the prisoners' release.

Others also reacted favorably. Later that morning Masclet showed the declaration to Madame de Staël, who voiced admiration, and then to Benjamin Constant, who "thought, as all do who have seen it, that it is impossible to express oneself with a precision more striking, a simplicity more noble, and a dignity more imposing." Masclet returned to the foreign ministry to dine with Talleyrand and

De Staël. The minister told him that he had not found the right opportunity to present the declaration at the Directory's plenary session but had read it to Barras, who "found it really quite nice" and planned to present it to the other directors at their meeting the next day.

The next morning, Masclet accompanied Talleyrand to the Luxembourg Palace. Along the way they discussed the geographical and political place that Lafayette might occupy in France. When they arrived, Barras expressed satisfaction with Lafayette's declaration, support for his release, and even openness to his return.[30]

Masclet made further use of Lafayette's declaration in the coming days. He asked Madame Simiane to have a copy sent to Fitzpatrick in England. He promised also to pass a translation "by another route" to James Perry, editor of the *Morning Chronicle.*[31]

Meanwhile the captives' impatience had reached a fever pitch. "They're in a terrible crisis of hope, of fear," Adrienne Lafayette wrote of her company. She herself had already bought clothes for the departure.[32] Paris papers published protests against delays. On 7 August a group of Constitutionals held an anniversary dinner celebrating their release from St. Lazare prison after Robespierre's fall. Masclet raised a toast to Lafayette's liberation, and "it was received with transport." Masclet anticipated each day's mail for word from Hamburg. Fox fretted to Fitzpatrick that "it is a sad thing that we do not hear any thing about the delivering of La Fayette and c[ompany]." At Bonaparte's Udine headquarters, Victor Maubourg felt "touched" by the interest both generals were now showing. He concluded "that a hundred thousand French would go to the walls of Vienna if the emperor does not sign" the release papers.[33] Premature reports heightened the tension in Paris. News came from Hamburg that César Maubourg had already sent his little dog from prison to his brother Victor in Italy. Madame Maisonneuve made ready to apply for passports from Director Reubell and, if necessary, the French minister of police, Pierre Sotin de la Coindière. Likewise Masclet applied for papers from the chief of the passport division in the Ministry of General Police, to depart for Hamburg with Madame Simiane.[34]

Early in September news reached Olmütz that Parish had met the emperor's conditions. Lafayette could not resist asking Pillet in Dresden that Mesdames Pusy and Maubourg solicit Thugut in writing. He dictated the entire letter and offered a blizzard of advice aimed at accelerating the release. He exclaimed that "we prisoners would do anything in the world" to shorten the years of imprisonment even by twenty-four hours, except compromise principles or friends.[35]

On 16 September, Romeuf reported to Bonaparte that Parish had fulfilled all conditions and that Buol's letter had reached Vienna on 27 August. Nevertheless there had been no sign of release in the past three weeks. Romeuf urged the general to act.[36]

Back in Paris, the French government had just undergone radical change. The coup of 18th Fructidor (4 September 1797), supported by Bonaparte's military forces, had purged moderates and royalists in the Directory, legislative councils, and press, ushering in a more radical regime. Director Barthélemy was under arrest and facing deportation. Director Carnot managed to flee his Luxembourg Palace bedroom through a window, garden gate, and nighttime streets. The coup put many of Lafayette's Parisian supporters under suspicion. In a letter to De Staël the day of the coup, Masclet described the ominous silence of Paris. The city gates were shut to prevent any departures. Arrests began. Many associated with Lafayette's cause fled the country. The president of a new Directory soon confirmed that Lafayette was banned from returning. In a speech before the purged Council of Five Hundred, Joseph Poullain-Grandprey, supporter of the coup, compared Lafayette to traitor Dumouriez. It also became clear that Lafayette was no longer welcome in France's "sister" state, the Batavian Republic.[37]

When word of the coup reached Vienna, Thugut knew that the French position in peace negotiations could only harden. But by that point, he had already issued instructions expediting release of the captives. On 7 September Thugut informed the emperor's aide Count Franz de Paula von Colloredo-Wallsee. "The affair to transfer the prisoners of Olmütz to Hamburg is arranged, and I presume that His Majesty will deign to approve my reaching an agreement with the Aulic War Council to transport all this caravan of Lafayette, his wife, children, and other companions in captivity to Hamburg and consign them to the American."[38] On 9 September, Thugut directed the war council to expedite the matter. The next day the council commissioned Major Auernhammer, the same cavalry officer who had accompanied Romeuf in Vienna, to lead the escort to Hamburg. The council also ordered the Moravian General Command to provide Auernhammer with an officer's pass for foreign travel. The State Chancellery was to arrange transit rights with states through which the group would pass. Auernhammer was to pay for postal horses and costs of room and board from army funds. The prisoner release was to occur without publicity. Adrienne Lafayette had already spent 513 florins 8 crosses in August to acquire two four-person carriages with accessories. Lafayette, Maubourg, and Pusy could share the first carriage, the Lafayette women the second. The major was to follow in his own vehicle, and shepherd the group as quickly as possible along the most direct postal station route, with stopovers at designated inns around noon and at night. Told to see that his wards received good treatment, he was to order food in the quantity and quality they had known in Olmütz and to prevent them from spreading harmful ideas, books, or money among the emperor's subjects.[39]

Olmütz commandant Schröder asked garrison surgeon Axter for final medical evaluations that focused on the captives' ability to endure a long trip. Axter concluded that they would all do well despite debilities. He recommended mild medicines to help them along the way.[40]

The reality was somewhat harsher than Axter indicated. In early summer, an informer in Olmütz, perhaps Ducoudray, had written Masson that the captives were wasting away. Adrienne Lafayette's symptoms had returned, including a painful leg wound and swollen arms. Axter's pleas to let her visit sulphuric waters nearby had gone unheeded. In late summer Madame Lafayette noted that she and her older daughter, Anastasie, had been experiencing "alarming" symptoms. When cooler weather returned, her husband resumed coughing and having frequent fevers. Pusy and Maubourg were in relatively good health, but they were much less robust than they had once been. Pontonnier had fared well for most of his custody, but lately he had fallen quite ill and was suffering more than anyone else.[41]

Thugut notified diplomats of the imminent transfer. On 1 September he sent a letter to Talleyrand, which Talleyrand showed to Madame de Staël's friend and his, Henriette Lucie de La Tour du Pin-Gouvernet at the foreign ministry. He also announced the news at Staël's home nearby. After Masclet had read the words, he determined to spread them abroad. By 20 September, *La Sentinelle* and other Parisian papers were reporting the news.[42]

Thugut notified the French command rather slowly. Gallo wrote Clarke and Bonaparte of the release on 16 September. On 19 September Gallo and fellow negotiator Baron Simon von Degelmann confirmed the news in a meeting with their counterparts in Passariano. Bonaparte responded "frostily," noting "that he had solicited the object for five months."[43]

Thugut also alerted Buol. On the morning of 18 September, Buol informed Masson that the Austrian cabinet had sent the release order to Olmütz. The news spread quickly through Hamburg-Altona, then to Plön and London. From there it crossed the Atlantic.[44]

Thugut told Buol that the emperor had ordered departure "without delay." Vienna had just made all necessary dispositions, including funds and escort by "an intelligent and trustworthy officer," who was to alert the Austrian envoy immediately on arriving in Hamburg. Thugut also provided the official reason for delivering the prisoners: "that, as His Majesty did not contract any definite commitment with the French that touches on the release of the prisoners named above, the motive of the particular interest that the United States of America appear to attach to it contributed greatly to bring His Majesty to this act of charity; that, for the rest, His Majesty will always be quite gratified, should opportunities arise, to give the United States of America genuine tokens of his friendship and benevolence."[45] The captives knew the truth. Soon after their release, they rejected the Austrian claim out of hand. They had been "torn from the prisons of Olmütz by the victories of the Republic and the interest of the French nation," Maubourg and

Pusy later wrote Buol. The Frenchmen attacked the pretense that they owed their freedom to Francis II, when they actually owed him their forty months of captivity. Lafayette deemed the "fallacious declaration of the Vienna court" to be an attempt "to dispense me from owing liberty and life to the victories and interest of my country and to the steps taken by its government." His wife agreed.[46]

At the last, Bonaparte was "their liberator," "the conqueror" of their jailors, as Lafayette, Maubourg, and Pusy addressed him after their release. John Adams later described Bonaparte to Lafayette as "your principal Deliverer from Olmutz." Lafayette adopted the phrase himself when he wrote Jefferson and McHenry.[47] He voiced the conviction that "had it not been for the glorious display of our military institutions, and uncommon exertions of the conquerors, we never should have left our prison but for the scaffold."[48] Lafayette's debt to Bonaparte become ironic after the general became Napoléon I, "Emperor of the French" and tyrant over much of Europe, and Lafayette himself served as figurehead of the democratic opposition.

Making his way to Dresden, the first major city on Lafayette's expected route after crossing the Bohemian border, Romeuf joined Pillet and the families of Pusy and Maubourg and sent anxious missives to Vienna, confirming that Parish and Lafayette would cooperate in the terms of the release and asking that the release be expeditious. Romeuf expected success and was frustrated at these delays. He made plans with Charles Maubourg to join Victor in Italy, while Mesdames Maubourg and Pusy considered pursuing visas to lobby in Vienna. Pillet sought support to send another envoy there.[49]

The Dresden group expressed bitter disappointment to allies in Hamburg and Paris that Thugut had not yet released the captives. Early on 25 September, Masclet arrived at Talleyrand's quarters to read aloud portions of letters just arrived, that reported delay. Someone else had told Talleyrand the news the day before, but he had not given it credence. Now the minister expressed shock "that after an assurance so precise, so positive, so official, one could think to defer even by a day to carry out the promise." Talleyrand said it proved Thugut's bad faith. He also felt it proved that Thugut intended to renew the war and avoid releasing the prisoners entirely. The matter would likely be clear within days. Given his sense of the new French regime, Talleyrand dismissed Masclet's suggestion that supporters appeal to the Directory. Instead the two men agreed to publish an article in the *Conservateur*, a new progovernment journal subsidized by the Directory. The article would reveal Austria's broken promises, describe the captives' situation, and report Lafayette's last declaration from Olmütz. Talleyrand assumed that Bonaparte was the most effective agent disposed to help. Talleyrand promised to send a special courier the next day, asking the general to act. He also promised to approach Barras, who seemed to be the only current director consistently supportive of release. Masclet alerted Madame Simiane and counseled her to take courage. He also determined to place an appropriate article with Dominique Garat, editor of the *Conservateur*.[50]

The plans proved unnecessary. On 18 September, final release formalities went forward. Lafayette was read once again the decision made by the Luxembourg military tribunal five years before, "that the existence of Lafayette was incompatible with the security of the governments of Europe." The prisoners signed receipts for confiscated property. Their jailors had stored it for the entire period of the Olmütz incarceration at the commandant's headquarters on the Upper Square. In a final act of defiance, the Lafayettes and Maubourg crossed out the noble titles preceding their names on the documents before adding their signatures. The captives distributed furniture bought with their own money to soldiers who had guarded and waited on them.

At 6:00 A.M. the next day, more than five years since Lafayette's arrest and two weeks after he had turned forty, the prison gate opened. He had spent a half decade in the prime of his life behind bars. He had not stepped outside his rooms for three years. Mary Square before him and the sky above must have seemed very broad; the outside air very sweet indeed. The Lafayettes, Maubourg, Pusy, and their servants boarded the loaded carriages. Virginie Lafayette later recalled that they were, "for a moment," able to see "the friend who had run such risks to alleviate the sufferings of our captivity," almost surely Passy. Other people tried to approach Lafayette at this moment and in the days to come. The escort saw to it that none could succeed until the party had left the emperor's lands.[51]

The trip to the border proved relatively uneventful. Ducoudray later claimed that he went along as an official French representative. He also recalled a mysterious count from Vienna, an agent of the Ministry of Police. Vienna, not the prisoners, had determined their route into freedom. As Adrienne Lafayette put it, the captives "could no more regulate their voyage than zoo animals being transported." The route took them onto the main highway southwest to Brünn, northwest toward Prague, then north-northwest, stopping a final time in the emperor's states at the border town of Peterswalde (Petrovice). Here a young Huguenot was awaiting the party to serve as translator; he was the son of Peter Villaume, a well-known pedagogue who had emigrated from Prussia to Denmark for political reasons. The group proceeded to the Saxon town of Bautzen, where Romeuf, Pillet, and the wives and families of Maubourg and Pusy were waiting. They included two daughters and two younger sons of Maubourg, his eldest son Florimond, and his brother Charles. They also included Pusy's five-year-old daughter, whom he saw for the first time on this occasion. Maubourg saw his children much more mature than he had known, and Lafayette greet friends and aides who were older versions of the men whom he remembered. After all exchanged embraces, tears, and some first words of renewed acquaintance, they became a single, expanded caravan that journeyed into Dresden.[52]

The news spread quickly. Gallo wrote Victor Maubourg in Italy "that your brother and his companions of misfortune are at liberty." Masson announced the news to the Paris circle from Hamburg, in a letter dated "29 Sept. in the 1st Year of the Liberty of the Prisoners of Olmütz": *They are finally free.* Word reached La Colombe in Philadelphia by 21 November. At the beginning of December, Washington received letters announcing the release, from La Colombe and U.S. envoys in London and The Hague.[53] Sir Morton Eden, British resident minister in Vienna, notified Lord Grenville by a dispatch of 23 September. There was no hint of disappointment, no indication that the release was important to British foreign policy.[54]

Once the convoy had passed the border, Major Auernhammer could no longer isolate his charges from the surrounding population. On 26 September, a large crowd formed before Lafayette's inn at Dresden. Auernhammer called in Saxon guards to keep order. After five years of isolation from the outside world, Lafayette enjoyed the attention enormously. He "took every opportunity to show himself to the curious," a local observer, Hans Krabbe, reported to brother-in-law August Hennings the next day. Leipzig was holding its huge fair at the time, but several hotel guests willingly vacated rooms to make way for the famous arrivals. Lafayette was gratified that hundreds of students welcomed him to Halle with music and a torch-lit parade. He addressed the cheering crowd in halting German. He was also delighted to meet an active supporter during his captivity, Professor Reinhold Forster. Virginie later recounted, "Particularly at Dresden, Leipsic [Leipzig], Halle, Hamburg, our journey was a prolonged triumph. Crowds thronged to see my father and his companions." A first newspaper fell into the party's hands, announcing the French coup. Major Auernhammer had made clear that his wards were not to write letters, but Adrienne Lafayette managed to slip out a note at Braunschweig to her father, Ayen.[55] Along the way Lafayette encountered an American artillery officer, a Lieutenant Guimpi, and expressed "the pleasing emotions I felt at the first sight, after so long a time, of an American uniform."[56]

Some of the former captives revived considerably in the course of the trip. Even while trying to maintain some pretense of control after leaving the emperor's lands, Auernhammer proved quite solicitous to his charges. Lafayette and daughter Anastasie suffered the least illness and recovered quickly. Within a couple weeks after arrival in Hamburg, Lafayette proclaimed that his poor health had been only momentary. By the beginning of 1798, Adrienne Lafayette could pronounce her husband "unbelievably restored."[57]

Others' health problems persisted. Pusy, Pontonnier, and Adrienne Lafayette suffered the most. Pusy was emaciated. Even by year's end he did not recover as his friends hoped. Pontonnier had experienced chest problems and nervous collapse shortly before release, and his companions worried about his survival on the trip north. Not until weeks later did Hamburg physicians declare him out of mortal danger, and Lafayette still voiced concern more than a year later.

Adrienne Lafayette was also in wretched condition. The rash that she had long complained of had expanded to cover much of her arms and entire left side. Her left foot bore a large open wound. The trip was an ordeal for her. She was still unable to walk and had pains in teeth and limbs. A voyage to America was out of the question. She had periods of remission, but she never recovered from the illness. She became bedridden in August 1807, perhaps because of the lead-based medicine she received. At midnight that Christmas Eve, she died at her aunt Tessé's townhouse in Paris.[58]

Her heroic initiative to rescue her husband and the suffering she endured as a result had earned Adrienne Lafayette widespread admiration. Roederer spoke for many in a spring 1797 issue of his *Journal de Paris* that "she is the most valuable jewel of the French Republic," deserving a victory crown as much as Bonaparte and other generals of the Republic's victorious armies.[59]

Supporters in Hamburg had been reconsidering where the former captives would go, given the emperor's demand that they promptly leave this "free imperial city." The new French government would not allow the Batavian Republic to accept them. Count Christian zu Rantzau, a liberal acquaintance of Hennings's, offered the group his home at Ratzeburg, a Danish Holstein island town fifty kilometers to the east, while he wintered in Copenhagen. Another possibility was Voght's estate of Flottbek, about six kilometers to the west, also in Danish Holstein. Lafayette's supporters looked elsewhere for various reasons. They feared that Voght's unfinished country home would prove too cold for the weak and ill and that Rantzau's palace would be too humid. They came to agree that the only feasible place was the Wittmold estate near Plön in northern Danish Holstein.[60] Here, far from the public eye and the emperor's control, Adrienne Lafayette's aunt Tessé and sister Pauline de Montagu ran a prosperous farm. They expected the family to stay at least the winter. The Lafayettes had looked forward for months to a sojourn there.[61]

On 27 September, Parish visited Buol to agree on how to receive the party and where it should then go. The imperial minister read him Thugut's order, "which says expressly that M. de Lafayette is not liberated at the instance of France, but merely to show the Emperor's consideration of the United States of America." Parish replied with gratitude, personally and on behalf of the United States. They agreed that Parish should initially receive the group at his house in Hamburg, where Buol would declare them free. Buol would have Auernhammer alert him as to the hour the company would arrive, and Buol would notify Parish. They hoped to keep from attracting the curious, by keeping the traveler's names confidential, a vain hope indeed. After a short stay, the group would continue on to the Wittmold estate. Buol notified Vienna of the arrangements, while Parish returned to Hamburg and informed Gouverneur Morris.[62]

U.S. Consul Williams was not privy to the plans. He was under the impression that, barring reasons of health, the Lafayettes would take Joy's ship to Philadelphia. Even on the eve of arrival, Williams mistook the family's intended winter quarters to be "lodgings about ten miles from Hamburg."[63] In most of the affair, Parish played Williams's rightful role. Even former diplomat Morris seemed better informed than Williams.

The Lafayette party approached the Elbe River in early October. Major Auernhammer rode ahead to Harburg on the southern bank and crossed in a launch to Hamburg. Here, on 2 October, he alerted Buol and Parish. The next evening, Parish came to town to prepare the official handover. Romeuf informed the local French envoy, Karl Friedrich Reinhard, of the arrival of Lafayette's group and the terms of transfer.

The party entered Hamburg, after two weeks in transit. In good weather the carriages reached Harburg on the evening of 3 October. The next morning a large American merchant ship of eight hundred tons, the *John*, saluted Lafayette's retinue and sent a barge to pick it up. The ship's Boston owner, George Joy, had been holding his vessel ready to carry the Lafayettes to Philadelphia. He prepared a light meal on board, where a crowd of well-wishers and such old friends as Cadignan welcomed Lafayette's party.

U.S. Consul Williams read a welcome in the name of local Americans. Lafayette replied with aplomb. He thanked the U.S. government, its diplomats, and his American rescuer Francis Huger. The resident Dutch minister, Abbema, gave a similar address in the name of the Batavian Republic. After the meal, Joy's barge hoisted an American flag. It carried the company into Hamburg's harbor, where many nations' ships displayed their colors in honor of the former prisoners. Shouts of welcome carried across the water from surrounding vessels.[64]

At 5:00 P.M. on 4 October 1797, Joy's launch brought its passengers to steps leading up to the harbor gatehouse (the Baumhaus). Lafayette's friends, supporters, and curious onlookers crowded around the inn, a place famous for its high veranda overlooking the water. A young, liberal physician, Heinrich de Chaufepié, waited in Parish's carriage at the adjacent bridge on Stubbenhuk Lane, to offer medical care. A twelve-year-old Hamburg boy was so entranced with the spectacle, the first time he had ever seen such a famous person, that he wrote down his experience as soon as he returned home. Years later the well-known Prussian diplomat and writer Karl Varnhagen von Ense published his childhood recollection of Lafayette's arrival:

My father and I stood at a favorable place, and saw him disembark, accompanied by his wife and his two daughters. The other two companions of his captivity,

Bureaux-Pusy and Latour-Maubourg, followed behind. He appeared afflicted, mild and well intentioned, but also firm and decisive. When he caught sight of the French cockade on the hats of those welcoming him, he greeted them delightedly by raising his own cockade high over his head. At every step up the stairs, he received new embraces, new hand clasps. With tears in his eyes, he blessed the soil of liberty that he again strode upon, for until this place he was still under the escort and supervision of an Austrian officer. The entire proceedings were quiet and simple. Only when he climbed into the carriage of the American consul Parish, I believe with the Hamburg Doctor Chaufepié, a thunderous "Vive Lafayette!" sounded from the thick mass of onlookers.[65]

Another eyewitness recalled how Lafayette wore "a thoughtful expression, marked by friendliness and satisfaction." At the moment he entered the carriage, a young man pointed out what a large crowd of onlookers surrounded him. "No matter," Lafayette replied, "I am used to it."[66]

Meanwhile, Buol had been hosting Morris and Parish in his home. Buol expressed irritation that the party had wasted time on Joy's ship instead of coming directly that morning by ferry. Around 4:00 P.M. Parish left to prepare the handover. Shortly after 5:00 P.M., a courier arrived at Buol's to announce the party's arrival. Buol and Morris rose from the dinner table and headed for Parish's residence on the Deichstrasse.

At the harbor the Lafayettes, Maubourg, and Pusy climbed into Parish's carriage. Other carriages followed, bringing Maubourg's wife, two daughters, and sister-in-law, as well as Louis Romeuf and René Pillet. The sensational effect of their appearance continued as the carriages worked their way along narrow alleys through crowds seeking to catch sight of the famous visitors.

The crowd entered and filled the foyer of Parish's home. Lafayette rushed to embrace Parish, while the Lafayette women clung to his arms. Parish led a weeping Adrienne Lafayette to a sofa and spent fifteen minutes calming her ecstatic husband. Buol joined them, and Parish introduced him to the family. Parish then beckoned Buol, his secretary, Auernhammer, Morris, and Lafayette into an inner room. There Auernhammer transferred custody to Buol, who formally announced the company's release with the understanding that it would leave Hamburg and sail to America. "Notwithstanding this," Morris later recalled, "it appeared to me that M. de Lafayette chose to consider himself as freed by the influence of General Bonaparte." Morris believed that his own efforts had played a key role, but said nothing at the time: "I did not choose to contest the matter, because, believing my applications at Vienna had procured his liberty, it would have looked like claiming acknowledgments." The former prisoners thanked Auernhammer and offered a substantial reward. He politely refused. Buol and the major left to send a report to Vienna. As Parish prepared to return to his country estate, Lafayette and his companions asked him to request a delay in the evening closure of the city gates. They wanted to have time first to visit the French resident minister before they departed to lodgings beyond.[67] Lafayette was now, had always really been, and would forever remain, a free man.

EPILOGUE

Waking Fettered Nations

Lafayette's flight from France in 1792 interrupted his formal political career, plunging him from high position to the status of an apparently powerless victim awaiting a potentially fatal outcome. But he was never powerless. Individuals sympathetic to him and his ideals and grateful for his military, political, and inspirational role in promoting constitutionally grounded liberty in America and Europe, kept contact with him, sustained him, and lobbied for his release. Most of these people lacked public office. Many were women in a world whose officials were men. Their ultimate effectiveness hinged on international networks that operated both behind the scenes and in public, in private homes, salons, government offices, press rooms and newspaper kiosks, cafés, postal stations, fortress garrisons, the prisons themselves, and the cross-border traffic in between. Eventually circumstances coincided to allow partisans to convince the army and government of France to force Austria to surrender Lafayette and his companions.

Lafayette's prison years represent a well-substantiated case of political captivity in early modern times. They reveal the mechanisms that governments applied to suppress people and ideas that they considered ideologically objectionable. They also demonstrate the political potential of individuals and groups largely lacking formal authority. Working cooperatively, imaginatively, and at times quite courageously, these people could bypass the machinery of suppression. By helping set countervailing official mechanisms in motion, they could even bring it to a halt.

State methods to contain, control, and eliminate religious dissidents had evolved over generations in Europe. In the eighteenth century, rulers such as the Prussian king and Austrian emperor turned from targeting those whom they deemed theologically objectionable to attacking those whom they considered political threats.[1]

In a way the age's revolutionary ideologies were just new forms of dissident religion. Some saw the French wars as ideological conflicts similar to the earlier wars of religion. Some considered them to be a struggle of faith with irreligion or demonic powers.[2] Lafayette later admitted that his own love of liberty carried "the enthusiasm of religion,"[3] that he was "religious toward liberty," that it was "a sacred obligation that I must acquit myself of."[4] He claimed that radical Jacobins slandered "the gospel of liberty" much as earlier tyrants had distorted "the gospel of Jesus Christ" to justify "religious massacres and an ecclesiastical aristocracy."[5] He referred to his jailors sometimes as "the Inquisition"[6] and called his imprisoned company "martyrs."[7] The Prussian and Austrian monarchs certainly thought that he wanted to replace age-old beliefs, practices, and aspirations with those of his own making. They welcomed the opportunity to remove him from action. What they did not appreciate was the depth and range of his support, reaching from members of their prison staffs to influential circles in major western cities, forming transatlantic networks of communication, financial assistance, and publicity.

In the end the French government and its military rightly deserve credit for forcing Lafayette's release. But they acted under the influence of persistent lobbying by individuals without official authority. They had already informed and otherwise cooperated with American diplomats and their superiors in Philadelphia, who—maintaining formal neutrality toward the warring European powers—tried to keep communications open with the prisoner, to give him and his family financial aid and political protection, and to broach privately the interest of the United States in Lafayette's eventual release. Fayettists had equipped minority members of Parliament with news of the latest prison developments to report on the floor of Commons. Their parliamentary addresses and the resulting debates, along with well-informed Fayettist editorials, entered the international press. They put the Austrian court on the defensive, leading to improved prison conditions and Vienna's ever greater readiness to find a way to rid itself of its burdensome guests. The publicity also shaped public opinion in France in favor of release, opinion that found expression on the floors of the French legislative chambers and exercised pressure on the Directory and their generals. Germaine de Staël and her circle lobbied these individuals personally and worked to insert associates into positions where they could exercise favorable official influence. Talleyrand became head of the foreign ministry in Paris, and Louis Romeuf a representative of generals Bonaparte and Clarke in Vienna. The evidence is highly persuasive that private individuals and groups cooperated successfully to influence the directors, Bonaparte, and Clarke on Lafayette's behalf.

Lafayette's long incarceration also sheds light on a key player in the emerging modern world. Following Lafayette's death in 1834, former president John Quincy Adams, then a member of the House of Representatives, delivered a eulogy before a joint session of Congress, including a brief but accurate description of Lafayette's arrest, captivity, and liberation.[8] Adams had observed these events as they unfolded, so he recognized how the prison years formed a distinct and dramatic chapter in the life of this "hero of two worlds." The incarceration offered a striking counterpoint to Lafayette's previous public roles in the American War of Independence and French Revolution. He had gone from being the adversary of "arbitrary government" to being its victim. He was forced to think, read, review his past, and consider possible futures. His case became a cause célèbre across the western world. This campaign not only kept him from being forgotten, but, at the right moment, roused military adversaries of his captors to compel his release.

For Lafayette the ordeal's immediate aftermath was relatively peaceful. He spent a two-year exile in Danish Holstein and Holland. After Bonaparte's coup of 18 Brumaire (9 November 1799), Lafayette slipped back into France and retired to his wife's château, La Grange, southeast of Paris. He became a gentleman farmer in conditions of "honorable poverty."[9]

His children pursued the family legacy, beginning with their choice of spouses. At Wittmold in May 1798, his daughter Anastasie had married Charles Maubourg, the youngest brother of Lafayette's fellow prisoner César. In 1802 George Lafayette married Françoise Emilie Destutt de Tracy, daughter of Antoine Louis Destutt de Tracy, a political philosopher who had been Lafayette's ally since working with him in the Estates General of 1789. In 1803 Virginie married another liberal aristocrat, Louis de Lasteyrie du Saillant. She eventually wrote a biography of her heroic mother, while Anastasie promoted relief of the poor while living in the household of a son-in-law who helped lead the Italian independence movement. George became a left-wing legislative deputy in 1827, contributed to the Revolution of 1848, and served thereafter as a member of the Constituent Assembly of the French Second Republic.

The elder Lafayette remained actively engaged in the cause of liberty though for many years behind the public stage. At the start of his Danish exile, he asked English abolitionist Thomas Clarkson for information on the campaign to halt British connivance in the slave trade. On the same day, he expressed hope to the French minister resident in Hamburg that his government would not forget political prisoners still in Austrian hands. Among them were Kościuszko's former aide Hugo Kołłątaj, who was transferred to Olmütz after Lafayette left.[10]

On their return to France, Lafayette's fellow state prisoners attained high rank. Bonaparte appointed Alexandre de Lameth and Jean de Bureaux-Pusy as prefects in a series of départements and named César de Latour-Maubourg a senator and then commandant at Cherbourg and Caen.

In contrast Lafayette chose to serve as a private adviser of democrats, a symbol of political opposition to one-man rule, and eventually an active conspirator against Bonaparte during the French Consulate and Empire. Lafayette refused Bonaparte's early offers of office in return for cooperation and opposed Bonaparte's creation of a life consulate for himself in 1802. Though George Lafayette served several years in the French army, suffering battle wounds and once saving his commanding general's life, Bonaparte personally prevented George's promotion above the rank of lieutenant out of anger at his father. Lafayette senior barely escaped exposure for complicity in a liberal conspiracy of 1808 to plan a new government following Bonaparte's eventual military defeat, and privately urged his abdication in 1814.[11] Until that abdication, Bonaparte saw to it that Lafayette remained on the political sidelines.[12] Thereafter Lafayette opposed the so-called charter imposed on the nation by a restored Louis XVIII. Instead he encouraged a legislatively approved constitution that limited executive power and preserved civil rights.[13]

Lafayette emerged into public life again during the "One Hundred Days" of Bonaparte's return to power in 1815. As a vice president of the Chamber of Representatives, Lafayette hoped to make the emperor's new tenure as conditional and short as possible while still preserving France against the allied invaders.[14]

Lafayette participated in negotiations over Bonaparte's second abdication in the wake of the Battle of Waterloo. Even after the king shut down the Chamber and arranged for a new, reactionary body to replace it, Lafayette continued to encourage constitutional provisions that would extend the suffrage, replace local appointees with elected officials, and guarantee freedom of the press. He opposed such royal prerogatives as arbitrary arrest and incarceration and called for abolishing special tribunals while guaranteeing rights of defendants to be informed of charges and have access to counsel and introducing juries to civil courts. He remained a correspondent in the international abolition movement.[15]

As a member of the Chamber of Deputies in 1818–24 and 1827–34—for the last years as a close ally of his son and fellow deputy—Lafayette helped to lead the democratic opposition and international movements for liberty. As always he promoted press freedom.[16] He encouraged national movements in Latin America (including Haiti), Spain, Portugal, Greece, Italy, Belgium, Ireland, Switzerland, Germany, and Poland.[17] Late in life he promoted giving women greater power to divorce their husbands.[18] He exercised his influence on behalf of political prisoners and those charged with political crimes, both in France and elsewhere. In February 1831 he delivered "a sensational speech" in the Chamber against Austria's long and cruel incarceration of Italian patriots Piero Maroncelli, Silvio Pellico, and others at the Spielberg in Brünn, a sibling institution of the barracks-prison in Olmütz.[19] He corresponded with prison reformers and called for abolition to capital punishment. His last speech sought French aid for Polish political exiles, some of whom he had harbored in his home. Two weeks before his death, he wrote a letter encouraging the United States to welcome these refugees.[20] The final letter in his memoirs praised British policies to end slavery.[21]

In the last great political campaign of his life, support of the Polish November Uprising of 1830–31 and its refugees, Lafayette seems to have closely imitated the work of his supporters during his prison years. He organized a support group in France, the French-Polish Committee, and linked it with others such as the Polish National Committee and the American-Polish Committee. He lobbied his government, spoke on the floor of the Chamber of Deputies, encouraged a campaign in the press, raised money, and arranged places of exile. He even sent a secret American agent into Prussia to help refugees in internment camps. The agent was caught and spent weeks in Prussian prisons.[22]

It is unknowable how much of this effort Lafayette would have undertaken without the personal experience of a five-year incarceration. His work for liberty had long preceded his capture. In prison it continued. There he emphasized to his wife, for instance, how important the completion of a mutual project was to him: to free the slaves on a plantation that they had bought at the South American coastal colony of Cayenne.[23] One may assume that he would have wanted to carry it to conclusion even if his own circumstances had been happier. But surely the depth of passion that he poured into later work and the strength of respect and attention that he inspired in others drew from his experience as a prisoner of state.

Shortly before Lafayette's release, an observer predicted that he would carry "the frightful imprint of his misfortunes for the rest of his life."[24] It at least left him with special sensitivities. As commissioner to the allies after the battle of Waterloo, Lafayette found himself unable to turn over Napoléon to incarceration. When the British foreign secretary, Robert Stewart, Viscount Castlereagh, demanded it, Lafayette replied, "I am astounded that, in asking of the French people such a despicable act, you would choose to address a prisoner of Olmütz." Lafayette even hoped to spare Napoléon by taking him to exile in the United States.[25] One motive was that Lafayette was still grateful to a person who had played a key role in his own release, even though that person had become his greatest political enemy. Another obvious motive was compassion for any prisoner.

Accompanied by his son, Lafayette returned to America in 1824–25 at the invitation of President James Monroe and Congress. Reminders of his captivity surfaced repeatedly. Enthusiastic crowds met him everywhere. They saw him as one of the last heroes of the War of Independence, as a martyr to despotism, and as an apostle of liberty. On the day of his arrival in Manhattan, some African Americans sought him out to thank him for working in the cause of their liberty too. Lafayette soon sought them out in turn and visited the African Free School of the New York Manumission Society.[26]

Lafayette's return to America in 1824. Marquis de Lafayette Prints Collection, Special Collections and College Archives, Skillman Library, Lafayette College

Lafayette was struck at the contrast between his enthusiastic reception in America and his earlier incarceration in Europe. A few weeks after arrival, his carriage entered Hartford, Connecticut. Daniel Wadsworth, a local notable sitting beside him, recalled that morning: "Lafayette was describing to me the sufferings he underwent at Olmütz, when we came to a place where the crowd had collected to welcome him. His description was rendered inaudible by the cheers which rent the air. Lafayette bowed to the people, and then, turning to me, said, with emphasis, 'These are, indeed, the extremes of human life!'"[27]

In New York, Philadelphia, Charleston, New Orleans, and Washington, Lafayette subjected himself to performances of two historically inaccurate dramas about his captivity: Samuel Woodworth's *La Fayette, or The Castle of Olmutz*[28] and Walter Lee's *La Fayette; or, The Fortress of Olmutz.*[29] When John Quincy Adams accompanied Lafayette to Eastern State Penitentiary, the new state prison under construction at Philadelphia, Lafayette spoke out against its planned practice of solitary confinement.[30]

Some Americans who gave important support to Lafayette in captivity were no longer alive. George Washington had died at Mt. Vernon in 1799, Angelica Church in New York City in 1814,[31] and Gouverneur Morris in Morrisiana, New York, in 1816. Justus Bollmann, who had become a U.S. citizen as "Erick Bollman," had died in Jamaica on a business trip in 1821.[32] All Lafayette could do was to express condolences and gratitude to their survivors, as he did to Bollmann's two daughters in Philadelphia.[33]

South Carolinians Dr. Francis Kinloch Huger and Thomas Pinckney were among the remaining persons who had sustained Lafayette in captivity. Soon after Lafayette's arrival, Huger slipped into the City Hotel in Manhattan to visit Lafayette for the first time since their fateful encounter in the wheat fields outside Olmütz. They attended the Park Theatre together to see the Woodworth play, surely a matter of dismay and mirth to them both. Huger accompanied Lafayette to West Point, where Huger's son was a cadet.[34]

Huger had been Thomas Pinckney's son-in-law since 1801. As Huger escorted Lafayette into Charleston in March 1825, they were driving in an open carriage down Meeting Street lined by blue banners of welcome, when Lafayette realized that the carriage behind them carried Pinckney. At the corner of George Street, Pinckney and Lafayette stepped out of their vehicles simultaneously to embrace. Lafayette publicly expressed gratitude for Pinckney's help. Privately he offered Huger a share in a large gift of money that the U.S. Congress had recently voted him: "You shared my prison, now share my wealth. I cannot be rich while you are poor." Huger turned him down. He accompanied Lafayette to Yorktown and then Savannah, where he took his final leave. Lafayette carried away a gold-framed miniature of Huger that Charleston's city fathers had given him. Shortly before his departure, Lafayette received a similar miniature of Huger for his birthday at a

White House dinner. Both reminders of his South Carolinian rescuer found permanent place at La Grange.[35]

The incarceration had brought new nobility to Lafayette's reputation, making him more than ever a symbol of the struggle for liberty. It exposed the utter falsehood of Jacobin accusations that he had sold out his country to its enemies. It helped make him, in the eyes of many supporters and adversaries, the incarnation of the hopes of democrats, abolitionists, judicial reformers, and those struggling for national independence, "transforming his life into a famous, symbolic text that was both admired and criticized."[36] Many remembered how he had resisted his captors and never lost confidence in the triumph of liberty. They found in his defiant hopes a reflection of their own unrelenting dreams for a juster world.

Liberty remained elusive. Ironically the young general credited as Lafayette's rescuer became one of Europe's greatest despots, who imprisoned hundreds for political or religious reasons.[37] Autocratic French regimes succeeded Emperor Napoléon's. Rulers elsewhere in Europe and beyond continued to repress political, intellectual and religious dissidents. In America slavery survived for decades to come.

But defeats as well as successes inspired grander visions. To his dying day, 5 May 1834, Lafayette expressed "belief that the struggle pointed toward some kind of historical apocalypse" and hope "that resembled the classical Christian promise of a better future world."[38] Fayettists saw his experience as a parable of the struggle that would eventually lead to the triumph of liberty over tyranny, good over evil. In a heap of bad poetry honoring Lafayette's American visit, one could find even his prison years take on that millennial meaning:

> Then, Olmutz! From thy dungeons sounds shall break,
> Whose thunders, thrilling like some martial blast,
> Shall fettered nations from long slumbers wake,
> Hurl thrones in dust—and strike proud Kings aghast![39]

NOTES

HKR3 HKR 1795:62–85, Kriegsarchiv, Vienna

HKR4 HKR 1797:33–342, Kriegsarchiv, Vienna

HKR5 HKR 1797:33–837, Kriegsarchiv, Vienna

HLB Hadtörténelmi Levéltár (Archive of War History), Budapest, Hungary

HStAD Hauptstaatsarchiv Düsseldorf

IPFB Institut für personengeschichtliche Forschung (Institute for Genealogical Research), Bensheim, Germany

KAW Kriegsarchiv, Österreichisches Staatsarchiv, Vienna

LCDC Manuscript Division, Library of Congress, Washington, D.C.

LCE Marquis de Lafayette Collections, Special Collections and College Archives, Lafayette College, Easton, Pa.

LCI Arthur H. and Mary Marden Dean Lafayette Collection (#4611), Rare and Manuscript Collections, Carl A. Kroch Library, Cornell University, Ithaca, N.Y.

LMB Lafayette Manuscripts, Manuscripts Department, Lilly Library, Indiana University, Bloomington, Ind.

LMC Lafayette Manuscripts, Special Collections, Regenstein Library, University of Chicago

LPLG Marquis de Lafayette Papers, Château La Grange, Courpalay, France

LPSM Collection of Papers of Marquis de Lafayette, Huntington Library, San Marino, Calif.

LSCN Lafayette and Spear Collections, Department of Literary and Historical Manuscripts, Pierpont Morgan Library, New York, N.Y.

MGPB B95 Moravskoslezske gubernium-prezidium (Moravian Governor's Office), Karton 249, Signature 60, Moravský zemský archiv v Brne (Archive of the Province of Moravia in Brno), Czech Republic

MZAB Moravský zemský archiv v Brne (Archive of the Province of Moravia in Brno), Czech Republic

NARA National Archives and Records Administration, College Park, Md.

NHA Nachlass Hennings August (August Hennings bequest), SUBH

NS Nachlass Sieveking (Sieveking bequest), uncatalogued, Mappe B-6, Staatsarchiv Hamburg

NWHKR Notenwechsel mit dem Hofkriegsrat (exchange of notes with the Aulic War Council)

PFPC Pinckney Family Papers, 1708–1878 (37/38), South Carolina Historical Society, Charleston, S.C.

SP William Short Papers, Library of Congress

StAH Staatsarchiv Hamburg

StKW Staatskanzlei, Haus-, Hof und Staatsarchiv, Österreichisches Staatsarchiv, Wien (State Chancellery, House, Court, and State Archive, Austrian State Archives, Vienna)

SUBH Handschriftensammlung, Staats- und Universitätsbibliothek (Manuscript Collection, State and University Library) Carl von Ossietzky Hamburg

VS   Varnhagen-Sammlung (Varnhagen Collection) 33, Biblioteka Jagiellonska (Jagiellonian Library), Krakow (Cracow), Poland

Preface

1. Though Louis XVI's incarceration was even more sensational and led to more intensive publicity for its duration, his imprisonment was much shorter (five months) and so did not produce the lengthy prisoner correspondence, both sanctioned and secret, that was created in Lafayette's case. Nor did any escape attempt by Louis lead to such detailed investigative reports.

2. After the breakup of the Austro-Hungarian Empire in 1918, the Austrian State Library sent the relevant military correspondence of the Hungarian General Command to Budapest, where it appears as General Command 1793-33-31, 1793-33-98, HLB. Because of World War II, relevant correspondence collected early on by Karl Varnhagen von Ense and deposited in the Prussian State Library in Berlin, is now in VS.

3. The most accurate and consistent early articles began appearing in early 1793 in the premier German-language journal of current political events, *Minerva* of Danish Altona. The articles were written by the journal's editor, Johann Wilhelm von Archenholz. An early substantial account of Lafayette's brief breakout was a pamphlet by "Mr. J.E.B." (would-be rescuer Justus Erich Bollmann) [1795]. The first overall description of Lafayette's imprisonment, based on correspondence and interviews, was an annotated poem published in Paris after the Jacobins' fall, by a Lafayette aide (Agrain, *Captivité de La Fayette,* 1797). Lafayette's friend Ségur published a short, accurate account shortly thereafter in *Histoire des principaux événemens du règne de Frédéric Guillaume I,* (1800); translated into English as *History of the Principle Events of the Reign of Frederic William II* (1801); see 3:275–88.

4. Lafayette's son, George Washington Lafayette, helped to publish many of his father's prison memoirs in volumes 3 and 4 (1837, 1838) of *Mémoires, correspondance et manuscrits.* Lafayette had asked former aide Louis Romeuf to collect prison correspondence specifically, but Romeuf's premature death in the Russian campaign of 1812 hindered timely publication. The Lafayette family handed the prison correspondence to Jules Thomas, who brought it to publication at the dawn of the twentieth century in *Correspondance Inédite . . . 1793–1801* (1903). Though Thomas's transcriptions are more reliable than George Lafayette's, they still contain significant deletions.

5. The archives at Chavaniac, acquired in the early twentieth century and added to by Paris antiquarian Dieudonné Fabius, went to Cornell in the 1960s, where they formed the bulk of the Arthur H. and Mary Marden Dean Lafayette Collection (LCI). Count René de Chambrun and Josée de Laval de Chambrun, owners of La Grange, opened its papers to other researchers and allowed staff of the Library of Congress to produce a comprehensive microfilm of the papers there (LPLG) in 1995–96. A copy is also at Cleveland State University. Maurois, *Adrienne* (1960), and Chambrun, *Prisons des La Fayette* (1977; lacking notes) drew on LCI and LPLG (LCI cited as "Collection Fabius," from a Bibliothèque nationale microfilm). However, they took little notice, beyond Büdinger, *Lafayette in Österreich* (1878), of extensive German-language sources.

6. HKR1-5 contains relevant Vienna manuscripts of the Hofkriegsrat (HKR). Büdinger's *Lafayette in Österreich,* a seventy-page pamphlet, was the first account to draw on them.

This pamphlet focused on the breakout, leaving out much other material on the incarceration. Latzko's *Lafayette* (1936) also used the Vienna manuscripts, calling them "archives of the Vienna police" (262), for a brief captivity account (229–90) that has minor errors and major gaps. Equal to the Vienna manuscripts in immediacy and detail is an extensive group of escape-related papers the police and judicial organs of the former Austrian imperial provincial government of Moravia-Silesia collected at its capital of Brünn (now Brno, in the eastern Czech Republic). Excerpts have appeared in the last generation in a few Czech articles virtually unknown to scholarship beyond the Czech Republic, available at the Moravský zemský archiv v Brne (MZAB, Archive of the Province of Moravia in Brno). The greatest modern biographer of Lafayette, Gottschalk, was linguistically well prepared to draw on the Vienna and Brno manuscripts. However, he died before publishing volumes on events beyond July 1790.

Introduction

1. The Prussian avant-garde near the Luxembourg village Frisange/Freiseng had received orders "toward midnight" on 18 August to decamp quietly and march toward the French border; anonymous (Prussian avant-garde officer), "Auszug aus dem Tagebuch" (diary entry for 18–19 August 1792), 210.

2. List of arrested officers, 19 August 1792, "10 P.M.," folder 2A, LPLG; Harnoncourt to Teschen, 19 August (11 P.M.), printed in Mortimer-Ternaux, *Histoire de la Terreur*, 3:441–42; to "Your Excellency" (Moitelle), 19 August, 11 P.M., Archives Modernes, Bibliothèque nationale, copy in box 88, GPC; to Bourbon, 20 August, in anonymous, "Neuere Pariser Nachrichten," 207; Douxchamps in Namur to a superior, 23 August, folder 2A, LPLG; Lafayette, *Mémoires*, 3:407–8. Early interviews of Lafayette and company (Archenholz "Historische Berichtigung einer Aeusserung des Generals von Mack betreffend" [June 1800], 535) confirm an encounter with pickets shortly after 9 P.M., versus later claims of "nearly eleven o'clock" (Ducoudray-Holstein, *Memoirs of Gilbert M. Lafayette* [1835], 173) or "towards eight o'clock" (Charavay, *Général La Fayette*, 330). Espinchal, *Journal of the Comte d'Espinchal*, 325–27 (entry for 19–29 August 1792), gives a fourth-hand, incorrect account.

3. According to Archenholz, "Historische Berichtigung einer Aeusserung des Generals von Mack betreffend" (June 1800), 533–38, 541–42, Rochefort troops numbered two hundred. He incorrectly claimed that the Frenchmen were lodged at the castle. Just after the arrest, Harnoncourt spoke of having fifty soldiers search the prisoners; to Teschen, 19 August 1792 (11 P.M.), in Mortimer-Ternaux, *Histoire de la Terreur*, 3:441.

4. The Pelican Inn is now Hôtel La Fayette at 87 rue Jacquet. A monument to Lafayette's arrest stands south of the hotel; see Clavery, "Épisode critique," 361–67.

5. Lafayette, *Mémoires*, 3:408. There were four French general officer ranks at the time, though the first was primarily honorary and the second a temporary commission: marshal (*maréchal de France*, abolished in 1793, then resurrected by Napoléon in 1804 as *maréchal d'Empire*); army general (*général d'armée* until 1793, then *général en chef*, a full general), division general (*lieutenant général* until 1793, then *général de division*, usually translated major general, and brigadier general (*maréchal de camp* until 1793, then *général de brigade*). Though his permanent rank was *général de division*, or major general, Lafayette had become a *général d'armée*, or army general, with his appointment in 1791 to command one of three

French armies. In that position he had rights to four aides de camp: a colonel, a major (*chef de bataillon* or *d'escadron*), and two captains. The rank *adjudant général,* or adjutant general (a general's administrative officer), was superior to colonel, and its holder was often addressed as "general," but it was not properly a general-officer rank, thus its replacement in 1800 with *adjudant commandant.* The rank *colonel* became *chef de brigade* in 1793, then reverted to *colonel* in 1803. See Charavay, *Les grades militaires sous la Révolution,* 2–16.

6. The highest standard Austrian ranks were field marshal (*Feldmarschall*), general (general of infantry, artillery or engineers: *Feldzeugmeister;* general of cavalry: *General der Kavallerie*), lieutenant general (*Feldmarschallieutenant*), and major general (*Generalmajor*); Bowden and Tarbox, *Armies on the Danube,* 34. Equivalent Prussian ranks were *Feldmarschall, General der Infanterie* or *General der Kavallerie, Generallieutenant,* and *Generalmajor,* Christopher Duffy, *The Army of Frederick the Great,* 33–34. The spelling *Leutnant* replaced *Lieutenant* late in the nineteenth century. There was no equivalent to the British rank of brigadier general in the Austrian and Prussian armies.

7. Contemporaries noted Maubourg's dramatic bursts of anger; see interim War Council (Hofkriegsrat) president Count Ferdinand von Tige to Thugut, 22 February 1797, NWHKR, K 143, StK, HHStAW; Chasteler, report to Thugut, 26 July, in Büdinger, *Lafayette in Österreich,* 54. Probably a jumbled version of the blowup appears in Stupffel to "Monseigneur" (Provence or Artois), 28 August 1792, box 84/6, LCI. Like Lafayette, Maubourg and other aristocrats supporting the Revolution did not use noble titles and the noble preposition "de" at this time, except in addressing counterrevolutionaries. The use of aristocratic names returned under Napoléon. For clear identification, however, I include "de."

8. 19 August 1792, folder 67bis, LPLG (published in *Gazette de Leyde* and Paris *Moniteur;* Agrain, *Captivité de La Fayette,* 39; Lafayette, *Mémoires,* 3:409n. Lafayette later defined "the right to come and go [freely]" as one of the "natural rights inherent in every society"; cited in Kramer, *Lafayette in Two Worlds,* 255.

9. Harnoncourt to Teschen, 19 August 1792, in Mortimer-Ternaux, *Histoire de la Terreur,* 3:441–42; to "Your Excellency" (Moitelle), 19 August, Archives Modernes, Bibliothèque nationale, copy in box 88, GPC; to Bourbon, 20 August, in anonymous, "Neuere Pariser Nachrichten," 207; Douxchamps in Namur to a anonymous, 23 August, folder 2A, LPLG; Espinchal, *Journal of the Comte d'Espinchal,* 325 (19–29 August entry); Metternich to Kaunitz, 27 August, FA 1792, Deutsch-Niederlande 13–80, KAW; Rivarol, *De la vie politique;* Lafayette, *Mémoires,* 3:408–9; see Cobenzl to Lebzeltern, 2 September, in Vivenot, *Quellen zur Geschichte der Revolutionskriege,* 2:180; Goethe, *Sämtliche Werke,* 28:35 (4 September entry).

10. National Assembly session, 21 August 1792, in *Archives Parlementaires,* 48:609; *Moniteur,* no. 240 (27 August 1792), in *Réimpression,* 13:530; Danton, *Discours,* 216 (14 October). The new regime intimidated newspapers into conforming; see Popkin, *Revolutionary News,* 135, 171. Later to flee to the Austrians himself, Dumouriez, Lafayette's successor as Northern Army commander, also called Lafayette "traitor"; to Le Brun, 24 August, in Barthélemy, *Papiers,* 1:253.

11. The Assembly decreed confiscation and sale of the Lafayette's property on 25 August 1792, the same day the public hangman broke the die of Lafayette's bronze medallion before city hall. A burst of laws against emigrants followed, banishing them on pain of death (23 October), seizing and selling their movable property (24 October), declaring them legally

dead (28 March 1793), and selling their land (3 June); see Jones, *Longman Companion,* 196, 199. Madame de Staël wrote Narbonne that Lafayette competed with Louis XVI as "the most hated man of France," 9 December, in Staël, *Correspondance générale,* 2, pt. 1:80.

12. Bray in Regensburg to Rohan-Polduc, 27 August 1792, in Bray *Mémoires,* 1:304–5; anonymous to Auckland, 20 August; Auckland to Morton Eden in Berlin, 24 August (enclosing anonymous letter excerpt from Luxembourg, 21 August), Add 34444, 111r, 150r–v, BL; to Grenville, 22 August, in Grenville, *Manuscripts of J. B. Fortescue,* 2:304; Morris to Jefferson, 22 August; Short to Jefferson, 24 August; Jefferson to Washington, 24 October, in Jefferson, *Papers* (1950–), 24:313, 323, 538–39; Littlepage to Lafayette, 12 September, Holladay Family Papers (Mss1 H7185a), Virginia Historical Society, Richmond; U.S. Treasury Secretary Oliver Wolcott Jr. to father, 8 October, in Wolcott *Memoirs,* 1:81.

13. Later "royalists ostentatiously used his noble title to annoy him"; Neely, *Lafayette and the Liberal Ideal,* 82.

14. Gottschalk, *Lafayette between the American and the French Revolution,* 10.

15. On 16 July 1793, Lafayette recalled how "it is four years ago today . . . that I gave myself the pleasure of demolishing the Bastille"; to Hénin, box 18/8, LCI.

16. On 11 June 1792, Coalition forces began probing Lafayette's army lines; Lafayette, *Mémoires,* 3:323. On 12 July, Lafayette traded commands with Marshal Luckner, taking over the Army of the North; Lynn, *Bayonets of the Republic,* 6. Correspondence detailing Lafayette's defense operations before fleeing appears in Lafayette, *Mémoires,* 3:359–71; also in Chief of Staff Laumoy, Northern Army bulletin (with Lafayette's note to Abancourt), 27 July; Le Veneur to Lafayette, 11 August, box 1/1, LMC; Lafayette to Dillon (Northern Army left-wing commander), 18 August, 67, LPLG. By Abancourt's order of 7 August, Lafayette's frontier extended from Dunkirk to Montmédy; Lafayette, *Mémoires,* 3:456n. Austrian-Prussian discussions from July to September 1792 on territorial "indemnity" for war on France included in the west French Flanders and Alsace-Lorraine for Austria and the Rhineland duchies Jülich and Berg for Prussia. The two allies had loftier goals in the east; Austria wanted the margraviates of Ansbach and Bayreuth in Franconia but, above all, Bavaria in exchange for the Austrian Netherlands; Prussia aimed at a large piece of Poland and at least contemplated Lusatia; Lord, *The Second Partition of Poland,* 217–18, 237–42, 310–53; Mori, *William Pitt,* 110, 145, 148.

17. Lafayette to Ardennes Department, 15 August 1792; Sedan council minutes, Sedan officials to Lafayette, Lafayette's prepared address to army, 18 August, folder 67, LPLG; Lafayette, *Mémoires,* 3:391–92, 463–64; Lafayette to Abancourt, 12 August, in Lafayette, *Mémoires,* 3:460–62; to Sedan council, 13 August; to Abancourt, 14 August, in *Archives Parlementaires,* 48:608–9, 313; Sedan council minutes, 14 August; Provisional Executive Council minutes, 11, 14, 17 August, in *Recueil* (1889), 1:lix–lx, 16; Lafayette, *Mémoires,* 3:388–94; Collinet, *Sedan il y a cent ans 1–2,* 1:113–16. The arrested Assembly commissioners were Quinette, Isnard, and Boudin; see Quinette and others, *Compte rendu.* On 15 August, Lafayette had troops assemble with town officials on a field at Sedan to reaffirm their oath. Refusal by many soldiers signaled widespread mistrust of Lafayette's leadership.

18. National Assembly sessions, 17, 19 August 1792, in *Archives Parlementaires,* 48:314–15, 387–89; Lafayette, *Mémoires,* 3:462n; Collinet, *Sedan il y a cent ans 1–2,* 1:113. The Council replaced Lafayette with Dumouriez, whom Lafayette mistrusted.

19. Collinet, *Sedan il y a cent ans 1–2*, 1:113; 2:44. While Dumouriez managed to flee certain death in April 1793, three other Northern Army commanders soon died under the Jacobin blade: Custine, Luckner, and Houchard; Lynn, *Bayonets of the Republic*, 13–14.

20. Lafayette to Pusy, 18 August 1792, reel 53, LPLG; to Adrienne de Noailles de Lafayette, 21 August, box 17/40, LCI; Lafayette, *Mémoires*, 3:400–401; see Moré, *The Chevalier de Pontgibaud*, 151 (La Colombe's alleged account); anonymous (Chambrun), "Lafayette échappe à la mort," reel 53, LPLG. Lafayette claimed he had forewarned only Maubourg and Laumoy; "Sur la vie," n.d. (after 1822), in Lafayette, *Mémoires*, 3:490; but the note to Pusy—with *tournie* (whirligig) perhaps code for flight—indicates otherwise.

21. Lafayette to Adrienne Lafayette, 21 August, 1792, to aunt Chavaniac, 25 August, box 17/39–40, LCI; to Archenholz, 27 March 1793, in Lafayette, *Lafayette Letters*, 10–13; Lafayette, *Mémoires*, 3:406–7. Two years earlier Lafayette had sheltered Paulus when Prussian troops crushed the Dutch patriot revolution. After his own arrest, Lafayette tried to smuggle news about himself to Paulus through La Colombe and Short and to encourage Short to work with Paulus to foster publicity. Pusy asked La Colombe to establish contact with Paulus, in whom Lafayette "places the most perfect confidence"; Lafayette to La Colombe, 10 December (first and second notes); Pusy to La Colombe, n.d. (ca. early December), folders 5E, 5B, LPLG; Gottschalk, *Lafayette between the American and the French Revolution*, 376, 388.

22. Lafayette, n.d. (ca.1810), "Compte rendu," in Jefferson, *Papers. Retirement Series* (2004–), 2:14. Lafayette left behind the army's chest with 1,100,000 livres; National Assembly session, 23 August 1792, in *Archives Parlementaires*, 48:667.

23. National Assembly session, 19 August 1792, in *Archives Parlementaires*, 48:387.

24. Ziekursch, "Zur Geschichte des Feldzuges," 20–77, especially 52–55.

25. To Sedan officials, 19 August 1792, in *Archives Parlementaires*, 48:609; to Pusy, 18 August, folder 382, LPLG; Lafayette, *Mémoires*, 3:402–6, 490–91. The last passage is from Lafayette's notes "Sur la vie . . . du Général Dumouriez," n.d. (after 1822).

26. Among published accounts of Lafayette's flight, capture, and initial incarceration, that of the greatest nineteenth-century Lafayette biography, Charavay, *Général La Fayette*, is particularly dependable; see 328–32. An earlier but less dependable source is Ducoudray-Holstein, *Memoirs of Gilbert M. Lafayette* (1835), 171–80. With Lafayette's help Ducoudray-Holstein cleaned up glaring errors in the first edition (1824), but many inaccuracies remained. For record of the flight in local archival sources, see Collinet, *Sedan il y a cent ans 1–2*, 1:113–18. Scholars have overlooked an especially valuable, early secondary source for Lafayette's flight, in part because the author imbedded the account within another subject —probably a strategy to avoid censorship; see Archenholz, "Historische Berichtigung einer Aeusserung des Generals von Mack betreffend." (June 1800), 533–42. In the days immediately after the release of Lafayette's party, Archenholz interviewed them at length.

27. Lafayette, *Mémoires*, 3:405n; Collinet, *Sedan il y a cent ans 1–2*, 1:114. Averhoult had helped Lafayette convince Sedan's council to arrest the commissioners.

28. Duroure's group joined Lafayette's at Rochefort; see Lafayette, *Mémoires*, 3:404, 490. Presumably this occurred after Harnoncourt had arrested the first, main group with Lafayette—judging by two early lists of arrestees dated 19 August, one in Harnoncourt to Teschen (11 P.M.), in Mortimer-Ternaux, *Histoire de la Terreur*, 3:441–42 (Duroure not included); the other in form of a signed protest by the arrestees to Namur commandant Moitelle (no hour

given, perhaps backdated, with Duroure included), facsimile in folder 67bis, LPLG. Duroure is also listed in Lafayette to Adrienne Lafayette, 21 August, box 17/40, LCI. A full list is in Douxchamps in Namur to anonymous, 23 August, folder 2A, LPLG.

29. *Dictionnaire des officiers,* 279–80, 291, 354–55.

30. See Lafayette to Lameth, 30 November 1797, box 19/11; to Masclet, n.d. (fall 1798), 19/19, LCI. Lafayette and Lameth's original alliance in the 1789 Estates General began dissolving in October 1789. Relations worsened after the king's flight to Varennes in June 1791. Publicist Mallet du Pan wrote Francis (Franz) II on 8 January 1795, that Lafayette and the Lameths headed rival Constitutional groups; see Mallet du Pan, *Correspondance inédite,* 1:48. Lafayette praised Pusy to Jefferson, 19 April 1799, folder 251, LPLG. On Lafayette's relations to Maubourg and Pusy, see Agrain, *Captivité de La Fayette,* 55, and an anonymous Hamburg article, n.d. (ca. early July 1796), box 96/3, LCI.

31. Vaublanc claims to have heard of the encounter with the peasant directly from Maubourg; see Vaublanc *Mémoires,* 177–78. Contemporary diary accounts of area weather include Espinchal, *Journal of the Comte d'Espinchal,* entry for 19 August 1792, 297; anonymous (avant-garde Prussian officer) 1800, cited in Espinchal's entry for 18–19 August, 210. Lafayette's map of the Austrian Netherlands was returned to him on his release; prisoners' money and effects, 18 September 1797, fol. 15, HKR5.

32. To Washington, 9 May 1799, in Lafayette, *The Letters of Lafayette to Washington,* 392; Lafayette, *Mémoires,* 3:407. Lafayette stressed being on Liège soil; to Archenholz, 27 March 1793, in Lafayette, *Lafayette Letters,* 13. Later he claimed there was no other way forward; see Lafayette, *Mémoires,* 3:407.

33. Generally reliable dates for Lafayette's prison residencies appear in Olivier, *Bibliographie des travaux,* 1979, 29.

34. I use Neier's definition of the term *political prisoner:* "someone who is incarcerated for his or her beliefs or for peaceful expression or association"; such individuals can include "those who have merely advocated violence" (Neier, "Confining Dissent," 393). Lafayette's captors indicated that his ideas of freedom in a constitutional order led to his incarceration as a "prisoner of state"—not his actions as a military officer fighting in the American war, maintaining civil order in France (primarily controlling populist mobs), or defending France against invasion.

Chapter 1. Prison Road into Prussia

1. Lord, *The Second Partition of Poland,* 273.

2. 21 August 1792, box 17/40, LCI.

3. The former monastery has been Hospice d'Hariscamp, a home for the elderly, since 1805.

4. Lafayette to Chavaniac, 25 August 1792, box 17/39–40, LCI.

5. Metternich to Teschen, 22 August 1792; to Kaunitz, 24 August, FA 1792, Deutsch-Niederlande 13–80, KAW.

6. Bernard, *From the Enlightenment to the Police State,* 192. Later it applied also to captives at Kufstein, Tyrol, and Eger, Hungary. Pufendorf, *Les Devoirs,* 298–99, states the classical view of natural law for a ruler acting even without explicit regulations: "sovereign powers are above all human and civil law" (book 2.9.3); and an absolute prince "is in the

right to govern the state as he judges appropriate, without having to consult anyone or follow certain fixed rules" (2.9.5).

7. Lafayette to Pusy, n.d. (ca. 1798), 19/2, LCI; Agrain, *Captivité de La Fayette*, 36–37; Chasteler, report to Thugut, 26 July 1797, in Büdinger, *Lafayette in Österreich*, 51.

8. Lafayette, "Sur un mémoire," n.d. (ca. 1830), in Lafayette, *Mémoires*, 3:503–4. Lafayette noted here that he asked "a celebrated professor of Göttingen" (probably Girtanner) not to address him as "marquis." On release from Olmütz, Lafayette struck the title out on a receipt listing his belongings before signing it; specifications of Lafayette's money and effects, 18 September 1797, fol. 15r, HKR5.

9. Lafayette to Chavaniac, 25 August 1792, box 17/39–40, LCI; see Mallet to Mounier, 5 April 1797, in Hérisson, *Autour d'une Révolution*, 283.

10. Lafayette to Hénin, 15 November 1793, box 18/28, LCI; Agrain, *Captivité de La Fayette*, 37; Archenholz "Historische Berichtigung einer Aeusserung des Generals von Mack betreffend" (June 1800), 538–39; Lafayette, *Mémoires*, 3:410. Ducoudray-Holstein, *Memoirs of Gilbert M. Lafayette* (1835), 175–76, mistakes Archduke Charles for Lorraine.

11. Lafayette to Pusy, n.d. (circa 1798), 19/2, LCI; Lafayette, *Mémoires*, 3:410.

12. Douxchamps in Namur to anonymous, 23 August 1792, folder 2A, LPLG; Chasteler, report to Thugut, 26 July 1797, in Büdinger, *Lafayette in Österreich*, 51.

13. Teschen to Paulus, 24 August 1792, in Büdinger, *Lafayette in Österreich*, appendix a, 36–37; Lafayette to La Rochefoucauld, 25 August; to Chavaniac, 25 August, boxes 18/2, 17/39–40, LCI; Agrain, *Captivité de La Fayette*, 39; Archenholz, "Noch ein Beitrag zu der Geschichte des Generals la Fayette" (October 1795), 113; Archenholz, "Historische Berichtigung einer Aeusserung des Generals von Mack betreffend" (June 1800), 539–40. Lafayette shared the money he had with his men for daily expenses.

14. To Hénin, 27 August 1792, box 18/3, LCI; Archenholz, "Historische Berichtigung einer Aeusserung des Generals von Mack betreffend" (June 1800), 539–40.

15. Cloquet, *Recollections of the Private Life of General Lafayette*, 1:13 ("laughing"); Lafayette to Tessé, 19 September 1792, box 18/7, LCI ("wallet"); Lameth, *Notes et Souvenirs*, 412n ("quill"); Stupffel to "Monseigneur" (Provence or Artois), 28 August, box 84/6, LCI ("8 million"); Harnoncourt to Bourbon, 20 August, in anonymous, "Neuere Pariser Nachrichten," 207–8; Douxchamps to anonymous, 23 August, folder 2A, LPLG; Teschen to Paulus, Mayer, 24 August, in Büdinger, *Lafayette in Österreich*, appendix a, 36–7; Staël to Narbonne, 25 August, in Staël, *Correspondance générale*, 2, pt. 1:1; Maubourg to Pillet, 5 March 1796, in Lafayette, *Correspondance inédite*, 295; Lafayette, *Mémoires*, 3:411.

16. Eden to Grenville, 2 October 1792, pp. 6–7, Foreign Office 64/26, no. 79, National Archives, Kew, U.K. Another officer acquired one of Lafayette's uniforms at Verdun; anonymous, "Auszug aus dem Tagebuch," 216–17. See Spalding, "How Lafayette Lost His Sword," for the odyssey of a sword now at Lafayette College (LCE).

17. Reuss to Teschen, 26 August 1792, in Vivenot, *Quellen zur Geschichte der Revolutionskriege*, 2:179–80.

18. Lafayette to Short, 16 September 1792, box 18/6, LCI; Archenholz, "Historische Berichtigung einer Aeusserung des Generals von Mack betreffend" (June 1800), 541; Agrain in Maastricht to Lafayette, 8 September, 18r–19r, GR11/91, Nr 26, GStAB; Lafayette, *Mémoires*, 3:411. Apparently assuming Lafayette's detention to be temporary, Agrain asked for money.

He named three other freed former officers, already departed for London. While some at Antwerp escaped, French troops freed others; see Lafayette to Reubell, 6 March 1798, folder 21, LPLG. U.S. diplomats provided funds for Lafayette through men who had fled with him, including Cadignan, Boinville, Masson, the Romeuf brothers, and La Colombe; U.S. envoys' advances for Lafayette, n.d. (ca. June 1798), folder 240, LPLG.

19. Lafayette, *Mémoires*, 3:411–12 (including Romeuf's record, sent later to Pusy), folder 5E, LPLG.

20. Hennings to Reinhard, 3 November 1797, NHA: 42, 64–65, SUBH.

21. To Pinckney, 4 July 1793, in Lafayette, *Correspondance inédite*, 207. After release Lafayette claimed "the moment I was their prisoner, I expected the worse"; to Jefferson, 19 April 1799, folder 251, LPLG. Lafayette later wrote of having been "Apostle and Martyr to the sacred doctrine"; to Madison, 1 December 1802, 22/45, LCI.

22. Adrienne Lafayette to Victor de Latour-Maubourg, 19 July 1797, box 100/31, LCI.

23. Lafayette to Hénin, 3 September 1792, folder 14, LPLG; to Short, 16 September, box 18/6, LCI. Lally soon noted that Lafayette was "a prisoner not *of war,* but *of state;*" to Lady Sheffield; 4 October, Add 34887, 232v, BL.

24. "Baron de Mareschal" (probably Hans von Marschall) to Lempens, 8 September 1792, FA 1792, Deutsch-Niederlande 9/62 4/4, KAW; Lafayette to Hénin, Short, 16 September, box 18/5–6, LCI; Lally to Angelica Church, 1 May (not "7") 1794, ACAC; Adrienne Lafayette to Tessé, 10 May 1796, folder 7B, LPLG; *Gazette de Leyde* 1792, no. 75 supplement (18 September), based on a 9 September letter from Luxembourg, copy in box 89, GPC; Lafayette to Gouverneur, 22 October 1832, cited in Section moderne, AB XXXVIII, 49, Archives nationales, Paris.

25. Teschen to Lafayette, 8 September 1792, in Vivenot, *Quellen zur Geschichte der Revolutionskriege,* 2:192; Lafayette to Hénin, 15 November 1793, box 18/28, LCI; Lafayette, *Mémoires,* 3:412–13 (a variant of Teschen's letter).

26. King Louis-Philippe recalled how Lafayette "was persecuted in France for wanting to defend the King and abroad for wanting to defend liberty in France" (Louis-Philippe, *Memoirs 1773–1793* [1977], 263); see Lafayette to Adrienne Lafayette, 21 August 1792, in Lafayette, *Mémoires,* 3:466; Maubourg to Pillet, Masson, 5 March 1796, in Lafayette, *Correspondance inédite,* 296.

27. Espinchal, *Journal of the Comte d'Espinchal,* 331 (1–11 September 1792 entry); Fersen, *Diary and Correspondence,* 265–66 (30 August entry); Eszterházy to Spielmann, 19 September, in Chuquet, *Lettres de 1792,* 236; Reuss to Spielmann, 19 September, in Vivenot, *Quellen zur Geschichte der Revolutionskriege,* 2:210; Masclet, undated note, vol. 5, BLPC.

28. Cited by Lafayette to Hénin, 15 November 1793, box 18/28–29, LCI; see Adrienne Lafayette to Masson, 30 August 1796, folders 7, 830, LPLG.

29. Cited by Mallet to Mounier, 5 April 1797, in Hérisson, *Autour d'une Révolution,* 283–84.

30. Lafayette to Hénin, 15 November 1793, box 18/28–29, LCI; Lafayette, *Mémoires,* 3:413.

31. Chinard, *La Déclaration des droits de l'homme,* 32; Lafayette's draft cited in ibid., 33–34.

32. Lafayette to Archenholz, 21 September 1793, in Lafayette, *Lafayette Letters,* 38–39; Louis-Philippe (himself fleeing into Austrian lines in 1793), *Memoirs 1773–1793,* 262; Adrienne Lafayette to Hénin, 15 September 1796, box 98/35, LCI; Ségur, *Histoire des principaux événemens,* 3:275. Ducoudray-Holstein, *Memoirs of Gilbert M. Lafayette* (1835), 176, took this remark to be Lafayette's. Cobenzl notified Frederick William (Friedrich Wilhelm) II of the captive's transfer, and Reuss of Francis II's say in their final disposition; to Francis II, 19 September 1792, box 89, GPC.

33. Ducoudray-Holstein, *Memoirs of Gilbert M. Lafayette* (1835), 185–86, claims that at Magdeburg soldiers brought the captives news of Louis XVI's death (21 January 1793), blamed them for it, and taunted them that Frederick William II could now order their execution. The Lafayettes attributed Vienna's hatred also to how Lafayette had diverted France's resources from Austrian political projects to the American war and had founded such a successful National Guard; Adrienne Lafayette to Victor de Latour-Maubourg, 19 July 1797, 100/31, LCI.

34. To Short, 16 September 1792, box 18/6, LCI.

35. Lafayette to Short, 16 September 1792, box 18/28, 6, LCI; Frederick William II (via Foreign Affairs Ministry, Berlin [Departement der auswärtigen Angelegenheiten]) to Lucchesini, 28 January 1794, 14r; Supreme War Council, Berlin (Oberkriegscollegium), to Foreign Affairs Ministry, Berlin, 28 January, 12r; Frederick William II to Prince Heinrich, n.d. (ca. 1 May), 59r, GR11/91, Nr 28, GStAB. Frederick William II's foreign minister, Haugwitz, also claimed to Lally that concern for the captives' safety had moved the king to bring them to Wesel; Lally to Angelica Church, 1 May (not "7") 1794, ACAC. Vienna's interest to be consulted by Frederick William II about the captives appears also in Cobenzl to Argenteau, 22 September 1792, in Vivenot, *Quellen zur Geschichte der Revolutionskriege,* 2:221–22.

36. Servants' given names and ages appear rarely in captivity manuscripts. Exceptions are a Prussian list of captives, 10 April 1794, 44r, Nr 28, GR11/91, GStAB ("Jean Marie Cantonnier [*sic*] dit Félix"; "Pierre dit Chavagnier"; Georg [Jules Grugeon] dit Beausseroi"; "Nicola[s] Jeandel"); a Latin medical report by Axter, 17 September 1797, folder 7C, LPLG (Grugeon, Compte, Pontonnier); and Hennings to Reinhard, 3 November, NHA 42:69, SUBH (Pontonnier, Compte). When he was released, the servant called "Compte" signed his name that way on a receipt for belongings (fol. 18, HKR5); his name appears elsewhere as "Comte" and even "Conte." On Compte as illiterate tailor's son, see Adrienne Lafayette to Pillet, 22 June 1796; Adrienne Lafayette to Hénin, 15 September 1796; Lafayette to Aunt Chavaniac, 10 November, 23 December 1797 (appendix to letters by Adrienne Lafayette), box 98/35, 100/10, 36–37, LCI. Ducoudray-Holstein, *Memoirs of Gilbert M. Lafayette* (1835) falsely names one of Lafayette's servants in captivity "Augustus Ferret" (182).

37. Pusy, deposition to Chasteler, 25 July 1797, in Archenholz and others, "Zur Geschichte der Freylassung" (October 1797), 173–74. A receipt for his belongings that Jandel signed on 18 September 1797 on prison release refers to him as "Nicolas Janti," but his crudely written signature reads "Jandel" (fol. 19, HKR5). Elsewhere his name appears as "Jeandel." Apparently Maubourg also took along a dearly loved poodle; Schröder to Botta, 5 February 1797; HKR to Botta, 25 April, 24v, HKR4; interim HKR president Tige to Thugut, 22 February 1797, NWHKR, K 143, StKW.

Transaction price (6)	Interest or discount (7)	Total Interests or discounts (5) − (6) (8)	Days to maturity (9)	Interests or discounts per day	
				Total (8) ÷ (9) (10)	per 100,000 (10) ÷ (5 or 6) (11)
92,000	D	8,000	180	44.44	44.44
−92,500	D	−7,500	176	42.61	42.61
230,000	D	20,000	180	111.11	44.44
500,000	I	45,000	162	277.78	55.56
−93,000	D	−7,000	174	40.22	40.22
636,500		58,500			
−230,000	I	−5,104	46	110.96	48.24

1. Security A was bought on June 1 at $92,000 and sold on June 5 at $92,500.

2. Securities B were bought on June 15 at $230,000. Two-fifths of these securities were sold on June 21 at $93,000 (the remaining three-fifths are still in the portfolio).

We can see how realized profits are reflected in the position book in Exhibit 13.1 by taking a balance after June 5, when security A was sold (see following table). The realized $500 profit remains in the "total interests or discounts" column and reduces the balance in the "transaction price" column. This profit of $500 is composed of two factors: (1) discounts earned during the holding period, and (2) a trading profit realized because of changes in the level of interest rates. To evaluate the performance of the portfolio manager, it is useful to separate these two components. The information in column 11 in Exhibit 13.1 helps us to separate these two profit components:

Realized Profits in Position Book

	Price at maturity	Transaction price	Total interests or discounts
June 1	100,000	92,000	8,000
June 5	−100,000	−92,500	−7,500
Balance	0	− 500	500

1. *Discounts earned.* $44.44 discount per day for the 4 days the investment was held from June 1 to June 5 $177.78

2. *Realized trading profit.* There has been a decrease in the discount in the amount of $1.83 per day ($44.44 − $42.61). This is due to a decrease in interest rates in the market. This is to be reflected for the remaining 176 days from June 5 to maturity[1]   322.22
Total profit $500.00

In the same manner, we can see that the $1,000 profits on the two-fifths of security B sold were earned as follows:

1. *Discounts earned.* $44.44 discount per day for each $100,000 for 6 days of investment holding $ 266.64

2. *Realized trading profit.* There has been a decrease in the discount in the amount of $4.22 per day ($44.44 − $40.22). This is to be reflected for the remaining 174 days from June 21 to maturity[2]   733.36
Total profit $1,000.00

UNREALIZED PROFITS AND LOSSES

On June 30, the end of this reporting period, the following items remain in the money market portfolio:

---

[1]The actual product of $1.83 for 176 days produces a total of $322.08. In practice the discounts are calculated with four decimal places. This produces a change in discount in the amount of $1.8308 per day and a realized trading profit of $322.22.
[2]Using four decimal places, the change in discount is $4.2147 per day.

1. Three-fifths of securities B, bought on June 15 at $230,000 (the other two-fifths were liquidated during the month)

2. Security C bought on June 18 at $500,000

3. Borrowings in the amount of $230,000 taken down on June 15

Exhibit 13.2 lists these instruments. The money market investments are identified in the price column at a total cost of $638,000 (column 2): however the market value of these securities is $641,700 (column 5). There is a total unrealized profit of $3,700. Like realized profits, the unrealized profit or loss reflected in the difference between market value and cost of a portfolio reflects two factors: (1) interests and discounts earned since the security was purchased, and (2) an unrealized trading gain or loss due to changes in the overall level of interest rates in the market.[3] In the work sheet in Exhibit 13.2 these two elements are separated.

In Exhibit 13.2 the "earned interests and discounts" column shows, for each of the instruments in the portfolio, interests and discounts which have accumulated from the day of the initial transaction to the closing date as follows:

1. In security B we earned $919.91, $44.44 in discounts per day for each $100,000 for 15 days.

2. In security C we earned $3,333.60, $55.56 in interests per day for each $100,000 for 12 days.

3. We owe $1,664.62 in interests, $48.25 per day for each $100,-000 of borrowings for 15 days.

Adding these accrued interests and discounts to the original price produces the adjusted value of these instruments in our books (column 4). Then, we can compare book values with market values (column 5) and make any necessary adjustment.

The subtotals in Exhibit 13.2 show that the securities held in the portfolio cost $638,000 initially and now have a market value of $641,700. The $3,700 increase in market price over cost is composed of earned interests and discounts in the amount of $4,253.51 less an adjustment of $553.51—because of an increase in interest rates in the market.

---

[3]When securities are held for investment purposes, which is not the case in a trading portfolio, it can be assumed that the securities will be held to maturity. In this case the only reported earnings will be those associated with earned interest and discounts, and the value of the portfolio will not be marked to market.

EXHIBIT 13.2

MONEY MARKET POSITION SHEET

Security or borrowing (1)	Transaction price (2)	Interests and discounts earned (3)	Adjusted book value (2) + (3) (4)	Market value (5)	Adjustment (5) − (4) (6)
Security B	138,000	919.91*	138,919.91	138,500.00	−419.91
C	500,000	3,333.60†	503,333.60	503,200.00	−133.60
	638,000	4,253.51	642,253.51	641,700.00	−553.51
Borrowing A	230,000	1,664.62‡	231,664.62	231,664.62	

*$44.44 × 1.38 hundred thousand × 15 days = $919.91

†$55.56 × 5 hundred thousand × 12 days = $3,333.60

‡$48.25 × 2.3 hundred thousand × 15 days = $1,664.62

For borrowings, the total amount owed has increased to $231,664.62 due to the accrued interests in the amount of $1,664.62 payable on the debt.

TOTAL PROFITS AND LOSSES

As shown above, the money market operations have produced the following:

1. A realized total profit of $1,500

2. An unrealized total profit of $3,700

3. Interest expenses in the amount of $1,664.62

Alternatively, we can say that the inventory of securities in the money market portfolio has a market value of $641,700, as shown in Exhibit 13.2. But the book value of this portfolio, as reflected in the money market ledger of Exhibit 13.1, appears as $636,500. Thus, the money market operations for this reporting period produced a total profit of $5,200, composed of interests and discounts earned, realized trading profits, and unrealized trading losses—as discussed above. In the same vein, the total amount owed to bank A at the end of the month is $231,664.62, while the money market ledger shows only $230,000.

Thus, the financial expenses of this money market portfolio for the period are $1,664.62.

Bookkeeping for Money Market Operations

Whenever we acquire a security, the traditional accounting entries are to debit the asset account "marketable securities" and to credit cash. Thus, when we acquire the various securities shown in Exhibit 13.1, the accounting entries are as follows:

		Debit	Credit
June 1	Marketable securities (security A)	92,000	
	Cash		92,000
June 15	Marketable securities (security B)	230,000	
	Cash		230,000
June 18	Marketable securities (security C)	500,000	
	Cash		500,000

When we sell securities, we have to reverse the above entries and, in addition, recognize any profit or loss realized in the security. As shown above, this profit or loss has two elements: interests and discounts earned and realized trading profit. Thus, when we sell security A and the two-fifths of security B the entries are as follows:

		Debit	Credit
June 5	Cash	92,500	
	Marketable securities (security A)		92,000.00
	Discounts and interests earned		177.78
	Realized trading profit		322.22
June 21	Cash	93,000	
	Marketable securities (Security B)		92,000.00
	Discounts and interests earned		266.64
	Realized trading profit		733.36

Finally, to bring the book value of the securities in the inventory to market values, we must reflect the discounts and interests earned in these securities and to "mark-to-market" their value. The accounting for interests and discounts earned is different depending on whether the security is traded on a discounted basis or accrues interests. For securities traded on a discounted basis, like security B, the amount of discounts earned is accompanied by an increase in the value of marketable securities. Thus, the discount earned on security B is accounted for as follows:

	Debit	Credit
June 30 Marketable securities (security B)	919.91	
Interests and dividends earned		919.91

For securities which pay interests at the end of the period the interests earned are accompanied by an increase in accrued income receivable. The interest earned on security C during the holding period is reported as follows:

	Debit	Credit
June 30 Accrued income receivable	3,333.60	
Interests and dividends earned		3,333.60

Finally, we must mark-to-market the value of the securities in inventory, for the securities in inventory at the end of June this total adjustment represents an unrealized trading loss of $553.51. Accounting for this adjustment separately for each security, we obtain the following entries:

	Debit	Credit
June 30 Unrealized trading loss	553.51	
Marketable securities (security B)		419.91
Marketable securities (security C)		133.60

If we add the entries for marketable securities presented above, plus accrued interest receivable, the grand total is $641,700—the market value of the securities at the end of the period. However, the money market position book in Exhibit 13.1 shows a cost for securities of $636,500. The difference between these two figures, $5,200, is equal to the sum of interests and dividends earned during the period, $4,697.93, the realized trading profits, $1,055.58, and less the unrealized trading loss of $553.51. The computation of these separate items was explained earlier, and their total of $5,200 can be verified against the entries above.

To bring the figures in the money market position book to market values we must make an adjustment for the total difference between the current market value of the portfolio and the cost reflected there. This is done by transferring $5,200 from the column "total interests or discounts" to the "transaction price" column. The new balance in the "transaction price" column, $641,700, provides the cost base for the next period. The new balance in the "interests or discounts" column, $54,300, reflects the unearned interests and discounts at the beginning of the next period. See Exhibit 13.3.

EXHIBIT 13.3

MONEY MARKET OPERATIONS: GENERAL LEDGER AFTER ADJUSTMENTS

Date (1)	Transaction (2) (+) Buy (−) Sell	Security (3)	Maturity (4)	Price at maturity (5)	Transaction price (6)	Interest or discount (7)	Total interests or discounts (5) − (6) (8)	Days to maturity (9)	Interest or discount per day Total (8) ÷ (9) (10)	per 100,000 (10) ÷ (5 or 6) (11)
		Investments								
June 1	+	A	December 1	100,000	92,000	D	8,000	180	44.44	44.44
June 5	−	A	December 1	−100,000	−92,500	D	−7,500	176	42.61	42.61
June 15	+	5 B	December 15	250,000	230,000	D	20,000	180	111.11	44.44
June 18	+	C	November 30	545,000	500,000	I	45,000	162	277.78	55.56
June 21	−	2/5 B	December 15	−100,000	−93,000	D	−7,000	174	40.22	40.22
Balances				695,000	636,500		58,500			
Adjustments*					+5,200		−5,200			
Net balance after adjustments				695,000	641,700		53,300			
		Borrowings								
	(−) Take down (+) Repay									
June 15	−	Bank A	July 31	−235,104.00	−230,000.00	I	−5,104.00	46	110.96	48.24
Adjustments: Accrued interests					−1,664.62		1,664.62			
Net balances				−235,104.00	−231,664.62		−3,439.38			

*The $5,200 adjustment is composed of $1,500 in realized profits and $3,700 net adjustment to reflect interests and discounts earned and to mark-to-market the value of the portfolio at the end of the period.

E X H I B I T 13.4

EXCHANGE POSITION BOOK

Date	Value date	Name of counterpart		Rate
		No. of contract		
June 1	June 3	1		2.3900
June 1	June 3	2		2.4000
June 1	September 3	3		2.3820
June 1	July 3	4		2.3940
June 1	December 3	5		2.3640
Balances				
Net balances				

The interest expense accrued on the borrowings during the period is reflected in the books through the following entries:

	Debit	Credit
June 30 Interest expense	1,664.62	
Interest payable		1,664.62

The interest expense is also incorporated in the borrowings section of the money market book by transferring the $1,664.62 from the "interests or discounts" column to the "transaction price" column. However, here the signs are the reverse of those in the adjustment of investments values above. This brings the new balance in the "transaction price" column to $231,664.62. This is the total amount owed as of the beginning of the next period. The new balance in the "interests or discounts" column $3,439.38 establishes the amount of interests payable that will become due in future periods. See Exhibit 13.3.

ACCOUNTING FOR FOREIGN EXCHANGE OPERATIONS

Recording Foreign Exchange Transactions

For each currency a separate page in a general exchange book should be kept. This book is commonly known as the *foreign exchange position book*. In each currency, every single transaction, regardless of its size or origin in the foreign exchange market (not in the money market),

| Foreign currency £ | | Local currency $ | |
Debit (buy)	Credit (sell)	Debit (buy)	Credit (sell)
110,000		262,900	
	100,000		240,000
200,000		476,400	
	1,000,000		2,394,000
1,000,000		2,364,000	
1,310,000	1,100,000	3,103,300	2,634,000
210,000		469,300	

should be entered in this book. An example of a position book, in this case for pounds sterling, is presented in Exhibit 13.4.

The position book registers every purchase and every sale in terms of two currencies: (1) the foreign currency for which the position book is kept (pounds sterling in our example) and (2) the local currency, that is, the currency of the country in which the operation takes place (U.S. dollars in this case). Purchases are treated as debits, and sales as credits. If the exchange transaction does not have a natural local currency equivalent, as is true when one foreign currency is purchased and another foreign currency is sold, an artificial local currency equivalent is assigned to that contract. For example, if a bank in the United States purchases £1 million at DM5.50/£, the notation means that the bank has purchased £1 million and sold DM5.5 million. Both currencies are foreign currencies to the U.S. bank, so there is no natural local currency equivalent. In this case, the trader assigns a rate of say, US$2.40/£ to the contract and establishes a local currency equivalent of US$2.4 million. The transaction is then entered in the position book for sterling as a sterling purchase at DM5.50/£ and as a local currency amount of US$2.4 million. Likewise, a sale of DM5.5 million is recorded in the position book for marks at DM5.50/£ with a local currency equivalent of US$2.4 million. The economic effect is the same as if the bank had purchased sterling at US$2.40/£ and sold marks at US$0.4364/DM. The choice of the arbitrary rate above is immaterial, but should reflect current market rates. Although the overall profit is not affected by the rate chosen, if the arbitrary rate differs substantially from the market rate, we arrive at sharply higher earnings in one currency and sharply lower earnings in another currency. This is undesirable because it distorts a profit and loss analysis of the exchange department on a currency-by-currency basis.

The other columns in the position book identify other particulars of the transaction, such as the date on which the transaction was closed, the rate (implicit in the expression of each transaction in terms of two currencies), the value date on which the transaction matures, and the name of the other party to the transaction, as well as the contract number. Then, at the end of the accounting period, a balance is taken for each column and a net balance is computed.

In the position book in Exhibit 13.4. we have recorded the following transactions, which, we assume, have all taken place on June 1:

1. Purchase £110,000 spot at $2.39/£

2. Sell £100,000 spot at $2.40/£

3. Purchase £200,000 three months outright at $2.3820/£

4. Sell £1,000,000 one month forward at $2.3940/£

5. Purchase £1,000,000 six months forward at $2.3640/£

The net balance line shows a net overbought position in the amount of £210,000, equivalent to $469,300.

Measuring Profits in Foreign Exchange Operations

Scanning the foreign exchange transactions reported in Exhibit 13.4 we can see that some foreign exchange contracts have been liquidated, while others remain in inventory at the end of the day. The profits or losses from liquidated contracts are realized profits or losses. For the outstanding exchange contracts, any change in the value between the time when they were acquired and the closing time is an unrealized profit or loss.

REALIZED PROFITS AND LOSSES

The two spot transactions reported in Exhibit 13.4 show that we bought £110,000 at $2.39 and sold £100,000 at $2.40. We realized a gain of $1,000 on the £100,000 sold, and £10,000 remain in inventory at the end of the period. We can see how profits realized from the two spot transactions are reflected in the position book by taking a balance just after the first two spot transactions, that is, after the purchase of £110,000 at $2.39 and the sale of £100,000 at $2.40, as shown in the table below. The net balance of $22,900 in local currency can be seen as the combination of the £10,000 still in inventory valued at the buying rate of $2.39, $23,900, less $0.01 profit per pound realized in the £100,000 sold, $1,000.

UNREALIZED PROFITS AND LOSSES

At the end of the period the position book for pounds shows the following items in inventory:

1. Transaction 1, £10,000 spot (the remaining £100,000 bought on that transactions were sold subsequently)

2. Transaction 3, a net outright purchase of forward pounds in the amount of £200,000

3. Transactions 4 and 5, a swap position of £1,000,000 with a sale for delivery on July 3 and a purchase for delivery on December 3

In Exhibit 13.5 the pound position at the end of the period is listed as being worth $470,300 at contract rates (column 6); however, at current market rates that position is worth $481,600 (column 7). That is, there is an unrealized profit of $11,300.

We can determine how much of the increase in market value of the

Realized Profits in Position Book

Rate	Foreign currency		Local currency	
	Debit (buy)	Credit (sell)	Debit (buy)	Credit (sell)
2.3900	110,000		262,900	
2.4000		100,000		240,000
Balance	110,000	100,000	262,900	240,000
Net balance	10,000		22,900	

EXHIBIT 13.5
TRADING POSITION WORK SHEET: DIRECT MARKET VALUATIONS

Position maturity	Long (L) or short (S) position (1)		Contract rate (2)	Market rate (3)	Market rate less contract rate (3) − (2) (4)	Unrealized profits (4) × (1) (5)	Contract value (1) × (2) (6)	Market value (1) × (3) (7)
Spot	L	10,000	2.3900	2.4000	+0.0100	+100	+23,900	+24,000
Forward								
September 3	L	200,000	2.3820	2.3880	+0.0060	+1,200	+476,400	+477,600
Swap								
July 3	S	1,000,000	2.3940	2.3960	+0.0020	−2,000	−2,394,000	−2,396,000
December 3	L	1,000,000	2.3640	2.3760	+0.0120	+12,000	+2,364,000	+2,376,000
						+11,300	470,300	481,600

position is due to changes in the spot rate, and how much is due to changes in swap rates.[4] This would provide a general view of how much of the $11,300 in unrealized profits comes from net exchange positions and how much from swap positions. Comparing the contract rate data (column 2) and the market rates (column 3) in Exhibit 13.5 we can explain the $11,300 in unrealized profits as follows:

SPOT   +£10,000

Change in spot rate:		
$2.3900/£ − $2.4000/£	$0.0100/£	
£10,000 × $0.0100/£		+ $100

THREE-MONTH   +£200,000

Change in spot rate:		
$2.3900/£ − $2.4000/£	+ $0.0100/£	
Change in three-month swap rate:		
$0.0080/£ − $0.0120/£	− 0.0040	
	$0.0060/£	
£200,000 × $0.0060/£		+$1,200

SWAP POSITION   £1,000,000

Sell position: one month; buy position: six months		
Change in swap rate between six and one months		
Initial swap rate:		
$2.3940/£ − $2.3640/£	$0.0300/£	
Ending swap rate:		
$2.3960/£ − $2.3760/£	0.0200	
	$0.0100/£	
£1,000,000 × $0.0100/£		+ $10,000
Total unrealized profits		+ $11,300

[4]For longer-term forward contracts which are linked to money market transactions, it will be preferable to use the so-called straight-line accounting method. In this method the original forward premium or discount is amortized over the life of the contract and converted into interest income or expense; exchange gains and losses in the outstanding contract reflect only changes in the spot rate. This approach is illustrated in the last section of this chapter, "Loan Financing through Swaps."

EXHIBIT 13.6

EXCHANGE PROFIT WORK SHEET

Net foreign currency position from position book (1)	Long or short (2)	Ending spot middle rate (3)	Value of position	
			At ending spot rate (4)	From position book (5)
£ 210,000	L	$2.40	$504,000	$469,300

TOTAL PROFITS AND LOSSES

As shown above, the foreign exchange operations for June 1 have produced the following:

1. A realized profit of $1,000

2. Unrealized profits of $11,300, composed of $1,300 profits in a net long exchange position, and $10,000 in a swap position

Alternatively, we could say that the market value of the pounds position is worth $481,600 at market rates, as shown in Exhibit 13.5, while in the position book in Exhibit 13.4 it appears at $469,300. Thus, we have a total of $12,300 in exchange profits for this period.

Another approach to calculating exchange profits and losses combines realized and unrealized gains and losses. This system, known as the *rebate system* is often used by exchange trading rooms. It first values everything at the current spot market rate, and then adjusts the forward transactions to reflect the appropriate market premium or discount. This system is applied in the *exchange profit work sheet* shown in Exhibit 13.6.

Columns 1, 2, and 5 in the exchange profit work sheet are copied from the position book in Exhibit 13.4. Column 1 shows the net foreign currency position of £210,000. Column 2 says that it is a long, or net overbought, position. Column 5 gives the historical cost of the position in terms of local currency, $469,300. As we showed in the position book in Exhibit 13.4, this local currency value of the position is the result of assigning to each transaction a local currency equivalent.

Unadjusted profit (4) − (5) (6)	Adjustment for forward contracts (7)	Adjusted profit (6) + (7) (8)
+ 34,700	− 22,400	+ 12,300

To translate the value of the £210,000 position at the current spot rate, we first establish a spot middle rate. This is indicated in column 3; it is $2.40/£. In column 4 we show the value of the pound position expressed at the current spot rate, $504,000 ($2.40/£ × £210,000). This is a crude current market value of the position; it assumes that the entire foreign currency position can be liquidated at the spot rate. The difference between this spot market value of the position, $504,000, and the value in the position book, $469,300, is $34,700. These profits are shown in column 6 as "unadjusted profit." Because the book value of the position, $469,300, was reduced by the $1,000 of realized profits, as shown earlier, the $34,700 unadjusted profit includes both realized profit and unrealized profits.

Now we have to adjust the value of the forward positions for the difference between the spot rate which we initially applied to those positions and the rate at which each of the forward positions can actually be liquidated. In our case, we estimated the market value of the entire position at the spot rate of $2.40. We know, however, that the forward sterling is selling at a discount against the dollar. The market rates on the outstanding forward contracts are below the spot rate of $2.40. We must adjust the profits computed in column 6.

The discount for forward sterling has been reduced from $0.0060 per month when the position was acquired to $0.0040 per month now. The *trading position work sheet* shown in Exhibit 13.7 lists the exchange positions by value date and provides the current market rates for each of them. In column 4 we compute the difference between the current spot rate at which each of the transactions was valued in the exchange profit work sheet and the current market rate for the various dates. This

EXHIBIT 13.7

TRADING POSITION WORK SHEET: SWAP RATE ADJUSTMENT

Position maturity	Long (L) or short (S) position (1)	Contract rate (2)	Market rate (3)	Market rate less closing spot* (4)	Revaluation adjustments (1) × (4) (5)
Spot	L	10,000	2.3900	2.4000	0.0000	0
Forward						
September 3	L	200,000	2.3820	2.3880	−0.0120	−2,400
Swap position						
July 3	S	1,000,000	2.3940	2.3960	−0.0040	+4,000
December 3	L	1,000,000	2.3640	2.3760	−0.0240	−24,000
						−$22,400

*Closing spot rate is $2.4000/£.

difference in rates multiplied by the size of the position is then entered in the column called "adjustments" (column 5).

No adjustment is required for the spot position. This was already valued at the current spot rate in the exchange profit work sheet. The September 3 maturity commands a 120-point discount. The position could be sold at $2.3880. Previously, it was evaluated at the spot rate of $2.40. Therefore, earnings were overstated by 120 points; this calls for a negative adjustment of $2,400. The July 3 sale of £1 million could be covered at $2.3960. Previously, we assumed we could purchase pounds to cover the position at the spot rate of $2.40, which was 40 points higher than the actual rate available in the market. Therefore, we must make a positive adjustment of $4,000. The December 3 purchase of £1 million could be sold at 240 points below spot, at $2.3760/£. Previously, we assumed a sale price of $2.40. Therefore, we have to make a negative adjustment of $24,000. The total of the "adjustments" column in Exhibit 13.7 is a negative figure of $22,400.

The negative net adjustment of $22,400 is inserted in column 7 of the exchange profit work sheet in Exhibit 13.6. The difference between the unadjusted profit in column 6 and the adjustment for future contracts in column 7 is the actual profit in the pounds position, $12,300. This figure appears in column 8. This total profit, $12,300, is the same as the sum of the realized and unrealized profits calculated earlier when we segregated the profits due to changes in the spot rate from the profits due to changes in the swap rate.

The procedures just described for pounds are applied to all currencies for which we have entries in the position book, and the grand total of column 8 in Exhibit 13.6 will show total exchange earnings for the period.

Bookkeeping for Foreign Exchange Operations

The spot transactions in the exchange markets can be treated in a manner similar to money market operations. The purchase of £110,000 spot in transaction 1 can be recorded as follows:

	Debit	Credit
June 1 Exchange position—pounds	262,900	
Cash		262,900

and the sale of £100,000 spot with the realization of $1,000 in profits in transaction 2 is entered as follows:

	Debit	Credit
June 1 Cash	240,000	
Exchange position—pounds		239,000
Realized trading profit		1,000

Forward transactions, although involving firm commitments, do not require any cash flow until the delivery date. Thus, the purchases and sales of foreign currency forward are reported as increases and decreases in the exchange position in that currency and the opposite movements are reflected in the exchange position of the home currency. The net of transactions 3, 4, and 5 is reported as follows:

	Debit	Credit
June 1 Exchange position—pounds	446,400	
Exchange position—dollars		446,400

Then, bringing the value of the exchange position to market value, involves the following entry:

	Debit	*Credit*
June 1 Exchange position—pounds	11,300	
Unrealized trading profit		11,300

The sum of the various entries for "exchange position—pounds" produces a total of $481,600—the market value of the position at the end of the period.

To bring the figures in the exchange position book to market values we must make an adjustment for the total difference between the current market value of the position and the cost reflected there. The market value of the pound position is $481,600 while the pound position book reflects a cost of $469,300. To reflect market values in the position book we must make an adjustment in the amount of $12,300. As discussed earlier, this adjustment represents $1,000 of realized trading profits and $11,300 of unrealized profits at the end of the period.

Of course, the value of the position in terms of pounds remains unchanged. Only the figures in local currency, dollars, are adjusted to reflect the market value of the position. The net balance after adjustments in the net position book reflects the asset value of the currency which will appear in the business's balance sheet. See Exhibit 13.8.

ACCOUNTING FOR JOINT EXCHANGE AND MONEY MARKET TRANSACTIONS

In this chapter we have shown how to account for treasury operations in the money market and the foreign exchange market. The procedures suggested measured gains and losses in interests and discounts from operations in the money market and gains and losses in exchange from operations in the exchange market. This separate reporting of money market and foreign exchange transactions can distort the picture for those operations which involve both markets—the so-called finance swaps. In these cases, although the net of the operation may be a profit, this net usually is composed of a larger profit in one market and a smaller profit or a loss in the other market. Separating the transaction components for reporting purposes distorts the combined net result of the total operation.

To avoid the distortion created by reporting the components of joint operations in different sets of accounts, these joint transactions must be identified and adjustments made to the records. The adjustments should remove the transactions from where they were reported originally and transfer them to a single account created for that purpose. This new account then will include both the money market and the exchange components of the transaction. Here we call such an account "sundry treasury profits and losses." If we want to keep track of the aggregate profit or loss from different activities of this type, we can add a subtitle to this account. Below we illustrate how to make the necessary adjustments for these activities using some of the problems discussed earlier in this book. The accounts created to show the joint effects are labeled "sundry treasury profits and losses—arbitrage," "sundry treasury profits and losses—forward quotes," and so forth.

In the transactions discussed in this section it is difficult to argue that they are either truly exchange or truly money market operations. That is why we have chosen an account which is neither an exchange account nor a money market account to show the combined effects: "sundry treasury profits and losses." However, there may be cases where the joint nature of the operation can be identified as being essentially a money market or an exchange transaction in disguise, depending on the case. In these cases we will still want to reflect all the components of the operation in one account; however, we will not need to use a new account. Instead, we will see that adjustments are made so all the component transactions are reflected on the relevant set of accounts. This is the case with the financing of loans through swaps. This is discussed in the following section.

Also, in the examples presented in this section, we will make the total adjustment at once. In practice, when more than one reporting period is involved, we will want to distribute these adjustments throughout the life of the joint transaction. A procedure for amortizing the adjustment through time is described in the following section, in the context of financing loans through swaps.

Covered Interest Arbitrage

In Chapter 5, we examined a case where there was an interest differential between the three-month pound and the dollar of 2.75 percent in favor of the pound. Simultaneously, the forward discount on the pound for a comparable period was 180 points, or 3 percent per annum discount from the spot price of $2.40/£. To take advantage of this market disequilibrium, we sold spot sterling against dollars and purchased forward

EXHIBIT 13.8

EXCHANGE POSITION BOOK AFTER ADJUSTMENTS

Date	Value date	Name of counterpart No. of contract	Rate
June 1	June 3	1	2.3900
June 1	June 3	2	2.4000
June 1	September 3	3	2.3820
June 1	July 3	4	2.3940
June 1	December 3	5	2.3640
Balances			
Net balances			
Adjustment*			
Net balances after adjustment			

*The $12,300 adjustment is composed of $1,000 in realized profit, and $11,300 adjustment to reflect the market value of the position at the end of the period.

sterling against dollars at the 3 percent per annum discount on the pound. The cash flows on the spot day, negative cash flow for sterling and positive cash flow for dollars, were squared in the money market through a sterling borrowing and a dollar placement. This was done at a net cost of 2.75 percent against us. The maturing of these two money market transactions squared the cash flows for the forward exchange transaction.[5]

If we follow the accounting conventions described in this chapter, this transaction will be recorded in our books as a large exchange profit, 3 percent, and a slightly smaller interest loss, 2.75 percent. The difference between the two figures, 0.25 percent, is the profit realized in the arbitrage. A large number of these transactions will distort the earnings picture shown under exchange and interest. A realistic picture of the total net profit in a covered interest arbitrage situation requires that adjustments be made to the original entries.

The objective of the adjustment is that both parts of the operation be

[5]This problem was also discussed in the section titled "Taking Advantage of Disequilibrium Situations: Covered Interest Arbitrage" in Chapter 8.

Foreign currency (£)		Local currency	
Debit (buy)	Credit (sell)	Debit (buy)	Credit (sell)
110,000		262,900	
	100,000		240,000
200,000		476,400	
	1,000,000		2,394,000
1,000,000		2,364,000	
1,310,000	1,100,000	3,103,300	2,634,000
210,000		469,300	
		12,300	
210,000		481,600	

reported together, preferably under a separate account. Such an account could be a miscellaneous account such as "sundry treasury profits and losses—arbitrage."

More specifically, in our example, the 180-point forward discount generating the exchange profit translates into a 3 percent interest differential. This profit already appears in the exchange accounts as a credit. To transfer this profit to the special account we have to debit the exchange accounts and credit the special account. The interest loss, a debit, is already measured in the money market accounts. We will want to transfer this loss from the regular accounts into the special account chosen to reflect this kind of transaction. Assuming an original amount of $400,000, the following entries may be made to achieve the desired adjustments:

	Debit	Credit
Exchange profits and losses	3,000	
Sundry treasury profits and losses—arbitrage		3,000
Sundry treasury profits and losses—arbitrage	2,750	
Interest expense		2,750

After netting the component $3,000 exchange profit and $2,750 interest loss, the $300 net profit from the complete operation is now reflected in one account: "sundry treasury profits and losses—arbitrage."

Creating a Forward Exchange Market

In Chapter 8, we discussed how to quote forward rates and create a forward exchange market when such a market does not exist. Essentially we arrived at the desired forward quote by undoing in the spot market the exchange position created by the forward transaction. To generate the cash flows needed in the spot market we borrowed the funds in one money market and invested the proceeds, after conversion in the spot market, in the other money market. That is, if we accepted the forward transaction we were forced to operate in two money markets. If we follow the procedures suggested for recording these transactions earlier in this chapter, two of the four transactions (the forward and spot exchanges) would be recorded as exchange transactions and the other two (borrowing and placing funds) as money market transactions.[6]

In the example we discussed in Chapter 8 we accepted to buy three-month dollars against Mexican pesos forward at Mex$12.5759/$, while in the spot market we converted dollars into pesos at Mex$12.4900/$— that is, an exchange loss of Mex$0.0859/$. The dollars needed for the spot transaction were borrowed for three months at 7.25 percent and the pesos obtained from the conversion were invested at 10 percent, also for three months; that is, an interest gain of 2.75 percent. Given the assumptions in that example, there was no profit or loss in this operation, since the exchange loss of Mex$0.0859/$ represents a 2.75 percent loss at the assumed spot rate. However, unless we make an adjustment, the exchange loss and the interest gain will be reported separately. To correct this distortion we can do the following bookkeeping entries, assuming a $400,000 transaction:

	Debit	*Credit*
Sundry treasury profits and losses— forward quotes	2,750	
Exchange profits and losses		2,750
Interest income	2,750	
Sundry treasury profits and losses— forward quotes		2,750

[6]See "Creating a Forward Exchange Market" in Chapter 8.

Exchange Transactions with All-In Price Quotes

It happens often that bank customers insist in getting all-in cost exchange quotes. They are interested in the net amount of cash they will receive from the bank after all charges have been made. In these cases it can happen that the bank will record the exchange transaction at this all-in cost while the accompanying money market operations are reported separately. This, again, will distort the reported figures.

A common example of this situation appears when the exporter comes to the bank to discount (sell) an export bill or time draft denominated in foreign currency. The bill is not due until, say, three months later. However, the exporter wishes to receive local currency immediately. The important issue for the exporter is how much local currency can he or she obtain by selling the bill to the bank today. The exporter is interested in an exchange rate for converting the dollars to be received three months hence into local currency received today.

In fact, the bank is making a loan to the exporter against the dollar inflow the bill will generate in 90 days; that is, the loan will be repaid by the issuer of the export bill. The bank will be providing financing to the exporter during the intervening three months. To finance this loan the bank has two options: (1) borrow dollars and convert the proceeds into local currency in the spot market, or (2) borrow local currency and cover the exchange position created by the dollar bill, in conjunction with the local currency borrowings, in the forward market. As an example, let's use the same situation we had in Chapter 11.[7]

MONEY MARKET, THREE-MONTH MATURITY

Eurodollars	11%
Local currency	6%

FOREIGN EXCHANGE MARKET

Spot rate	LC2.2000/$
Three-month swap rate (5% p.a. interest differential)	0.0275
Three-month forward rate	LC2.1725/$

In the first approach, the bank borrows and lends in dollars at 11 percent (we are assuming no profit). The dollar loan will be repaid, in fact, by the collection of the export bill. When the customer exchanges the dollar loan proceeds into local currency in the spot market at LC2.2000/$, the bank reverses the operation to balance the exchange position at the same rate. Money market operations show no gain or

[7]See "Financing Trade When Order Is Received," in Chapter 11.

loss. Exchange operations show no gain or loss. This reflects accurately the net effect of the total operation.

In the second approach, the bank borrows and lends directly in local currency at 6 percent. So there is no profit or loss reported in interests. Since the bank has made a loan in local currency while having an export bill in dollars, it will want to cover this exchange position by selling dollars against local currency at LC2.1725/$ for three-month delivery. In the exchange book there is a purchase of dollars against local currency, the export bill, and a sale of dollars against the local currency at the three-month forward rate of LC2.1725. Again, there is not a profit or loss in exchange. Neither the recording of the interests, nor of the exchange transactions, distorts the fact that there is no profit in this whole operation.

When the customer wants an all-in cost exchange rate, the bank must incorporate the cost of the loan to the customer into an exchange rate. From above, we know that the cost of the loan is 11 percent per annum. The loan is for three months. If we want to convert the interest cost into an exchange figure we must apply the three-month rate to the spot rate of LC2.2000/$. This is equivalent to LC0.0605/$ ($0.11/12 \times 3 \times 2.2000$). Thus, the all-in cost exchange rate is LC2.1395/$ (which is equal to 2.2000 less 0.0605). The bank will report in the exchange book a purchase of the export bill in dollars at LC2.1395/$. The other transactions in the exchange book and in the money books will depend on how the operation is actually financed by the bank.

If the bank finances the loan by borrowing dollars and converting the proceeds into local currency in the spot market, the exchange account will show the purchase of a three-month export bill at LC2.1395/$ and a spot sale of dollars against local currency at LC2.2000/$; an exchange gain of LC0.0605/$. The interest account will show the 11 percent interest cost on the dollar borrowings. Assuming a $1 million export bill, the adjustments needed would be as follows:

	Debit	Credit
Exchange profits and losses	60,500	
Sundry treasury profits and losses—		
export bills		60,500
(LC0.0605/$ $\times$ 1,000,000 reported exchange gain)		
Sundry treasury profits and losses—		
export bills	60,500	
Interest expense		60,500
(0.11/12 $\times$ 3 $\times$ 1,000,000 $\times$ 2.20)		

On the other hand, if the loan is financed in local currency, the interest expense account will reflect the 6 percent cost of local funds. The exchange accounts will show the purchase of the export bill at LC2.1395/\$ and a sale of three-month dollars against local currency at LC2.1725/\$. In this case the necessary adjustments would be as follows:

	Debit	Credit
Exchange profits and losses	33,000	
Sundry treasury profits and losses—		
export bills		33,000
(LC2.1725/\$ − LC2.1395/\$) × 1,000,000 reported		
exchange gain		
Sundry treasury profits and losses—		
export bills	33,000	
Interest expense		33,000
(0.06/12 × 3 × 1,000,000 × 2.20)		

In both financing approaches, the adjustment entries bring into one single account, "sundry treasury profits and losses—export bills," the fact that there was no profit in the transaction as a whole. The actual financing choice would depend on the bank position.

Loan Financing through Swaps

It often happens that the local currency in which an international bank lends is not readily available to the lending institution. In these cases the standard procedure to finance the loan is to borrow the needed funds in the Euromarkets and "swap" them into the local currency. That is, a Eurocurrency is borrowed while the loan is in local currency. To protect against the exchange risk derived from such a transaction, the bank buys the Eurocurrency in the forward market against the local currency. In the funding strategy just described, the cost of the funds to the bank equals the interest rate paid on the Eurocurrency plus the premium or discount which the Eurocurrency carries in the forward market against the local currency. However, given the reporting system described in this chapter, the swap transaction will be reported together with the other exchange transactions. As a result we have two problems, the cost of funds as reported in the money market books is distorted, and so are the accounts for exchange transactions. In addition, the distortions are likely to be longer-lived than the ones discussed in the preceding section, because the maturity of the lending operation will tend to produce longer-term forward contracts. Given the revaluation procedures used to measure exchange and money market operations, the distortion will be further compounded with every reporting period.

To cope with the reporting problems created by the funding of loans through "swaps" we want to have procedures which (1) convert the cost of the forward operation into interest costs and (2) distribute the adjustments throughout the life of the operation. That is, the cost of the cover should be allocated in the same way as accrued interest income and interest expense are distributed throughout the life of the loan.

As an illustration, assume that on July 16 we made a loan in pesos and financed the loan with Eurodollar borrowings. To cover the exchange position we sold pesos against dollars for delivery on September 30. The main reason for the borrowings and the cover transaction is to finance the loan in pesos. The loan and the borrowings are recorded with the money market accounts. However, the spot conversion from dollars into pesos and the forward operation—a swap—appear together with every other exchange transaction in the position book for pesos. Because the main reason for the exchange transactions is a funding decision—we should transform the swap costs into interests and have these interests transferred to the accounts which record borrowings and loans.

In the rate scenario in Exhibit 13.9, the September 30 forward peso is at a discount against the U.S. dollar of $0.0023/Mex$ (equal to 0.041490 for the forward rate less the 0.043790 spot rate). Since the forward cover involves selling pesos against dollars for future delivery, this discount is against us. It represents an increase in borrowing costs over the interests paid on U.S. dollars. Given that the cover transaction involves Mex$110 million, the forward discount on the peso against the U.S. dollar, represents $253,000 more in borrowing costs (equal to Mex$110 × $0.0023/Mex$ discount). This amount should be removed from the exchange books and added to interest expenses on money market operations. However, because the interest on borrowings and loans are not reported all at once, but accrued and realized throughout the life of the respective loans, we want to distribute the forward discount, now transformed into interest expenses, throughout the life of the forward contract. Thus, we prepare an amortization schedule that calculates the amount of interest expense to be transferred from the exchange accounts into interest expense throughout the two-and-a-half months until the forward contract matures. This schedule is presented in Exhibit 13.9. Every month we will credit the position book for pesos and debit interest expenses for the amount of amortization scheduled for that month.

EXHIBIT 13.9

AMORTIZATION SCHEDULE FOR SWAP COSTS IN LOAN FUNDING THROUGH SWAPS

RATES AS OF JULY 16

Spot	$0.043790/Mex$
Forward value September 30	$0.041490/Mex$
Swap rate	$0.002300/Mex$

Amount of forward contract: Mex$110,000,000

Amount to be amortized: Mex$110,000,000 $\times$ 0.0023 = $253,000

Date	Total amortization (1)	Unamortized amount* (2)	Accrued amortization (3)	Amortization this month (1) − [(2) + (3)] (4)
July 31	253,000	203,065.78	—	49,934.22
August 31	253,000	99,868.42	49,934.22	103,197.36
September 30	253,000	—	153,131.58	99,868.42
				253,000.00

*Unamortized amount = $\dfrac{253,000 \text{ (total amortization)}}{76} \times$ number of days from the first of next month to date of maturity

After the pesos obtained from the spot transaction are lent out, we are left with a net short position in pesos, value September 30, in the amount of Mex$110 millions. Earlier in this chapter we showed how unrealized exchange profits and losses on forward positions can be explained in terms of changes in spot rates and changes in swap rates. However, the forward contracts involved in swap funding are not subject to fluctuations in value because of changes in swap rates. We can say that, from the point of view of exchange transactions, there is a hedge against changes in swap rates. There is a guarantee that an amount equivalent to the initial swap rate will be transferred from the exchange accounts into the money market accounts following the amortization schedule. The only exposure to changes in exchange rates is the exposure to changes in the spot rate.

The exchange profit work sheet presented in Exhibit 13.10 is a variation of the exchange profit work sheet presented earlier. The first six

EXHIBIT 13.10

EXCHANGE PROFIT WORK SHEET
FOR LOAN FUNDING THROUGH SWAPS

| | | | Value of position | | |
| | Net foreign currency position | Long or short | End of month spot middle rate | At ending spot rate | From position book* |
Date	(1)	(2)	(3)	(1) × (3) (4)	(5)
July 31	110,000,000	S	0.043950	−4,834,500	−4,563,900.00
August 31	110,000,000	S	0.043950	−4,834,500	−4,631,434.22
September 30	110,000,000	S	0.043750	−4,812,500	−4,734,631.64

*Initial book value in preceding period plus net profit or loss (column 8) in that period.

†From amortization schedule, column 2.

‡From amortization schedule, column 4.

columns are the same in both work sheets. Essentially, in these columns the position is valued at the current spot rate and compared with the value in the position book to produce a figure for "unadjusted profits." The "unadjusted profits" are segregated into two parts: amounts to be amortized in the future (column 7) and the profit and loss for the period (column 8). This profit and loss, in turn, is segregated into two components: a portion to be charged to interest expense according to the initial amortization schedule (column 9) and a residual exchange gain or loss (column 10).

We can see that the profit or loss accrued in the exchange accounts each month (column 10) is a function of the change in the spot rate from the time when the forward transaction took place, to the time when the revaluation is being made. The initial spot rate was $0.043790. When on July 31 the peso spot rate appreciates to $0.043950, this produces an exchange loss in the amount of $17,600. Given our short position of Mex$110 million, the appreciation of $0.00016 per peso represents a loss of $17,600. Fortunately, by the end of September 30, this loss is reversed as the peso depreciates against the U.S. dollar, and an exchange gain of $22,000 is reported.

The accounting entries to accompany these adjustments at the end of the first period, July 31, are as follows:

Unadjusted profit or loss (4) − (5) (6)	Unamortized amount† (7)	Net profit or loss (6) − (7) (8)	Interest paid (−) or earned (+) (9)	Exchange gain (+) or loss (−) (8) − (9) (10)
−270,600.00	203,065.78	−67,534.22	−49,934.22	−17,600
−203,065.78	99,868.42	−103,197.36	−103,197.36	—
−77,868.44	—	−77,868.44	−99,868.42	+22,000

	Debit	Credit
July 31 Unrealized exchange profits and losses	17,600.00	
Interest expense	49,934.22	
Exchange position—pesos		67,534.22

The forward discount which is scheduled to be converted into interest expense in future periods is excluded from the valuation of the peso position at the end of the period (Mex$203,065.78 at the end of July 31). The remaining change in valuation (Mex$67,534.22 at the end of July) is then distributed between unrealized exchange profits and losses and interest expense for the period.

CHAPTER 14

Risks in
Treasury Operations

In this book we have mentioned often the risks inherent in different operations in the money and exchange markets. However, that discussion focused on the risks specific to each of those transactions. Now we shall assess those risks in terms of treasury operations in general. This will serve to qualify the profitability of treasury operations—as measured in the preceding chapter—and to control the risks acceptable in these operations—as described in the next chapter.

There are three major types of risks involved in the operations in the money market and the exchange market: credit risk, rate risk, and liquidity risk.[1]

CREDIT RISK

The credit risk has to do simply with the ability of the other party to a transaction to meet the agreed-upon obligations. In financial markets, the ability to meet a contracted obligation translates into the ability to pay when the obligation to deliver funds matures.

[1]It should be noted that in this chapter we are using the term "risk" to mean the danger of realizing a loss, or a profit smaller than the one anticipated. This is in contrast to the statistical definition of risk, where risk is measured in terms of the distribution of possible outcomes around their average.

Credit Risk in the Money Market

In the money market, the credit risk is very obvious. In this market, one borrows and lends, or places, funds. From our point of view, there is no credit risk when we do the borrowing; however, on the lending (or placing) side, there is always the risk that the borrower will be unable to repay the funds we have lent. In spite of a very profitable rate on the loan, if the borrower is not able to pay back the debt, the funds manager is sure to have a loss.

Credit Risk in the Foreign Exchange Market

In the foreign exchange market the credit risk of the other party being unable to pay has a different impact depending on whether the inability to pay occurs *before the value date* or *on the same value date* of the foreign exchange contract. The less serious case appears when the inability to pay is discovered before the value date of a contract. In this case, the funds manager is expecting a cash inflow in that currency to take place on the contracted date. Chances are that an outflow had already been planned to ensure the proper use of the inflow promised by the forward contract. However, if the other party to the transaction does not meet the specified obligation and the funds manager needs the funds, he or she will have to go to the market to obtain those funds. The actual gain or loss in that transaction depends on the then-prevailing rate of the desired currency relative to the rate contracted through the now-defaulted contract for the given value date. This risk traditionally was called the 10 percent risk. The 10 percent referred to the size of the usual revaluation during the fixed-rate system which prevailed from the end of World War II until 1971. Since then, given the wider fluctuations in exchange rates, this risk is better referred to as the *20 percent risk.* Note that this risk occurs when the other party to the transaction defaults *prior to maturity* of the contract.

A more serious credit risk in the foreign exchange market is the one that has appeared prominently in a few major losses in commercial banks. This situation occurs when the other party to a transaction goes bankrupt *on the day of maturity* and settlement of the contract and after the first part of the transaction has been completed. Given the time differences among various financial centers, one party may transfer the funds corresponding to his or her part of the transaction during regular office hours while the other party decides to declare bankruptcy before opening on the day on which the transaction is to take place. This loss amounts to 100 percent of the funds involved.[2]

A widely publicized example which illustrates the credit risk in foreign exchange transactions is the failure of the German Herstatt Bank on Wednesday, June 26, 1974. The bank was very active in foreign exchange; in fact, it was this business that led, in large part, to the bank's failure. In a move which has led to much controversy, the German authorities closed the Herstatt Bank early in the afternoon of that Wednesday. The financial and nonfinancial institutions who had exchange business with Herstatt were divided into two groups: those that had exchange contracts outstanding with Herstatt maturing *after* June 26, and those with exchange contracts that matured *on* June 26.

Suppose the rate for marks at that time was US$0.40/DM, and another bank had sold marks to Herstatt, maturing in July 1974, at US$0.48/DM. Herstatt did not perform under this contract, and the bank which sold to Herstatt at US$0.48/DM had to sell the marks again to another bank at the then-prevailing rate of US$0.40/DM. This is the 20 percent loss potential we mentioned earlier. Obviously, this kind of situation can lead to larger or smaller losses, as the case may be, or even produce a profit. In the latter instance, however, the bankrupt bank would probably file a claim.

Those parties who had exchange transactions with Herstatt maturing on June 26 were really in trouble, particularly if they had sold European currencies, including marks, to Herstatt and purchased U.S. dollars against them. The European currencies were paid to Herstatt on Wednesday morning, German time. However, Herstatt was closed before it had a chance to pay the U.S. dollars on Wednesday morning, New York time, which is Wednesday afternoon in Europe. Everybody having exchange transactions maturing that morning initially lost 100 percent of the amount involved in the exchange transaction and was treated just like the regular depositors of the bank.[3]

This *clean risk at liquidation* of exchange contracts prevails even when different time zones are not involved. The operations in financial institutions are automated to such an extent that a payment could probably not be stopped on the same business day, even if one were to hear

---

[2]This loss could be larger if adverse rate movements occur simultaneously with bankruptcy at time of maturity.
[3]The eventual loss will usually be less than 100 percent. The amount recovered depends on the settlement of the bankruptcy proceedings.

at some point in the morning that a partner in an exchange transaction was going bankrupt.

Sovereign Risk

A subgroup within the credit risk is the *sovereign risk*. At any point in time, a given country has the prerogative of closing its foreign exchange window. Particularly in countries whose currencies are very sparsely traded in the market, the central bank can be the only source of foreign exchange. Thus, we can have the situation of a very good credit risk in a company located in a country with a high sovereign risk. For example, one can be fairly certain that the corporation will be able to generate the necessary local currency to repay a loan we have made in foreign currency. However, if the central bank makes it impossible to convert the local currency into foreign exchange, the proceeds from the repayment of the loan will not be available in the desired foreign currency.

The sovereign risk is even more direct when lending to governments themselves. The additional dimension of a possible change in the government or in the policies of the same government can easily invalidate any previous contract and, therefore, any hope of receiving a payment for the loan in hard currency.

RATE RISK

We saw in previous chapters that one way in which one can profit in the financial markets is by anticipating correctly changes in market rates. It is this anticipation that leads the funds manager to produce "mismatched" cash-flow positions and be exposed to undesirable fluctuations in rates, the rate risk.

Rate Risk in the Money Market

In the money market, the rate risk arises when the maturities of the placement and the borrowings are not matched. For example, when we lend funds for six months while borrowing with a one-month maturity, the interest rate on the six-month loan has been locked in from the beginning. However, at the end of the first month, additional borrowings are necessary to repay the initial debt or to roll over the debt. But, at the beginning of the transaction, we do not know with certainty what the interest rate will be at that time. Most likely, the funds manager in this situation is speculating that interest rates will decline after a month. If the assumption proves correct, the funds manager would have locked in a high interest rate on the loan for six months, while refinancing the operation at a lower interest rate after the initial first month. If the initial expectation proves to be wrong and interest rates actually increase and keep doing so for the remainder of the loan period, however, the funds manager will be forced to obtain financing (to borrow) at rates which might prove to be higher than the one at which the funds were placed or lent initially.

Rate Risk in the Foreign Exchange Market

In foreign exchange transactions the rate risk appears in two forms: (1) in net exchange positions, and (2) in swap positions or mismatched maturities. The most obvious case of rate risk is the maintenance of a *net exchange position* in a given currency. If the position is long or overbought and there is a depreciation of the currency, a loss is sure to occur. On the other hand, if an upvaluation occurs while the funds manager is holding a long net exchange position, there will be a profit from such a change in exchange rates. The opposite results would occur if the net exchange position were short or oversold in that currency.

The other way in which rate risk appears when one operates in the foreign exchange market is through *swap positions.* As explained in previous chapters, a swap transaction does not affect the *net exchange position.* By definition, a swap involves a simultaneous buy and sale of currency for two different maturities. For example, the funds manager may buy German marks against U.S. dollars for three-month delivery and sell German marks against U.S. dollars for one-month delivery. Let's say that the forward mark is selling at a premium against the dollar. In this case, in order to make a profit, the funds manager must be expecting that, when the one-month transaction matures, it will be possible to square the two-month gap at a premium larger than the one that prevailed initially. If the mark had been selling at a discount, the funds manager, when entering into this specific swap, would have expected that the discount would decrease.

This expectation of an increase in the premium or a decrease in the discount of the mark against the dollar must be based on a change in relative interest rates. The interest differential must change in favor of the dollar. If the initial situation was one of a forward premium on the mark against the dollar, then, in this case, the interest differential was in favor of the dollar. In other words, the interest rate for dollars was higher than the one for marks, and the forecast implied that the interest differential would become even more strongly in favor of the dollar. If the initial situation was one of a discount on the mark against the dollar, then the interest differential must have been in favor of the mark. Therefore, the expectation behind the swap transaction described earlier must have been that the differential would narrow (become less favorable to the mark) either because the mark rate would decrease or the dollar rate would increase.

The previous paragraph clearly points out the connection between the forward exchange market and the money market. The rate risks in the forward exchange market, when one is dealing in swap transactions, are dependent on the same assumptions and outcomes as in the money market. A swap position, after all, is not really an exchange position. Profits and losses in a swap position depend exclusively on the development of interest rates for the two currencies involved. *A swap position is a money market position disguised with exchange contracts.*

One major distinction between the rate risk in money market operations and swap transactions is that, when operating in the money market, we are forecasting only the rates for one currency. When operating in the foreign exchange market through a swap, it becomes necessary to take into account the future interest rates for two currencies, a slightly more complicated task!

LIQUIDITY RISK

The liquidity type of risk is closely associated with rate risk. Liquidity risks arise because the cash flows in a transaction are not "square." These cash flows are not balanced on purpose, because of the expectation of a change in rate (hence the rate risk). However, there is also a risk which arises from the question of ability to obtain the funds when a cash inflow has not been prearranged; this is the liquidity risk.

Liquidity Risk in the Money Market

In the money market, the liquidity risk appears when the funds are placed for a period longer than the source of funds which made the placement possible. Using the same example that we used in the discussion of the rate risk, if we lend funds for six months while borrowing for only one month, a risk exists that at the end of the month when refinancing must be arranged, it will not be found. One example of such a situation is seen if the initial source of funds is a certificate of deposit (CD) with one-month maturity. At the end of the month, the CD is presented for redemption, and funds must be found to pay the initial lender. The usual procedure is to issue another CD. However, in the intervening month the market for CDs may have disappeared because of regulations imposed by the central bank. In an extreme case, a very tight money market may make it impossible to raise funds in the market, regardless of the rate offered; this is liquidity risk. However, this risk usually is more relevant in terms of rate risk. There is always a price at which funds can be raised by creditworthy borrowers! Raising funds under these conditions (rate risk) might prove not to be very profitable, but bankruptcy because of loss of liquidity can usually be avoided. The exception, clearly, is any case in which the entity in question becomes a very poor credit risk and no one is willing to lend funds to it at any rate, nor are there any financial assets to be sold or pledged.

Liquidity Risk in the Foreign Exchange Market

The liquidity risk in the foreign exchange market also arises from uncertainty of the ability to obtain the funds in the currency desired. This problem is much more acute in the foreign exchange market than in the money market. This imbalance between the risks in the two markets arises from two factors: (1) greater inclination on the part of monetary authorities to impose funds availability controls on the foreign exchange market than on the local money market, and (2) the narrowness and shallowness of foreign exchange markets when compared with the money markets for the same currencies. In the example we used in the discussion of rate risk, we described a swap transaction where we bought three-month marks against dollars and sold one-month marks against dollars. At the end of the first month, in the absence of any further transactions, marks must be purchased in the spot market to fulfill the forward contract entered into one month before. If the Bundesbank (the West German central bank) decides to close its foreign exchange window because of instabilities in the market, we will be at the mercy of sellers of marks in the market. These other sellers are likely to be unable to deal in very large quantities. If the transaction is for a fairly large amount, say DM100 million or more, it may be very hard to complete the desired transaction. If it is completed, it will surely take place at disadvantageous rates (the rate risk). If the transaction is not completed, this may mean almost-certain bankruptcy to some financial institutions.

EVALUATION OF COMPARATIVE RISKS

We have seen that the various types of financial risks are present in transactions in both the money market and the foreign exchange market. However, for a given operation the *degree* of each of these risks will vary depending on whether the money market or the foreign exchange market is chosen to achieve the desired objective.

As an illustration of how the degree of each of the risks varies depending on the specific approach chosen, we shall make use of the example discussed in Chapter 8 where an interest change was anticipated. The market scenario is reproduced in Exhibit 14.1. In this case, the initial market is in equilibrium; the interest rate differential equals the premium/discount in the forward exchange market. However, a change in the interest rate differential is forecast. We have a case of the dollar and the pound sterling, with the initial interest differential being 3 percent in favor of the pound. It is forecast that the interest rate on the pound will decrease by 1 percent in a month, thus reducing the interest differential to 2 percent and changing the discount on the forward pound accordingly.

To take advantage of this information in the money market, we would want to lend, or place, pounds for a longer period at the present high rate and finance the transaction with borrowings of a shorter maturity. When the borrowings mature, we can refinance the transaction by borrowing for five months, now at the lower interest rate. The cash flows accompanying this transaction are reproduced in Part A of Exhibit 14.1. In the example where we lend funds for six months at 13 percent and finance them initially with one-month borrowings, the profit is derived from the lower interest rate, 12 percent, obtained to refinance the loan for five months when the one-month borrowings mature. Dealing with £1 million, we can make a total profit of $10,000 with the interest differential of 1 percent per annum in our favor for five months.[4]

The expected interest reduction on the pound translates into an expected smaller discount on the forward pound. We expect the swap rate of the pound against the dollar (a discount) to decrease. Therefore, we

---

[4]The profit is £15,000 for value date July 1, less £10,833 for value date February 1, equal to £4,167. The profit of £4,167 at $2.40/£ equals $10,000. For a more detailed discussion of this example see "Taking Advantage of Expected Changes in Interest Rates" in Chapter 8.

EXHIBIT 14.1

ACTING ON ANTICIPATED CHANGES IN INTEREST RATES:
MONEY MARKET AND EXCHANGE MARKET APPROACHES COMPARED

MARKET SCENARIO

	Money market (maturities up to six months)	Foreign exchange market
Initial Situation		
Pound sterling	13%	Spot rate: $2.4000/£ 3% discount on pounds
U.S. dollar	10%	One-month swap rate: $0.0060/£
Situation Anticipated for One Month Later		
Pound sterling	12%	Spot rate: $2.4000/£ 2% discount on pounds
U.S. dollar	10%	One-month swap rate: $0.0040/£

---

*+ = cash inflow; − = cash outflow; NCF = no cash flow.

CASH FLOWS

Date	Transaction	Currency* £	$
	A. MONEY MARKET APPROACH		
January 1	Borrowed funds received (13 percent for one month)	+1,000,000	
	Investment made (13 percent for six months)	−1,000,000	
	Net cash flows	0	
February 1	Borrowed funds repayment (includes interest)	−1,010,833	
	Borrowed funds received (12 percent for five months)	+1,000,000	
	Net cash flows	− 10,833	
July 1	Investment repayment received, including interest	+1,065,000	
	Borrowed funds repayment, including interest	−1,050,000	
	Net cash flows	+ 15,000	
	B. FOREIGN EXCHANGE MARKET APPROACH		
January 1	Purchase of pounds against dollars value date July 1	NCF	NCF
	Sale of pounds against dollars value date February 1	NCF	NCF
	Net cash flows	0	0
February 1	Sale of pounds against dollars from January 1 contract	−1,000,000	+2,394,000
	Purchase of pounds against dollars in spot market	+1,000,000	−2,400,000
	Sale of pounds against dollars value date July 1	NCF	NCF
	Net cash flows	0	− 6,000
July 1	Purchase of pounds against dollars from January 1 contract	+1,000,000	−2,364,000
	Sale of pounds against dollars from February 1 contract	−1,000,000	+2,380,000
	Net cash flows	0	+ 16,000
Net exchange positions		0	+ 10,000

want to purchase the forward pounds now and sell them after the swap rate has decreased. To take advantage of this information in the exchange market, without assuming a net exchange position, we must do it through a swap transaction.

In the first swap position, we arrange the sterling purchase for a relatively long maturity. The sterling sale is arranged for a relatively short maturity. We hope that when the maturity of the sell transaction arrives, our forecast has come true, and that we can enter a new swap —purchase spot and sell forward sterling—at a lower swap rate. The market scenario and the cash flows accompanying this transaction are reproduced in Part B of Exhibit 14.1. In this example, the initial swap transaction is:

Purchase pounds against
dollars for six months

at a swap rate of $0.0060/£
per month

Sell pounds against dollars
for one month

At the end of one month, when the one-month contract matures and our forecast for the decline in the interest rate of the pound has proven correct, we enter another swap transaction:

Purchase pounds against
dollars spot

at a swap rate of US$0.0040/£
per month

Sell pounds against dollars
for five months

Again, the profit here originates from the $0.0020/£ difference in swap rate enjoyed for five months. The equivalent interest rate is 1 percent per annum. The total profit is also $10,000. Let's now analyze the various risks in each of these approaches.

Comparative Credit Risks

The credit risk depends entirely on the nature and abilities of the party with whom we are contracting to fulfill its part of the transaction. If the other party turns out to be a bad credit risk and one is using the money market route, one stands to lose 100 percent of the funds lent to that party. If one is using the forward exchange market, the 100 percent loss can occur only if the timing permits the other party to go bankrupt after we have completed our part of the transaction by transferring the necessary funds. In other words, using the money market approach produces a 100 percent credit risk throughout the entire life of the transaction. The exchange approach produces some risk throughout the life of the transaction. The exact amount of that risk is the difference between the rate in the exchange contract which is not completed and the rate which we can obtain in the market for the same value date. This so-called 20 percent risk prevails, except on the delivery date itself when the clean risk of liquidation exposes the entire amount.

Comparative Rate Risks

The expectation of profit in the above transactions is all predicated on the basis of a change in the pound interest rate. When we used the money market, we were concerned only with the interest rate for the pound. However, when we used the foreign exchange market, we were concerned with changes in the interest differential; therefore, we are susceptible to changes in two different rates, the rate for the pound and the rate for the U.S. dollar. In our example, we change only the interest rate for the pound; however, one could have gained the same profit in the foreign exchange market if the U.S. dollar interest rate had increased by 1 percent. In either case, the interest *differential* would have decreased by 1 percent, and the discount for the pound would have decreased by 1 percent also. So, on the one hand, the foreign exchange market makes it possible to realize a profit even if a similar event takes place; on the other hand, now we are forecasting the behavior of two rates in contrast with the single rate involved when we operate in the money market. For example, even if the expected decrease in the interest rate for pounds from 13 to 12 percent takes place, it is possible that the interest rate for dollars will drop from 10 to 8 percent over the same period. Now, the interest differential will be 4 percent, producing a monthly swap rate of $0.0080, a $0.0020/£ per month cost to close the five-month gap. This situation will cause a loss, although the rate forecast for a drop in the pound interest rate was correct.

Comparative Liquidity Risks

In the money market, at the end of one month, we are forced to roll over our borrowings, that is, to approach a lender. In the foreign exchange market, at the end of the first month, we have only to go to the spot market. There is almost always somebody willing to sell the desired currency although we may not like the rate, but that is a different type of risk. In addition, there is a cosmetic problem. When we use the money market, borrowings appear in the balance sheet. This may upset some of the multiple ratios which a financial institution must maintain to keep within government regulations. Forward exchange transactions are, in a way, off the balance sheet.

Thus, it appears that, from the point of view of the liquidity risk, there is a slight advantage in using the foreign exchange market instead of the money market, particularly if one is anticipating not being such a good credit risk when the borrowings have to be rolled over!

Overall Assessment

The table below gives an overview on a risk-by-risk basis. A positive sign indicates the approach that is preferable to take advantage of an expected change in an interest rate for a currency.

Overall Assessment of Risk

	Money market approach	Exchange approach
Credit risk	−	+
Rate risk	+	−
Liquidity risk	−	+

If we are dealing with first-rate institutions and are part of that select group ourselves, the liquidity and credit risks play a minor role as compared with the rate risk where anticipated profits may evaporate or even become losses because of a faulty forecast. Once we start dealing with anyone other than the very best names in the world, however, the credit risk becomes more important. Furthermore, if we are not among the most prestigious institutions, we have to be much more concerned with our liquidity risk.

PROBLEM

PROBLEM 14.1

Assume that five-year dollars are quoted at 12 percent per annum in the interbank market, that is, LIBOR is 12 percent per annum. A customer wishes to borrow dollars for five years and demands a competitive quote. It is the bank's policy to get at least a 1.50 percent per annum spread on all loans. However, the customer is not willing to pay more than 13 percent, which would give the bank only a 1 percent profit margin. The loan officer makes the loan anyway at 13 percent, but does not cover the transaction with a five-year borrowing at 12 percent in the Eurodollar market. Instead, he borrows three-month dollars at 11 percent and argues that he expects the average cost of a series of short-term borrowings to be 11.50 percent per annum, or 0.50 percent per annum cheaper than the present 12 percent cost of five-year money. He also intends to occasionally borrow low-interest-rate currencies, such as Swiss francs, instead of dollars. Through this cross-currency borrowing he expects to cut the average borrowing cost by yet another 0.50 percent per annum. Thus, the expected average cost of funding the 13 percent loan is 11 percent per annum, and the expected profit is 2 percent per annum. What are your comments on the risks in this funding strategy?

ANSWER

The strategy is very risky and probably it is at variance with the bank's policy.

It appears that the bank expects to earn 1.50 percent per annum for its credit risk, that is, the possibility that the borrower cannot repay the loan. If the bank does not incur any other risk than the credit risk, it has to lend at 13.50 percent. In the absence of a nonbank borrower, the bank can place the dollars for five years at 12 percent with another bank at a lesser credit risk. As the loan was made at 13 percent, and not at 13.50 percent, the bank is not being fully compensated for its credit risk.

The proposed funding strategy involves three more risks, for which there is no adequate compensation:

1. *Liquidity risk.* The bank borrows for three months only, even though the loan has been committed for five years. At the end of the three-month borrowing period the money market could be very tight, or the bank's credit standing could be tarnished, or both. There is clearly the risk that the bank could have difficulties getting the money for a rollover.

2. *Interest rate risk.* Instead of the expected lower dollar interest rates, interests could in fact rise to very much higher

levels. This would produce a negative interest rate spread on the loan.

3. *Exchange rate risk.* In those cases where the bank borrows in nondollar, low-interest-rate currencies, the expectation is that the interest savings will exceed a possible exchange loss when the borrowed currency appreciates. But the exchange loss could also be larger than the interest savings and produce an all-in cost for the generated dollars in excess of the dollar interest rate.

In conclusion, the bank gets only 1 percent for absorbing all these risks. This is 0.50 percent per annum less than what is required to absorb the credit risk alone and it ignores all the risks involved in the funding strategy.

It is always useful to understand *all* the risks involved in a given set of transactions and then price them accordingly. A good rule for pricing might be called "compartmentalization of risks and rewards." This means that we identify all the individual risks taken and establish, for each risk, the minimum compensation or spread we require expressed in basis points. Then we add up all the compensations needed to absorb all the risks or to render services. This aggregate then should be added to our basic cost of funds to arrive at a proper price. If that desired price is not competitive, we might be well advised *not* to do the business.

CHAPTER 15

Control of
Treasury Operations

We have identified three major financial risks in treasury operations: credit risk, rate risk, and liquidity risk. In this chapter we shall discuss ways of controlling these risks as they apply to operations in the foreign exchange and money markets. In the last section we also discuss the control of other risks attending these operations.

CREDIT RISK

The risk that the other party to a financial transaction may become unable to pay us the amount contracted on the date it is due, can be controlled by limiting the total amount that the other party may owe us at any time. This total amount is commonly called a *line of credit.*

These lines of credit should specify separate amounts for exchange transactions and money market transactions. If several operators have authority to extend credit to a single party, as international banks operating in the international money market can do, it may be useful to establish at headquarters one global line for exchange transactions and one global line for money market placements. The individual operators should then receive allocations from this total line.

Credit Risk in the Money Market

The credit risk in money market operations is controlled primarily by establishing lines for placements with each borrower. These lines will limit the amount and tenor under which these placements can be made. For example, a line for a given party might read: "US$10 million, or equivalent, for money market placements up to twelve months, with a sublimit of US$5 million, or equivalent, for money market placements up to six months." These individual lines of credit should also insure that no one borrower accounts for an unduly high percentage of the total money market portfolio. The maximum impact that bankruptcy of a given borrower can have, given the total size of the portfolio, must be limited.

When a portfolio consists not only of placements with banks, but also contains commercial paper and other debt instruments from nonbanks, lines of credit should be established also by industry. This provides economic diversification, so that we can have some protection against adverse developments in specific industries which would affect all companies in that industry.

For a financial institution accepting deposits, credit risk also exists in these deposits. More specifically, the risk consists of believing that good funds have been received or will be received with the deposit when this may not be the case. For example, we may accept an overnight deposit on Monday and repay the principal with interest on Tuesday. The credit risk in this operation will appear if our control system failed to detect that the funds actually were not received on Monday. In this case, the "repayment" on Tuesday is just a "payment" subject to the same credit risk as a loan. Credit risk on deposits also exists between the time when the deposit is negotiated and the value date for the deposit. For example, if on Monday we accept a one-year deposit value Wednesday from an investor at 10 percent, we have a credit risk if the given investor files for bankruptcy on Tuesday. The credit risk appears if on Monday, when we learned about the 10 percent deposit value Wednesday, we arrange for a placement in the same amount value Wednesday, say, at 11.50 percent. If the 10 percent deposit does not materialize on Wednesday, because of the bankruptcy of the depositor, we will have to borrow an equivalent amount of funds to be able to deliver on the placement we made for Wednesday. If in the meantime interest rates on deposits have increased from 10 percent to 12 percent, there will be a *credit loss* of 0.50 percent. The protection against these risks are a control system which can identify at the end of every day whether or not deposits have become good funds and an understanding of the economic conditions of the depositors.

Credit Risk in the Foreign Exchange Market

Credit risk in foreign exchange operations is either the so-called 20 percent or a 100 percent risk, depending on whether the other party to the contract defaults *before* or *at* the maturity date.[1] Thus, any operator in the foreign exchange market should have both a limit on the aggregate amount of exchange contracts outstanding with a particular party, to cover the so-called *20 percent risk;* and a sublimit on transactions maturing on any one day, to cover the *100 percent clean risk at liquidation* of the contract.

A bank might be willing to have a total of US$10 million outstanding in exchange contracts with a given customer and to bear the 20 percent risk on this total. However, the line might specifically stipulate that no more than US$2 million may mature on a single day. This means that the bank can have US$2 million worth of contracts maturing on everyday of a week Monday through Friday. This would make an aggregate of US$10 million, and the total maturity per day would not exceed US$2 million. A maximum loss in this situation would, in theory, be as follows: The customer defaults on Monday, and the bank suffers a 100 percent loss on the US$2 million maturing on that day, assuming the bank has already paid for its part of the contract, plus whatever is lost because of adverse rate movements on Monday. If we assume that this rate deterioration does not exceed 20 percent, the loss due to rate changes would be US$2 million, that is, 20 percent of US$10 million. The total loss on the entire US$10 million outstanding at the beginning of the week would be US$4 million—the US$2 million principal maturing on Monday plus the US$2 million loss from adverse rate movements.

The actual foreign exchange line in the above example could be worded as follows: "US$10 million or equivalent, for aggregate exchange transactions outstanding with a sublimit of US$2 million, or equivalent, for transactions maturing on any one day." Of course, by defining the sublimit so that it controls contracts maturing on any one day, it is assumed that the bank has a system for assuring itself at the end of each day that "good" counterpart funds have been received in its depository. If it does not have such a system, or if liquidation is not made by direct credit to its account (for example, if the bank receives payment by means of a check which has to be cleared to make sure the funds are good), the sublimit will have to be redefined so that it reflects the exposure more precisely.

The international trade practices of many businesses make it necessary for them to buy and sell certain currencies in order to settle their accounts in various countries. In these cases, it is wise for a bank to have specific knowledge as to which currencies its customers must buy

---

[1]As discussed in the preceding chapter, this 100 percent risk could be even larger if adverse rate movements occur simultaneously with the default at maturity.

and sell as a result of their normal business. Then, the exchange lines can be more specific and may possibly be limited to transactions in these specific currencies. These sublimits will alert the bank whenever a customer decides to deal in currencies which are not related to that customer's usual commercial business transactions. The bank may very well honor the request, but it may be useful to note that such transactions are out of the ordinary for the customer.

In the case of trading partners with whom we deal in a variety of currencies, and from whom we both buy and sell currencies, the 20 percent credit risk should be controlled by valuing outstanding contracts periodically at market rates, that is, "marking-to-market" these contracts. This procedure amounts to simulating the bankruptcy of the given trading partner and determining the rates at which every single contract could be replaced. A comparison of the actual rate on each contract with the rate at which it could be replaced would identify a positive or a negative variance. An aggregation of all the positive and negative variances for all the contracts outstanding with the given counterparty would indicate the true market risk with that partner. In most cases this risk would be less than 20 percent of all the outstanding contracts with that party, and it could even be positive. In the latter situation, it would mean that the contracts could be replaced at rates more favorable than the rates on the contracts. Under these circumstances, these contracts would be a source of funds which could be used to offset uncollectable receivables with that party, if that party declared bankruptcy.

To implement the procedure of marking-to-market the outstanding contracts with a given party, one could group the outstanding contracts with that party by month, or even half month, and establish prevailing market rates for each currency and each period. In the cases when the amounts involved for a given period are very large, market rates should be adjusted to reflect the likely effect on these rates if such a large amount were to be transacted.

Sovereign Risk or Cross-Border Risk

A bank extending credit in foreign countries must develop a system to measure the total amount of funds, including money market and exchange transactions, exposed to sovereign or cross-border risk for each country. One way of doing this is, first, to establish a maximum amount of credit exposure allowed for each country. If there are several independent operators with authority to extend credit to businesses within a country or to the country itself, it may be practical to ask them to report transactions to a suitable central point at the end of each business day. This procedure can be continued until total outstanding credits for a given country are approaching, for example, 80 percent of the limit. At that time, all operators should be advised that they must obtain approval for additional transactions prior to extending credit to that particular country. This system permits instant decision making by all operators until the 80 percent limit is reached. After 80 percent of the credit line has been extended, the operators must use caution, and the bank is guaranteed that the credit limit will not be exceeded.

RATE RISK

Changes in Interest Rates

There are two types of rates that affect the performance of treasury operations: interest rates and exchange rates. Changes in interest rates determine the profitability of (1) *money market positions,* in which the maturities of borrowings and placements are not the same, and (2) *swap exchange positions,* in which the purchase and sale of a currency have different value dates. The risk of adverse changes in interest rates while holding these positions can be controlled by imposing limits on the net positive and net negative cash positions allowed to develop during given periods of time such as daily, weekly, monthly, quarterly, and so forth. These limits also serve to control the liquidity risk in treasury operations. In fact we will want to develop a report, the cash-flow report, which can be used to control both rate risk and liquidity risk. We do this in the discussion of control of liquidity risk later in this chapter.

Changes in Exchange Rates

The risk of adverse changes in exchange rates can be controlled by limiting the size of *net exchange positions.* Changes in the spot rate and in forward outright rates may have a direct impact on the value of a net exchange position. A limit must be established for net overnight exchange positions in each currency, including the local currency of the home country. The reason for the *overnight limit* is that political and economic events occurring outside that particular country's business hours may have an important effect on exchange rates. The trader, not working at night, cannot react immediately to these changes and is, therefore, particularly vulnerable. For example, important announcements of a political and economic nature are often made purposely after the markets in that particular country are closed and traders are not in the trading room; however, traders in other parts of the world do have an opportunity to react to the news and affect market rates. During the day, traders should also be limited in their net positions, but they may be permitted larger positions than overnight. This larger limit is necessary to enable the traders to respond to the foreign exchange needs of their customers. The *daylight limit* is usually a multiple of the overnight limit.

Depending on the type of currency, the net overnight and daylight limits may be split, with different limits imposed depending on whether the position is a net overbought or a net oversold one in that specific currency. For example, if a currency is a strong candidate for devaluation, the net overbought position limit would be smaller than the net oversold position limit. In case of an upvaluation-prone currency, the relationship of the limits would be reversed.

In addition to the limits just mentioned, some banks establish a so-called *override limit.* This is a limit for aggregate net positions in all currencies traded. For example, a trader may have a limit of US$1 million equivalent for each of ten different currencies with an override limit of US$6 million for the aggregate of all positions. Without the override limit, the trader could have an aggregate net position of US$10 million, which would be the case if the full US$1 million limit in each of the ten currencies were to be used. The override limit prevents the trader from reaching the net position limit in all ten currencies and restricts that individual's aggregate net position to US$6 million. It is very important to impose a net position limit on the local currency and to include it within the override limit. Otherwise, traders can either buy or sell their maximum limit for all other currencies against local currency. This would, of course, create a very large net overbought or net oversold exchange position in local currency which, like any other currency, may be subject to devaluations or upvaluations.

LIQUIDITY RISK

The risk of not being able to obtain funds when they are needed, the liquidity risk, appears whenever cash flows are not matched by currency and maturity. That is, there is a liquidity risk whenever we have one of the three major types of positions discussed in this book: net exchange position, swap position, and money market position.

A large net exchange position may represent a substantial liquidity risk if the currencies involved are not very marketable and an excessively large amount matures on a given day. In this case, the trader may not be able to sell all the currency originally purchased to obtain other needed currencies. To obtain the needed currencies, the trader would be forced to borrow them in their respective money markets. This could prove to be difficult, particularly in a floating-rate environment in which central banks cannot be expected to buy or sell foreign currencies at a fixed rate. Thus, the cash-flow limits referred to above also serve to control the liquidity risk in these transactions.

The liquidity risk in swap exchange positions and money market positions can be controlled through limits on maximum amounts that can be due for refinancing during different units of time period, that is, maximum negative cash positions per time period. The data needed to enforce these limits can be gathered in what we call the *cash-flow report*. As mentioned earlier, this report can be used also to control the rate risk on swap positions and money market positions. Another tool to control the liquidity risk in these positions is to impose limits on the amounts due from different lending sources. The data for these controls can be gathered in what we call a *liability-mix report*.

The Cash-Flow Report

The simplified cash-flow report shown in the exhibits consists of four blocks. In each block the columns represent different currencies; the rows indicate different maturity brackets. (See Exhibit 15.1.) Block 1 shows maturing net assets and liabilities, currency by currency, on a noncumulative basis for each maturity. Block 2 shows the same type of information for net cash flows resulting from maturing forward exchange contracts. Block 3 is a consolidation of blocks 1 and 2. It adds the cell (in block 1) for a given currency and maturity for the net cash flow resulting from net assets and liabilities to the corresponding cell (in block 2) for forward exchange contracts. Block 4 is the same as block 3, but on a cumulative basis.[2]

To illustrate how the form works, we will show how the cash-flow gaps discussed in a previous case would be reflected in the cash-flow

---

[2] The charts for the cash-flow report presented in the exhibits in this chapter have been simplified. The maturity brackets can be broken down into many more rows such as daily for the first week, weekly for the rest of the first month, and monthly for the rest of the year.

E X H I B I T   15.1

SAMPLE CASH-FLOW REPORT

	1. Net Assets and Liabilities		2. Foreign Exchange Contracts Net Bought and Sold	
	£	$	£	$
Demand				
Spot				
One month				
Two-to-five months				
Six months				

	3. Consolidation		4. Cumulative		Total
	£	$	£	$	
Demand					
Spot					
One month					
Two-to-five months					
Six months					

report. We choose the case where the funds manager wishes to take advantage of an anticipated decline in the pound interest rate. This case was discussed first in Chapter 8, and in Chapter 14 we used it again to analyze comparative risks.

Let's begin with the money market approach. We place six-month pounds and borrow one-month pounds. (See Exhibit 15.2.) The net cash flow in block 1 of these two money market transactions is an outflow of pounds after one month (repayment of the one-month borrowing) and an inflow of pounds after six months. There is no dollar cash flow in block 1, and there are no cash flows in pounds or dollars in block 2. Therefore, block 3 shows the same cash flows as block 1. Block 4 differs from block 3 because it is cumulative. It clearly indicates that there is

EXHIBIT 15.2

CASH-FLOW REPORT: MONEY MARKET CASH-FLOW GAP

PLACE SIX-MONTH POUNDS AND BORROW ONE-MONTH POUNDS

	1. Net Assets and Liabilities		2. Foreign Exchange Contracts Net Bought and Sold	
	£	$	£	$
Demand				
Spot				
One month	−			
Two-to-five months				
Six months	+			

	3. Consolidation		4. Cumulative		Total
	£	$	£	$	
Demand					
Spot					
One month	−		−		−
Two-to-five months			−		−
Six months	+				

a negative cash flow for pounds from one to five months. However, the net cumulative cash flow for six months is zero (blank), because at that time our placement matures; that is, we get our money back, and there is no more negative cash flow.

Now let's depict the foreign exchange approach on the cash-flow report. Exhibit 15.3 reflects in block 2 the sale of one-month pounds against dollars (outflow of pounds, inflow of dollars) and the purchase of six-month pounds against dollars (inflow of pounds, outflow of dollars). Block 3 is a repetition of block 2 because there was no activity in block 1. Block 4 shows the activity in block 3 on a cumulative basis. It

EXHIBIT 15.3

CASH-FLOW REPORT: FOREIGN EXCHANGE CASH-FLOW GAP

**SELL ONE-MONTH POUNDS AGAINST DOLLARS AND
BUY SIX-MONTH POUNDS AGAINST DOLLARS**

	1. Net Assets and Liabilities		*2. Foreign Exchange Contracts Net Bought and Sold*	
	£	$	£	$
Demand				
Spot				
One month			−	+
Two-to-five months				
Six months			+	−

	3. Consolidation		*4. Cumulative*		*Total*
	£	$	£	$	
Demand					
Spot					
One month	−	+	−	+	
Two-to-five months			−	+	
Six months	+	−			

is very obvious that there is a negative cash flow for five months in pounds and a positive cash flow for five months in dollars. In month 6, the cumulative outflows equal inflows in each currency.

We know from descriptions in previous chapters that gaps, that is, mismatched maturities for cash flows, can be established through exchange contracts and through money market transactions. Regardless of whether the exchange approach or the money market approach is used, this example shows that the impact on cash flows is the same.

As mentioned earlier, the cash-flow report can be used to control rate risk as well as liquidity risk in swap positions and money market positions. All net positive cash flows for a given maturity represent a rate risk. All net negative cash flows for a given maturity represent both a rate risk and a liquidity risk. To control these risks management should establish limits on maximum cumulative positive and negative cash flows for each currency traded.

In establishing the limits on cumulative cash flows, the time factor must also be considered. The rate risk is a function of both amount and time. As an example, the rate risk is substantially the same whether the exposure is $100 million for three months or $50 million for six months. Therefore, management must have an awareness not only of the size (dollar amount) of a gap, but also for how long it is (number of months). Also, a rate risk or a liquidity risk of a given amount is different depending on how far in the future the respective positive or negative cash flow occurs. The rate risk in a $100 million, three-month gap is smaller if the position is from spot until three months from now, than if it is from six months to nine months from now. The greater market liquidity in shorter maturities makes it easier and faster to cover a three-month gap between spot and three months later than a three-month gap between six and nine months from now. Also, to the extent that market expectations change in the same direction as changes in the level of interest rates, the impact of rate changes will be larger on the longer maturities. For example, three-month from spot money may be 10 percent and three-month money six months from now may be 11 percent—an upward-sloping yield curve. Let's say that three-month from spot money drops from 10 percent to 9 percent as part of a general decline in interest rates. If the yield curve also changes from upward to downward sloping, the three-month money beginning six months from now may no longer be 1 percent higher than three-month from spot, but rather 1 percent lower. That will put it at 8 percent, or 3 percent below the 11 percent level where it was before. In this situation the rate three months from spot moved from 10 percent to 9 percent while the three-month rate, six months forward moved from 11 percent to 8 percent. Forward gaps can be riskier than positions beginning from spot.

Another measure of aggregate exposure to liquidity risk can be obtained by aggregating cumulative cash-flow gaps, regardless of currency. Thus, a column called "total" appears on the extreme right side of block 4 in the cash-flow reports in Exhibits 15.2 and 15.3. In this column the reports show the net positive or negative cumulative cash flows of all currencies combined for the particular maturity bracket in that row. The cash-flow report showing the money market cash-flow gap in Exhibit 15.2 shows negative entries in this column. However, gaps resulting from exchange transactions are netted out because, as the word "exchange" suggests, on each occasion that there is a purchase of a currency, there is also a sale of another currency. Each maturing exchange contract creates two cash flows: a positive cash flow in the currency purchased and a negative cash flow in the currency sold. For "total" liquidity purposes the two flows are offsetting. Thus, the cash-flow report showing the foreign exchange cash-flow gap in Exhibit 15.3 does not have any entry in the total column.

There are two major items which require special attention regarding their appearance on the cash-flow report. The first is demand deposits. Any bank has substantial demand deposits which, theoretically, can be withdrawn on any day, but, as a practical matter, they are probably the most stable deposits in the bank. If all these demand deposits are shown in the demand column of the liquidity report, the entries will indicate a very large negative cumulative cash flow. This problem must be approached with common sense, and one solution is to classify demand deposits bearing interest at a rate close to the interbank money market in the demand column. Non-interest-bearing demand deposits, or those bearing interest at rates substantially below the interbank money market level, should be placed in the three- or six-month column.

The second type of special item is the revolving Euroterm loan which was described in Chapter 2. In order to measure their rate risk, such loans should be recorded in the cash-flow report by rollover date, that is, the date on which the negotiated interest rate ceases to be in effect, and a new interest rate based on the then-prevailing interbank offered rate is set. We recommend that system because, from the viewpoint of a rate risk, the taking of a deposit matching the interest period chosen by the borrower is the most conservative form of borrowing or funding. However, for the measurement of liquidity, we should use the expiration date of the entire loan commitment, which is usually several years in the future. Firms with a heavy volume of revolving-term loans should have two cash-flow reports: one with revolving-term loans recorded by interest periods (rate risk oriented) and one with revolving-term loans recorded by ultimate expiration date (liquidity risk oriented).

If a company has several independent operators in the international money markets and exchange markets, the enterprise will find it worthwhile to consolidate periodically their individual liquidity reports and to create a master report which will show the overall net positive and negative cumulative cash flows for each currency. It is conceivable that each operator may have taken a position within the specified cumulative cash-flow limits, but that the aggregate of all the operators' positions may seem excessive to senior management. In this case, a reduction of the institution's overall position may be initiated. This would be done best by taking a counter position at the institution's headquarters, so that the individual operators—who, after all, were within their given limits—are not disturbed.

We have shown in the previous paragraph the value of the cash-flow report to limit cumulative positive or negative cash flows and to control different operators in their adherence to established limits. There is an additional advantage associated with this report. In many cases, the cash-flow report will reflect fundamental funding techniques of a specific country. This information can be useful to review personnel in the headquarters of international banks. As an example, let's analyze the cash-flow report for a German bank presented in Exhibit 15.4.

We see in block 1 of Exhibit 15.4 a positive cash flow in one- to three-month local currency (DM). This is not surprising because a German bank naturally makes loans in German marks which it expects to collect a few months later; the collections create the positive cash flow in the DM column. We also see negative cash flows for U.S. dollars in block 1. They can only be the result of dollar deposits received which must be repaid over the next few months, thus creating the negative cash flows in the US$ column. At this point, the examiner of the liquidity report may be concerned because the German branch is apparently lending marks and borrowing dollars, which would make it necessary to maintain a very sizable net overbought position in marks against dollars. However, as we study block 2, we recognize an outflow of marks in the one- to three-month area and an approximately corresponding inflow of dollars. These cash flows are the result of forward exchange transactions. Now the whole report begins to make sense. The bank made loans in marks, borrowed dollars, converted these dollars into marks in the spot exchange market, and covered in the forward exchange market, i.e., sold forward marks and purchased forward dollars. This means that the bank has no net exchange position and a negative cumulative cash-flow position which results, by and large, from demand deposits. The consolidation of the cash flows from assets and liabilities and exchange purchases and sales are almost balanced. The explanation for this funding approach must be that the branch finds it cheaper to borrow dollars and swap them into marks than simply to borrow marks.[3]

---

[3]See "Raising Needed Funds in a Given Currency" in Chapter 9.

EXHIBIT 15.4

CASH-FLOW REPORT FOR A GERMAN BANK

FUNDING MARK LOANS WITH DOLLAR DEPOSITS

	1. Net Assets and Liabilities		2. Foreign Exchange Contracts Net Bought and Sold	
	DM	$	DM	$
Demand	(20)	(10)		
Spot			(15)	14
One month	40	(37)	(38)	39
Two months	50	(46)	(49)	47
Three months	60	(63)	(61)	62

	3. Consolidation		4. Cumulative		Total
	DM	$	DM	$	
Demand	(20)	(10)	(20)	(10)	(30)
Spot	(15)	14	(35)	4	(31)
One month	2	2	(33)	6	(27)
Two months	1	1	(32)	7	(25)
Three months	(1)	(1)	(33)	6	(27)

The Liability-Mix Report

The liquidity risk in exchange transactions and money market assets covered by the cash-flow report are controlled further through the lines of credit discussed earlier in this chapter. However, control of the liquidity risk in our borrowings requires further disaggregation of the data contained in the cash-flow report.

For the same reasons that we considered it advisable to establish lines of credit for different borrowers, industries, and countries, we can expect other participants in the market who lend to us to establish similar lines of credit toward us. Thus, for liquidity purposes, we want to control the amount of funds that we must obtain from each individual source of funds. These controls on different sources should be done along two different lines: one, in terms of the proportion that specific sources of funds represent in our total liabilities; and two, in terms of the proportion that our borrowings from a specific source represent in the total of funds supplied by that source—market share. No one source of funds should represent a very large percentage of our liabilities; and we should not absorb a very large share of any one market for funds.

Liquidity is obviously improved when we stretch the maturities of our liabilities and, in addition, stagger the maturities of liabilities when they mature. The diversification of sources of funds and the stretching of maturities usually means a slightly higher cost of the money. This is the cost of liquidity, which at times may mean the price to stay in business.

Exhibit 15.5 presents an analysis of the liabilities of a bank along the lines suggested here. The first column of numbers provides the amount of funds obtained from the given source. The next column to the right expresses these numbers as a percentage of total liabilities. Each of these percentages should have an upper limit. These limits may have to vary from country to country to reflect the specific sources of funds available in each country. The next column to the right shows the percentage that our borrowings represent in each of the given markets. For example, demand deposits in this particular bank represent 2 percent of total demand deposits in that country; and the certificates of

---

EXHIBIT 15.5
SAMPLE LIABILITY-MIX REPORT

Instrument	Amount (in million $)	% of total liabilities	% share of market	Avg. tenor	Avg. rate
Demand deposits	67	14	2.0	Demand	0.0
Savings deposits	71	15	1.4	Demand	4.5
Time deposits	107	22	2.0	5 months	6.3
Certificates of deposit	34	7	10.0	2 months	7.2
Interbank loans—call	33	7	10.0	24 hours	10.5
Interbank loans—time	80	17	11.0	1.5 months	9.9
Swaps with other banks	48	10	8.0	2.5 months	9.4
Other swaps	2	—		2.0 months	9.7
Others (including capital)	41	8			
Total	483	100			

deposits issued by this bank take 10 percent of the market for these instruments in that country. We will want to set a limit for the percentage that we will take from each of the markets listed in the report. Additional information as to the liquidity of these liabilities can be obtained by providing the average tenor of each of the sources of funds.

For each individual or institution who contributes a significant proportion of our money market liabilities a roster should be maintained. In this roster limits should be set for the maximum overall amounts owed to that party and for the amounts allowed to mature per day, per week, per month and so forth. In addition, it may also be advisable to avoid maturities of deposits from the same customer on two consecutive days and allow at least one day in between without a maturity. Thus, if one of these important lenders chooses to stop placing funds with us, only a fraction of the total amount placed with us will have to be refinanced with another party on any given day, week, or month.

Before leaving the topic of liquidity risk it may be well to discuss the change that occurred in modern liquidity management—particularly in large commercial banks—over the last thirty years, at least in the United States. In the 1950s the typical balance sheet of a bank would show on the asset side 60 percent in loans and 40 percent in government bonds. On the liability side there were customer deposits and capital. Liquidity was managed on the *asset side.* If there was an inflow of funds (a loan repaid or a new deposit received) the bank would buy more bonds. If there was an outflow of funds (a new loan or a deposit withdrawn) the bank would sell bonds. Liquidity management was on the asset side! Today, big banks and nonbanks manage their liquidity on the *liability side* of the balance sheet. They structure their liabilities in such a way that they can rollover maturing liabilities with great ease and generate new liabilities (borrow new fresh money) without problems. As a result, a third block of liabilities has emerged in commercial banks, in addition to customer deposits and capital. That third block is called "money market funds."[4]

These money market funds are obtained and managed by the money desk in the bank's treasury department. These are cold-nosed, arms-length type of deposits. They are not based on any relationship with the depositor. Instead, this money is invested by sharp-penciled people, who are seeking the highest return offered by a group of organizations with an acceptable credit standing. This kind of money will move from

---

[4]This is not to be confused with the financial institutions named money market mutual funds. See the section titled "Money Market Funds" in Chapter 10.

one investment outlet to another for as little as five basis points. Organizations attempting to attract these funds must first of all enjoy the best possible reputation. In addition, they must apply the diversification techniques suggested above to maintain a broad liability mix; that is, to have many different sources of funds, tap these sources with different instruments, and maintain for each of these sources and for each of the instruments a low market share. With that kind of liquidity-management on the liability side banks are not only protecting against lack of liquidity, but more important, they can restructure the asset side. Loans can be made with the funds previously invested in government securities for liquidity purposes, and more loans can be made with the additional sources of funds.

MISCELLANEOUS CONTROLS

Aggregate Limits

We have described tools to limit and control the credit, rate, and liquidity risks. The aggregate limit proposed here does not control any particular risk which would not be controlled already by one of the above-mentioned limits. The aggregate limit is a limit for total unliquidated exchange contracts outstanding with all other banks, corporations, and individuals. It is strictly a volume indicator and functions as a red flag whenever there is an increase in unliquidated exchange contracts. For example, if the aggregate contracts outstanding increase without a corresponding increase in earnings and without any other good explanation, and if this increase in volume is accompanied by a general increase in operating costs such as telephone and telex expenses, a careful examination of the entire operation seems advisable.

On the other hand, there may be a good reason for changes in outstanding balances and, therefore, in limits. For example, the volume of unliquidated exchange contracts rose substantially when floating rates became a reality after August 1971. Importers and exporters who had previously handled their exchange needs on a spot basis whenever they needed a certain currency then began to protect their interests through forward purchases and sales. A spot contract is settled within a few business days, but a forward contract, by definition, is not settled until several months in the future. Therefore, the aggregate limit for unliquidated exchange contracts had to be substantially increased, and there was a very good reason to do so.

Confirmations

Whenever wholesale exchange and money market transactions are closed, a confirmation is sent to the other party to the contract. If the other party is a bank, there will usually be an incoming confirmation from that bank which can be compared with a copy of the outgoing confirmation. If such an incoming confirmation is not expected, or if transactions are carried out with commercial customers and individuals, it is wise to send out a confirmation in duplicate and request a return copy signed by the other party. The importance of this process cannot be emphasized enough. Operating errors of any kind can usually be detected in the period between the day the contract is closed and the settlement date. These details include the name of the other party, the rate, the amount placed or borrowed or purchased or sold, the currencies involved, the value date of the transaction, and the account and/or banks where amounts should be received or paid.

In the hectic atmosphere of a trading room, it is inevitable that some of these details will, on occasion, be recorded improperly. The confirmation slip makes it possible to identify these errors and to avoid substantial costs and penalties.

Protection against Fraud

Generally, foreign exchange and money market operations are no exception to the rule that if enough smart people gang up against an institution, no rule or control will totally protect it against such an assault. However, there are a few guidelines which provide reasonable protection and make life at least more difficult for the fraudulent operator. The incoming confirmations of exchange and money market contracts play a key role in this context. All business partners should be advised that these confirmations must be sent to the attention of an auditing (or some other) department which is completely unconnected to the trading room. The incoming information should be compared in detail with the outgoing confirmation, and any discrepancies should be carefully appraised. If the discrepancy is significant, it should be investigated independently. If the discrepancy is small, a copy of the confirmation may be given to the trader for clarification with the counterparty, since the trader will probably have daily contact with the other party anyhow. In any event, it is important for the audit department to follow up on all these discrepancies and to ensure that new confirmations are obtained for any agreed changes in terms.

The importance of this procedure is that it makes it impossible for a trader to enter into a contract, mail out the original of a confirmation, and then destroy all copies. This technique would enable a trader to build up positions without the knowledge of the bank's management. If the incoming confirmation is directed to the trader, it could be destroyed as well, and nobody would ever know about the position. The trader, when selling this position, will make up a ticket for the originally destroyed contract and pass it on together with the sales contract so that the position is square again. Receipt of the incoming confirmation by an independent audit department will immediately uncover this kind of activity.

An additional protection is the use of serially numbered manifold forms for confirmations. There should be exact accounting and comprehensive explanation for any forms not used.

Another form of fraud is to deal at off-market rates with cooperating parties who are willing to share the resulting profits or provide other forms of kickbacks. To protect against this, a daily rate sheet should be maintained where, on an hour-by-hour basis, the exchange rates, interest rates, and key forward rates (one, three, and six months) are recorded. In a jumpy market, these entries should be made whenever there is a significant change in rates. In addition, the handwritten contract should be time-stamped by the trader immediately after preparing the ticket and before passing it on for entry in the position book. This procedure permits retroactive comparison between the market rates recorded on the rate sheet and the rates at which business was closed on an almost minute-by-minute basis.

This system not only protects against deliberate transactions at off-market rates, but it is also useful in solving rate discrepancies in transactions with other banks and customers. For example, the rate for pounds against dollars moves during a given day between \$2.3800/£ and \$2.4000/£; a customer buys pounds at \$2.3950/£. The customer may think that the pounds are being bought at \$2.3850/£ instead of \$2.3950/£. The rate sheet described earlier will be helpful in clarifying the discrepancy to the satisfaction of both parties involved.

We have only touched upon some of the necessary controls. It cannot be stressed enough that a sound operational backup department and an effective control system are essential for any institution which is actively engaged in operations in the foreign exchange and money markets.

Currency Symbols

Country	Currency	Symbol
Australia	dollar	A$
Austria	schilling	Sch
Belgium	franc	BF
Canada	dollar	Can$
Denmark	krone	DKr
Finland	markka	Fmk
France	franc	FF
Gr. Britain	pound	£
Greece	drachma	Dr
Hong Kong	dollar	HK$
Indonesia	rupiah	Rp
Italy	lira	Lit
Japan	yen	¥
Kuwait	dinar	KD
Malaysia	dollar	Mal$
Mexico	peso	Mex$
Netherlands	guilder	Hfl
Philippines	peso	₱
Saudi Arabia	riyal	SR
Singapore	dollar	S$
South Africa	rand	R
Spain	peseta	Pta
Switzerland	franc	SwF
Thailand	baht	ThB
United States	dollar	US$ ($)
Venezuela	bolivar	B
West Germany	mark	DM

The following publications (most of them produced by governmental or international agencies) are sources for the economic, financial, and trade data necessary to make decisions relating to the foreign exchange and money markets. This list is divided into two parts. The first part gives sources of information for a variety of areas; the second part gives sources for particular countries. In addition, most major international banks regularly publish newsletters and other periodicals which contain useful information.

A. GENERAL

Bank for International Settlements. *Annual Report.* Basel.

Commission of the European Communities. *Economic Situation in the Community.* Brussels (quarterly).

The Economist. London (weekly).

Economist Intelligence Unit. *European Trends.* London (quarterly).

———. *Quarterly Economic Review:* (selected countries). London.

The Financial Times. London (daily).

International Monetary Fund, *Balance of Payments Yearbook.* Washington (annual with monthly updates).

———, *International Financial Statistics.* Washington (monthly).

Organization for Economic Cooperation and Development, *Main Economic Indicators.* Paris (monthly with quarterly and irregular supplements).

————, *OECD Economic Outlook.* Paris (semiannual).

————, *OECD Economic Survey:* (selected countries). Paris (annual).

————, *OECD Financial Statistics.* Paris (semiannual with bimonthly supplements).

Statistical Office of the European Community, *Basic Statistics of the Community.* Brussels (annual).

————, *General Statistics.* Luxemburg (monthly).

United Nations, *Monthly Bulletin of Statistics.* New York.

————, *Statistical Yearbook.* New York.

B. SPECIFIC COUNTRIES

Austria

Austrian Economy in Figures. Vienna: Creditanstalt-Bankverein (annual).

Austria's Monetary Situation. Vienna: Oesterreichische Nationalbank (monthly).

Der Oesterreichische Betriebswirt. Vienna: Hochschule fur Welthandel (quarterly).

Oesterreichische Nationalbank, *Bericht Uber das Geschaftsjahr mit Rechnungsabschluss.* Vienna (monthly).

Oesterreichisches Bank-Archiv. Vienna: Oesterreichische Bankwissenschaftliche Gesellschaft (monthly).

Statistiches Zentralamt, *Statistisches Handbuch fur die Republik Oesterreich.* Vienna (annual).

Belgium

Banque Nationale de Belgique, *Bulletin.* Brussels (monthly).

————, *Rapports.* Brussels (annual).

Institut National de Statistique, *Annuaire Statistique de la Belgique.* Brussels (monthly).

Canada

Canada: The Annual Handbook of Present Conditions and Recent Progress. Ottawa: Statistics Canada.

Canada Year Book. Ottawa: Statistics Canada (annual).

Canadian Statistical Review. Ottawa: Statistics Canada (monthly).

Economic Council of Canada, *Review*. Ottawa (annual).

System of National Accounts: Aggregate Productivity Measures. Ottawa: Statistics Canada (annual).

System of National Accounts: The Canadian Balance of International Payments. Ottawa: Statistics Canada (annual).

France

Banque. Paris (monthly).

Banque de France, *Bulletin Trimestriel*. Paris (quarterly).

Banque Nationale de Paris, *Revue Economique*. Paris (quarterly).

Institut National de la Statistique et des Etudes Economiques, *Annuaire Statistique de la France*. Paris (annual).

————, *Bulletin Mensuel de Statistique*. Paris (monthly).

Italy

Banca d'Italia, *Bolletino*. Rome (bimonthly).

Instituto Centrale de Statistica, *Annuario Statistico Italiano*. Rome (annual).

Japan

Bank of Japan, *Economic Statistics Annual*. Tokyo.

————, *Economic Statistics Monthly*. Tokyo.

————, *Monthly Economic Review*. Tokyo

Ministry of Finance, *Monthly Finance Review*. Tokyo.

Netherlands

Centraal Bureau voor de Statistiek, *Statistical Yearbook of the Netherlands*. The Hague (annual).

Nederlandsche Bank, *Report Presented to the Annual Meeting of Stockholders*. The Hague.

Switzerland

Schweizerische Nationalbank, *Rapport.* Berne (annual).

Schweizerische Nationalbank, Statistisches Bureau, *Monatsbericht.* Zurich (monthly).

United Kingdom

Bank of England. *Quarterly Bulletin.* London.

———, *Report.* London (annual).

Great Britain Central Statistical Office, *Economic Trends.* London (monthly).

———, *Financial Statistics.* London (monthly).

Overseas Trade Statistics of the United Kingdom. London: Her Majesty's Stationery Office (monthly).

United States

Department of Commerce, *Survey of Current Business.* Washington (monthly).

Department of the Treasury, *Treasury Bulletin.* Washington (monthly).

Federal Reserve System, Board of Governors, *Federal Reserve Bulletin.* Washington (monthly).

———, *Selected Interest and Exchange Rates.* Washington (weekly).

West Germany

Deutsche Bundesbank, *Monatsbericht, Statistische Beiheft.* Frankfurt (monthly).

———, *Monthly Report.* Frankfurt.

———, *Report.* Frankfurt (annual).

Aggregate limit   The total volume of all unliquidated contracts allowed to be outstanding at any one time. This limit is only a total volume indicator and is not affected by the characteristics of the particular parties involved in a contract.

Appreciation   A gradual increase in the value of a currency, usually occurring over several days or weeks as the result of market forces of supply and demand in a system of *floating exchange rates.* By contrast, an *upvaluation* is an official government act which produces a substantial increase in an exchange rate, usually overnight.

Arbitrage   The process of taking advantage of the existence of different prices for the same product (or its substitute) at the same time but in different markets. The different markets can be different geographic locations for the same financial asset or different financial assets in one or more geographic locations. Arbitrage between different locations can involve two or more currencies and occurs, for example, when the price for Swiss francs against U.S. dollars in Zurich is higher than the price for Swiss francs against U.S. dollars in New York. In this case profits can be obtained by purchasing Swiss francs against U.S. dollars in New York and, at the same time, selling Swiss francs against U.S. dollars in Zurich. More than two currencies could be involved if the price for Swiss francs in Amsterdam expressed in guilders were higher than the price for Swiss francs in New York expressed in U.S. dollars. Profits in this case could be derived from purchasing Swiss francs against U.S. dollars in New York and, simultaneously, selling Swiss francs against guilders in Amsterdam. Since, at this point, there is a net *long* position in guilders and a net *short* position in dollars, an additional transaction is necessary: Guilders must be sold against U.S. dollars to eliminate any risk. For an example of arbitrage between different financial assets, see *Covered interest arbitrage.*

Asian currency unit A trading department of a bank in Singapore which has received a license from the monetary authority in Singapore to deal in *external currencies*. Although the unit is called Asian currency, it trades in all external currencies, not just Asian ones.

Asian dollar See *External dollar*.

Asian dollar market See *External dollar market*.

Ask rate See *Offer rate*.

Balance of payments A financial statement prepared for a given country summarizing the flows of goods, services, and funds between the residents of this country and the residents of the rest of the world during a certain period of time. The balance of payments is prepared using the concept of double-entry bookkeeping where the total of debits equals the total of credits (total sources of funds equal total uses of funds).

Balance of trade The net of imports and exports of goods and services reported in the *balance of payments*.

Balloon payment The simultaneous return of the principal and interest on a loan at the end of the loan period.

Bankers' acceptance A *money market instrument* providing relatively low interest rate credit to the borrower and a marketable security to the bank. Bankers' acceptances are created as follows: First, a bank's customer draws a bill, or draft, on the bank. Second, the bank "accepts" the bill. By this acceptance, the bank promises to pay the face value of the bill to its holders. The resulting instrument is a two-name paper (the customer's and the bank's are on it); thus, it is highly marketable. The bank charges an "acceptance fee" for accepting the draft; so, the cost of a banker's acceptance to the customer is the going *discount rate* for bankers' acceptances in the market plus the fee charged by the bank. The discount rate for bankers' acceptances is approximately the same as the rate for *commercial paper* and *certificates of deposit*.

Basic balance The net of the following accounts in the *balance of payments:* exports and imports of goods and services, *unilateral transfers,* and long-term capital flows.

Basis risk This risk exists in two types of situations. The first type is a case when an operator uses, for example, a Treasury bill to hedge an interest rate risk in Eurodollars. The interest rates for T-bills and Eurodollars do not always move exactly parallel to each other. The risk of this lack of parallel movement is a basis risk. The other type of basis risk occurs when the period of time for which a financial risk exists is not identical with the period of time for which the hedge is arranged, for example, when a three-month interest risk in a revolving Eurodollar loan is hedged with a six-month futures contract in Eurodollars. A change in the shape of the *yield curve* can bring about nonparallel movements in interest rates for the two different maturities.

Bid rate The price at which the quoting party is prepared to purchase a currency or accept a deposit. If the bid rate is accepted by the party to whom it was quoted, then that party will sell currency or place/lend money at that price. The opposite transaction takes place at the *offer rate*.

Bilateral exchange contract An exchange contract for a local currency against a foreign currency. See also *Multilateral exchange contract.*

Bond A security which shows the liability of the issuing party. It is usually a negotiable instrument with a fixed *interest rate* and a fixed maturity date which is longer than a year.

Break a deposit/loan The advancement of the maturity date of a deposit or a loan upon the request of a customer. In the case of a deposit, the maturity acceleration means that the customer would like his money back prior to the originally negotiated maturity date. In the case of a loan, the customer would like to repay the loan prior to the originally negotiated maturity date. Banks will usually charge a penalty for breaking a deposit or a loan, especially if interest rates have moved up (in the case of a deposit) or down (in the case of a loan).

Break-even exchange rate The particular spot *exchange rate* which must prevail at the maturity of a deposit or debt in a foreign currency (which has not been *covered* in the *forward market*) so that there will be no advantage to any party from *interest rate differentials*. For example, if the Swiss franc interest rate is 5 percent, and the pound interest rate is 12 percent, it may be desirable for the holder of Swiss francs to convert the Swiss francs into pounds and invest them at 12 percent. If this is done without a forward *cover,* an interest gain of 7 percent will be derived. Then, the investor can afford an exchange loss of up to 7 percent which might result from a *depreciation* of the *exchange rate* of the pound against the Swiss franc. Thus, the break-even exchange rate for this transaction would be that spot rate which is 7 percent per annum below the exchange rate at which the original conversion from Swiss francs to pounds took place.

Bretton Woods conference A meeting of representatives of non-Communist countries in Bretton Woods, New Hampshire, in 1944. The participants agreed on the characteristics of the international monetary system which prevailed through 1971. This system was called the "Bretton Woods system" and was a *fixed exchange rate system.*

Broker An individual who introduces the two parties in a transaction to each other. The parties could be a buyer and a seller of foreign currencies or a borrower and a lender of a given currency. The broker charges a fee for this service. Brokers usually do not take a position for themselves; they only arrange for transactions among other parties. In dealing with brokers, financial institutions should insist that the broker disclose the name of the other party to the transaction immediately after the deal is closed. This procedure ensures that the broker does not take a position on his own account, even if only for a few minutes.

Brokerage fee   The charge made by a *broker* for his or her service.

Call money   Funds placed with a financial institution without a fixed maturity date. The money can be "called" (withdrawn) at any time with a telephone call. There is "same day" call money, which means that the call must be made (usually) before 10 o'clock in the morning. There is also "24-hour," "48-hour," and "7-day" call money, which means that the money must be called 1, 2, or 7 calendar days prior to the actual repayment date. While these are the most common varieties of call money, two parties can obviously agree on different types.

Capital accounts   The accounts in the *balance of payments* which measure the changes in liabilities and financial claims of local residents on foreigners and of foreigners on local residents. For example, the purchase of a *bond* issued by a German company by a U.S. resident increases liabilities to foreigners in the German balance of payments. In the U.S. balance of payments, foreign financial assets, or claims on foreigners, have increased.

Cash flow   The increases and decreases in an institution's or an individual's balances in a particular currency.

Cash-flow report   A record of an institution's inflows and outflows of funds in a particular currency, whether the flows are created by *money market* contracts or *foreign exchange* contracts.

Central bank   A bank acting on behalf of a country's government with the right to issue the country's currency and the responsibility to manage the country's money supply, *interest rate* levels, and credit availability. It also manages the level of the country's *foreign exchange reserves* and the external value of its currency.

Certificate of deposit (CD)   A placement of funds for a certain period of time with a bank for which the depositor of the funds receives a confirmation which makes the deposit receipt a negotiable instrument. Investment bankers create a secondary market where CDs can be purchased and sold prior to maturity. Investors usually accept a smaller interest rate on CDs than on regular time deposits because the investment is more liquid, that is, the CD can be converted into cash at any time without asking the bank to *break the deposit*. CDs were originally invented in the United States in the early sixties and were used in the domestic U.S. money market. They were later also used for *external dollars* in several financial centers. The technique is so attractive that the instrument has also been introduced into the *domestic money market* of several other countries. See *Near-money*.

Chain   A method of calculating *cross rates*. For example, if a trader knows the *exchange rate* for marks against dollars and for French francs against dollars, the chain makes possible a calculation of the *cross rate* for marks against French francs.

Clean risk at liquidation A type of *credit risk* which occurs when exchange contracts mature. There may be a brief interval (usually no more than a few hours) during which one of the parties to the contract has fulfilled its obligations, but the other party has not. During this period, the first party is subject to a 100 percent credit risk, on the chance that, in the interval, the second party may become bankrupt and its assets become frozen before it can fulfill its part of the contract.

Commercial paper A *money market instrument* which shows that there has been a *money market* transaction between two nonfinancial institutions. For example, a petroleum company with excess funds may purchase commercial paper issued by an automobile company which needs funds. In this case, the petroleum company is, in effect, lending funds to the automobile company for the period during which it holds the commercial paper. Only the largest companies have access to the commercial paper market. It is particularly developed in the United States because bank regulations do not allow interest to be earned on bank deposits for periods of less than 14 days. Consequently, the main activity in the U.S. commercial paper market is for periods of less than a month. The very largest companies *place* their commercial paper directly with investors. Other companies use the services of a *broker,* who places the commercial paper for a fee. Usually, companies borrowing in the commercial paper market have confirmed back-up lines of credit with commercial banks. These lines can be used for borrowing if money is not available in the commercial paper market.

Compensated value date A day on which both parts of a *foreign exchange* contract are supposed to be consummated. By contrast, a contract with *noncompensated value dates* requires the delivery of one currency on a different day from the delivery of the other. In the latter transaction, the party which receives delivery first can avoid any *clean risk at liquidation* and can possibly obtain further profits from the *float* resulting from receiving and investing one currency a day or more before paying out the other.

Confirmation A record of the terms of a *foreign exchange* or *money market* transaction sent out by each party to the transaction to each other before the actual consummation of the transaction itself. The confirmation contains the exact details of the transaction and thus serves legal, practical, and antifraud purposes.

Correspondent bank A bank located in one geographic area which accepts deposits from a bank in another region and provides services on behalf of this other bank. Internationally, many banks maintain one account with a correspondent bank in each major country so as to be able to make payments in all major currencies. Correspondent banks are usually established on a reciprocal basis, with the two banks maintaining local currency accounts with each other. For example, American bank A maintains a pound account with British bank B, and in turn British bank B maintains a U.S. dollar account with American bank A. Both banks usually maintain reasonable working balances in their accounts so that A can receive and make payments in pounds and B can receive and make payments in U.S. dollars.

Country limit   An amount of money which a financial institution has established as the maximum it is willing to lend borrowers in a given country regardless of the type of borrower or the currencies involved.

Cover   To lock in advance the *interest rate* and/or the *exchange rate* on funds which will mature or be required at some future date. For example, if an American company has a deposit of funds in pounds which will mature in three months, it can sell those pounds for U.S. dollars in the *foreign exchange market* for delivery on the date of the maturity of the deposit. By doing so, the company is setting in advance the exchange rate at which it will convert its pound deposit into dollars; it is thus protected against any decline in the value of pounds against dollars during the intervening three months.

Covered interest arbitrage   The process of taking advantage of a disparity between the *net accessible interest differential* between two currencies and the forward exchange *premium* or *discount* on the two currencies against each other. For example, if the interest rate for pounds is 10 percent and 7 percent for dollars, while the *swap rate* between them equals 3.5 percent, it is possible to borrow pounds at 10 percent, *swap* them through the *forward exchange market* at a discount of 3.5 percent (which provides dollars at 6.5 percent), and invest the dollars at 7 percent, for a profit of 0.5 percent.

Crawling peg system   An *exchange rate* system in which the exchange rate is adjusted every few weeks, usually to reflect prevailing rates of inflation. In between adjustments, a *fixed exchange rate system* prevails. In Brazil, for example, where a crawling peg system has been in use for some time, the Brazilian cruzeiro *devalues* about ten times a year.

Credit risk   In lending operations, the likelihood that a borrower will not be able to repay the principal or pay the interest. In *foreign exchange* operations, the *clean risk at liquidation*.

Cross-currency interest accrual   In money market operations with interest payments and receipts in different currencies, the interest flows are exposed to the risk of exchange fluctuations. This risk, unless hedged, can be significant when interest rates are high.

Cross-currency risk   The risk associated with maintaining opposite *net exchange positions* in two foreign currencies as the result of one transaction. For example, if an American operator borrows Swiss francs at 5 percent and invests the proceeds in pounds at 12 percent, the cross-currency risk is the chance that the pounds will *depreciate* in value against the Swiss francs to such an extent that there will be a loss on the transaction in spite of the favorable *interest rate differential.*

Cross rate   An *exchange rate* calculated from two other bilateral exchange rates (two different currencies compared to the same third currency). For example, if we know the exchange rates for both marks and French francs against U.S. dollars, we can compute the exchange rate for marks against French francs.

Currency liquidity   In a multicurrency-investment portfolio the liquidity of a given foreign currency has to be viewed in terms of exchange liquidity and instrument liquidity. *Exchange liquidity* depends upon the ease with which a currency can be converted into and out of another major currency, usually the U.S. dollar. In the past the British pound, the German mark, the Swiss franc, the Canadian dollar, and the Japanese yen had an excellent exchange liquidity. Very sizable amounts could be purchased and sold in these currencies without affecting market rates in a notable way. *Instrument liquidity* depends upon the ease with which a negotiable instrument denominated in that currency can be purchased and sold without noticeably affecting the market rate for that instrument. For example, if a funds manager wishes to diversify from U.S. dollars into yen, he or she may go through two steps: First convert the dollars into yen in the exchange market, and then invest the yen in a yen-denominated security. If after a period of time the funds manager needs to get back the original U.S. dollars, two steps are again required: First, sell the yen-denominated securities—affected by the instrument's liquidity and then convert the yen into dollars in the exchange market—affected by the yen exchange liquidity. Both types, exchange liquidity and instrument liquidity, determine the overall liquidity of a given currency in a portfolio.

Current account balance   The net of the following accounts in the *balance of payments:* exports and imports in goods and services, and *unilateral transfers.*

Daylight limit   The maximum net exchange position which an institution will allow during business hours. See *Overnight limit*.

Deflation   A price decrease for the same type and amount of goods and services.

Demand deposit   Funds in a currently active account (a checking account) which can be withdrawn at any time without notice. Depending on local regulations demand deposits may or may not be interest bearing.

Depreciation   A decline in the value of a currency. Depreciation is a gradual decline, usually occurring over several days or weeks on account of market forces of supply or demand. *Devaluation,* by contrast, is an official government act which produces a substantial decline in *exchange rates,* usually overnight.

Devaluation   See *Depreciation.*

Direct investment   The purchase of enough shares of equity ownership in a company in a foreign country to involve some degree of managerial control.

Dirty float   A *floating exchange rate* system in which some government intervention still takes place. A government may announce that it will let its currency *float,* that is, it will let the currency's value be determined by the forces of supply and demand in the market. However, the government may secretly allow its *central bank* to intervene in the exchange market to avoid too much *appreciation* of the currency (hurts exports) or too much *depreciation* (increases *inflation*). This is also called a *managed float.* See *Floating exchange rates.*

Discount (noun)   The amount (usually expressed by a *per annum* percentage rate—the *swap rate*) by which the *forward exchange rate* of one currency against another currency is less than the *spot exchange rate* between the two currencies.

Discount (verb)   To subtract from a loan, when it is first made, the amount of interest which will be due when the loan has to be repaid.

Discount rate   The *interest rate* used to *discount* a loan (see preceding definition). The discount rate most commonly discussed is the rate at which a *central bank* is prepared to purchase eligible *money market instruments* or to lend to *commercial banks* against eligible collateral. Through upward and downward adjustments of the official discount rate, and through increases and decreases in the rediscount lines established for commercial banks, a central bank can influence the general level of interest rates and the lending capacity of the banking system.

Domestic money market   The places where a local currency is borrowed and deposited by financial institutions and other major corporations.

Domestic U.S. dollars   The assets and liabilities denominated in U.S. dollars on the books of financial institutions in the United States subject to domestic banking regulations.

Effective interest rate   The amount of money, expressed as a *per annum* percentage, actually paid on a loan or deposit. The effective interest rate may differ from the *nominal interest rate,* depending on interest payment schedules. For instance, when the interest is deducted from a loan when the loan is first made (see *Discount*), the actual proceeds available to the borrower are less than the nominal loan principal used to calculate the interest payments. The effective interest rate in this case is the interest payments expressed as a percentage of the actual proceeds on a *per annum* basis.

Eligible value date   A normal business day on which a payment to settle a *money market* transaction can be made. An eligible value date for a *foreign exchange* transaction must be a business day in the home countries of *both* of the currencies involved.

Engineered swap transaction A *spot* transaction and an offsetting *forward* transaction (for example, sell pounds for dollars spot; buy pounds for dollars forward) in which each of the two transactions is carried out with a different party.

Eurobond A *bond* denominated in an *external currency* and traded in an *external market*. See *Bond*.

Eurocurrency See *External currency*.

Eurodollar See *External dollar*.

Eurodollar market See *External dollar market*.

Euromarket See *External market*.

European currency band See *European Monetary Union*.

European Monetary Union An agreement among some of the countries of the European Common Market and some other European countries to restrict the fluctuations among participating currencies to a given maximum spread.

Eurorate See *External interest rate*.

Exchange controls The regulation of *foreign exchange* transactions by a government/*central bank* to avoid an excessive expansion of the local *money supply* or depletion of the country's *exchange reserves*. Such controls are usually imposed when a country has undesirably large capital inflows or outflows.

Exchange profit work sheet A record of *foreign exchange* gains and losses.

Exchange rate The amount of one currency that can be bought by or sold for a certain amount of another currency.

Exchange rate differential The difference between the two *exchange rates* in a *swap transaction*.

Exchange reserves The total amount of freely convertible foreign currencies held by a country's *central bank*.

Explicit interest rate See *Nominal interest rate*.

Exposure The amount by which inflows in a given currency are less or greater than outflows in that currency. See *Net exchange position*.

External currency A currency which is an asset or liability in a financial institution outside the regulations affecting domestic deposits in the currency's home country. For example, pounds on deposit in Paris are external pounds. Such funds are also called *Eurocurrencies* or *offshore currencies*.

External dollar The U.S. dollar assets or liabilities on the books of financial institutions outside the regulations affecting domestic deposits in the United States. These funds are also called *Eurodollars, Asian dollars,* or *offshore* *dollars* to indicate that they are being held outside of the country. Thus, they are not subject to the same government regulations as *domestic U.S. dollars.* See *International banking facility*.

External dollar market   The places where *external dollars* are traded. Also called *Eurodollar market, Asian dollar market,* or *offshore dollar market.*

External interest rate   The *interest rate* applicable to *external currencies.*

External market   Any place where a currency is traded outside of that currency's home country, that is, a place where *external currencies* are traded.

Fed Funds   Money deposited with the U.S. Federal Reserve Bank and often used for U.S. interbank overnight borrowings.

Finance swap transaction   A financial operation in which one swap in the exchange market is accompanied by two money market transactions.

Financial center   A city or country where a large number (relative to other places in the world) of financial transactions take place. International financial centers arise in places with little or no governmental regulation constraining the inflow or outflow of foreign currencies and with an adequate amount of political stability.

Fiscal policy   The management of government expenditures and income to accomplish desired economic goals.

Fixed exchange rate system   A system in which the values of various countries' currencies are tied to one major currency (such as the U.S. dollar), gold, or *special drawing rights.* The term should not be taken literally because fluctuations within a range of 1 or 2 percent on either side of the fixed rate are usually permitted in such a system. The *Bretton Woods conference* set up such a system. See *Floating exchange rate system.*

Flat interest rate   A simple percentage interest rate which ignores the element of time. For example, 5 percent flat of $100 is $5. If a flat interest rate is charged over a certain period of time, then it can be converted into a *per annum interest rate.* Thus, 5 percent flat of $100 over three months would equal 20 percent per annum.

Float(noun)   The money available between the actual receipt of funds and the scheduled payment of those funds (usually for only a day or two). During this interval, the beneficiary of the float can deposit the funds in the *money market* and earn interest. Thus, it can be said that a positive float earns money and a negative float costs money.

Float(verb)   To move the value of *exchange rates* up or down according to the forces of supply and demand in the market.

Floating exchange rate system   A system in which the values of various countries' currencies relative to each other are established by the forces of supply and demand in the market without intervention by the governments which are behind the currencies. See *Dirty float*. Frequently, when a currency under a *fixed exchange rate system* is under pressure to *upvalue* or *devalue*, its government will allow it to *float* for a period of time in order to let the market determine the level at which the currency should be fixed again.

Foreign exchange   In any one country, the currencies of all other countries.

Foreign exchange market   The places where one country's currency can be bought with or sold for another country's currency. This market, as well as the *money market,* is not a geographic location, as the term might suggest; instead, the market is the collection of *foreign exchange* and *money market* traders with offices in their respective banks who are connected with each other around the world via telephone and telex.

Forward exchange rate   The price of foreign currencies for delivery (on a *value date*) some time in the future. Normally, transactions which mature within a calendar week are called *spot* transactions. Any transaction with a longer value date is a *forward exchange* transaction.

Forward market   A market in which foreign currency, and some money market instruments, are traded for future delivery. There are *no* margin requirements to be met in this market. Most transactions are closed directly between the buying and selling parties, and it is difficult to cancel a contract. A forward contract is expected to be settled with actual deliveries being made. The usual way to eliminate the economic impact of an outstanding contract is to arrange an (offsetting) contract for the same amount and maturity with another market participant. However, even though the economic impact has been neutralized there are now two (offsetting) contracts outstanding. In the absence of margin requirements like those in the *futures* market, operators in the forward market must establish lines of credit before they can trade with another party. See *Credit risk*.

Futures market   A market in which contracts are traded for future delivery of commodities (coffee, gold), currencies (marks, pounds), and financial instruments (Treasury bills, certificates of deposit). The purchase or sale of a futures contract requires that a deposit, called *margin*, be maintained with a broker. The market is designed in such a way that it is easy to get out of a contract or cancel it. The vast majority of the participants, the buyers and sellers of futures contracts, do not intend to take delivery or deliver, what they bought or sold. Futures contracts are used as an investment vehicle (*speculating* on future price changes) and as a vehicle for *hedging* positions. As an example, a manufacturer of gold jewelry who has bought gold on the spot or cash market will *sell* gold in the futures market until the time when the jewelry is completed and sold in the wholesale or retail market. At that time the manufacturer will *buy* gold in the futures market. If the price of gold rose in the meantime, he loses on the futures contract but obtains a higher price for his gold jewelry. If the price of gold fell in the meantime, he makes a profit on the futures contract but obtains a lower price for his gold jewelry. The sale of a futures contract protected him against fluctuations in the price of gold; however, he never intended to deliver gold under that contract. The initial *margin* deposit is usually around 5 percent of the market value of the contract. Thereafter, the contract is marked-to-market at the end of every day. Depending on the price movements for the respective contract, there are positive and negative *variation margins* reflecting the size of the profits and losses made in the futures market. If an operator cannot meet a *margin call* in the case of an adverse price movement, the broker will immediately close out the futures contract, take the loss realized out of the initial margin, and return the remaining money from the margin deposit to the operator. Because of the availability of margin deposits, credit lines are not required in order to enter in a futures contract. If the futures contract was indeed a hedge against an existing commercial risk, the positive and negative *variation margins* do not represent net profits and losses. However, the interest earned or paid on these margins has an economic impact, which can be neutralized by putting a *tail* on the futures contract.

Gap   The period, in *foreign exchange* transactions, between the maturities for purchases and the maturities for sales of each foreign currency (exchange gap). In *money market* transactions, the period between the maturities of placements (loans) and the maturities of borrowings (deposits) of each currency (money market gap). The former occurs when a currency is purchased against one currency and sold against another, each time for different maturities. The money market gap is created by lending a certain amount of a certain currency for a longer or shorter period than the same amount of the same currency is borrowed. See *Swap position*.

Hard currency   The currency of a country with large *exchange reserves* and a surplus in its *balance of payments*. The *exchange rates* of such a currency would be apt to be stable or possibly candidates for *upvaluation*.

Hedge   The elimination of a *net exchange position* or a money market *gap* (an *interest rate position*) through an offsetting transaction. See *Cover*.

Inflation   A price increase for the same type and amount of goods and services. If a country consistently has a higher rate of inflation than other countries, its products will become less competitive in the world markets, and the country may have to *devalue* its currency.

Interest period   The period for which an *interest rate* is fixed for a *revolving-term loan*.

Interest rate   The amount (generally expressed as a *per annum* percentage) of money charged for allowing another party the use of one's money.

Interest rate differential   The difference between the *interest rates* on two different currencies. Also the *swap rate* between two currencies expressed as a *per annum* percentage premium or discount. The formula for calculating it is

$$\frac{\text{Swap rate} \times 100 \times \text{time}}{\text{Spot rate} \times \text{time}}$$

It is essentially the annualized *net accessible interest differential* between the two currencies.

Interest rate position   See money market *Gap* and money market *Position*.

Interest withholding tax   The amount of money which, in some countries, must be withheld by the borrower from any interest the borrower pays. This tax is levied, for the most part, on interest paid to foreigners.

International banking facility (IBF)   In the United States, a bank which is allowed to accept deposits in any currency, including U.S. dollars, without having to be subject to most of the regulations applied to domestic U.S. dollar deposits. To be eligible to be an IBF the banking unit must deal only with non-U.S. residents or other IBFs.

International Monetary Fund (IMF)   An international organization created under the *Bretton Woods Agreement*. The IMF's resources are composed of money received from member countries. These resources constitute a pool which participant countries can draw upon during short-term *balance of payments* difficulties. During the period of *fixed exchange rates* that prevailed until 1971, the IMF was supposed to be consulted before a country *upvalued* or *devalued* its currency.

Intervention   The actions of a *central bank* designed to influence the *foreign exchange* rate of its currency. The bank can use its *exchange reserves* to buy its currency if it is under too much downward pressure, or to sell its currency if it is under too much upward pressure.

Lag   To defer payment of a debt. A company with a subsidiary in a *hard currency* country which has capital inflow controls will often encourage the subsidiary to lag its payments in order to take advantage of higher interest rates available in the *domestic money market* (as opposed to the *external markets*) and a possible *upvaluation* of the hard currency.

Lead   To prepay a debt. A company with a subsidiary in a *soft currency* country which has capital outflow controls will often encourage the subsidiary to prepay any money due to the home office to avoid the risk of the soft currency's *depreciating* relative to the home currency.

LIBOR   See *London interbank offered rate*.

Liquidity   The ability to meet financial obligations without delay.

Liquidity risk   The chance that it may be impossible to meet financial obligations without delay. Even though a corporation may have a sufficient amount of total assets, it will be exposed to liquidity risk whenever there is a difference between the maturities of assets and liabilities, a *gap* resulting from *foreign exchange* or *money market transactions*. Thus, if a bank *covers* a six-month placement of funds with only a three-month deposit (borrowing), it may be difficult or impossible for the company to *roll over* that deposit for an additional three months if it suffers a deterioration of its credit standing or a tightening of the *money market*. See *Currency liquidity*.

London interbank offered rate (LIBOR) The *interest rate* at which prime banks offer foreign currency to other prime banks in London. This rate is often used as the basis for pricing *Eurodollar* and other *Eurocurrency* loans. The lender and the borrower agree to a markup over the *LIBOR*, and the total of LIBOR plus the markup makes the *effective interest rate* for the loan.

Long To have greater inflows than outflows of a given currency. In *foreign exchange* operations, long positions arise when the amount purchased of a given currency is greater than the amount sold. In *money market* operations, a long position arises from investing a given currency for a shorter period of time than it is borrowed. For security brokers, a long position occurs when the amount of a security owned by the broker exceeds the amount of that security contracted to be delivered. See *Short*.

Make a market To deal so frequently and in such volume in a given asset as to make it possible for others to buy or sell that asset at almost any time.

Managed float See *Dirty float*.

Margin The deposit made with a broker when buying or selling a security *on margin* or when buying or selling a futures contract. The margin protects the broker against the customer's inability to meet a *margin call* for payment of a negative *variation margin*. Given that the objective of the margin is to establish the credit worthiness of the customer, this margin most often is not made in cash but takes the form of a prime marketable security or a guaranty, or letter of credit, from a bank.

Margin call A call from a broker requesting an increase in the deposit maintained as *margin* against outstanding transactions in order to cover a negative *variation margin*.

Mark-to-market To value an exchange contract or a money market investment at market rates. This is usually done to determine the profitability of outstanding contracts and investments held in inventory.

Monetary policy The management of several tools at the disposal of a *central bank* in order to achieve desired economic goals. The tools of monetary policy include control of *reserve requirements*, the *discount rate*, and *open market operations*.

Money market The places where funds can be borrowed or deposited.

Money market instruments The negotiable documents which show someone's obligation to pay a certain amount of money on a specific date, usually within a year. The most popular money market instruments are *bankers' acceptances, treasury bills, commercial paper,* and *certificates of deposit*.

Money supply   The currency in circulation plus *demand deposits* at *commercial banks.* Broader definitions of money supply also include different types of *time deposits.*

Multilateral exchange contract   An exchange contract involving two foreign currencies against each other, for example, a contract for U.S. dollars against French francs which is made in London or a contract for pounds against marks made in New York. Also called an *arbitrage exchange contract* perhaps because of the need for such a contract whenever *arbitrage* between locations involves more than two currencies. See *Bilateral contract* and *Chain*.

Near-money (near-cash)   Securities which, while not actually currency themselves, are almost as negotiable as currency, for example, *Treasury bills.*

Negative interest   A fee charged by a bank for accepting a deposit from a customer. This can happen when a currency is under pressure to *appreciate.* A *central bank* in this situation can establish capital import controls and limit the amount of deposits which a bank can receive from nonresidents. If market participants want to deposit more money in the country than the central bank will allow, *interest rates* will drop initially to zero, and, if the pressure continues, produce negative interest. Any taxes which a central bank may impose on foreign deposits can also create negative interest.

Net accessible interest differential   The difference between the *interest rates* which can actually be obtained on two currencies. This difference is usually the basis of the *swap rate* between the two currencies and, in most cases, is derived from *external interest rates* rather than domestic interest rates. These *external rates,* or *Eurorates,* are free from *reserve requirements* (which would increase the interest rate) and from *exchange controls* (which would limit access to the money).

Net borrowed reserves   The total amount of money borrowed by member banks from the Federal Reserve Bank.

Net exchange position   An imbalance between all the assets and purchases of a currency, on the one hand, and all the liabilities and sales of that currency, on the other hand. The size of the exchange position is not affected by maturity dates.

Nominal interest rate   The *interest rate* stated as a percentage of the face value of a loan. Depending on the frequency of interest collection over the life of the loan, the nominal rate may differ from the *effective interest rate.*

Nonborrowed reserves   The total amount of money maintained by member banks as reserve requirements with the Federal Reserve Bank minus the *net borrowed reserves*.

Noncompensated value date   See *Compensated value date.*

Offer rate   The price at which a quoting party is prepared to sell or lend currency. This is the same price at which the party to whom the rate is quoted will buy or borrow if it desires to do business with the quoting party. The opposite transactions take place at the *bid rate*.

Official reserves See *Exchange reserves*.

Offshore currency See *External currency*.

Offshore dollar See *External dollar*.

Offshore dollar market See *External dollar market*.

Offshore rate See *External interest rate*.

Open market operation The actions of a *central bank* in its local *money market* to reduce or increase the *money supply*. For example, the purchase of government *bonds* and *treasury bills* will increase the money supply while the opposite actions will decrease it.

Option exchange contract A contract for *foreign exchange* without a fixed maturity date. In this type of contract, a period of time is stated during which the person who has the option can choose any day for liquidation and settlement of the contract. The contract must state which party has the option (the buyer or the seller) and is usually employed when the date on which foreign exchange will be needed or will be available for sale is not known precisely. This can happen when the availability of foreign exchange depends on uncertainties regarding the production of goods or the arrival of a ship. These options are different from options in securities trading because option exchange contracts must be carried out by the final date of the contract. A security option need never be exercised. The traditional option is also available in the exchange market and called true option.

Outright forward rate A *forward exchange rate* which is expressed in terms of the actual price of one currency against another, rather than, as is customary, by the *swap rate*. The outright forward rate can be calculated by adding the *swap premium* to the *spot rate* or by subtracting the *swap discount* from the spot rate.

Overall balance The net of all accounts in the *balance of payments* excluding transactions in *official reserves*.

Overbought The position of a *foreign exchange* operator who has bought a larger amount of a certain currency than he has sold.

Overnight position A *foreign exchange* or *money market* position maintained overnight. There is more risk involved in such a position than one maintained during the day because political and economic events may take place at night, when the operator cannot react immediately to them.

Overnight position limit The maximum *exposure* an institution is willing to maintain in a given currency after business hours. See *Overnight position*.

Override limit The total amount of money (measured in terms of an institution's domestic currency) which the institution is willing to commit to *all foreign exchange net positions*.

Oversold   The position of a *foreign exchange* operator who has sold a larger amount of a certain currency than he has bought.

Per annum (p.a.)   Over the period of a year.

Place   To lend; usually this term refers to one bank lending to another.

Political risk   See *Sovereign risk.*

Portfolio investment   In the *balance of payments,* the acquisition of the bonds which have a maturity of more than a year or the stocks of a foreign business.

Position   A situation created through *foreign exchange* contracts (exchange position) or *money market* contracts (money market position) in which changes in *interest rates* or *exchange rates* could create profits or losses for the operator.

Position book   A detailed, on-going record of an institution's dealings in a particular currency.

Premium   The amount (usually expressed as a *per annum* percentage rate—the *swap rate*) by which the *forward exchange rate* of one currency against another currency is greater than the *spot exchange rate* between the two currencies.

Price quotation system   A method of giving *exchange rates* in which a certain specified amount of a foreign currency (1 or 100, usually) is compared to the proper amount of local currency.

Rate risk   In the *money market,* the chance that *interest rates* may rise when an operator has a negative money market *gap* (a *short* position), or that interest rates may go down when the operator has a positive money market gap (a *long* position). In the exchange market, the chance that the *spot rate* may rise when the operator has a net *oversold* position (a *short* position), or that the spot rate may go down when the operator has a net *overbought* position (a *long* position).

Reciprocal rate   The price of one currency in terms of a second currency, when the price of the second currency is given in terms of the first.

Repurchase agreement   A contract in which the seller of an asset agrees to buy back the asset he sold on a specific date. This technique is frequently used when a bank, for regulatory reasons, cannot accept a deposit from a customer and pay interest on such a deposit. In such a case, the bank can sell a security, a *Treasury bill* or a *bond,* for example, to its customer and agree in writing to repurchase this security on the date the customer wants to have his money back.

Reserve requirement   An amount of money (usually a percentage of commercial deposits) which *commercial banks* in most countries are required to keep on deposit with the *central bank.* Originally, these requirements were designed to protect the solvency of banks; today, central banks adjust requirements, for the most part, as a tool to affect the *money supply* and the *liquidity* of the entire banking system, that is, its ability to make loans.

Revaluation   See *Upvaluation.*

Revolving-term loan   A loan commitment from a bank to lend money for a number of years with the *interest rate* undergoing periodic adjustments. The revolving feature refers only to the interest rate and not to the actual availability of the money.

Risks   See *Credit risk, Liquidity risk,* and *Rate risk.*

Rollover   The extension of a maturing *foreign exchange* contract in the exchange market or of a loan or deposit in the *money market.*

Rollover date   The end of an *interest period* in a *revolving-term loan.*

Seven-day-notice money   See *Call money.*

Short   To have greater outflows than inflows of a given currency. In *foreign exchange* operations, short positions arise when the amount of a given currency sold is greater than the amount purchased. In *money market* operations, a short position arises from borrowing a given currency for a shorter period of time than it is invested. For security brokers, a short position occurs when the amount of contracts to deliver a security exceeds the amount of the security owned by the broker. See *Long.*

Smithsonian Agreement   An agreement reached at the Smithsonian Institution in December 1971 by the major nations of the non-Communist world. This agreement set new parity rates after the general floating period which prevailed between August and December of that year. This attempt to maintain a *fixed exchange rate system* was abandoned in March 1973. See *European Monetary Union.*

Soft currency   The currency of a country with low *exchange reserves* and a deficit in the *balance of payments.* The *exchange rate* of such a currency would be considered to be a candidate for *devaluation.*

Sovereign risk   The risk that the government of a country may interfere with the repayment of a debt. For example, a borrower in a foreign country may be economically sound and capable of repaying the loan in local currency. However, his country's government may not permit him to repay a loan to a foreign bank because of a lack of *foreign exchange* or for political reasons. The bank making the loan in the first place must take this sovereign risk into account and reflect it in the *interest rate.*

Special drawing rights (SDRs)   International paper money created and distributed by the *International Monetary Fund* to governments in quantities and at times dictated by special agreements among IMF member countries. The value of SDRs is determined by the weighted value of a "basket" of major currencies.

Spot exchange rate   The price of foreign currencies for delivery in two business days. In practice, transactions with *value dates* within a week are called spot transactions.

Spread   The difference between the *bid rate* and the *offer rate* in an *exchange rate* quotation or an interest quotation. This difference is not identical with the profit margin because traders seldom buy and sell at their bid and offer rates at the same time. In another sense (for example, *Eurodollar* loans priced at a *markup* over LIBOR), spread means a *markup* over cost, and in this context the spread *is* identical with the profit margin.

Square exchange position   See *Square-off.*

Square-off   To make the inflows of a given currency equal to the outflows of that currency for all maturity dates. This produces a *square exchange position* in that currency.

Swap   The purchase of one currency against another currency for one maturity date and the simultaneous reversal of that exchange contract for a different maturity. Usually, a swap transaction involves a *spot* maturity date against a *forward* maturity date, and its net effect is the same as two *money market* transactions.

Swap position   A situation in which the scheduled inflows of a given currency are equal to the scheduled outflows, but the maturities of those flows are purposely mismatched (for example, the *forward* sale of a million pounds against dollars for six months, and the forward purchase of a million pounds against dollars for only one month). The expectation in a swap position is that the *swap rate* will change, and that the *gap* can be closed at a profit.

Swap rate   The difference between the *spot exchange rate* of a given currency and its *forward exchange rate.*

Swap-swap   A *swap* transaction involving one *forward* maturity date against another forward maturity date.

Tail   Amount in a futures contract tailored to protect an operator in a hedged position against the cost of interest payables in case of negative *variation margins.* For example, an operator who buys a commodity in the spot, or cash, market and sells it for delivery several months ahead in the futures market. The difference between the spot purchase price and the futures sales price is higher than the cost of borrowing the money needed to pay for the spot or cash purchases. The operator appears to be fully covered. However, if the price for this commodity rises, the operator will have a negative variation margin on the futures contract sold. The margin payment itself is not a loss, but the interest cost of the margin payment is. The money for the margin payment either is no longer available for investment or has to be borrowed. This risk is eliminated by initially selling a slightly lesser amount of the commodity in the futures market than what is purchased in the spot market. As a result, a net overbought position is created, which generates a profit when the price of the commodity rises. This net overbought position, or in a reverse situation a net oversold position, is called a *tail*. The size of the tail has to be such that the profit in this case from the net overbought position exactly offsets the interest cost of the negative variation margin. The size of the tail is a function of the remaining life of the transaction and the level of interest rates; therefore, it must be recalculated daily.

Take down   The receipt of the principal of a loan by the borrower.

Terms   The currency in which an item (including another currency) is priced. Thus, if 1 U.S. dollar equals 4 French francs, the price of a dollar is FF4 in French terms. It also refers to the maturity in a *money market* transaction, for example, a short-term loan.

Time deposit   The placement of funds with a financial institution for a fixed period of time, usually more than a month.

Trade accounts   Those parts of the *balance of payments* which reflect money spent abroad by the citizens of a country on goods and services and the money spent by foreigners in the given country for goods and services.

Trading position work sheet   A record of transactions not yet completed in a particular currency.

Treasury bills   The obligations of a country's treasury department. Because of the unquestioned quality of their issuer and their usually short-term maturities, Treasury bills are the most marketable *money market instrument*.

Trending of rates   Quoting a slightly higher or lower *two-way rate* in order to reflect a preference for either purchasing or selling. For example, if the general market rate is 50 bid and 60 offer, a seller might quote 47-57 to give potential buyers an incentive to buy at 57 rather than elsewhere at 60. In the same situation a buyer might quote 53-63 to give potential sellers an incentive to sell at 53 rather than elsewhere at 50. Trending is one reason why exchange and interest rates often are not exactly the same with different market participants. This is also true for interest rates, both in the domestic and Eurocurrency markets.

Two-way rate   An *exchange rate* or an *interest rate* quotation which contains both a *bid rate* and an *offer rate*. The size of the *spread* between the two rates indicates the relative quality of the quotation.

Unilateral transfers   The account in the *balance of payments* which reflects money sent out of a country and money sent into the country from abroad which is not in exchange for goods, services, or financial assets. Usually, this account reflects money sent by workers in one country to their families in another country.

Upvaluation   Also commonly called *revaluation*. See *Appreciation*.

Value [or] Value date The day on which a financial transaction is to be settled, that is, on which payments are actually made and received. The specification of a value date is an important part of any *foreign exchange* or *money market* transaction.

Variation margins Positive or negative changes in the value of a security bought on *margin* or a futures contract. These variations must be paid in cash on a daily basis. All outstanding securities bought or sold on margin and futures contracts are *marked-to-market.* Those that made money receive their positive margins in cash and those that lost money must pay their negative margins, also in cash. As a result, the clearing brokers are always square and their liquidity is not affected.

Volume quotation system A method of giving *exchange rates* in which a certain specified amount of local currency (usually 1 or 100) is compared to a varying amount of foreign currency. The most prominent country using the volume quotation system is Great Britain.

Wash A transaction which produces neither profit nor loss.

Yield curve The interest rates for each different tenor or maturity of a financial instrument. A graph of the yield curve has interest rates on the vertical axis and time-to-maturity on the horizontal axis. When longer maturities have higher interest rates than shorter maturities, the curve is called a positive or upward-sloping yield curve. The opposite type of curve is called a negative, downward-sloping, or inverted yield curve. When interest rates are the same for all maturities, we call it a flat yield curve.

Index

Index